Get the First Bestselling Biblic[illegible] Based on This Book!

For a Limited Time Only in eBook

FREE

This is Not Your Sunday School Noah's Ark.

This book you are reading, *When Giants Were Upon the Earth*, is the research for the entire bestselling series, *Chronicles of the Nephilim*.

The first novel in the series is *Noah Primeval*. It tells of the events that lead to the Great Flood, with Noah at the very center of the storyline of God's chosen Seed. See how the Nephilim, the Sons of God and the Watchers fit into the War of the Seed. Faithful to the Scriptures. Open to Biblical imagination. Get it in eBook now!

See page 319 for how to get this ebook FREE.

The Appendices of
Chronicles of the Nephilim

When Giants Were Upon the Earth

The Watchers, the Nephilim, and the Biblical Cosmic War of the Seed

By Brian Godawa

WHEN GIANTS WERE UPON THE EARTH
3rd Edition

Embedded Pictures Publishing
9830 Vidor Drive #302
Los Angeles, CA 90035
310.948.0224
www.embeddedpictures.com

ISBN: 978-0-9911434-4-3 (Paperback)

Scripture quotations taken from *The Holy Bible: English Standard Version*. Wheaton: Standard Bible Society, 2001, unless indicated NASB.

NASB Scripture quotations taken from *New American Standard Bible: 1995 Update*. LaHabra, CA: The Lockman Foundation, 1995.

Dedicated to

The fans of *Chronicles of the Nephilim*

Table of Contents

Foreword
By Dr. Michael S. Heiser

The believing Church is in crisis.

I'm not talking about the current socio-political hostility that is progressively marginalizing and even villainizing Christianity. I'm speaking of something more lethal—an internal predicament. The Church has historically held its ground against enemy attack and emerged stronger. But it's the enemy from within that's a greater concern. Christianity is in danger of morphing from the "pillar and buttress of the truth" (1 Tim. 3:15) to a shallow parody of itself or a meaningless amalgam of disconnected Bible verses and incoherent hokum. If it happens, we'll have only ourselves to blame.

I've been a Christian for over thirty years. I wear the hats of lay person, elder, scholar, professor, writer, novelist, speaker, and blogger. Everything I do and have done as a Christian has been oriented by that thing believers claim to consider inspired, divine revelation: the Bible. In more than three decades of personal engagement with the biblical text and observation of many versions of public, private, and celebrity Christianity, I've gained some perspective.

As a biblical studies professor, I've seen the current generation and the one to follow in my classrooms. There are glimmers of hope, but the view isn't inspiring. As a scholar, I've had steady interaction with fellow academics in biblical studies and theology. Besides listening to themselves talk, scholars enjoy talking to other scholars. Academic societies are like country clubs for geeks. Sadly, few conversations are about specifically helping the person in the pew get better access to primary sources so they can sift through the intellectual rubbish they see on the internet or YouTube (or church). As a key content contributor to the nation's largest and most successful Bible software company, I've learned a lot about the Christian consumer. I know what pastors and lay people read and don't read, what is preached or not preached. God help us. Lastly, as someone whose fiction has vaulted him inside the fringe communities of religion, parapsychology, and the paranormal, I no longer have to wonder what it would be like if Erich von Däniken led a Bible study, or if Billy Graham and Shirley MacLaine had children together.

I've spent some time in the past few years wondering about how it came to this and what to do about it. That's where Brian Godawa and his work come in. He's trying to be part of the remedy for some of what ails us. The present book, along with his *Chronicles of the Nephilim* fantasy series from which its content derives, are demonstrations of the sincerity of his efforts. But before I explain why I whole-heartedly believe that's the case, I need to give you the lay of the Christian land as I see it. You'll only know Brian is part of the solution when you clearly grasp the problems.

Believing Christianity operates in three realms. I have friends and enemies in all of them. Let's imagine them as three concentric circles.

In the outermost ring, the largest, we have what happens in church. This is where we find pastors and their congregations, the laity. Part of this ring is composed of folks with a long attachment to the faith. Church is where they go to hear about the Bible, to hear stories and truths from their childhood. It's a familiar community. The rest of the population are seekers or newcomers. These are folks who are there due to intellectual curiosity, a personal relationship, or the need to redefine community.

Because this ring has the most people, one might expect to find the most engagement with the Bible. That simply isn't true, especially today. Few read the Bible with regularity. *That's what church is for, isn't it*? One would also think the pastor's primary distraction is fixing this problem of biblical illiteracy. Not so. Whether generational believers or seekers, the focus has become what is known in church growth circles as "felt needs." Where biblical knowledge is not a felt need, where it fails to stimulate the intellect and the imagination, the Bible won't be the priority.

This is one crisis.

Churches have become places with little tolerance for serious biblical content. That's impractical, so the mantra goes—what felt need does it address? As time goes on, people become conditioned to expecting little from the Bible. Preaching gets reduced to Bible stories with adult illustrations. The Bible no longer surprises or stimulates. It is stripped of both its wonder and transformative power. In the absence of a divine revelation that holds our attention and motivates us as spiritual warriors, we've created an evangelical Gnosticism—we're on our own for a spiritual buzz, and so we'll get it where we can.

Moving inwardly, the next ring is occupied by those largely self-exiled from the outermost ring. The motivations vary, but boredom and intellectual atrophy are the most common. They want to learn Scripture in a serious way. They know that Bible reading isn't Bible study. They've been going to church for a solid meal for years, and the intravenous drip they get isn't cutting it. They're starving for content. Who can blame them?

Those who emerge as teachers in this space know more than most anyone in the outermost ring, even most pastors. But they are not scholars, despite the fact that most who occupy this ring look at them that way, and they come to fancy themselves as such. Scholars are taught and tested by other scholars. The teachers in this realm are self taught and tested by no one. Neither they, nor the people who follow them, know what they don't know.

Since these teachers occupy the top of the intellectual pecking order that emerges in this realm, they cannot know when they stray from sound method, teaching, and theology. If they have sufficient humility to desire such accountability, they may never find it, since most scholars have long detached themselves from such assistance. But the greater concern are those who are intoxicated by the idea of having a following. These are the theological hipsters and hucksters of the current generation. Their devotees are not equipped to challenge them, and have become accustomed to filter anything anyone else says through the wise sage that commands their attention. They can say anything to their pupils, no matter how outlandish or idiosyncratic and get away with it.

That's another crisis.

The final (and smallest) ring is the innermost—the domain of the scholars. Here we find the deepest engagement with Scripture and, as I hinted earlier, the farthest detachment from the people who need the fruit of their labors.

The irony is that, despite the greatest depth in scriptural knowledge, this ring has the most dysfunction when it comes to ministry—the other two rings. This is expected with respect to non-confessional scholars, but it's also common within the evangelical ranks.

There are naturally exceptions, but all too often the brightest minds who have the most time and expertise for engaging Scripture cloister themselves and become fixated on reputation within the guild. They overwhelmingly view the nonsense absorbed (and taught) in the other two rings as simply not worth their time. Many who have discovered blogging and social media use it to debate among or congratulate themselves in cyberspace. The web is a just new way to avoid the biblically unwashed masses.

This is also a crisis.

Brian Godawa offers a remedy to each crisis. *The Chronicles of the Nephilim* does the impossible—it turns serious academic scholarship in ancient primary sources into engaging entertainment. Fiction and fantasy are tried-and-true vehicles for transmitting theological truths and biblical concepts. This is what reaches the masses.

Brian's work also addresses what's wrong with the other two realms. Each volume of *The Chronicles of the Nephilim* contains resources and commentary for exploring the biblical text in its own context. *When Giants Were Upon the Earth* collects all that information and expands on it. It's a biblical-theological feast.

But don't mistake the feast for smorgasbord theology. As someone Brian has tapped as a resource, I can tell you his focus is on peer-reviewed biblical scholarship. His sources are not his own opinions. He's not grinding axes and "solving" conspiracies. He's not pretending questions are answers. He knows the difference between supernatural possibilities grounded in the biblical text and sanctified speculation. He's not building a fiefdom—he wants you to learn what he's learned. That's the purpose of this book. It's a blessing to recommend it to you.

Dr. Michael S. Heiser
PhD, Hebrew Bible and Semitic Studies
University of Wisconsin-Madison
Academic Editor, Logos Bible Software
Bellingham, WA

Preface

When I began writing *Chronicles of the Nephilim*, I never thought it would become such a vast enterprise that would change my life. It was like the opening of Elisha's servant's eyes to see the heavenly host I had been missing.

This book began when I decided to add some appendices onto the first volume *Noah Primeval.* I thought it might provide some interest for those who wanted to explore the Biblical and ancient historical foundation behind the fiction of the novel.

I've always been kind of "bipolar" in my love of both imagination and intellectual analysis. I was inspired by Michael Crichton novels because he used to provide an appendix at the end of each of his books explaining some of the real science behind his fictional morality tales about the dangers of unfettered science and technology. So I decided to mimic a master with my own appendices at the end of my novels.

I didn't realize what a strong and positive reaction I would get from that addition. A significant number of readers thanked me for providing the research I had done. Some even said they enjoyed the appendices as much as the novels. I thought I stumbled upon an effective helpful supplement, so I decided to do the same thing in every novel. I provided an appendix after each book that covered the Biblical and ancient Near Eastern research behind that particular story.

What I soon realized was that the appendices were not merely unconnected pieces of scholarship. They were much like the novels. They created a theological progression of the very same Cosmic War of the Seed storyline that my Biblical fantasy novels were offering.

I decided that I wanted to provide that more intellectual and theological development in a single unified volume for those who wanted to study the Biblical and ancient historical material exclusively.

So I offer this compilation of all the appendices of the *Chronicles of the Nephilim*. To add some value, I have included some extra material not in the original appendices, such as my analysis of the book of 1 Enoch. But I have also included the appendices for the last two Chronicles, *David Ascendant* and *Jesus Triumphant* before the release of those novels.

Of course, there will be some overlap of material in the chapters, but I kept them that way because each chapter provides a different context of the information that may shed new light the reader did not see in previous chapters.

Enjoy.

Imagine.

Believe.

Brian Godawa
Author, Chronicles of the Nephilim
March, 2014

Chapter 1
The Book of Enoch: Scripture, Heresy, or What?

In recent years, there has been a rise of interest in the subject of giants called "Nephilim" and the Sons of God called "Watchers" in the Bible. Much of this interest swirls around the End Times crowd and involves speculation that approaches the absurd. Visions abound of an impending return to "the days of Noah," with cloned Nephilim among us, the Antichrist coming in a UFO, and Watchers masquerading as alien saviors. It makes for fascinating and entertaining reading. But regardless of such flights of futuristic fanciful fantastique, the fact remains, the Bible does talk about a bizarre event in antediluvian days (before the Flood) that involves these strange Nephilim creatures – whatever they are.

> Genesis 6:1–4
> When man began to multiply on the face of the land and daughters were born to them, the sons of God saw that the daughters of man were attractive. And they took as their wives any they chose. Then the LORD said, "My Spirit shall not abide in man forever, for he is flesh: his days shall be 120 years." The Nephilim were on the earth in those days, and also afterward, when the sons of God came in to the daughters of man and they bore children to them. These were the mighty men who were of old, the men of renown.[1]

There is an ongoing historical controversy over what exactly happened in those ancient days. Several views have been held by orthodox Christian Church fathers and later theologians. The most popular view in ancient

---

[1] Most Bible passages quoted in this book are from *The Holy Bible: English Standard Version* (Wheaton: Standard Bible Society, 2001). Variations are from the *New American Standard Bible*: 1995 Update (LaHabra, CA: The Lockman Foundation, 1995).

Judaism and the early Church was that the Sons of God were supernatural angelic beings who mated with human woman and their offspring were giants. More recent scholarly views argue that the Sons of God were either tyrannical kings who claimed divinity in their royal lineage, or human descendants from the "righteous" line of Seth who violated holiness and intermarried with the "unrighteous" line of the daughters of Cain. In these modern views, the Nephilim tend to be understood merely as mighty warriors of an ancient era.

I will not be arguing for any of these views in this chapter, but rather, I will be addressing the ancient Book of Enoch because it has made a significant impact on the current Watchers/Nephilim controversy. The theological scandal is that the book includes a very clear supernatural interpretation of Genesis 6 with angelic Watchers mating with humans who birth giants that walk among us. But even more, it expands upon that view with a detailed story of how these Watchers influenced mankind with occultic revelations and how the patriarch Enoch condemned the Watchers and their giant offspring who had become violent bloodthirsty cannibals.

If the book is a reliable source, it certainly adds to the controversial flames with this fantastic interpretation, but honest pursuers of truth should not discount any textual assessment because of a fear of undesired conclusions. We must follow the truth no matter where it leads us.

Many Christians are now quoting the Book of Enoch as if it were Scripture, or at least a true interpretation of Scripture in order to prove their supernatural view. Others are dismissing it as obvious fabricated legend without merit, or worse, heresy. Regardless of one's interpretation, this esoteric ancient manuscript warrants an examination because of its popular and scholarly influence in its mysterious connection to the Bible.

Enoch in the Bible

The ancient patriarch Enoch is surely one of the most enigmatic characters in all of Bible history. Outside of genealogies, he is only mentioned in one brief sentence in the Old Testament. But that single sentence has drawn volumes of speculation because it is so fascinating and mysterious.

In Genesis 4:17 we read about a son of Cain named Enoch, after whom, a city was built. But this is not our man. The Enoch we are looking at is the son of Jared, before the Flood, whose son was Methuselah, the oldest man in the Bible (Gen. 5:19-21). The text says that Enoch only lived 365 years, compared to the much longer time spans of those around him, reaching as high as Adam's 930 years and Jared's 962 (Methuselah's record was 969).

Whether these ages are literal or symbolic, Enoch was on earth for only a short time because, as the text says, "Enoch walked with God, and he was not, for God took him" (Gen. 5:24). The phrase "walked with God" is used of

Noah right after this and its context is righteousness and purity in a wicked generation filled with violence and corruption (Gen. 6:9-12). But it also carries the connotation of a direct and immediate relationship with God beyond mere obedience.[2] Enoch had a holy intimacy with the Creator that separated him from the world around him.

This righteousness sheds light on the unique phrase that Enoch "was not, for God took him" (5:23). As Old Testament scholar Gordon Wenham points out, the idea of "was not" cannot merely be a poetic way of saying "died," because every other reference to the death of the men in that same genealogy is "and he died" (eight times). In contrast, Enoch is the only one with this peculiar wording "and he was not." But this reflects the same wording used of Elijah's translation to heaven in a chariot of fire, thus avoiding death (2 Kgs 2:1-10).[3]

The New Testament confirms this interpretation of translation to heaven in Hebrews 11:

> Hebrews 11:5
> By faith Enoch was taken up so that he should not see death, and he was not found, because God had taken him. Now before he was taken he was commended as having pleased God.

The writer of Hebrews holds up Enoch as an example of the righteousness of faith under the Old Covenant. Even before Messiah came, even in the primeval era of humankind, faith was the expression of right standing before God.

The only other reference to Enoch is in the epistle of Jude where Enoch is quoted as a righteous man condemning the wicked of his generation.

> Jude 14–15
> It was also about these [evil blasphemers] that Enoch, the seventh from Adam, prophesied, saying, "Behold, the Lord comes with ten thousands of his holy ones, to execute judgment on all and to convict all the ungodly of all their deeds of ungodliness that they have committed in such an ungodly way, and of all the harsh things that ungodly sinners have spoken against him."

---

[2] Claus Westermann, *A Continental Commentary: Genesis 1–11* (Minneapolis, MN: Fortress Press, 1994), 358.

[3] Gordon J. Wenham, *Genesis 1–15, vol. 1, Word Biblical Commentary* (Dallas: Word, Incorporated, 1998), 128.

I will have more to say about this passage shortly, but for now, let me just make the point that the three Biblical passages about Enoch paint a picture of a righteous man, in holy communion with God, during a time of great evil before the Flood, who prophesied judgment upon evildoers, and as a result of his God pleasing faith, was translated into heaven by God before he could die.

It is easy to see why Enoch has captivated the imagination of believers through history with his mysterious introduction, cryptic behavior, and aura of holiness. And it is also easy to see why he captivated the imagination of ancient Jews writing extra-Biblical literature during the Second Temple period.

The Books of Enoch

There are actually three "Books of Enoch." They are numbered but also go by the names of the language they are written in. Thus 1 Enoch is referred to as Ethiopian Enoch, 2 Enoch is called Slavonic Enoch, and 3 Enoch is called Hebrew Enoch. They are all considered to be Pseudepigrapha. Though this word literally means "false writings," or writings attributed to an author who did not write them, J.H. Charlesworth argues that "rather than being spurious the documents considered as belonging to the Pseudepigrapha are works written in honor of and inspired by Old Testament heroes."[4]

This newer denotation illustrates the attempt to distance the literature from the notion of deliberate deception and to highlight its sacred value to the community of faith. One is reminded of how the Pentateuch is often attributed to Moses, yet it remains anonymous and shows distinct signs that argue against his sole authorship.[5]

Loren Stuckenbruck complains that the modern notion of "falseness" in Pseudepigraphal authorship is an anachronism that fails to capture the ancient acceptance of anonymous writers using "ideal" authorship as a means of uniting the ancient past with the present and future in sacred connection. "They presented themselves, in effect, as voices about the readers' remote past out of the remote past… This, in turn, would make it possible for the audience to participate imaginatively in *that* world in order to re-imagine and gain perspective on the present."[6]

As Charlesworth explains, the Pseudepigrapha includes a large body of manuscripts from various locations and authors that were composed around

---

[4] James Charlesworth, *The Pseudepigrapha and Modern Research, With a Supplement (Septuagint and Cognate Studies Series, No. 7)* (United Kingdom, Scholars Press, 1981), p 25.

[5] Duane A. Garrett, *Rethinking Genesis: The Sources and Authorship of the First Book of the Pentateuch* (Grand Rapids, Baker Bookhouse, 1991). Richard Elliott Friedman, "Torah (Pentateuch)," ed. David Noel Freedman, *The Anchor Yale Bible Dictionary* (New York: Doubleday, 1992), 618.

[6] Loren T. Stuckenbruck, "The Epistle of Enoch: Genre and Authorial Presentation," *Dead Sea Discoveries 17* (2010) 395-96.

the period from 200 B.C. to about A.D. 200. They are either Jewish or Christian in origin, they are often attributed to ideal figures in Israel's past, and they usually claim to contain God's message, building upon ideas and narratives of the Old Testament.[7] Some of the other well known Pseudepigrapha include Jubilees, The Testaments of the Twelve Patriarchs, Psalms of Solomon, the Apocalypses of Ezra and Baruch and many others.[8]

Though 2 and 3 Enoch also contain material about the patriarch Enoch and his alleged visions and experiences, they do not carry the weight or influence that 1 Enoch has had on ancient Judaism and Christianity. 2 and 3 Enoch are both written much later and are plagued by diverse traditions of manuscript variations. 2 Enoch was most likely written sometime in the 2nd century after Christ. 3 Enoch shows evidence of later Jewish mysticism and claims authorship by a Rabbi Ishmael relating his visions of Enoch written anywhere from the 3rd to the 6th century A.D.[9]

But the book that is traditionally intended when referring to "the book of Enoch" is the Ethiopian 1 Enoch. Its oldest sections are considered to have been written as early as 300 B.C., but the only complete manuscript we have available is an Ethiopic translation from 400-500 A.D.[10] Though early Church Fathers and the Ethiopian Church had been familiar with the text, it had been considered lost to Western scholarship until its rediscovery and introduction in the 1800s. The most recent discoveries in the 1950s of Enoch fragments among the Dead Sea Scrolls in Qumran suggest that the original language was Aramaic.

What is the Book of 1 Enoch?

1Enoch belongs to the genre of literature called "apocalyptic" or "apocalypticism." "Apocalypse" in Greek simply means "revelation" or "disclosure." John Collins, an expert in apocalyptic literature defines it as a genre "with a narrative framework, in which a revelation is mediated by an otherworldly being to a human recipient, disclosing a transcendent reality which is both temporal, insofar as it envisages eschatological salvation, and spatial, insofar as it involves another, supernatural world."[11] Yarbro Collins adds a point of clarification to the definition that apocalyptic is "intended to interpret present,

---

[7] J. H. Charlesworth, "Introduction for the General Reader," in *The Old Testament Pseudepigrapha, vol. 1* (New York; London: Yale University Press, 1983), xxv.
[8] See James H. Charlesworth, *The Old Testament Pseudepigrapha*. Vol. 1. And Vol. 2. (New York; London: Yale University Press, 1983) for the largest collection of these writings in one volume.
[9] Francis I. Andersen, "Enoch, Second Book Of," ed. David Noel Freedman, *The Anchor Yale Bible Dictionary* (New York: Doubleday, 1992), 516–517. Philip S. Alexander, "Enoch, Third Book Of," *AYBD*, 524.
[10] George W. E. Nickelsburg, *1 Enoch: a Commentary on the Book of 1 Enoch,* ed. Klaus Baltzer, Hermeneia—a Critical and Historical Commentary on the Bible (Minneapolis, MN: Fortress, 2001), 1, 9.
[11] John J. Collins, "The Jewish Apocalypses," ed. John Joseph Collins, *Semeia* 14 (1979): 22.

earthly circumstances in light of the supernatural world and of the future, and to influence both the understanding and the behavior of the audience by means of divine authority."[12]

Apocalyptic literature has the common elements of 1) being written as comfort to people who are suffering contemporary oppression 2) by referring to God's victory in history over oppressive forces 3) using fantastic imagery to express spiritual reality 4) in esoteric or symbolic terms in order to avoid outright suppression by the reigning powers in authority.

The well known books in the Bible of Daniel and Revelation are considered apocalyptic in their genre as Daniel and John are ushered into heaven and receive revelation about coming earthly historical events cloaked in poetic language to communicate the spiritual and theological meaning behind those events. They too are written as comfort to believers suffering persecution. They both contain symbolic fantastic imagery and are esoteric significations of governing authorities.

Most scholars believe that the Book of Enoch is really five different books that were written in different time periods and redacted together by editors until it became its current version before A.D. 100. But there is no manuscript evidence for this theory and the oldest version that we have of the books are fragments among the Dead Sea Scrolls that indicate all five in one corpus.[13]

The five different "books" are subdivided with their approximate dates thus:[14]

1. The Book of the Watchers (Chapters 1–36) 3rd century B.C.
2. The Book of Parables (37–71) 1st century B.C.
3. The Book of Heavenly Luminaries (72–82) 3rd century B.C.
4. The Book of Dream Visions (83–90) 2nd century B.C.
5. The Book of the Epistle of Enoch (91–107) 2nd century B.C.

1. The Book of the Watchers (Chaps. 1-36). This is the book that carries the most amount of interest for our examination. It most likely predates the Hellenistic period, being completed by the middle of the 3rd century B.C.[15] It is announced as an oracle of judgment by Enoch. It tells a detailed narrative of two hundred heavenly Watchers who rebel against God in heaven led by

---

[12] John J. Collins, "Apocalypses and Apocalypticism: Early Jewish Apocalypticism)," ed. David Noel Freedman, *The Anchor Yale Bible Dictionary* (New York: Doubleday, 1992), 283.

[13] Most ancient written texts are preceded by many years of oral tradition. So the date of composition or even the date of the latest manuscript is not indicative of the true age of the text, which is probably much older. In other words, they didn't just make up a book of Enoch around 300 to 200 B.C., they were transcribing oral traditions and maybe even written sources that were much more ancient.

[14] Nickelsburg, *1 Enoch: a Commentary*, 7. Also, E. Isaac, "A New Translation and Introduction," in *The Old Testament Pseudepigrapha*, vol. 1 (New York; London: Yale University Press, 1983), 7.

[15] Nickelsburg, *1 Enoch: a Commentary*, 7.

Semyaza and Azazel. They come to earth on Mount Hermon, mate with human women, and produce bloodthirsty hybrid giants as their progeny, leading to the Great Flood. It contains details about the Watchers and their names, along with the occultic secrets they reveal to mankind that violate the holy separation of heaven and earth. It describes Enoch's heavenly commission as a prophet and accounts of his cosmic journeys into heaven to proclaim judgment upon these foes of God.

2. The Book of Parables (Chaps. 37-71). This appears to be the latest portion of Enochic texts, dating to about the end of the 1st century B.C. It is a recounting of Enoch's cosmic journey and vision of judgment upon the fallen angels and their wicked human counterparts, juxtaposed against the elevation of "the holy, the righteous, the elect." It also includes descriptions of astronomical phenomena such as the source of the wind and rain. The unique and important contribution of these chapters is the vision of God's throne room drawn from the book of Isaiah and Daniel 7 that depicts the "Ancient of Days," the heavenly host that surrounds the throne, and the "Son of Man" as vice regent, also referred to as the Elect One, the Righteous One, and the Messiah (Anointed One). Scholars point to this book as influential in the development of the doctrine of the Son of Man leading to the New Testament Gospels.[16]

3. The Book of Heavenly Luminaries (Chaps. 72-82). These are probably the earliest of Enochian texts with roots in the Persian period between 500 and 300 B.C.[17] It describes Uriel the angel showing Enoch the astronomical, cosmological and calendrical laws that verify the authority of the solar calendar.

4. The Book of Dream Visions (Chaps. 83-90). Enoch recounts two dreams he saw to his son Methuselah before his marriage. The first dream is a brief warning about the coming Flood. The second dream is a complex allegory using animals to represent the history of the world from Adam to the Hellenistic period they were in, with a projection into the future judgment. The date for this book is around 165 B.C., the time of the Maccabean revolt, which is roughly where the history allegory ends.

5. The Epistle of Enoch (Chaps. 92-105). Composed sometime in the 2nd century B.C., this document records Enoch's exhortation to his children

[16] George W. E. Nickelsburg, "Son of Man," ed. David Noel Freedman, *The Anchor Yale Bible Dictionary* (New York: Doubleday, 1992), 139.
[17] Nickelsburg, *1 Enoch: a Commentary*, 7.

to remain righteous in their wicked generation. He predicts woes of suffering, shame, misery, and judgment for the wicked who are rich, oppress the righteous, and worship idols. He predicts justice, comfort, eternal life, and glorification like the stars for those who remain pure.

6. Additional "Books" (Chaps. 106+). These last pieces are like appendices added onto the book of Enoch as additional chapters. Two chapters detail the miraculous birth narrative of Noah. The infant Noah's face and hair are said to glow white. His father Lamech is frightened that he may be the offspring of a Watcher, but he is reassured by Enoch that this is not the case, but rather that Noah is pure and holy, called to be God's remnant. Then one chapter, 108, is an additional exhortation by Enoch to Methuselah of the judgment of good and evil in the latter days.

Lastly, is the Book of Giants. Until the 1950s, the Book of Giants was only known as a Manichean gnostic text from the late 3rd century A.D. But the discoveries of the Dead Sea Scrolls at Qumran in the 1950s uncovered fragments of an original Book of Giants in Aramaic from the 2nd century B.C. that was the basis for the Manichean expanded alterations.[18] Enochian expert J.T. Milik argues that the Book of Giants should be considered part of the corpus of 1 Enoch texts, but scholars are divided over this conclusion.[19]

Although we only have precious few fragments of this book, the story can be pieced together of the fall of the Watchers and their mating with humans, producing defiled giant offspring. But the unique aspect of this manuscript is its elaboration of the personal exploits of the giants from their perspective. Several giant sons of the Watchers named Ohya and Hahya (sons of Semyaza) and Mahway have dream visions of the Deluge. Interestingly, the Mesopotamian giant king Gilgamesh shows up in this tale as well, and he helps the giants seek out Enoch to discover the interpretation of their dreams. Enoch responds with a tablet declaring the great Flood to come as their judgment and his own challenge to them to pray for mercy.[20]

---

[18] James C. VanderKam and Peter W. Flint, *The Meaning of the Dead Sea Scrolls: Their Significance for Understanding the Bible, Judaism, Jesus, and Christianity*, 1st ed. (New York: HarperSanFrancisco, 2002), 196.

[19] Devorah Dimant, "The Biography of Enoch and the Books of Enoch," *Vetus Testamentum*, 33:1 (1983), 16; Loren T. Stuckenbruck, "The Early Traditions Related To 1 Enoch From The Dead Sea Scrolls:An Overview And Assessment," *The Early Enoch Literature*: *Supplements to the Journal for the Study of Judaism*, Ed., Gabriele Boccaccini and John J. Collins (Boston: Brill, 2007) 59-63.

[20] Translations of the fragments and their summary can be found in Michael O. Wise, Martin G. Abegg Jr., and Edward M. Cook, *The Dead Sea Scrolls: A New Translation* (New York: HarperOne, 2005), 290-295.

The Book of Enoch and the Canon

The book of Enoch may be fascinating religious and spiritual storytelling. But there are a myriad of such texts from the Second Temple period of ancient Judaism. What makes Enoch special? Just how was the book of Enoch thought of by ancient Jews before Christ, or for that matter, by Christians after him?

The canonization of the Old Testament is well documented in Jewish and Christian scholarship.[21] Though claims have been made for the canonicity of 1 Enoch by some early Church Fathers, it was not considered to be Scripture by any of the ancient traditions.

The traditional thirty-nine books that we now call the Old Testament, was referred to in the New Testament and other Second Temple literature as "the Law, the Prophets, and the Psalms" (Luke 24:44).[22] There is no manuscript or historical evidence that 1 Enoch was ever a part of this traditional threefold designation.

The earliest manuscripts we have of Old Testament canonical writings are from 400-300 B.C. from the library of Qumran.[23] But as Bauckham points out, the Enoch literature and other apocryphal works at Qumran were evidently valued as literary works by the Essene community but were not included in their canon of Scripture.[24]

The Septuagint (LXX) was considered the authoritative Greek translation from around 200-100 B.C. and was quoted or alluded to by Jesus and the apostles.[25] The LXX did include additional apocryphal books along with the traditional threefold division, but 1 Enoch was not one of them.[26]

The Hebrew Masoretic texts (MT), compiled between A.D. 500 and 900 by Jewish scribes, is considered by both Christians and Jews to be one of the most authoritative set of manuscripts reflecting the ancient Jewish canon.[27] 1 Enoch was never a part of this set.

The only manuscript collection that does include 1 Enoch as canonical is the Ethiopic canon of the Coptic Church. But this designation was solidified

---

[21] Roger T. Beckwith, The Old Testament Canon of the New Testament Church and Its Background in Early Judaism (London: SPCK, 1985); F.F. Bruce, The Canon of Scripture (Downers Grove: IL, InterVarsity Press, 1988).
[22] Beckwith, *The Old Testament Canon*, 111.
[23] Gleason Archer Jr., *A Survey of Old Testament Introduction*, 3rd. ed. (Chicago: Moody Press, 1994), 41.
[24] Richard J. Bauckham, *2 Peter, Jude*, vol. 50, Word Biblical Commentary (Dallas: Word, Incorporated, 1998), 96.
[25] Richard N. Longenecker, *Biblical Exegesis in the Apostolic Period, 2nd ed.* (Grand Rapids, MI; Vancouver: W.B. Eerdmans; Regent College Pub., 1999), 45, 137.
[26] Bruce, Frederick Fyvie (2010-11-17). *The Canon of Scripture* (p. 43). Intervarsity Press - A. Kindle Edition.
[27] Geoffrey W. Bromiley, ed., *The International Standard Bible Encyclopedia, Revised* (Wm. B. Eerdmans, 1979–1988), 799.

sometime in the 13th century A.D. in response to Western pressure and under Muslim influence.[28]

Outside the Canon. In his commentary on 1 Enoch, George Nickelsburg catalogues the widespread influence that the book of Enoch had on both Jewish and Christian literature. Though the Old Testament canon never included 1 Enoch, its Watchers/giants storyline was quoted as spiritually authoritative in other significant Second Temple Jewish literature such as the Wisdom of Jesus ben Sira, the Genesis Apocryphon, Wisdom of Solomon, Philo of Alexandria, Josephus, 2 and 3 Enoch, The Life of Adam and Eve, as well as some of the Targumim.[29]

The book of Jubilees, a highly regarded Jewish text, written sometime in the 2nd century B.C., draws explicitly from 1 Enoch as Scripture under the claim that Enoch had received his vision from the angels of God:

> Jubilees 4:17-22
> [Enoch] wrote in a book the signs of the heaven… And he was therefore with the angels of God six jubilees of years. And they showed him everything which is on earth and in the heavens, the dominion of the sun. And he wrote everything, and bore witness to the Watchers, the ones who sinned with the daughters of men because they began to mingle themselves with the daughters of men so that they might be polluted. And Enoch bore witness against all of them.[30]

Because the Christian Church arose within a milieu of Jewish apocalypticism, Enochic texts and traditions had much influence on Christian thought outside the New Testament. 1 Enoch translator E. Isaac writes, "1 Enoch played a significant role in the early Church; it was used by the authors of the Epistle of Barnabas, the Apocalypse of Peter, and a number of apologetic works. Many Church Fathers, including Justin Martyr, Irenaeus, Origen, and Clement of Alexandria, either knew 1 Enoch or were inspired by it. Among those who were familiar with 1 Enoch, Tertullian had an exceptionally high regard for it."[31]

Indeed, the epistle of Barnabas, young Origen, Clement of Alexandria, and Tertullian all considered 1 Enoch to be Scripture. Tertullian wrote in "Concerning The Genuineness Of "The Prophecy Of Enoch," "I am aware that

---

[28] Beckwith, *The Old Testament Canon*, 479-481
[29] Nickelsburg, *1 Enoch: a Commentary*, 71-82.
[30] Charlesworth, *The Old Testament Pseudepigrapha vol. 1*, 62.
[31] E. Isaac, "A New Translation and Introduction," in *The Old Testament Pseudepigrapha*, vol. 1 (New York; London: Yale University Press, 1983), 8.

the Scripture of Enoch, which has assigned this order (of action) to angels, is not received by some, because it is not admitted into the Jewish canon either...But since Enoch in the same Scripture has preached likewise concerning the Lord, nothing at all must be rejected *by* us which pertains *to* us; and we read that "every Scripture suitable for edification is divinely inspired."...To these considerations is added the fact that Enoch possesses a testimony in the Apostle Jude."[32]

Church father Justin Martyr quotes 1 Enoch's angelic mating with women and their revelation of occultic arts to humans as an apologetic argument explaining the true origin of gods mating with women in pagan mythologies.[33]

Isaac concludes that starting in the 4th century, Enoch fell into disfavor in the West with the negative reviews of influential theologians like Julius Africanus, Augustine, Hilary, and Jerome. He then explains that it was the medieval mind that relegated 1 Enoch to virtual oblivion outside of Ethiopia before it was resurrected in 1773 by the discovery of Scottish explorer James Bruce, who returned to Europe with several manuscripts of the Ethiopic Enoch.[34]

Though skepticism of 1 Enoch was surely warranted, Nickelsburg suggests that some skeptics were influenced by biases apart from Biblical arguments. For instance, the gnostic manipulation of Enochic texts by the Manichean heresy made both Jerome and Augustine uncomfortable with its popularity, leading them to dismiss it as apocryphal.[35] Augustine, having a personal background in Manicheanism, displayed a tendency to react against the interpretation of angels with corporeal bodies because of its alleged affinity to his Gnostic past.[36] With his singular influence on the Western Church, Augustine laid the foundation for the rejection of Enochian concepts within that tradition.

But we must learn our lesson from Augustine's fallacy of guilt by association. Just because some aberrant sects or non-Christian cults may value 1 Enoch does not make it an unworthy text, especially since it has a long pedigree of acceptance within the historic orthodox Christian faith. After all,

---

[32] Tertullian, "On the Apparel of Women," in The Ante-Nicene Fathers: Fathers of the Third Century: Tertullian, Part Fourth; Minucius Felix; Commodian; Origen, Parts First and Second, ed. Alexander Roberts, James Donaldson, and A. Cleveland Coxe, trans. S. Thelwall, vol. 4 (Buffalo, NY: Christian Literature Company, 1885), 15.

[33] Justin Martyr, "The Second Apology of Justin," in *The Ante-Nicene Fathers: The Apostolic Fathers with Justin Martyr and Irenaeus,* ed. Alexander Roberts, James Donaldson, and A. Cleveland Coxe, vol. 1 (Buffalo, NY: Christian Literature Company, 1885), 190.

[34] E. Isaac, "A New Translation and Introduction," in *The Old Testament Pseudepigrapha*, 8.

[35] Nickelsburg, *1 Enoch: a Commentary*, 102.

[36] Robert C. Newman, "The Ancient Exegesis Of Genesis 6:2, 4," *Grace Theological Journal* 5,1 (1984) 26.

non-Christian cults of all kinds do the same thing with the Bible. Abuse of a text does not negate proper use.

The Book of Enoch and the New Testament

Though the book of 1 Enoch is not considered Scripture, this does not invalidate its claims to accuracy or reliable spiritual information. Orthodox Christian believers maintain that only the Old and New Testaments are the "God-breathed" or inspired Word of God (2Tim. 3:15-16). That is, they are the sole infallible authority of God's revelation to humankind. But in our desire to affirm the absolute canonical truth value of God's Word, we too often dismiss the contingent truth value of non-canonical works. We can become guilty of "dehumanizing" the authorship of Scriptures in our desire to maintain a priority of the authorship of God. The truth is that the authorship of Scripture, like the incarnation of Christ, is rooted in both human and divine origins.[37]

The doctrine of the Inspiration of Scripture is not like the claims of Islam. We do not believe that the human authors merely recorded the words of God like secretaries taking audible dictation. Nor does Inspiration mean that God magically controlled the hands of the authors to write what he alone wanted, like some kind of automatic writing from a spirit. Rather, God providentially breathed his intent into the words that men were writing in very human contexts, employing very human sources.[38]

It may surprise those who hold a high view of Scripture that some of the New Testament writers used the book of Enoch as source material. They may even bristle at the suggestion and seek to deny it or downplay it because of the implications they fear of connecting holy writ to human writ. But it is important to understand that the admitted use of non-canonical sources by writers of Scripture was an all too common activity of God.

There are well over fifty references in the Scriptures to just over twenty non-canonical source texts used by Biblical authors that are lost to history. These are non-Biblical sources that the writers of Scripture *actually mention* as being sources of information for their writing of Scripture. Noted scholar James Charlesworth lists a few of them in his examination of lost writings related to the Bible:

The Book of the Wars of Yahweh (Num. 21:14)

---

[37] The Chicago Statement on Biblical Inerrancy and Exposition states, "We affirm that inspiration was the work in which God by His Spirit, through human writers, gave us His Word." http://www.bible-researcher.com/chicago1.html accessed Jan. 26, 2014.

[38] The Chicago Statement on Biblical Inerrancy and Exposition: "Although the human writers' personalities were expressed in what they wrote, the words were divinely constituted," and "We must pay the most careful attention to its claims and character as a human production." http://www.bible-researcher.com/chicago1.html accessed Jan. 26, 2014.

The Book of the Just [or Jasher] (Josh. 10:13, 2 Sam. 1:18)
The Book of the Acts of Solomon (1 Kgs. 11:41)
The Book of the Annals of the Kings of Israel
(1 Kgs. 14:19, 2 Chr. 33:18; cf. 2 Chr. 20:34)
The Book of the Annals of the Kings of Judah
(1 Kgs. 14:29, 15:7)
The Annals of Samuel the seer (1 Chr. 29:29)
The History of Nathan the prophet (2 Chr. 9:29)
The Annals of Shemaiah the prophet and of Iddo the seer
(2 Chr. 12:15)
The Annals of Jehu son of Hanani (2 Chr. 20:34)
An unknown and untitled writing of Isaiah (2 Chr. 26:22)
The Annals of Hozai (2 Chr. 33:18)
An unknown lament for Josiah by Jeremiah (2 Chr. 35:25).[39]

With a repertoire of non-Biblical source texts like this acknowledged by the very writers of Scripture, Christians simply cannot afford to dismiss influential non-canonical texts as irrelevant or unworthy of studious respect. Especially those who proclaim *sola scriptura*, since the Scriptures themselves grant such explicit respect to their sources.

Unfortunately all of these sources are lost to history, except one: 1 Enoch.[40] This book of Enoch is one such source whose direct and indirect influence can be seen on significant portions of the New Testament. As a matter of fact, 1 Enoch is quoted directly in the epistle of Jude. But before we examine that explicit example, let's take a look at the implicit impact of Enoch on the New Testament.

Son of Man. Nickelsburg lays out evidence for the influence of 1 Enoch on the New Testament appropriation of Son of Man Christology. Though Daniel 7 is clearly a source for Jesus' self-designation as Son of Man, Nickelsburg argues that it cannot explain the totality of the Son of Man doctrine as portrayed in the Gospels, a doctrine that reveals development in the Intertestamental period through 1 Enoch in particular.

---

[39] J. H. Charlesworth, "Introduction for the General Reader," in *The Old Testament Pseudepigrapha*, vol. 1 (New York; London: Yale University Press, 1983), xxi. For a closer examination of these non-canonical source text references, see Duane Christensen, (1998), "Lost Books of the Bible," *Bible Review*, 14[5]:24-31, October.

[40] There is another extant manuscript, the Book of Jasher, that some claim is the source material quoted in Joshua and 2Samuel. But its authenticity is hotly debated by scholars. For a discussion of the issues, see Ken Johnson, ThD., *Ancient Book of Jasher: A New Annotated Edition*, (Lexington, KY: BibleFacts Ministry, 2008).

Daniel 7 portrays a vision of the Son of Man on a cloud approaching the throne of the Ancient of Days, surrounded by ten thousands of his holy ones and receiving a kingdom of glory and dominion as vice regent of that throne.

But Nickelsburg argues that the New Testament Son of Man engages in more judicial responsibilities than Daniel's kingly ruler. For instance, in Daniel 7, the Son of Man is enthroned *after* judgment. But in passages such as Mark 8:38 and Matt. 10:32-33, the Son of Man comes *in* judgment, which is more like Enoch's *interpretation* of Daniel 7 in the Parables of Enoch than simple dependence on Daniel 7.[41]

Mark 13:26-27 speaks of those who will see the Son of Man coming to gather his "chosen ones," in a manner made familiar in the resurrection imagery of 1 Enoch 51; 61:2-5 and 62:14-15.

The parable of the sheep and the goats told by Jesus in Matt. 25:31-46 speaks of the Son of Man coming in his glory with his angels before his throne. He then divides them up unto eternal life and eternal damnation. While this is surely reflective of the throne imagery in Daniel 7, what is not is the judgment of nations and their consignment by the angels to torment or glory based on their treatment of the "elect ones" we read about in 1 Enoch:[42]

> 1 Enoch 62:5-15
> One half portion of them shall glance at the other half; they shall be terrified and dejected; and pain shall seize them when they see that Son of Man sitting on the throne of his glory... But the Lord of the Spirits himself will cause them to be frantic, so that they shall rush and depart from his presence... So he will deliver them to the angels for punishments in order that vengeance shall be executed on them—oppressors of his children and his elect ones... The righteous and elect ones shall be saved on that day; and from thenceforth they shall never see the faces of the sinners and the oppressors. The Lord of the Spirits will abide over them; they shall eat and rest and rise with that Son of Man forever and ever. The righteous and elect ones shall rise from the earth and shall cease being of downcast face. They shall wear the garments of glory.[43]

As Isaacs concludes, "There is little doubt that 1 Enoch was influential in molding New Testament doctrines concerning the nature of the Messiah, the

[41] Nickelsburg, *1 Enoch: a Commentary*, 83.
[42] George W. E. Nickelsburg, "Son of Man," ed. David Noel Freedman, *The Anchor Yale Bible Dictionary* (New York: Doubleday, 1992), 144.
[43] Charlesworth, *The Old Testament Pseudepigrapha*, vol. 1, 43.

Son of Man, the messianic kingdom, demonology, the future, resurrection, final judgment, the whole eschatological theater, and symbolism. No wonder, therefore, that the book was highly regarded by many of the earliest apostolic and Church Fathers."[44]

Enoch and the New Testament. R.H. Charles, one of the earliest experts on the Pseudepigrapha and Enoch, listed about sixty examples where the language of the New Testament reflected possible Enochian influence. He concluded, "*1Enoch* has had more influence on the *New Testament* than has any other apocryphal or pseudepigraphic work.[45]

Here is just a sampling of these many linguistic connections:[46]

New Testament	1Enoch
1 *John* 1:7. 'walk in the light'.	92:4. 'walk in eternal light'.
2:8. 'the darkness is past'.	58:5. 'the darkness is past'.
15. 'Love not the world nor the things that are in the world'.	108:8. 'love … nor any of the good things which are in the world'.
Rev. 2:7. 'the tree of life'. Cf. 22:2, 14, 19.	25:4–6. The tree of life.
3:5. 'clothed in white raiment'.	90:31. 'clothed in white'.
20. 'I will come in to him and will sup with him and he with me'.	62:14. 'and with that Son of Man shall they (i.e. the righteous) eat and lie down and rise up'.
6:15. Compare the fear of the kings of the earth, and the princes, and the chief captains, and the rich, and the strong, when they see 'the face of him that sitteth on the throne'.	62:3. 'the kings, and the mighty, and the exalted 5… shall be terrified… and pain shall seize them when they see that Son of Man sitting on the throne of his glory'.
15. 'He that sitteth on the throne shall dwell among them'.	45:4. 'I will cause Mine Elect One to dwell among them'.
9:1. 'I saw a star from heaven fallen to the earth'.	86:1. 'And I saw … and behold a star fell from heaven'.
20:13. 'the sea gave up the dead …, and death and Hades gave up the dead which were in them'.	51:1. 'in those days shall the earth also give back that which has been entrusted to it, and Sheol also shall give back … and hell shall give back …'.

[44] E. Isaac, "A New Translation and Introduction," in Charlesworth, *The Old Testament Pseudepigrapha*, vol. 1, 0.
[45] Robert Henry Charles, ed., *Pseudepigrapha of the Old Testament*, vol. 2 (Bellingham, WA: Logos Bible Software, 2004), 178.
[46] Charles, *Pseudepigrapha of the Old Testament*, vol. 2, 178.

20:15. 'cast into the lake of fire'.	90:26. 'cast into this fiery abyss'.
Rom. 8:38. 'angels … principalities … powers'. Cf. *Eph.* 1:21; *Col.* 1:16	61:10. 'angels of power and … angels of principalities'.
1 *Cor.* 6:11. 'justified in the name of the Lord Jesus'.	48:7. 'in his (i.e. the Messiah's) name they are saved'.
2 *Cor.* 4:6. 'to give the light of the knowledge of the glory of God in the face of Jesus Christ'.	38:4. 'the Lord of Spirits has *caused His light to appear* (*emended*) on the face of the holy, righteous and elect'.
Col. 2:3. 'in whom are hid all the treasures of wisdom and knowledge'.	46:3. 'the Son of Man … who reveals all the treasures of that which is hidden'.
1 *Thess.* 5:3. 'then sudden destruction cometh upon them as travail upon a woman with child'.	62:4. 'Then shall pain come upon them as on a woman in travail'.
2 Thess. 6:15. 'King of kings and Lord of lords'.	9:4. 'Lord of lords … King of kings'.
Heb. 4:13. 'there is no creature that is not manifest in His sight: but all things are naked and laid open before the eyes of Him with whom we have to do'.	9:5. 'all things are naked and open in Thy sight, and Thou seest all things, and nothing can hide itself from Thee'.
12:9. 'Father of Spirits'.	37:2. 'Lord of Spirits' (and *passim* in Parables).
Acts 3:14. 'the Righteous One' (= Christ).	53:6. 'the Righteous and Elect One' (= Messiah).
John 5:22. 'He hath committed all judgement unto the Son'.	69:27. 'the sum of judgement was given unto the Son of Man'.
Luke 9:35. 'This is My Son, the Elect One'.	40:5. 'the Elect One' (i.e. the Messiah). Cf. 45:3, 4 'Mine Elect One'; 49:2, 4.
Matt. 19:28. 'when the Son of Man shall sit on the throne of His glory'.	62:5. 'When they see that Son of Man sitting on the throne of his glory'.
'ye also shall sit on twelve thrones'.	108:12. 'I will seat each on the throne of his honour'.
25:41. 'prepared for the devil and his angels'.	54:4, 5. 'chains … prepared for the hosts of Azâzêl'.

The argument could be made that the examples of linguistic overlap between the book of Enoch and the New Testament are circumstantial or even cultural coincidence. After all, didn't the Old Testament use terms like walking in light and darkness? Didn't everyone of that time period use metaphors such as kingly gods sitting on their thrones?

Not entirely. That is, as Charles points out, four titles appear *for the first time* in 1 Enoch's Book of Parables *applied to a personal Messiah*.[47] "Christ" or "The Anointed One" applies to priests or royalty in the Old Testament, but is transformed into the ideal Messianic King first in 1 Enoch 48:10 and 52:4 before the New Testament. "The Righteous One" and "the Elect One" likewise first appear with Messianic designation in 1 Enoch 38:2; 53:6; 40:5; 49:2 and others. As noted above, even the "Son of Man" was transformed in his identity from Old Testament king to New Testament judge by way of 1 Enoch.

As Charles argues, the notions of Sheol, resurrection, demonology and future life that are barely mentioned in the Old Testament, are expanded upon in 1 Enoch in a way that corresponds to the New Testament usage of the terms.[48] The sheer volume and repetition of phrases and concepts between 1 Enoch and the New Testament may not prove absolute dependence, but certainly suggest a strong familiarity and interaction with that tradition of ideas – a tradition of Second Temple literature that all points back to its own dependence upon 1 Enoch.[49] The preponderance of the evidence supports Charles' claim that, "Doctrines in Enoch…had an undoubted share in moulding the corresponding New Testament doctrines, or are at all events necessary to the comprehension of the latter."[50]

Enoch and Jude. The strongest cases for New Testament literary dependence upon Enochic texts are the epistles of Jude, and 1 and 2 Peter.[51] Of all three of these passages, Jude is the most explicit in that the apostle literally quotes 1 Enoch 1:9 when he writes,

> Jude 14–15
> It was also about these that Enoch, the seventh from Adam, prophesied, saying, "Behold, the Lord comes with ten thousands of his holy ones, to execute judgment on all and to convict all the ungodly of all their deeds of ungodliness that they have committed in such an ungodly way, and of all the harsh things that ungodly sinners have spoken against him.

Here is the original text of 1 Enoch being quoted:

---

[47] Charles, *Pseudepigrapha of the Old Testament*, vol. 2, 182–185.
[48] Charles, *Pseudepigrapha of the Old Testament*, vol. 2, 182–185.
[49] See Nickelsburg's description of Second Temple literature's dependence on 1 Enoch: Nickelsburg, *1 Enoch: a Commentary*, 68-80. See the classic article by H.J. Lawlor. "Early Citations from the Book of Enoch." *Journal of Philology* 25 (1897): 164-225.
[50] Charles, *Pseudepigrapha of the Old Testament*, vol. 2, 182.
[51] I will not address 2 Peter 2:4-11 because it is a virtual paraphrase of Jude that does not provide any new information about 1 Enoch's influence on the New Testament other than being a second witness of confirmation of that influence.

> 1 Enoch 1:9
> And behold! He cometh with ten thousands of His holy ones to execute judgement upon all, and to destroy all the ungodly: And to convict all flesh of all the works of their ungodliness which they have ungodly committed, and of all the hard things which ungodly sinners have spoken against Him.[52]

While most Biblical scholars accept Jude's quotation as being the prophecy from 1 Enoch, some deny this by arguing that Jude is merely quoting from a *common source* of 1 Enoch. This approach to interpretation hints at artful ad hoc dodging by pushing back the source into a "safe" past of unretrievable sources. But more importantly, it wouldn't be consistently applied to other New Testament quotations. For instance, those same exegetes would surely *not* claim that Matthew's quotation in Matt. 2:5-6 of a "prophet" that Messiah would be born in Bethlehem was from a further removed "common source" with Isaiah rather than from Isaiah himself. The list of these New Testament examples would of course be manifold.

Another approach to denying the influence of 1 Enoch on Jude is typified by Douglas Moo's commentary on Jude. He writes, "To be sure, Jude claims that Enoch 'prophesied.' But this word need not mean 'wrote an inspired prophetic book'; it could well mean simply 'uttered in this instance a prophecy.'"[53]

On the face of it, this is a logical option, but not a probable one, unless one is willing to maintain a hermeneutical double standard. Yet again, applying this standard consistently forces one to conclude that Matthew was not affirming the total book of Isaiah when he quoted the prophecies, but only specific instances of prophecies from Isaiah. Something of which Moo would not want to be found guilty.

Of course, there are cases where apostles quote a saying as a singular cultural reference without connection to the rest of the source. Paul quotes the Stoic Aratus on Mars Hill this way (Acts 17:28), as well as Epimenedes of Crete (Titus 1:12), and Menander (1 Cor. 15:33). But the difference here is that Jude does not merely quote a verse from the book of 1 Enoch. *He also follows the content patterns of 1 Enoch along with allusions and echoes of its phrases and language throughout his epistle.*

---

[52] Charles, *Pseudepigrapha of the Old Testament*, vol. 2, 189.

[53] Douglas J. Moo, *The NIV Application Commentary: 2 Peter and Jude* (Grand Rapids, Mich.: Zondervan Publishing House, 1996], 272-74.

Greeting. To start with, Jude's greeting reflects the same exact greeting as 1 Enoch in appealing to the preservation of the elect, followed by God's mercy or kindness and the multiplication of blessings (see chart below for comparison verses).

Theme. Jude also echoes 1 Enoch in its primary apocalyptic theme of the punishment of the ungodly. Both texts are addressing the evil of their day as an unveiling or fulfillment of past prophetic proclamation. They both appeal to ancient examples of judgment as the promise of judgment upon the present ungodly. In 1 Enoch's case, it was the angelic Watchers corrupting humanity with occultic teaching that was probably an analogy with the ungodly corruption of Hellenism on Judaism.[54] In Jude's case, he refers to those same angels as an analogy with the ungodly corruption of antinomian false teachers (Jude 4).

Memes. Jude uses what commentator Richard Bauckham calls "midrash" in his exegesis. That is, he weaves together quotations, allusions, reminiscences and catchwords of other older texts to apply it to his contemporary situation.[55] Thus specific phrases or memes become anchor points of connection between the ancient text (1 Enoch) and the present dilemma (Jude's 1st century Church).

Some of those memes are referred to later in the letter when describing the nature of the ungodly. Jude seems to follow Enoch's descriptions of these wicked sinners point for point. Carroll Osburn concludes that Jude must have used Enoch 80:2-8 as the "essential framework for Jude's metaphorical construction" because Jude warns of the impending punishment of the ungodly and then follows the precise order of Enoch's description of them as first waterless clouds (Jude 12; 1 En. 80:2); second, unfruitful trees (Jude 12; 1 En. 80:3); and fourth, wandering stars (Jude 13; 1 En. 80:6). The third metaphor of turbulent waters being found in 1 Enoch 67:5-7.[56]

When Jude introduces Enoch as "the seventh from Adam," this is not merely a number attained by adding up the lineage from the genealogy of Genesis 5:3-19. The phrase "seventh from Adam" is a common identifier used outside the Old Testament in Second Temple literature starting with 1 En. 60:6 and 93:3.[57]

---

[54] E. Isaac, "A New Translation and Introduction," in *The Old Testament Pseudepigrapha*, vol. 1 (New York; London: Yale University Press, 1983), 8.

[55] Richard J. Bauckham, *2 Peter, Jude, vol. 50*, Word Biblical Commentary (Dallas: Word, Incorporated, 1998), 4. Also, Walter M. Dunnett, "The Hermeneutics Of Jude And 2 Peter: The Use Of Ancient Jewish Traditions," JETS 31/3 (September 1988) 289.

[56] Carroll D. Osburn, "7 Enoch 80:2-8 (67:5-7) and Jude 12-13," *The Catholic Biblical Quarterly* 47, 1985, 297.

[57] See also, Jubilees 7:39, and the Talmudic Lev. Rab. 29:11.

The Fallen Watchers. Another Enochian motif that finds a strong presence in Jude is the Book of the Watchers storyline of 1 Enoch 1-36. The "wandering stars" that Jude later condemns in v. 13 is a common ancient Jewish idiom in both the Old Testament and the Pseudepigrapha for divine celestial beings. In the ancient world, the stars were called the "host of heaven" and were equated with deities.[58] In the Old Testament, the stars of heaven are also called "heavenly host" and are likened to the pagan deities (Deut. 4:19), as well as the angelic Sons of God around his throne (Psa. 89:5-7, Job 38:7). So it is within this tradition that 1 Enoch also likens the fallen angelic Watchers to imprisoned stars.

> 1 Enoch 18:14-15
> the angel said (to me), "This place is the (ultimate) end of heaven and earth: it is the prison house for the stars and the powers of heaven... they are the ones which have transgressed the commandments of God."[59]

Next, Jude sets up these "wandering stars" as ungodly villains motivated by sensual immorality and denial of the Lord (v. 4), the exact same description in 1 Enoch 67:10 of those angels who "debauch their bodies" and "deny the Lord." This repetitious theme of fleshly defilement and rejection of authority (v. 8) are all traits of the "angels who did not keep their own domain, but abandoned their proper abode" (v. 6). But who are these angels, what is their proper abode, and what is their violation?

Bauckham explains that "Jude's reference is directly dependent on *1 Enoch* 6–19, which is the earliest extant account of the fall of the Watchers...and he shows himself closely familiar with those chapters."[60] Those Watchers "abandoned the high holy and eternal heaven and slept with women and defiled [themselves] with the daughters of the people, taking wives... and begetting giant sons." (1 En. 15:3). As Jude says, these angelic beings who rebelled against God were put in "eternal bonds for the judgment of the great day" (v.6), or as 1 Enoch says, they were "bound underneath the rocks of the ground until the day of their judgment" (1 En. 10:12).

It is acknowledged by most experts in Second Temple Jewish literature that the Enochian Book of the Watchers is an expansive interpretation of Genesis 6:1-

---

[58] H. Niehr, "Host of Heaven," Toorn, K. van der, Bob Becking, and Pieter Willem van der Horst. *Dictionary of Deities and Demons in the Bible DDD*. 2nd extensively rev. ed. Leiden; Boston; Grand Rapids, Mich.: Brill; Eerdmans, 1999., 428-29; I. Zatelli, "Astrology and the Worship of the Stars in the Bible," *ZAW* 103 (1991): 86-99.

[59] Charlesworth, *The Old Testament Pseudepigrapha*, vol. 1, 23.

[60] Bauckham, *2 Peter, Jude*, 51.

4 that led up to the Flood as God's judgment. The Sons of God are the angelic Watchers who left their heavenly abode and mated with human women. Their offspring are the Nephilim, or giants that bring havoc on the earth.

But the point being made here by Jude is the violation of the heavenly/earthly divide of created flesh. The "gross immorality" of Sodom and Gomorrah, the pursuit of "strange flesh" (v. 7) that Jude speaks about in this context, is not the traditional notion of homosexuality that most believers think of when they hear the term Sodom and Gomorrah. The sin of the men of Sodom was not that they were going after men, but that they were going after *angels*. They wanted to violate that heavenly earthly separation of flesh. They were seeking the same primeval sin of Genesis 6 that was partly responsible for bringing about the Flood.

The Greek words for "gross immorality" (*ek porneuo*) indicates a heightened form of sexual immorality, and the Greek words for "strange flesh" (*heteros sarx*) indicate the pursuit of something different from one's natural flesh. This "strange flesh" cannot be a reference to homosexuality for several reasons. First, homosexuality is not the pursuit of *hetero* or different gender, it is the pursuit of *homo* or same gender. Secondly, homosexual behavior involves the *same* human male flesh, not different flesh as it would with angels. Thirdly, when the New Testament refers to the unnaturalness of homosexual acts it uses the Greek phrase, *para physin*, which means "contrary to nature" (Romans 1:26). The Bible certainly does condemn homosexuality as sin, but the sin of Sodom that is referenced by Jude and Peter is not so much homosexuality, but interspecies sexuality between angels and humans.

This connection of Sodom and Gomorrah to the Watchers' sexual sin and the Noahic Flood is a poetic doublet used by Jude that does not occur in the Old Testament. But it is a common occurrence in multiple Second Temple texts that draw from 1 Enoch.[61] Here are just a couple examples that illustrate the connection: [62]

[61] There is one other New Testament passage that links Sodom with the days of Noah: Luke 17:26-34. The reference then is to the nature of surprise judgment upon clueless sinners, not about the sin of angels and their giant progeny.
[62] See also Sirach 16:7-8; 2 En. 34:1.

Testament of Naphtali 3:4-5
Do not become like Sodom, which departed from the order of nature. Likewise the Watchers departed from nature's order; the Lord pronounced a curse on them at the Flood.[63]

3 Maccabees 2:4-5
Thou didst destroy those who aforetime did iniquity, among whom were giants trusting in their strength and boldness, bringing upon them a boundless flood of water. Thou didst burn up with fire and brimstone the men of Sodom, workers of arrogance, who had become known of all for their crimes, and didst make them an example to those who should come after. [64]

Jubilees 20:4-5
[L]et them not take to themselves wives from the daughters of Canaan; for the seed of Canaan will be rooted out of the land. And he told them of the judgment of the giants, and the judgment of the Sodomites, how they had been judged on account of their wickedness, and had died on account of their fornication, and uncleanness, and mutual corruption through fornication.[65]

Jude's linking of Sodom with the days of Noah and the sexual sin of the Watchers is a literary doublet that reinforces the Enochian Watcher paradigm. Combined with the other Enochian allusions, echoes, and linguistic memes in Jude this certainly provides a preponderance of evidence of the extensive dependency of Jude upon 1 Enoch far beyond the single quotation in verses 14-15.

Enoch and 2 Peter. 2 Peter 2:4-11 is understood by Bible scholars as having literary dependence upon Jude so it repeats these same memes of the fallen angels "bound in chains," and the Noah's Flood/Sodom doublet along with judgment. The language is redundant with Jude, but Peter adds one element to the mix that further elucidates this Enochic connection. Lest anyone misunderstand Jude's reference to the location of the binding of the angels, Peter locates it right in Sheol, as Enoch did. He writes that God "did

---

[63] James H. Charlesworth, *The Old Testament Pseudepigrapha*, vol. 1 (New York; London: Yale University Press, 1983), 812.
[64] Robert Henry Charles, "3 Mac 2:5," *Apocrypha of the Old Testament, Volume 1*. ed. Bellingham, WA: Logos Research Systems, Inc., 2004, 164.
[65] Charles, *Pseudepigrapha of the Old Testament*, vol. 1, 42.

not spare the angels when they sinned, *but cast them into hell* and committed them to chains of gloomy darkness" (v. 4). The word for "hell" in this passage is *tartaroo*, not *gehenna*, the traditional designation for the English translation of hell. *Tartaroo* is a Greek word that refers to Tartarus, the deepest location in Sheol,[66] where it was said in Greek lore that the gigantic Titans were chained.[67] Enoch however says this is where the fallen angels, the Watchers, were chained (1 En. 63:10-64:1).

The following chart is a helpful graphic summary of the content patterns and linguistic echoes of 1 Enoch that weave throughout Jude:[68]

Jude	1 Enoch
1–2 To those who are called, beloved in God the Father and kept for Jesus Christ: May mercy, peace, and love be multiplied to you.	1:8 And to all the righteous he will grant peace. He will preserve the elect, and kindness shall be upon them. They shall all belong to God and they shall prosper and be blessed; and the light of God shall shine unto them.
4 certain people…who long ago were designated for this condemnation	108:7 Things sealed in heaven… about to befall sinners
Jude 4 For certain people…designated for this condemnation, <u>ungodly people</u>	1:9 to destroy all the <u>ungodly</u>… the works of <u>ungodliness</u> which they have <u>ungodly</u> committed, and of all the hard things which <u>ungodly</u> sinners have spoken against Him.
4 who pervert the grace of our God into sensuality and deny our only Master and Lord, Jesus Christ	67:10; 48:10; 38:2 they believe in the debauchery of their bodies and deny the spirit of the Lord.
6 And angels who did not keep their own domain, but abandoned their proper abode…	12:4; 15:3 the Watchers who have abandoned the high heaven, the holy eternal place…
6 …went after strange flesh	12:4; 15:3 …and defiled themselves with women
6 He has kept in eternal bonds under darkness for the judgment of the great day	10:12 bind [the Watchers] for seventy generations underneath the rocks of the ground until the day of their judgment.

---

[66] Τάρτἄρος, H.G. Liddell, A Lexicon: Abridged from Liddell and Scott's Greek-English Lexicon (Oak Harbor, WA: Logos Research Systems, Inc., 1996), 793.
[67] See Hesiod, *Theogony* lines 720-739.
[68] I've culled these examples from my own research as well as Douglas Van Dorn, *Giants: Sons of the Gods* (Kindle Location 4850). Waters of Creation. Kindle Edition.

6 / 2 Peter 2:4 …cast them into Tartarus.	63:10 …being cast into the oppressive Sheol.
12 …waterless clouds…	100:11; 80:2 … every cloud…rain shall be withheld
12 …fruitless trees…	80:3 …fruit of the trees shall be withheld…
12 …raging waters…	67:5-7; 101:4 … a great turbulence and the stirring of the waters…
13 …wandering stars…	80:6; 46:6 …stars change their courses…
…the gloom of utter darkness has been reserved forever…	…darkness shall be their dwelling… (46:6)
14 *It was* also about these men *that* Enoch, *in* the seventh *generation* from Adam, prophesied…	60:8 wherein my grandfather [Enoch] was taken, the seventh from Adam.
14–15 Enoch…prophesied, saying, "Behold, the Lord came with many thousands of His holy ones, to execute judgment upon all, and to convict all the ungodly of all their ungodly deeds which they have done in an ungodly way, and of all the harsh things which ungodly sinners have spoken against Him."	1:9 Behold, he will arrive with ten million of the holy ones in order to execute judgment upon all. He will destroy the wicked ones and censure all flesh on account of everything that they have done, that which the sinners and the wicked ones committed against him.

Enoch and 1 Peter. 1 Peter 3:18-20 is a controversial passage that is relevant to our discussion of Enochian influence on the New Testament.

> 1 Peter 3:18-20
> For Christ also suffered once for sins, the righteous for the unrighteous, that he might bring us to God, being put to death in the flesh but made alive in the spirit, in which he went and proclaimed to the spirits in prison, because they formerly did not obey, when God's patience waited in the days of Noah, while the ark was being prepared, in which a few, that is, eight persons, were brought safely through water.

This is one of the most notoriously difficult passages in the New Testament to exegete, so we must proceed with caution and humility. Some scholars argue that this passage is poetically describing Jesus Christ's earthly ministry of preaching the Gospel to the "spiritually imprisoned" on earth after he rose from the dead. But the reflections of the Enochian Watcher incident are too strong to ignore.

The spirits to which Christ proclaims are not described as those humans living on earth, but rather as those spirits who are imprisoned or bound because of their disobedience *in the days of Noah*, not in the days of Christ. This again points to the disobedient angels before the Flood in 1 Enoch 10, who along with Azazel, are bound and imprisoned in Sheol, the underworld, until their judgment.

In this traditional understanding, Christ descends into Sheol or "hell" as the Apostle's Creed calls it,[69] and proclaims his triumph to those angelic spirits, the Watchers, who had sought to defy God and establish their own kingdom of rebellion.

As Nickelsburg points out, Christ's journey to Sheol is a mirror image of Enoch's own journey through Sheol in 1 Enoch 17-22, where he too sees the bound angels in prison awaiting their judgment.[70]

> 1 Enoch 18:13; 19:1-2
> This place is the (ultimate) end of heaven and earth: it is the prison house for the stars [angels] and the powers of heaven…"Here shall stand in many different appearances the spirits of the angels which have united themselves with women. They have defiled the people and will lead them into error so that they will offer sacrifices to the demons as unto gods, until the great day of judgment"[71]

But this single passage is not the only place where 1 Peter reflects Enochian influence. Nickelsburg argues that the entire book of 1 Peter follows the language and structure of 1 Enoch 108, illustrating a strong likelihood of familiarity and respect if not dependence. Here is the chart he provides:[72]

1 Peter	1 Enoch 108
3:12 those who do evil	2, 6, 10 those who do evil
1:23 perishable seed	3b seed will perish

[69] The Apostle's Creed is the most universally accepted creed of Christendom. For the full text see http://en.wikipedia.org/wiki/Apostles'_Creed.
[70] Nickelsburg, *1 Enoch: a Commentary*, 86.
[71] Charlesworth, *The Old Testament Pseudepigrapha*, vol. 1, 23. Enoch defines this place as Sheol in 103:7.
[72] Nickelsburg, *1 Enoch: a Commentary*, 560.

3:19-20 spirits in prison	3-6 spirits punished
3:20 Noah, sons saved	(106:16, 18) Noah, sons saved
1:10-12 Prophets, books, angels	6-7 Prophets, books, angels
1:8 Love Christ	8, 10 Love God, heaven
1:7, 18 Disdain silver, gold	8 Disdain silver, gold
2:2 Desire milk	8 Do not desire food
1:24 Flesh as grass	9 Breath that passes
Faith tested	Spirits tested
1:7 Found praiseworthy	9 Found pure
3:9 Bless, blessing	9-10 Bless, blessing
3:16; 4:4, 16 Reproach, insult, abuse	7, 10 Reproach, insult, abuse
2:9 Blessing by contrast	10 Blessing by contrast
2:9 Summoned from darkness to light	11 Summoned from darkness to light
5:4, 6 Exaltation	12 Exaltation
1:17; 2:23 Righteous Judgment	13 Righteous Judgment

The Book of Enoch for Christians Today

1 Enoch is a fascinating ancient manuscript with a long historical pedigree of value and respect within Judaism and Christianity. It is the only known source text explicitly attributed in Scripture that we possess with some manuscript certainty. It provides a helpful look into Second Temple Judaism and the development of Intertestamental interpretations that have influenced the New Testament doctrines of Messiah and his kingdom, the Son of Man, demons, resurrection, final judgment, and other eschatological imagery.

Evangelical Christians who uphold a high view of Scripture and its inspiration are uncomfortable with 1 Enoch because of its controversial ideas like the Watchers/Giants storyline and its astronomy based on ancient cosmology. Because the book is divided into five "books" or sections that were redacted over several centuries, skepticism of its contents is understandable.

But the preponderance of evidence shows that not only does the New Testament letter of Jude quote directly from 1 Enoch 1 (Book of the Watchers), but the entire letter and its alternate version in 2 Peter, show signs of literary and theological dependency on the rest of the Book of the Watchers (Chaps. 1-36), as well as chapter 80 (Book of Luminaries), chapter 46 (Book of Parables), and chapter 100 (Epistle of Enoch). 2 Peter shows evidence of structural and thematic dependency on 1 Enoch 17-22 and 108 (Additional Books). But the fact is, the entire New Testament shows such a multitude of allusions and linguistic echoes of the entire corpus of 1 Enoch, that one can safely say, the book and its basic interpretations may not be Scripture, but are surely legitimated by the Bible and are therefore worthy of study and high regard by the Christian Church.

Noah Primeval

Appendices

Chapter 2
The Sons of God
(Newly Expanded from *Noah Primeval*)

Deut. 6:4
"Hear, O Israel: The LORD our God, the LORD is one."

Psa. 82:1
God has taken his place in the divine council; in the midst of the gods he holds judgment.

A major premise of *Chronicles of the Nephilim* is that the gods of the ancient world were real spiritual beings with supernatural powers. Thus, the mythical literature and artistic engravings of the gods that have been uncovered by ancient Near Eastern archaeology reflect a certain amount of factual reality. The twist is that these gods are actually fallen divine angelic beings called "sons of God" (*bene ha elohim* in Hebrew) in the Bible. These sons of God had rebelled against God's divine council in heaven and came to earth in order to corrupt God's creation and deceive mankind into worshipping them in place of the real God. While this is not polytheism, neither is it absolute monotheism. It is Biblical monotheism, which will become clear shortly.

Though I have clearly engaged in imaginative creative license and fantasy in the novel, it is not without Biblical theological foundation. The purpose of this essay is to make an argument that in principle the Bible does in fact suggest a paradigm that reflects something similar to the theological interpretation presented in the novel. For that reason I might call *Chronicles of the Nephilim* theological novels.

Are the Sons of God Human or Divine?

One of the key passages that drives *Noah Primeval*, indeed the entire *Chronicles* saga, is Genesis 6:1-4.

> Genesis 6:1–4
> 1 When man began to multiply on the face of the land and daughters were born to them, 2 the sons of God saw that the daughters of man were attractive. And they took as their wives any they chose. 3 Then the LORD said, "My Spirit shall not abide in man forever, for he is flesh: his days shall be 120 years." 4 The Nephilim were on the earth in those days, and also afterward, when the sons of God came in to the daughters of man and they bore children to them. These were the mighty men who were of old, the men of renown.

This passage has been a source of exegetical struggle for millennia. The major questions we want to answer here are: Who are the Sons of God and who are the Nephilim? We will get into the Nephilim in a later chapter. First, let's take a look at the Sons of God.

Robert Newman has analyzed the history of interpretation of this passage to show that the supernatural interpretation of the Sons of God as being heavenly angelic beings was virtually unanimous in the ancient world until the first century after Christ.[1] This view basically believed that the Sons of God were rebellious divine beings from God's heavenly host, also called "Watchers," who came from heaven to earth and mated with human beings, thus violating the heavenly/earthly division that God established. The hybrid offspring of this abominable union was the giants called Nephilim. We will be examining this supernatural view later, and the Nephilim after that. For now let's look at the non-supernatural view of the Sons of God.

Newman points out that all the ancient Jewish views before Christ understood the Sons of God to be angelic. But by the time of the second century A.D., some of the Targumim, or Jewish commentaries on the Torah, began interpreting the Sons of God as human dynastic rulers or judges. This was most likely because the Rabbinic writers were reacting to the powerful rise of Christianity in their world. They had rejected Jesus as Messiah and the notion of a hybrid god-man coming from heaven and calling himself the "only begotten" Son of God, was too close to that supernatural view of the angelic Sons of God. Their non-supernatural interpretation springs from a theological reaction against Christianity.

The Sethite View. The non-supernatural view of the Sons of God as human beings began in the Christian world with Julius Africanus. It gripped

---

[1] Robert C. Newman, "The Ancient Exegesis of Genesis 6:2, 4, *Grace Theological Journal* 5,1 (1984) 13-36.

the Western Church through the support of Augustine and later Luther, Calvin, and Aquinas.[2] This "Sethite View" as it became known, claimed that the Sons of God in Genesis 6 were humans from the "righteous" lineage of Seth. Let Julius Africanus state the basic principles for us:

> The descendants of Seth are called the sons of God on account of the righteous men and patriarchs who have sprung from him, even down to the Saviour Himself; but that the descendants of Cain are named the seed of men, as having nothing divine in them, on account of the wickedness of their race and the inequality of their nature, being a mixed people, and having stirred the indignation of God.[3]

In this view, Cain's lineage is considered evil or condemned because it came from the first murderer, and his legacy led to Lamech, another murderer and polygamist (Gen. 4:19, 23). In contrast, Seth's lineage is considered elect or chosen by God because he replaced the bloodline of the innocent righteous victim Abel (Gen. 4:25).[4] Genesis 4:26 says "To Seth also a son was born, and he called his name Enosh. At that time people began to call upon the name of the LORD."

The picture here is that, in context, Seth's line called upon God. Chapter 5 is then the genealogy of this righteous line that leads to the righteous Noah. Then Genesis 6 talks about the fall of those righteous Sethites ("Sons of God") who should have remained separate from the unrighteous line of Cain ("daughters of men"). Instead, they took wives, and much like the intermarrying that God forbade the Israelites to engage in with the Canaanites, this intermixing led to great evil on the earth that resulted in the Flood. So the picture is one of violating the holiness code of separation between the godly and the godless.

There are multiple problems with this interpretation that make it untenable. Firstly, the Hebrew text of Gen. 4:26 does not say that Seth's line called upon the name of the Lord, but only that there was a general calling upon the name of the Lord. The Jewish Targumim even interpreted the Hebrew behind "began to call upon the name of the Lord" as actually meaning "began to make idols

---

[2] Van Dorn, Douglas (2013-01-21). *Giants: Sons of the Gods* (Kindle Locations 413-415). Waters of Creation. Kindle Edition.

[3] Dionysius of Alexandria, "The Extant Fragments of the Five Books of the Chronography of Julius Africanus," in *The Ante-Nicene Fathers: Fathers of the Third Century: Gregory Thaumaturgus, Dionysius the Great, Julius Africanus, Anatolius and Minor Writers, Methodius, Arnobius,* ed. Alexander Roberts, James Donaldson, and A. Cleveland Coxe, trans. S. D. F. Salmond, vol. 6 (Buffalo, NY: Christian Literature Company, 1886), 131.

[4] Abel offered an acceptable sacrifice to God, thus

and calling their idols by the name of the Lord."[5] This is a complete reversal of the typical understanding, as the Brown Driver Briggs Hebrew Lexicon reveals that the word for "began" can mean "pollute, defile, profane, or desecrate."[6] So it is possible that this text is referring to the sinfulness of humanity that will lead to the Flood. If one claims the context is Sethite, then those Sethites were not considered righteous, but wicked. But whether this was a profaning of or a calling upon God, the text does not link it exclusively to Seth's line, but to people in general.

Secondly, the "Sons of God" are nowhere in Scripture ever signified as the descendants of Seth. In fact, every single use of "Sons of God" elsewhere in the Old Testament is always a reference to angelic beings. (We will look at this shortly). In the New Testament, Adam is called a Son of God because he was the only human who was a direct creation of God, like the angels (Luke 3:38). Every human after Adam comes through Adam and is thus a son or daughter of Adam. Even Eve was not created directly by God, but out of Adam's own flesh. Paul writes that all unregenerate humanity is cursed "in Adam" (1 Cor. 15:22). Jesus is called the "unique Son of God" (John 3:16), because he was part of that heavenly host (Dan. 7:9-10), but was uncreated (Heb. 1:3-4). This is why believers in Christ are considered as "sons of God," because they are born from above with the seed of Christ to become like him (Gal. 3:26-27; Luke 20:36; 1 Cor. 15:49 – more on this later).

Thirdly, nowhere in the Bible is Seth called a Son of God. He is called a Son of Adam in the New Testament (Luke 3:38), but he is never called a Son of God. In the Old Testament, his birth was uniquely described as being "in the image and likeness of Adam," in a reflection of Adam's own creation (Gen 5:3). But this means he is distinctly described in terms of being a son of Adam, *not a Son of God.*

Fourthly, nowhere else in the Old Testament are the female descendants of Cain called "daughters of men." In fact, Genesis 6:1 defines the daughters of men for us: "man began to multiply on the face of the land and daughters were born to them." The Hebrew word for "man" is "*ha Adam*," or "the Adam." So the text itself tells us that the daughters of men are the generic "daughters of Adam," not the specific "daughters of Cain." But the daughters of Adam includes the bloodlines of both Cain *and* Seth. So for the contrast of Sons of God and daughters of men to make sense, the Sons of God cannot be

---

[5] Kevin Cathcart, Michael Maher, and Martin McNamara, eds., *The Aramaic Bible: The Targum Onqelos to Genesis*, trans. Bernard Grossfeld, vol. 6 (Collegeville, MN: The Liturgical Press, 1990), 50; *Targum Pseudo-Jonathan: Genesis*, trans. Michael Maher, vol. 1 (Collegeville, MN: The Liturgical Press, 1992), 35; *Targum Neofiti 1: Genesis*, trans. Martin McNamara, vol. 1 (Collegeville, MN: The Liturgical Press, 1992), 69.

[6] Francis Brown, Samuel Rolles Driver, and Charles Augustus Briggs, *Enhanced Brown-Driver-Briggs Hebrew and English Lexicon* (Oak Harbor, WA: Logos Research Systems, 2000), 320.

a reference to the human lineage of Cain, but a lineage of something that contrasts with human beings in general.

Fifthly, If the bloodline of Seth is considered righteous, and the bloodline of Cain, unrighteous, then there is a major contradiction occurring in Genesis 6, because it now depicts the "righteous" line of Seth as becoming corrupted by their union with the Cainite daughters. Since Noah comes from the lineage of Seth, he would be part of this corruption. But the text goes out of its way to specify that Noah was "blameless in his generation" (Gen. 6:9). The Hebrew word for "blameless" is *tamim*, which is a word that everywhere else in the Old Testament is used of physically unblemished sacrificial animals.[7] Noah was untainted by the lineage of the Sons of God. But if the Sons of God are the corrupted bloodline of Seth, then the text is at odds with itself in establishing the corruption of Noah's bloodline then denying it.

Sixthly, if one believes that these Sons of God are mere humans, then how is it that their union with other mere human women creates the offspring of Nephilim giants? These giants are not mere random anomalies, but a bloodline of giants that end up inhabiting the Promised Land in giant clans much later (Num. 13:32-33). We will explain why Nephilim are clearly giants in a later chapter. But the point is that mere human cohabitation with humans does not explain the giant offspring that are the result of that union. If the Nephilim are indeed giants, then the Sethite View crumbles.

Divine Kingship View. This view argues that the Sons of God in Genesis 6 are human kings or magistrates that claimed divinity or stood as representatives in the place of God over the people. As a major proponent of this view, Meredith Kline points out that it was a common behavior of ancient pagan kings to claim to be sons of gods who were patrons of their cities.[8] Cain is shown to be the first city builder (Gen. 4:17), thus tying the evil legacy of Cain to those dynastic urban rulers.

In this view, even the Bible claims a certain god-like prerogative of those in authority. To stand before the judges or rulers of Israel was considered the equivalent of standing before God in his representatives (Deut. 19:17; Ex. 22:8, 9, 28). Psalm 82 is a passage where God allegedly calls human judges "gods" for their rulership over the people. He then condemns them for failing to rule according to the Creator's standards. "How long will you judge unjustly and show partiality to the wicked?... I said, 'You are gods, sons of the Most High, all of you; nevertheless, like men you shall die, and fall like any prince'" (82:2, 6-7).

---

[7] Lev. 1:3, 10; 3:1, 6: 4:3, 23, 28, 32; 5:15, 18; 6:6; 9:2, 3; etc.

[8] Meredith Kline, "Divine Kingship and Genesis 6:1–4," *WTJ* 24 (1962): 187–204.

But what then is the sin of marrying daughters of men? Earlier Jewish commentators considered it the intermarriage of royalty with plebeians. But this view was more an expression of Rabbinic Judaism's fear of contamination with Gentiles than a Biblically legitimate interpretation, since the Genesis 6 intermarriages resulted in the Nephilim offspring called *gibborim*, or "mighty men who were of old, men of renown" (Gen. 6:4). Such glorious terms would not be used of the bastard sons of polluted royalty.

Kline suggests instead that the union of Sons of God with daughters of men was the polygamous marriages of tyrant kings. The last of Cain's line mentioned before this event is Lamech, who was a bigamist and a tyrant (Gen. 4:19, 23-24). The first *gibborim* on the earth after the Flood was Nimrod, another tyrant who was connected to that idolatrous city and tower of Babel (Gen 10:8-12). The sin of the Sons of God was polygamy, "characteristic institution of the ancient oriental despot's court. In this transgression the [Sons of God] flagrantly violated the sacred trust of their office as guardians of the general ordinances of God for human conduct. The princes born into these royal houses of the [Sons of God] were the Nephilim-Gibborim (vs. 4), the mighty tyrants who Lamech-like esteemed their might to be their right."[9]

The Divine Kingship View, like its non-supernatural ancestor, the Sethite View, also suffers a multitude of problems that make it untenable as well. Some of them, the same as their predecessor. Firstly, while it is true that ancient pagan kings did consider themselves offspring of deity, or demigods, nowhere in the Bible is the term "Sons of God" used in reference to such rulers outside this passage.[10] It is always used of the angelic beings of God's heavenly host (see later).

But even the representational view of judges standing in the place of God is not ever connected to the concept of divine sonship only to direct representation of God. Deuteronomy 19:17 says, "then both parties to the dispute shall appear before the LORD, before the priests and the judges who are in office." We see here that the judges may represent God's authority, but this is explicitly in their judging office, not in any special familial connection to God. They are not called "sons" or "gods" in any capacity. In fact, they are themselves subject to God's Law by which they adjudicate: so in this sense, both judge and judged stand before God.

Secondly, Psalm 82 is referring to judges in authority, but they are not human judges, they are divine judges. The first verse of that Psalm states, "God has taken his place in the *divine* council; in the midst of the *gods* he holds judgment." This passage will be examined in more detail later, but a

---

[9] Kline, "Divine Kingship," 196.

[10] When God was describing how Aaron could be Moses' mouthpiece he told Moses to tell Aaron what to say, and Moses would thus "be as God to him" (Ex. 4:16). But this is a verb metaphor for behavior, not a description of identity.

concurrent Psalm 89, fills out this "divine council" or divine assembly as being in the skies, not on earth, and consisting of members of his heavenly host, (Psa. 89:5-8). To assume that these judges are human begs the question when all the language refers to heavenly beings.

Thirdly, the contrast of Sons of God with daughters of men is not expressed in any terms reminiscent of royalty or kingship whatsoever. Only in Nimrod *after* the Flood, do we see language of kings and kingdoms (Gen. 10:8-12) which is very different from Genesis 6. It is most likely that there were antediluvian kingdoms, as ancient sources attest, but they are conspicuously absent in Genesis 6, which suggests a different theological focus for this God/man contrast. The passage begins the comparison by describing the birth of daughters to the growing population of men. This would be entirely unnecessary if the distinction was between royalty and commoners. It would be stating the obvious. Of course daughters come from men. Where else would daughters come from? There is simply no need to say that men were giving birth to daughters unless the point of contrast is their identity as human. And if the Sons of God are indeed only humans masquerading as divine, then the point of contrast is a false one.

The origin of the offspring of this union is of fundamental importance to the author. He sees the need to explain the ancestry of the Nephilim because of their mighty historical presence and effect. But surely he is not saying that polygamy is the heinous sin that inherently breeds monsters of tyranny that cause God to destroy the world. Polygamy is tolerated in the Old Testament, and it is never affirmed as ideal, but it is nowhere condemned as inherently evil or an abomination, like adultery, homosexuality, fornication, and bestiality is. Even the Messiah king of Israel, David, was a polygamist and gave birth to both good and bad seed through his many wives, as did his son, Solomon. Indeed, Messiah came through a lineage of polygamists (Matthew 1). Again, I am not making an argument *for* polygamy, but rather an argument *against* polygamy being a "high handed sin" worthy of world destruction.

No, what we have here is not a violation of monogamy, but an unholy union of the heavenly and the earthly. The human men give birth to daughters who mate with the Sons of God, and the result is the Nephilim, whose very hybrid nature is the source of their wickedness. The contrast of Sons of God with daughters of men makes sense if the point of difference is between divinity and humanity, not social status or hierarchy.

Fourthly, as stated before, the Nephilim will be easily proven to be the ancestors of the clans of giants in the Promised Land, which does not comport with mere human parentage. If the Nephilim/gibborim were tyrannical offspring who brought violence upon the land, then it would not make sense for Moses to make a genetic connection between them and the Anakim giants he faced down in the Promised Land (Num. 13:32-33).

The Supernatural View. The view that has weathered all these attempts to naturalize or demythologize the Bible text is the supernatural view that interprets the Sons of God as angelic beings who came to earth and mated with human woman to give birth to hybrid giants called Nephilim. This sin of heavenly/earthly contamination became a factor in bringing the Deluge of judgment upon the corrupted earth. But before embarking on an examination of this supernatural view of the Sons of God, it is important that we first take a look at the big picture of divinity in the heavenly places that sets the stage and leads us into the supernatural Biblical worldview of Sons of God and men.

The Plurality of the Divine

Jewish monotheism and Christian Trinitarianism affirm the oneness of God's being. Christianity contains an additional doctrinal nuance of three persons, Father, Son and Holy Spirit, who share the same substance while maintaining separate persons. In this way, the Christian is able to both affirm God's oneness (unity) *and* his threeness (diversity). Simply put, God is three persons in one being, *not* three beings.

Jews, Muslims and atheists who seem to assume that a monotheistic worldview cannot provide for diversity within the divine realm have often accused Christians of being polytheists. I call this Jewish/Muslim viewpoint, "absolute monotheism" as opposed to Biblical monotheism. What would shock most readers of the Bible is that the same Old Testament that proclaims the *Shema* about God being "one," also describes a cosmic worldview that includes a hierarchy in heaven of divine beings, a kind of governmental bureaucracy of operations that counsels with God, and carries out his decrees in heaven and earth. Biblical scholars refer to this hierarchy as the divine council, or divine assembly and it consists of beings that are referred to in the Bible as *gods*.

Before examining the texts about the divine council it is important to understand that the English word "God" can be misleading in Biblical interpretation. The most common Hebrew word translated in English as "God" in the Bible is *Elohim*. But God has many names in the text and each of them is used to describe different aspects of his person. *El*, often refers to God's powerful preeminence; *El Elyon* (God Most High) indicates God as possessor of heaven and earth; *Adonai* means God as lord or master; and *Yahweh* is the covenantal name for the God of Israel as distinguished from any other deity. *Elohim*, though it is the most common Hebrew word for God in the Old Testament, was also a word that was used of angels (Psa. 8:5; Heb. 2:7), gods or idols of pagan nations (Psa. 138:1), supernatural beings of the divine council (Psa. 82:6), departed spirits of humans (1Sam. 28:13), and demons (Deut.

32:17).[11] Scholar Michael S. Heiser has pointed out that the Hebrew word Elohim was more of a reference to a plane of existence than to a substance of being. In this way, Yahweh was *Elohim*, but no other elohim was Yahweh. Yahweh is incomparably *THE* Elohim of elohim (Deut. 10:17).[12]

Of Gods and Elohim

A common understanding of absolute monotheism is that when the Bible refers to other gods it does not mean that the gods are real beings but merely *beliefs* in real beings that do not exist. For instance, when Deuteronomy 32:43 proclaims "rejoice with him, O heavens, bow down to him, all gods," this is a poetic way of saying "what you believe are gods are not gods at all because Yahweh is the only God that exists." What seems to support this interpretation is the fact that a few verses before this (v. 39), God says, "See now, that I, even I am he, and there is no god [elohim] beside me." Does this not clearly indicate that God is the only God [elohim] that really exists out of all the "gods" [elohim] that others believe in?

Not in its Biblical context it doesn't.

When the text is examined in its full context of the chapter and rest of the Bible we discover a very different notion about God and gods. The phrase "I am, and there is none beside me" was an ancient Biblical slogan of incomparability of sovereignty, not exclusivity of existence. It was a way of saying that a certain authority was the most powerful *compared to* all other authorities. It did not mean that there were no other authorities that existed. We see this sloganeering in two distinct passages, one of the ruling power of Babylon claiming proudly in her heart, "I am, and there is no one beside me" (Isa. 47:8) and the other of the city of Nineveh boasting in her heart, "I am, and there is no one else" (Zeph. 2:15). The powers of Babylon and Nineveh are obviously not saying that there are no other powers or cities that exist beside them, because they had to conquer other cities and rule over them. In the same way, Yahweh uses that colloquial phrase, not to deny the existence of other gods, but to express his incomparable sovereignty over them.[13]

---

[11] Geoffrey W. Bromiley, "God, Names of," *The International Standard Bible Encyclopedia, Revised.* Wm. B. Eerdmans, 1988; 2002, p. 504-508.

[12] Michael S. Heiser, *The Myth That is True: Rediscovering the Cosmic Narrative of the Bible*, unpublished manuscript, 2011, p 25-29. Available online at www.michaelsheiser.com. I have read quite a few scholars on the divine council, but Michael Heiser has been the most helpful and represents the major influence on this essay.

[13] Michael S. Heiser, "Monotheism, Polytheism, Monolatry, or Henotheism? Toward an Assessment of Divine Plurality in the Hebrew Bible" (2008). Faculty Publications and Presentations. Paper 277, p. 12-15, http://digitalcommons.liberty.edu/cgi/viewcontent.cgi?article=1276&context=lts_fac_pubs&sei-redir=1#search=%22heiser+Monotheism,+Polytheism,+Monolatry,+or+Henotheism%22 accessed March 23, 2011.

In concert with this phrase is the key reference to gods early in Deuteronomy 32. Israel is chastised for falling away from Yahweh after he gave Israel the Promised Land: "They sacrificed to demons not God, to gods they had never known, to new gods that had come recently, whom your fathers had never dreaded" (Deut. 32:17). In this important text we learn that the idols or gods of the other nations that Israel worshipped were real beings that existed called "demons." At the same time, they are called, "gods" and "not God," which indicates that they exist as real gods, but are not THE God of Israel.

Psalm 106 repeats this same exact theme of Israel worshipping the gods of other nations and making sacrifices to those gods that were in fact demonic.

> Psa. 106:34-37
> They did not destroy the peoples, as the LORD commanded them, but they <u>mixed with the nations</u> and learned to do as they did.
> They served their <u>idols</u>, which became a snare to them. They sacrificed their sons and their daughters to the <u>demons</u>.

One rendering of the Septuagint (LXX) version of Psalm 95:5-6 reaffirms this reality of national gods being demons whose deity was less than the Creator, "For great is the Lord, and praiseworthy exceedingly. More awesome he is than all the gods. For all the gods of the nations are demons, but the Lord made the heavens."[14] Another LXX verse, Isa. 65:11, speaks of Israel's idolatry: "But ye are they that have left me, and forget my holy mountain, and prepare a table for [a demon], and fill up the drink-offering to Fortune [a foreign goddess].[15]

The non-canonical book of 1 Enoch, upon which some of *Noah Primeval* is based, affirms this very notion of gods as demons, the fallen angels of Genesis 6: "The angels which have united themselves with women. They have defiled the people and will lead them into error so that they will offer sacrifices to the demons as unto gods."[16]

The New Testament carries over this idea of demonic reality of beings behind the idols that pagans offered sacrifices to and worshipped: "No, I imply that what pagans sacrifice they offer to demons and not to God. I do not want

---

[14] Randall Tan, David A. deSilva, and Logos Bible Software. *The Lexham Greek-English Interlinear Septuagint*. Logos Bible Software, 2009. Baruch 4:7 in the Apocrypha echoes this Scriptural theme as well when speaking of Israel's apostasy: "For you provoked him who made you, by sacrificing to demons and not to God."

[15] Lancelot Charles Lee Brenton, *The Septuagint Version of the Old Testament: English Translation* (London: Samuel Bagster and Sons, 1870), Is 65:11. Randall Tan and David A. deSilva, Logos Bible Software, *The Lexham Greek-English Interlinear Septuagint* (Logos Bible Software, 2009), Is 65:11.

[16] 1 Enoch 19:1, James H. Charlesworth, *The Old Testament Pseudepigrapha: Volume 1*, (New York; London: Yale University Press, 1983).

you to be participants with demons (1Cor. 10:20)." In Revelation 9:20, the Apostle John defines the worship of gold and silver idols as being the worship of demons. The physical objects were certainly without deity as they could not "see or hear or walk," but the gods behind those objects were real beings with evil intent.

Returning to Deuteronomy 32 and going back a few more verses in context, we read of a reality-changing incident that occurred at Babel:

> Deut. 32:8-9
> When the Most High gave to the nations their inheritance, when he divided mankind, he fixed the borders of the peoples according to the number of the sons of God. But the LORD's portion is his people, Jacob his allotted heritage.

The reference to the creation of nations through the division of mankind and fixing of the borders of nations is clearly a reference to the event of the Tower of Babel in Genesis 11 and the dispersion of the peoples into the 70 nations listed in Genesis 10.

But then there is a strange reference to those nations being "fixed" according to the number of the sons of God.[17] We'll explain in a moment that those sons of God are from the assembly of the divine council of God. But after that the text says that God saved Jacob (God's own people) for his "allotment." Even though Jacob was not born until long after the Babel incident, this is an anachronistic way of referring to what would become God's people, because right after Babel, we read about God's calling of Abraham who was the grandfather of Jacob (Isa. 41:8; Rom. 11:26). So God allots nations and their geographic territory to these sons of God to rule over as their inheritance, but he allots the people of Jacob to himself, along with their geographical territory of Canaan (Gen. 17:8).

The idea of Yahweh "allotting" geographical territories to these sons of God who really existed and were worshipped as gods (idols) shows up again in several places in Deuteronomy:

> Deut. 4:19-20
> And beware lest you raise your eyes to heaven, and when you see the sun and the moon and the stars, all the host of heaven,

[17] The astute reader will notice that some Bible translations read "according to the sons of Israel." The ESV reflects the latest consensus of scholarship that the Septuagint (LXX) and the Dead Sea Scrolls (DSS) segment of this verse is the earlier and more accurate reading than the later Masoretic Text (MT) of the same. See Heiser, Michael, "Does Deuteronomy 32:17 Assume or Deny the Reality of Other Gods?" (2008). Faculty Publications and Presentations. Paper 322, p 137-145. http://digitalcommons.liberty.edu/lts_fac_pubs/322/

> you be drawn away and bow down to them and serve them, things that the LORD your God has allotted to all the peoples under the whole heaven.
>
> Deut. 29:26
> They went and served other gods and worshiped them, gods whom they have not known and whom He had not allotted to them.

"Host of heaven" was a term that referred to astronomical bodies that were also considered to be gods or members of the divine council.[18] The *Encyclopedia Judaica* notes that, "in many cultures the sky, the sun, the moon, and the known planets were conceived as personal gods. These gods were responsible for all or some aspects of existence. Prayers were addressed to them, offerings were made to them, and their opinions on important matters were sought through divination."[19]

But it was not merely the pagans who made this connection of heavenly physical bodies with heavenly spiritual powers. The Old Testament itself equates the sun, moon, and stars with the angelic "sons of God" who surround God's throne, calling them both the "host of heaven" (Deut. 4:19; 32:8-9).[20] Jewish commentator Jeffrey Tigay writes, "[These passages] seem to reflect a Biblical view that… as punishment for man's repeated spurning of His authority in primordial times (Gen. 3-11), God deprived mankind at large of true knowledge of Himself and ordained that it should worship idols and subordinate celestial beings."[21]

There is more than just a symbolic connection between the physical heavens and the spiritual heavens in the Bible. In some passages, the stars of heaven are linked *interchangeably* with angelic heavenly beings, also referred to as "holy ones" or "sons of God" (Psa. 89:5-7; Job 1:6).[22]

---

[18] H. Niehr, "Host of Heaven," Toorn, K. van der, Bob Becking, and Pieter Willem van der Horst. *Dictionary of Deities and Demons in the Bible DDD*. 2nd extensively rev. ed. Leiden; Boston; Grand Rapids, Mich.: Brill; Eerdmans, 1999., 428-29; I. Zatelli, "Astrology and the Worship of the Stars in the Bible," *ZAW* 103 (1991): 86-99.

[19] "Astrology", *Encyclopaedia Judaica* Michael Berenbaum and Fred Skolnik, eds. 2nd ed. Detroit: Macmillan Reference USA, 2007, p. 8424.

[20] See also Deut 4:19; Deut 17:3; 2King 23:4-5; 1King 22:19; Neh 9:6.

[21] Jeffrey Tigay, *JPS Torah Commentary: Deuteronomy* (Philadelphia: The Jewish Publication Society, 1996): 435; as quoted in Michael S. Heiser, "Deuteronomy 32:8 and the Sons of God," Bibliotheca Sacra 158 (January-March 2001): 72; online: http://thedivinecouncil.com/.
[Copyright © 2001 Dallas Theological Seminary;, online: http://thedivinecouncil.com/

[22] See also Job 38:4-7; Neh. 9:6; Psa 148:2-3, 1King 22:29 & 2King 21:5. In Isa 14:12-14 the king of Babylon is likened to the planet Venus (Morningstar) seeking to reign above the other stars of heaven, which are equivalent to the sons of God who surround God's throne on the "mount of assembly" or "divine council" (see Psa 89:5-7 and Psa 82).

Daniel 10:10-21 speaks of these divine "host of heaven" allotted with authority over pagan nations as spiritual "princes" or rulers battling with the archangels Gabriel and Michael.

> Daniel 10:13, 20
> [13] The prince of the kingdom of Persia withstood me twenty-one days, but Michael, one of the chief princes, came to help me… [20] "But now I will return to fight against the prince of Persia; and when I go out, behold, the prince of Greece will come.

Some Second Temple non-canonical Jewish texts illustrate an ancient tradition of understanding this interpretation of the gods of the nations as real spirit beings that rule over those nations:

> Jubilees 15:31-32
> (There are) many nations and many people, and they all belong to him, but over all of them he caused spirits to rule so that they might lead them astray from following him. But over Israel he did not cause any angel or spirit to rule because he alone is their ruler and he will protect them.

> Targum Jonathan, Deuteronomy 32, Section LIII
> When the Most High made allotment of the world unto the nations which proceeded from the sons of Noach [Noah], in the separation of the writings and languages of the children of men at the time of the division, He cast the lot among the seventy angels, the princes of the nations with whom is the revelation to oversee the city. [23]

In conclusion, the entire narrative of Deuteronomy 32 tells the story of God dispersing the nations at Babel and allotting the nations to be ruled by "gods" who were demonic fallen divine beings called sons of God. God then allots the people of Israel for himself, through Abraham, and their territory of Canaan. But God's people fall away from him and worship these other gods and are judged for their apostasy.

---

[23] See also 1 Enoch 89:59; 90:25, 3Enoch 48C:9, DSS War Scroll 1Q33 Col. xvii:7, Targum Jonathan, Genesis 11, Section II; Philo, On the Posterity of Cain and His Exile 25.89; Concerning Noah's Work as a Planter 14.59; On the Migration of Abraham 36.202; 1 Clement 29; Origen, First Principles 1.5.1. Thanks to Don Enevoldsen for some of these passages. Walter Wink footnotes a plenitude of texts about the 70 angel "gods" over the 70 nations in the Targums in Walter Wink. *Naming the Powers: The Language of Power in the New Testament* (The Powers : Volume One) (Kindle Locations 2235-2242). Kindle Edition.

We will now see that Yahweh will judge these gods as well.

Psalm 82

Bearing in mind this notion of Yahweh allotting gods over the Gentile nations while maintaining Canaan and Israel for himself, read this following important Psalm 82 where Yahweh now judges those gods for injustice and proclaims the Gospel that he will eventually take back the nations from those gods.

> Psa. 82:1-8
> God [elohim] has taken his place in the divine council;
> in the midst of the gods [elohim] he holds judgment:
> "How long will you judge unjustly
> and show partiality to the wicked? *Selah*
> Give justice to the weak and the fatherless;
> maintain the right of the afflicted and the destitute.
> Rescue the weak and the needy;
> deliver them from the hand of the wicked."
>
> They have neither knowledge nor understanding,
> they walk about in darkness;
> all the foundations of the earth are shaken.
>
> I said, "You are gods [elohim]
> sons of the Most High, all of you;
> nevertheless, like men you shall die,
> and fall like any prince."
> Arise, O God, judge the earth;
> for you shall inherit all the nations!

So from this text we see that God has a divine council that stands around him, and it consists of "gods" who are judging rulers over the nations and are also called *sons of the Most High* (synonymous with "sons of God"). Because they have not ruled justly, God will bring them low in judgment and take the nations away from them. Sound familiar? It's the same exact story as Deuteronomy 32:8-9 and Isaiah 24:21-22.

> Isaiah 24:21–22
> On that day the LORD will punish the host of heaven, in heaven, and the kings of the earth, on the earth. They will be

> gathered together as prisoners in a pit; they will be shut up in a prison, and after many days they will be punished.[24]

One of the Dead Sea Scrolls written in the first century B.C., reinforces this ancient Jewish interpretation of Psalm 82 as punishment focused on the divine council of gods, with Satan as their chief, allotted judicial authority over the nations:

> its interpretation concerns Satan and the spirits of his lot [who] rebelled by turning away from the precepts of God to ... And Melchizedek will avenge the vengeance of the judgements of God ... and he will drag [them from the hand of] Satan and from the hand of all the sp[irits of] his [lot]. And all the 'gods [of Justice'] will come to his aid [to] attend to the de[struction] of Satan.[25]

The idea that the Bible should talk about existent gods other than Yahweh is certainly uncomfortable for absolute monotheists. But our received definitions of monotheism are more often than not determined by our cultural traditions, many of which originate in theological controversies of other eras that create the baggage of non-Biblical agendas.

According to the Evangelical Protestant principle of *Sola Scriptura*, that the Bible alone is the final authority of doctrine, not tradition, believers are obligated to first find out what the Bible text says and then adjust their theology to be in line with Scripture, not the other way around. All too often we find individuals ignoring or redefining a Biblical text because it does not fit their preconceived notion of what the Bible *should* say, rather than what it actually says. The existence of other gods in Scripture is one of those issues.

In light of this theological fear, some try to reinterpret this reference of gods or sons of God in Psalm 82 as a poetic expression of human judges or rulers on earth metaphorically taking the place of God, the ultimate judge, by determining justice in his likeness and image. But there are three big reasons why this cannot be so: First, the terminology in the passage contradicts the notion of human judges and fails to connect that term ("sons of God") to human beings anywhere else in the Bible; Second, the Bible elsewhere

---

[24] Interestingly, this passage of Isaiah is not clear about what judgment in history it is referring to. But the language earlier in the text is similar to Psalm 82 and to the Flood when it says, "For the windows of heaven are opened, and the foundations of the earth tremble. 19 The earth is utterly broken, the earth is split apart, the earth is violently shaken. 20 The earth staggers like a drunken man; it sways like a hut; its transgression lies heavy upon it, and it falls, and will not rise again." So this may be another passage that uses a Flood reference tied in with the Watchers and their punishment.

[25] *11QMelch* Geza Vermes, *The Dead Sea Scrolls in English*, Revised and extended 4th ed. (Sheffield: Sheffield Academic Press, 1995), 361.

explicitly reveals a divine council or assembly of supernatural sons of God that are judges over geographical allotments of nations that is more consistent with this passage; Third, a heavenly divine council of supernatural sons of God is more consistent with the ancient Near Eastern (ANE) worldview of the Biblical times that Israel shared with her neighbors. We'll take a closer look at each of these following.

Human or Divine Beings?

Though the sons of God in Psalm 82 and elsewhere in the Old Testament have been understood as supernatural, angelic, or divine beings through most of Jewish and Christian history, it is fair to say that there has also been a minor tradition of scholars and theologians who have interpreted these beings as tyrannical human kings or judges.[26] They claim that the scenario in which we see these sons of God is a courtroom, the liturgy they engage in is legal formality, and the terminology they use is forensic (related to lawsuits), thus leading them to conclude that these are poetic descriptions of the responsibility of natural human authorities over their subjects on earth.

And they would be supernaturally wrong.

The setting, liturgy and language are indeed all courtroom-oriented in their context, but that courtroom is God's heavenly courtroom because that is how God reveals his own judgments to his people and the nations.

But don't take my word for it. Let's let Jesus exegete this passage for us.

In John 10, learned Jews in the Temple challenge Jesus about his identity as Christ. Jesus says that he and the Father are one, a clear claim of deity in the Hebrew culture, which results in the Jews picking up stones to stone him because he, being a man, made himself out to be God (10:33). Their particular Rabbinic absolute monotheism did not allow for the existence of divinity other than the Father. Jesus responds by appealing to this very passage we are discussing: "Jesus answered them, "Is it not written in your Law, 'I said, you are gods'? If he called them gods to whom the word of God came—and Scripture cannot be broken—do you say of him whom the Father consecrated and sent into the world, 'You are blaspheming,' because I said, 'I am the Son of God'?" (10:34-36).

If the judges in Psalm 82 "to whom the word of God came" were considered to be men rather than gods by Jesus, then his appeal to the passage

---

[26] Some prominent examples are: The Jewish Rabbinic Targums and Babylonian Talmud; Ramban (Nachmanides), *Commentary on the Torah: Genesis*, trans. Charles B. Chavel (New York: Shilo Publishing House, 1971); William H. Green, "The Sons of God and the Daughters of Men," in *The Unity of the Book of Genesis* (New York: Charles Scribner's Sons, 1910); Meredith G. Kline, *Kingdom Prologue: Genesis Foundations for a Covenantal Worldview*, (Overland Park: KS; Two Age Press, 2000); James B. Jordan, *Primeval Saints: Studies in the Patriarchs of Genesis* (Moscow, ID: Canon Press, 2001).

to justify his claims of deity would be nonsensical. He would essentially be saying "I am a god in the same way that human judges were human representatives of God." But this would not be controversial, it would divest Jesus of all deity, and they would certainly not seek to stone him. No, Jesus is affirming the divinity of the sons of God in Psalm 82 and chastising the Jews that their own Scriptures allow for the existence of divine beings (gods) other than the Father, so it would not be inherently unscriptural for another being, such as himself, to claim divinity. Of course, Jesus is the species-unique Son of God (John 1:18),[27] the "visible Yahweh" co-regent over the divine council (Dan. 7:13-14). But Jesus' point is that the diversity of deity is not unknown in the Old Testament.[28]

Jesus is arguing for the Trinitarian concept of divine diversity as being compatible with Old Testament monotheism, which was not compatible with man-made traditions of absolute monotheism that Rabbinic Jews followed. Remember, in the Bible, the concept of "god" (elohim) was about a plane of existence not necessarily a "being" of existence, so there were many gods (many elohim) that existed on that supernatural plane, yet only one God of gods (Elohim of elohim) who created all things, including those other elohim or sons of God.

This is precisely the nuanced distinction that the Apostle Paul refers to when he addresses the issue of food sacrificed to idols—that is, physical images of deities on earth. He considers idols as having "no real existence," but then refers to other "gods" in the heavens or on earth *who do exist*, but are *not the same* as the One Creator God:

> 1 Cor. 8:4-6
> Therefore, as to the eating of food offered to idols, we know that "an idol has no real existence," and that "there is no God but one." For although there may be so-called gods in heaven or on earth—as indeed there are many "gods" and many "lords"—yet for us there is one God, the Father, from whom are all things and for whom we exist, and one Lord, Jesus Christ, through whom are all things and through whom we exist.

---

[27] Heiser points about that the Greek word for "only begotten" son of God is *monogenes*, which is better translated as "unique," in the same way that Isaac was not Abraham's only son, but was referred to as his "only son" in this sense of uniqueness (Heb 11:17). Heiser *The Myth That is True,* p. 28-29.

[28] Michael S. Heiser, "Deuteronomy 32:8 and the Sons of God" http://www.thedivinecouncil.com/DT32BibSac.pdf, accessed March 23, 2011, p 20-21. See also, "Michael S. Heiser, "Mormonism's Use of Psalm 82," The FARMS Review, 19/1, 2007, http://www.thedivinecouncil.com/John10Psa82excerpt.pdf accessed March 23, 2011.

> 1 Cor. 10:18-20
> Consider the people of Israel: are not those who eat the sacrifices participants in the altar? What do I imply then? That food offered to idols is anything, or that an idol is anything? No, I imply that what pagans sacrifice they offer to demons and not to God. I do not want you to be participants with demons.

In 1 Corinthians, as in Revelation 9:20 quoted earlier, gods are not merely figments of imagination without existence in a world where the Trinity is the sole deity residing in the spiritual realm. Rather, physical idols (*images*) are "nothing," and "have no real existence" in that they are the representatives of the deities, not the deities themselves. But the deities behind those idols are real demonic beings; the gods of the nations who are not THE God, for they themselves were created by God and are therefore essentially incomparable to the God through whom are all things and through whom we exist.

The terminology used by Paul in the first passage contrasting the many gods and lords with the one God and Lord of Christianity reflects the client-patron relationship that ANE cultures shared. As K.L. Noll explains in his text on ancient Canaan and Israel, "Lord" was the proper designation for a patron in a patron-client relationship. There may have been many gods, but for ancient Israel, there was only one Lord, and that was Yahweh."[29]

This is certainly difficult for a modern mind to wrap itself around because we have been taught to think that there are only two diametrically opposed options: Either absolute diversity as in polytheism (many gods of similar essence) or absolute unity as in absolute monotheism that excludes the possibility of any other divine beings less than the One God.[30] As we have already seen, the Bible seems to indicate that there are other "gods" who are not of the same species as God the Father or God the Son, yet they do exist as supernatural entities with ruling power over the nations outside of God's people. Some scholars have used the term *monolatry* of this view rather than monotheism, because monotheism excludes the existence of any other gods, while monolatry allows for the existence of other gods, but demands the worship of one God who is essentially different from all other gods.[31]

---

[29] K.L. Noll, *Canaan and Israel in Antiquity: An Introduction*, New York: NY; Shefffield Academic Press, 2001, p. 212.

[30] Another possibility, henotheism, is the belief that there are many gods but one god is supreme over them all. But this is nothing more than an exalted polytheism because that supreme god is not a different species, whereas Biblical monotheism or *monolatry* maintains Yahweh as being of a different substance, essence, or species than the other gods it speaks of.

[31] Michael S. Heiser, The Divine Council In Late Canonical And Non-Canonical Second Temple Jewish Literature (Madison, WI: University of Wisconsin, 2004), 10.

Psalm 89 fills out the picture of the heavenly divine council as opposed to an earthly human one that is composed of these sons of God who are comparably less than Yahweh:

> Psa. 89:5-8
> Let the heavens praise your wonders, O LORD,
> your faithfulness in the assembly of the holy ones!
> For who in the skies can be compared to the LORD?
> Who among the heavenly beings (Hebrew: *sons of God*) is like the LORD,
> a God greatly to be feared in the council of the holy ones,
> and awesome above all who are around him?
> Oh LORD God of hosts…

Here, the sons of God are referred to as an assembly or council of holy ones that surround Yahweh in a heavenly court "in the skies," not in an earthly court or council of humans, thus reinforcing the supernatural distinction from earthly judges. Israel is sometimes called, "a holy nation" (Ex. 19:6), a "holy people" (Isa. 62:12), "holy ones" (Psa. 16:3), and other derivatives of that concept, but the Hebrew word for "holy ones" (*qedoshim*) is used often in the Bible to refer to these supernatural sons of God, as the "ten thousands of his holy ones," surrounding God's heavenly throne.[32] Verse 7 affirms this heavenly assembly with the phrase, "above all who are around him," and verse 8 contextualizes it with the phrase, "LORD God of hosts," which also refers to the heavenly host.

Daniel calls these heavenly *holy ones* "watchers" in Daniel 4 (verses 13, 17, and 23) and the New Testament book of Jude quotes the non-canonical book of Enoch regarding God coming with ten thousand of his holy ones who were also these sons of God from heaven (Jude 14).[33] The Dead Sea Scrolls of Qumran also uses the term "holy ones" in many passages to refer to angelic

---

[32] Deut 33:1-4; Job 5:1; 15:15; Psa 89:5, 7; Dan 8:13; 14:7; Zech 14:5; Jude 14. Michael S. Heiser points out that even though the MT of Deut 33:1-4 appears to reference the congregation of Israel as "holy ones," the Septuagint version of this verse, which the New Testament authors seem to quote, applies the term to "angels" at Sinai through whom God gave the law (Acts 7:52-53; Heb 2:1-2; Gal 3:19) Heiser, *The Myth That is True,* p. 149-152. In Daniel 7 it appears that the holy ones in God's divine council in heaven (7:27) are spoken of in fusion (7:21-22, 25) with the "saints" or holy ones in earthly Israel (7:18). The beasts of earthly kingdoms ruled over by their Watcher Princes are at war with Israel and its Watchers led by Michael. And in Deut 33:2-3 the term "holy ones" is used of both Israelites *and* supernatural beings in the same paragraph.

[33] And behold! He cometh with ten thousands of His holy ones, To execute judgment upon all, And to destroy all the ungodly. (Enoch 1:9)
And his activities had to do with the Watchers, and his days were with the holy ones. (Enoch 12:2)
And it came to pass after this that my spirit was translated And it ascended into the heavens: And I saw the holy sons of God. (Enoch 71:1)

beings from God's heavenly throne, making this a common Semitic understanding congenial with the worldview of Daniel.[34]

So there is Biblical unanimity in describing a heavenly host of ten thousands of sons of God, called gods, watchers, and holy ones who surround God's throne in the heavens as an assembly, and who counsel with God and worship him, and some of whom were given to rule over human nations in the past (also called "demons"), but have lost that privilege at some point. These gods are clearly *not* human judges on earth; they are supernatural elohim in the heavenly divine council.

Biblical Narratives of the Divine Council

The idea of a divine council of sons of God surrounding Yahweh as a hierarchical assembly is not merely mined from poetic passages in the Psalms; it is explicitly described in narratives that seem to settle any question of the matter. The two main passages are 1Kings 22 and Job 1-2.

In 1 Kings 22, the evil King Ahab of Israel seeks out prophets to tell him that his wicked intentions of invading Ramoth-gilead will be condoned by Yahweh. Many of the prophets encourage Ahab to do so with God's blessing. The prophet Micaiah however describes this vision of what actually happened:

> 1 Kings 22:19-22
> And Micaiah said, "Therefore hear the word of the LORD: I saw the <u>LORD sitting on his throne</u>, and all <u>the host of heaven standing beside him on his right hand and on his left</u>; and the LORD said, 'Who will entice Ahab, that he may go up and fall at Ramoth-gilead?' And one said one thing, and another said another. Then a spirit came forward and stood before the LORD, saying, 'I will entice him.' And the LORD said to him, 'By what means?' And he said, 'I will go out, and will be a lying spirit in the mouth of all his prophets.' And he said, 'You are to entice him, and you shall succeed; <u>go out and do so</u>.'

So, here we see an explicit description of how the Divine council of God operates. The "host of heaven" surround God's throne and God throws out a

[34] See these DSS passages: 1QM 1:16; 10:11–12; 12:1, 4, 7; 15:14; 1QS 11:7–8; 1QH 3:21–22; 10:35; 1QDM 4:1; 1QSb 1:5; 1Q 36:1; 1QapGen 2:1. John Joseph Collins, Frank Moore Cross and Adela Yarbro Collins, *Daniel: A Commentary on the Book of Daniel, Hermeneia—a critical and historical commentary on the Bible* (Minneapolis: Fortress Press, 1993), 313-314. The sectarian Jews from Qumran who safeguarded the Dead Sea Scrolls believed they were united with the angels in heaven, so they occasionally used the term "holy ones" to refer to those humans, but this reinforces the usage of the term as related to the angelic beings.

question that they then deliberate through council until God accepts one of the ideas offered by a spiritual being. God then gives that spirit the authority to go and perform the will of the council led by Yahweh.

Job 1 and 2 picture a very similar scene of God's heavenly assembly "presenting themselves" in a legal procession "before the Lord" with the added element of the prosecuting "adversary" (the Hebrew word *ha satan* means "the adversary"):

> Job 1:6-12
> Now there was a day when the sons of God came to present themselves before the LORD, and the adversary also came among them... And the LORD said to the adversary, "Behold, all that he has is in your hand. Only against him do not stretch out your hand." So the adversary went out from the presence of the LORD.

> Job 2:1-6
> Again there was a day when the sons of God came to present themselves before the LORD, and the adversary also came among them to present himself before the LORD… And the LORD said to the adversary, "Have you considered my servant Job, that there is none like him on the earth, a blameless and upright man, who fears God and turns away from evil?...And the LORD said to the adversary, "Behold, he is in your hand; only spare his life."

Once again, God counsels with his divine assembly of sons of God, asking questions and deliberating, in this case with the adversary, or "the satan." And then God gives the adversary the responsibility of carrying out the will of God's overseen council meeting. These sons of God are the same heavenly host who were present when God was creating the foundations of the earth and sang for joy as in the Psalm passages we already looked at (Job 38:7). These could not possibly be human rulers in an earthly court.

The last passage that describes a scene exactly like the previous two is in Zechariah:

> Zech. 2:13-3:7
> Be silent, all flesh, before the LORD, for he has roused himself from his holy dwelling. Then he showed me Joshua the high priest standing before the angel of the LORD, and Satan ["the adversary"] standing at his right hand to accuse him... Now Joshua was standing before the angel, clothed

> with filthy garments. And the angel said to those who were standing before him, "Remove the filthy garments from him."...And the angel of the LORD solemnly assured Joshua, "Thus says the LORD of hosts..."

In this vision of Zechariah he sees into God's holy dwelling where Yahweh has brought his heavenly host standing before him and the satan standing ready to accuse Joshua before the heavenly court. Yahweh is called "Lord of hosts" because he is surrounded by that heavenly host of the sons of God (Remembering that the name of God used in a passage reflects a distinct aspect of his identity or character related to that passage).

Scholars point out that this vision of Zechariah is exemplary of another thread throughout the Old Testament of the covenant lawsuit. As we have seen in Job, 1Kings, and Zechariah, there are legal procedures that the divine council engages in when deliberating judgment upon Israel or another guilty nation or king.[35] We have seen the summoning of the host and defendant, a presentation or standing before God, the judge's call for testimony from the council, accusation of an adversary or the prophet himself, and judgments carried out by council members. These same elements are assumed in other passages with a more implicit presence. Examples would be Isaiah's vision of the heavenly throne of seraphim with the plural imperatives by God "Who will go for us?" (Isa. 6) or "Comfort my people and cry out" (Isa. 40), or in Ezekiel's throne room vision (Ezek. 1). In these passages, God asks a question to an unknown group of beings. That group is no doubt the divine council around his throne. Jeremiah and Amos have even indicated that the mark of a true prophet versus a false prophet is that the true prophet has actually stood in the divine council and received his directions from God and his holy ones, while the false prophet has not (Jer. 23:18, 22; Amos 3:7).

Ancient Near Eastern Parallels

We have seen that the term *sons of God* is used interchangeably in the Bible with other words such as gods, demons (in some cases), heavenly host, host of heaven, watchers, holy ones, assembly, and divine council. But there is a third reason why the sons of God are not human judges but divine heavenly beings, and that is because the same divine council or assembly of gods shows up in ancient Near Eastern stories from Israel's neighbors. In other words, Israel shared a common cultural environment with her contemporaries that

[35] Herbert B. Huffmon "The Covenant Lawsuit in the Prophets" *Journal of Biblical Literature*, Vol. 78, No. 4 (Dec., 1959), pp. 285-295; Wheeler Robinson, H., "The Council of Yahweh," *Journal of Theological Studies*, 45 (1944) p.151-158.

provides a context for interpreting the intended meaning of the Biblical text.[36] If we want to understand the meaning of a mysterious term or concept in the Bible we must exegete the broader cultural context within which Israel operated. Though this is not finally determinative of Biblical meaning, it carries great weight considering that Israel shared much in common with her neighbors in terms of language, worldview, symbols, and imagination.

Thorkild Jacobsen, one of the foremost authorities on Mesopotamian religion explained the origins of the divine council as a projection of the terrestrial conditions of the primitive form of human governmental democracy that existed in ancient Mesopotamia.[37] Though this worldview of divine world and cosmos ruled by the gods through a divine assembly was not monolithic and unchanging, scholar Patrick D. Miller has argued that it nevertheless remained fairly constant, and was clearly a part of the Biblical worldview as well.[38]

The Mesopotamian/Sumerian worldview that Abraham was immersed in before his calling by Yahweh involved a divine council of gods that functioned in part as a court of law that ruled over the affairs of men, including the authority to grant kingship to both gods and men. The divine council met in assembly under the god of heaven and "father of the gods," An (later, *Anu*), but also with him was Enlil, the god of storm. Either of them would broach a matter to be considered which would then be discussed and debated by the "great gods" or "Anunnaki," whose number included the fifty senior gods as well as "the seven gods who determine fate."[39] As Jacobsen put it, "Through such general discussion—"asking one another," as the Babylonians expressed it—the issues were clarified and the various gods had opportunity to voice their opinions for or against."[40] The executive duties of carrying out the decisions of the assembly seemed to have rested with Enlil as a kind of co-regent with An.

The *Enuma Elish*, the Akkadian creation myth of the Babylonians who presided over Israel's exile also depicted a divine council of gods convened around the supreme god Marduk whose operations reflected the same

---

[36] John Walton called it a "common cognitive environment." John H. Walton. *Ancient Near Eastern Thought and the Old Testament: Introducing the Conceptual World of the Hebrew Bible.* Grand Rapids, MI: Baker, 2006; p 21.

[37] Thorkild Jacobsen, "Primitive Democracy in Ancient Mesopotamia," *Journal of Near Eastern Studies*, Vol. 2, No. 3 (Jul., 1943), 167.

[38] Patrick D. Miller, "Cosmology And World Order In The Old Testament The Divine Council As Cosmic-Political Symbol" *Israelite Religion and Biblical Theology: Collected Essays by Patrick D. Miller*, NY: Sheffield Academic Press, 2000, p 425.

[39] The seven gods who determine fate are portrayed in the novel *Noah Primeval* as An, the god of heaven, Enlil the god of storm, Enki the god of water, Ninhursag the earth goddess, Nanna the moon god, Utu the sun god and Inanna the goddess of sex and war.

[40] *Jacobsen*, "Primitive Democracy," 168-169.

heavenly bureaucracy.[41] But as Heiser points out, the consensus of scholars is that the Ugaritic pantheon of Canaan was the closest conceptual precursor to the Israelite version of the divine council.[42] The linguistic parallels are numerous and their comparison yields fruitful understanding of the Hebrew worldview, both in its similarities and differences.

Among the many parallels that Heiser draws out between the Canaanite and Israelite divine council are the following:

> Ugaritic terms of the divine council include, "assembly of the gods," and "assembly of the sons of God." The Hebrew Bible uses the terms, "sons of God," "assembly of the holy ones" (Psa. 89:6), and "gods" "in the council of God" (Job 15:8).
>
> In Ugaritic mythology, El was the supreme god and Baal was his vice-regent who ruled over the other gods of the council. In the Hebrew Bible, El/Elohim/Yahweh is the creator God, but he also has a vice-regent, the Son of Man/Angel of the Lord who was a visible incarnation of Yahweh who ruled over the divine council (Dan 7). Christians would eventually argue that this "second Yahweh" was in fact the pre-incarnate Messiah, Jesus.
>
> In Ugaritic mythology, El lived in a tent on a cosmic mountain in the north (*Sapon*) "at the source of two rivers," where the divine assembly would meet to deliberate and El would dispense his decrees. The mountain was a connection between heaven and earth, that is the earthly temple and its counterpart in heaven. In the Hebrew Bible, Yahweh's sanctuary is also in a tent (tabernacle) on a cosmic mountain, Zion (Psa 48:1-2), that is in the heights of the north (*Sapon*). This mountain is poetically linked to Eden, which is the source of rivers (Ezek 28:13-16) and its precursor, Mount Sinai was where God dispensed his word with his heavenly host (Deut 33:1-2; Ps 68:15-17).[43]

Though there are more congruencies between Canaanite and Hebrew concepts of the divine council than listed here, there are certainly many incongruencies as well, not the least of which was the polytheistic worldview

---

[41] Min Suc Kee, "The Heavenly Council and its Type-scene," *Journal for the Study of the Old Testament* Vol 31.3 (2007): 259-273.
[42] Heiser, The Divine Council, 8.
[43] Heiser, *The Divine Council*, 34-41.

of Canaan versus the monolatrous worldview of Israel. Gerald Cooke's classic article, "The Sons of (the) God(s)" lists the distinguishing characteristics in the Hebrew divine council of Sons of God:

> The full mythological representation is absent: the individualization, personalization and specification of function which characterized this idea-complex in other cultures of the Near East finds little parallel in the Hebrew-Jewish records... The recognition or assignment of functions in the heavenly company is never specific as in non-Israelite mythologies: they appear only in the more general functions of praising Yahweh and his holiness, serving as members of the royal court, entering into counsel with Yahweh, exercising judgment over the peoples, and doing Yahweh's bidding. Nor are the interrelations of the gods treated in Israelite tradition as in other traditions. Members of the heavenly company remain essentially characterless functionaries even when they appear singly as "the spirit," "the satan," or a "messenger." Yahweh's relationship to the lesser beings appears only in the formalized title "sons," which seems to describe only the classification of these beings as divine; Yahweh is never associated in paternal relationship with any particular one(s) of these beings, as are many of the gods of pagan pantheons; if Yahweh's "fatherhood" vis-à-vis these divine beings can be spoken of at all, it has only the formal meaning found in the idea of the "father" (i.e., head and leader) of a group of prophets; members of the heavenly company are never called "sons of Yahweh"; worship of any of the heavenly court besides the supreme Judge, Yahweh, is never countenanced by prophetic Yahwism. Members of the heavenly company never threaten his authority as supreme Judge and King.[44]

So the similarities between the worldviews need not mean absolute identity, but rather a common linguistic understanding that may help modern interpreters to understand the Bible in its own historical and cultural context. As Miller concluded, "The mythopoeic conception of the heavenly assembly, the divine council, is the Bible's way of pointing to a transcendent ordering and governing of the universe, of which all human governments and

---

[44] Gerald Cooke, "The Sons of (the) God(s)," *Zeitschrift für die alttestamentliche Wissenschaft*, n.s.:35:1 (1964), p 45-46.

institutions are a reflection, but even more it is the machinery by which the just rule of God is effective, that is, powerful, in the universe."[45]

[45] Miller, "Cosmology And World Order," p 442.

Chapter 3
The Nephilim

Gen. 6:4
The Nephilim were on the earth in those days, and also afterward, when the sons of God came in to the daughters of men, and they bore children to them. Those were the mighty men who were of old, men of renown.

Num. 13:33
And there we saw the Nephilim (the sons of Anak, who come from the Nephilim), and we seemed to ourselves like grasshoppers, and so we seemed to them."

The meaning of the Biblical word *Nephilim* has been a matter of unending controversy in Church history. That the word is still not translated into an English defined word but *transliterated* in most Bible translations is evidence of the fact that no agreement can be made over its original meaning. The two passages quoted above are the only two places in the Bible where the Hebrew word *Nephilim* is used. What would surprise some Bible readers is that these are not the only places where the Nephilim are *talked about* in Scripture. *Nephilim* has a theological thread that begins in Genesis 6 and goes through all the way to the New Testament.

The main opposing interpretations of this word come down to whether it is a reference to mighty leaders of some kind or to giants of abnormal human height. In my novel, *Noah Primeval* I take the perspective that these are giants and that these Bible passages are not merely obscure and unconnected factual references to an historical oddity, but rather that they are part of a diabolical supernatural plan of "sons of God" who are fallen from God's divine council of heavenly host. While my novel is obviously speculative fiction, it is nevertheless loosely based upon what I believe is a theological thread revealed in the Bible that becomes clear upon closer inspection of the text.

Taking a closer look at the first passage, Genesis 6:4, in context we read:

> Genesis 6:1-4
> When man began to multiply on the face of the land and daughters were born to them, the sons of God saw that the daughters of man were attractive. And they took as their wives any they chose. Then the LORD said, "My Spirit shall not abide in man forever, for he is flesh: his days shall be 120 years." The Nephilim were on the earth in those days, and also afterward, when the sons of God came in to the daughters of man and they bore children to them. These were the mighty men who were of old, the men of renown.

Genesis 6 is the opening lines to the story of Noah's flood. It talks about man reproducing upon the face of the earth and "sons of God" taking women as wives. I have already documented extensively elsewhere that the phrase *sons of God* in the Bible is a proven attribution to supernatural members of God's divine council. The emphasis in the text is on the separation of heavenly and earthly flesh.[1]

The New Testament agrees with the supernatural interpretation of divine/human cohabitation because it actually alludes to this very violation of fleshly categories and resultant punishment in 2 Peter and Jude, letters that show a strong literary interdependency on one another. If you compare the two passages you see the sensual violation of human and angelic flesh that is located in Genesis 6:

> 2Peter 2:4-10
> For if God did not spare angels when they sinned, but cast them into hell (*tartarus*) and committed them to chains of gloomy darkness to be kept until the judgment; if he did not spare the ancient world, but preserved Noah, a herald of righteousness, with seven others, when he brought a flood upon the world of the ungodly; if by turning the cities of Sodom and Gomorrah to ashes he condemned them to extinction, making them an example of what is going to happen to the ungodly;... then the Lord knows how to rescue the godly from trials, and to keep the unrighteous under punishment until the day of judgment, and especially those who indulge in the lust of defiling passion and despise authority.

[1] For a refutation of the sons of God as human rulers, judges or potentates, see Appendix A, "The Sons of God."

> Jude 6-7
> And angels who did not keep their own domain, but abandoned their proper abode, he has kept in eternal chains under gloomy darkness until the judgment of the great day—just as Sodom and Gomorrah and the surrounding cities, which likewise indulged in gross immorality and pursued strange flesh, serve as an example by undergoing a punishment of eternal fire.

Both these passages speak of the same angels who sinned before the flood of Noah, and who were committed to chains of gloomy darkness. 1 Peter 3:19-20 calls these imprisoned angels "disobedient." According to our study, the angelic sons of God are spoken of as sinning in Genesis 6, so these must be the same angels referred to by the authors of the New Testament. But just what is their sin?

Both Peter and Jude link the sin of those fallen angels with the sin of Sodom and Gomorrah, which is described as indulging in "gross immorality" by pursuing "strange flesh." The Greek words for "gross immorality" (*ek porneuo*) indicates a heightened form of sexual immorality, and the Greek words for "strange flesh" (*heteros sarx*) indicate the pursuit of something different from one's natural flesh. This "strange flesh" cannot be a reference to homosexuality for several reasons. First, homosexuality is not the pursuit of *hetero* or different gender, it is the pursuit of *homo* or same gender. Secondly, homosexual behavior involves the *same* human male flesh (*sarx*), not different flesh as it would with angels. Thirdly, when the New Testament refers to the unnaturalness of homosexual acts it uses the Greek phrase, *para physin*, which means "contrary to nature" (Romans 1:26). The Bible certainly does condemn homosexuality as sin, but the sin of Sodom that Jude and Peter focus on is not so much homosexuality, as interspecies sexuality between angels and humans.[2]

Angels on earth can have a physical presence. Bible students know that the men in Sodom were seeking to engage in sexual penetration of these same angels who visited Lot in his home. So here, men seeking sex with angels is not merely a homosexual act, it is a violation of the heavenly and earthly flesh distinction that the Scriptures seem to reinforce. So Peter and Jude link the angels sinning before the flood to the violation of a sexual separation of angels

---

[2] This observation is qualified by the fact that in Genesis 19, the Sodomites do not apparently know that the two men are angels. In Judges 19, the same exact scenario as Sodom is played out with Benjaminites in Gibeah seeking homosexual copulation with a visiting Levite (angels are not involved). Jude seems to draw out the angelic/human copulation angle in his interpretation. In full Biblical context, it may be most consistent to say that the sin of Sodom includes both homosexuality *and* angelic/human violation.

and humankind. The New Testament commentary on Genesis 6:1 affirms the supernatural view of the sons of God as having sex with humans.

It has been long known by scholars that the letter of *Jude* not only quotes a verse from the non-canonical book of *1 Enoch* (v. 14 with 1 Enoch 1:9),[3] but that Jude 6-7 and 2 Peter 2:4-10 both paraphrase content from *1 Enoch*, thus supporting the notion that the inspired authors intended an Enochian interpretation of "angels" called the Watchers (sons of God) having sexual intercourse with humans. *1 Enoch* extrapolates the Nephilim pre-flood story from the Bible as speaking of angels violating their supernatural separation and having sex with humans who bear them giants.[4]

Any question regarding the authenticity of this interpretation in Jude and Peter is quickly answered by another commonality that the New Testament authors share with the Enochian interpretation. Their combination of the angelic sexual sin with the sexual sin of Sodom is a poetic doublet that does not occur in the Old Testament, but does appear in multiple Second Temple Jewish manuscripts circulating in the New Testament time period. Jude and Peter are alluding to a common understanding of their culture that the angelic sin (and its hybrid fruit of giants) was an unnatural sexual violation of the divine and human separation. Here are some of those texts:

> Sirach 16:7-8
> He forgave not the <u>giants of old</u>, [the fruit of angelic sin]
> Who revolted in their might.
> He spared not the place where Lot sojourned,
> Who were arrogant in their pride.[5]

---

[3] Richard J. Bauckham, Vol. 50, *Word Biblical Commentary: 2 Peter, Jude*. Word Biblical Commentary. Dallas: Word, Incorporated, 2002. Here is the Jude passage: "[T]hat Enoch, the seventh from Adam, prophesied, saying, "Behold, the Lord comes with ten thousands of his holy ones, to execute judgment on all and to convict all the ungodly of all their deeds of ungodliness that they have committed in such an ungodly way, and of all the harsh things that ungodly sinners have spoken against him." Here is 1 Enoch 1:9, the text from the actual book that Jude quotes: "And behold! He cometh with ten thousands of His holy ones to execute judgement upon all, and to destroy all the ungodly: And to convict all flesh of all the works of their ungodliness which they have ungodly committed, and of all the hard things which ungodly sinners have spoken against Him.

[4] See 1 Enoch 6-19 and 86-88, especially 7:1-2; 15-16; 106:17. Richard Bauckham observes, "This was how the account of the "sons of God" in Gen 6:1–4 was universally understood (so far as our evidence goes) until the mid-second century A.D. (*1 Enoch* 6–19; 21; 86–88; 106:13–15, 17; *Jub.* 4:15, 22; 5:1; CD 2:17–19; 1QapGen 2:1; *Tg. Ps.-J. Gen.* 6:1–4; *T. Reub.* 5:6–7; *T. Napht.* 3:5; *2 Apoc. Bar.* 56:10–14)." Bauckham, Richard J. Vol. 50, *Word Biblical Commentary : 2 Peter, Jude*. Word Biblical Commentary. Dallas: Word, Incorporated, 2002, p 51. Other Second Temple Jewish writings support this ancient interpretation of pre-diluvian Nephilim/human offspring as giants: 3 Baruch 4:10; Wisdom 14:6; 3 Maccabees 2:4; Sirach 16:7.

[5] *Apocrypha of the Old Testament, Volume 1,* ed. Robert Henry Charles, Sir 16:7–8. Bellingham, WA: Logos Research Systems, Inc., 2004, 372.

Testament of Naphtali 3:4-5
[D]iscern the Lord who made all things, so that you do not become like Sodom, which departed from the order of nature. Likewise the Watchers departed from nature's order; the Lord pronounced a curse on them at the Flood.[6]

3 Maccabees 2:4-5
Thou didst destroy those who aforetime did iniquity, among whom were giants trusting in their strength and boldness, bringing upon them a boundless flood of water. Thou didst burn up with fire and brimstone the men of Sodom, workers of arrogance, who had become known of all for their crimes, and didst make them an example to those who should come after.[7]
[notice "making an example for those after" that is also in Jude 7]

Jubilees 20:4-5
[L]et them not take to themselves wives from the daughters of Canaan; for the seed of Canaan will be rooted out of the land. And he told them of the judgment of the giants, and the judgment of the Sodomites, how they had been judged on account of their wickedness, and had died on account of their fornication, and uncleanness, and mutual corruption through fornication.[8]

This is critical for understanding the Nephilim as unholy giant progeny because the Nephilim are the result of this sexual union between angel and human.

Some respond that angelic beings cannot have sex with humans because of Jesus' statement in Matthew 22. Jesus is confronted by Sadducees who are trying to force Jesus to deny the future Resurrection of the dead. They construct a hypothetical of a woman with multiple husbands due to their multiple deaths, and then ask him whose wife she is at the Resurrection, hoping to stump Jesus on the horns of a dilemma. Jesus replies, "You are mistaken, not understanding the Scriptures nor the power of God. "For in the

---

[6] Charlesworth, James H. *The Old Testament Pseudepigrapha: Volume 1*. New York; London: Yale University Press, 1983, 812

[7] *Apocrypha of the Old Testament, Volume 1.* ed. Robert Henry Charles, 3 Mac 2:5. Bellingham, WA: Logos Research Systems, Inc., 2004, 164.

[8] *Pseudepigrapha of the Old Testament Volume 1.* ed. Robert Henry Charles. Bellingham, WA: Logos Research Systems, Inc., 2004, 42.

resurrection they neither marry nor are given in marriage, but are like angels in heaven (Matt. 22:29-30)." Because of this, it is alleged that angels cannot have sexual intercourse with humans.

But this is not at all what Jesus is saying. Firstly, Jesus is not talking about sexual intercourse, but the Torah laws of marriage. Secondly, he is not talking about what angels *cannot* do, but what they *do not* do. Angels in heaven who obey God do not marry. This has no implication on what a fallen angel is capable of physically doing when coming to earth. Thirdly, Jesus is talking about angels in heaven, their natural abode, not angels on earth who left that abode to engage in unnatural liaisons with human flesh (as we saw in 2 Peter 2 and Jude). The angels in heaven that Jesus is talking about *are not* the angelic sons of God who left heaven, came to earth, and violated God's separation of those domains by having intercourse with human women.

Returning to Genesis 6:1-4, let's take a look at the second part of the passage:

> Genesis 6:3-4
> Then the LORD said, "My Spirit shall not abide in man forever, for he is flesh: his days shall be 120 years." The Nephilim were on the earth in those days, and also afterward, when the sons of God came in to the daughters of man and they bore children to them. These were the mighty men who were of old, the men of renown.

Some believe that the Nephilim were not the result of the sexual union between the sons of God and the daughters of men, but rather Nephilim were simply mighty warriors who happened to be around during those times before and after the incident of the sons of God. But this view would make nonsense of the text by inserting something (Nephilim) that has no connection to what is being talked about, namely the sexual unions and the flood. The pericope of verses 1-4 are a lead up to the proclamation of the flood in verses 5-8. The contextual reading of this concise unit of text begins talking about the sexual union of the sons of God with the daughters of men, then makes a reference to God's announcement to destroy the world in 120 years, which then references the Nephilim in context with that judgment, and then bookends the pericope with a reference back to the supernatural sexual union again, thus linking everything between those "bookends" as a parenthetical explanation of what it was all about, which leads to the Flood in verse 5-8.

Bookend About sex	Gen. 6:2	the sons of God saw that the daughters of man were attractive. And they took as their wives any they chose.

Parenthetical (The Flood as consequence)	Gen. 6:3-4a	the LORD said, "My Spirit shall not abide in man forever, for he is flesh: his days shall be 120 years." The Nephilim were on the earth in those days, and also afterward,
Bookend About sex	Gen 6:4b	…when the sons of God came in to the daughters of man and they bore children to them. These were the mighty men who were of old, the men of renown.

The Nephilim were around before and after *the flood*, not just the intermarriage incident, and they were the offspring result of that union.[9] Numbers 13:33 confirms this interpretation by saying that the Anakim at the time of Joshua were descendants of the Nephilim, so the Nephilim were clearly around before *and after* the flood.

But the question remains, what does the Hebrew word *Nephilim* mean? Some scholars looking at the root word claim that it means "fallen ones" because that is what the Hebrew means, "to fall." But there is a problem, and that is that the Septuagint (LXX) which is sometimes quoted by the New Testament authors as authoritative, translates this word as "giants."[10] Did those ancient Hellenized Jews not know the true meaning of the word? Or did they know something we do not?

Indeed, most all the ancient Jewish sources understood this term to mean "giant." We have already listed some passages from Sirach, The Testament of Naphtali, and Jubilees. But here are some more from other Second Temple Jewish texts:

> Jubilees 5:1
> And when the children of men began to multiply on the surface of the earth and daughters were born to them, that the angels of the LORD saw… that they were good to look at. And they took wives for themselves from all of those whom they chose. And they bore children for them; <u>and they were the giants</u>.[11]

---

[9] C. Westermann concludes, "There is every reason to think that the Nephilim in 4a refers to mythical semi-divine beings, the fruit of the marriages of the gods with humans, who are connected with the overstepping of the bound presumed in the divine judgment of v. 3. "They came to (them)": " 'to come to' refers in this connection only to the male who visits a woman's quarters, 30:16; 38:16" (E.A. Speiser, AncB). This sentence states expressly that children were the fruit of the union of the sons of the gods with the daughters of men, and clearly, they must be something special; they could not be just plain ordinary mortals." Claus Westermann, *A Continental Commentary: Genesis 1-11*, (Minneapolis, MN: Fortress Press, 1994), p 378.

[10] Genesis 6:4; Randall Tan, David A. deSilva, and Logos Bible Software. *The Lexham Greek-English Interlinear Septuagint*. Logos Bible Software, 2009.

[11] James H. Charlesworth, *The Old Testament Pseudepigrapha and the New Testament: Expansions of the "Old Testament" and Legends, Wisdom, and Philosophical Literature, Prayers, Psalms and Odes, Fragments of Lost Judeo-Hellenistic Works*, vol. 2 (New Haven; London: Yale University Press, 1985), 64.

Jubilees 29:9
But formerly the land of Gilead was called "the land of Raphaim" because it was the land of the Raphaim. And the Raphaim were born as giants whose height was ten cubits, nine cubits, eight cubits, or down to seven cubits.[12]

Baruch 3:26
[26] There were the giants born that were famous of old, Great of stature, *and* expert in war.[13]

Josephus Antiquities 1:73
for many angels of God accompanied with women, and begat sons that proved unjust, and despisers of all that was good, on account of the confidence they had in their own strength; for the tradition is, That these men did what resembled the acts of those whom the Grecians call giants.[14]

Biblical scholar Michael S. Heiser has revealed a Biblical reference that virtually seals the proof that *Nephilim* are giants, not "fallen ones." In his article "The Meaning of the Word *Nephilim*: Fact vs. Fantasy,"[15] he explains that Hebrew is a consonantal language, which means it only spells words with consonants and leaves the reader to fill in the vowels. The ancient language of Aramaic is also consonantal and has an influence on the Hebrew text at various places. There are many Aramaic words in the Bible, and some chapters, such as Daniel 2-7, are written in Aramaic. In later copies, vowel markers were added to the consonants in order to aid in pronunciation. He then explains that the Hebrew word NPHL which is translated into English as *Nephilim* has different meanings depending on the morphology or form of the word. Evidently the morphological form of the word in Genesis and Numbers is not that of the Hebrew meaning "fallen ones," but that of the Aramaic meaning "giants." And the Bible clinches this argument in Numbers 13:33:

Num. 13:33
And there we saw the Nephilim (the sons of Anak, who come from the Nephilim), and we seemed to ourselves like grasshoppers, and so we seemed to them."

---

[12] Charlesworth, *The Old Testament Pseudepigrapha,* vol. 2, 111.
[13] Robert Henry Charles, ed., *Apocrypha of the Old Testament*, vol. 1 (Bellingham, WA: Logos Bible Software, 2004), 589.
[14] Flavius Josephus and William Whiston, *The Works of Josephus : Complete and Unabridged* (Peabody: Hendrickson, 1996).
[15] Michael S. Heiser, "The Meaning of the Word *Nephilim*: Fact vs. Fantasy" http://www.acidtestpress.com/

Heiser shows that the first spelling of Nephilim in the verse is the Hebrew spelling, but the second spelling of Nephilim is a variation that is clearly the Aramaic spelling of "giants." And should there really be any question when the text then describes these Anakim who are descendants of the Nephilim as being gigantic in stature such that they felt like small grasshoppers?

Now, let's take a look at the Anakim and the other giants that the Bible speaks about. The Anakim or "sons of Anak" are unquestionably defined as giants throughout the Bible because of their tall height (Num. 13:33; Deut. 1:28; 2:10, 21; 9:2). One of the most famous of all those Anakim giants was Goliath.[16] He stood at 9 feet 9 inches tall.[17] His coat of mail alone weighed about 125 pounds, the weight of his spearhead was 15 pounds (1 Sam. 17:4-7). There is no doubt Goliath was unnaturally huge in stature. And his brother Lahmi was of the same genetic material (1 Chron. 20:5). Philistia had a big problem with these Anakim giants, as 1 Chronicles 20:4-8 attests to no less than four of them who had to be killed by King David's men in an apparent campaign against the giants.

But if we go back in time from David to Joshua and the conquest of the Promised Land, we see that the giant Anakim that David was fighting were merely the leftovers from Joshua's own campaign to wipe them out:

> Josh. 11:21-22
> Then Joshua came at that time and <u>cut off the Anakim</u> from the hill country, from Hebron, from Debir, from Anab and from all the hill country of Judah and from all the hill country of Israel. <u>Joshua utterly destroyed them</u> with their cities. There were <u>no Anakim left</u> in the land of the sons of Israel; only in Gaza, in Gath, and in Ashdod some remained.

As it turns out, the Anakim were not the only giants in the land. Evidently the land in and around Canaan was crawling with giants that were called by different names in different locations, such as the Emim, Rephaim, Zamzummim, Horim, Avvim and possibly Caphtorim:

> Deut. 2:10-11, 20-23
> (The <u>Emim</u> formerly lived there, a people <u>great and many, and tall as the Anakim</u>. Like the Anakim they are also counted as <u>Rephaim</u>, but the Moabites call them <u>Emim</u>… (It is also

[16] Joshua 11:21 says that the only Anakim left by the time of David were in Gaza, Ashdod and Gath, Goliath's home.

[17] David Tsumura, *The First Book of Samuel, The New International Commentary on the Old Testament* (Grand Rapids, MI: Wm. B. Eerdmans Publishing Co., 2007), 441.

> counted as a land of Rephaim. Rephaim formerly lived there—but the Ammonites call them Zamzummim— a people great and many, and tall as the Anakim; but the LORD destroyed them before the Ammonites, and they dispossessed them and settled in their place as he did for the people of Esau, who live in Seir, when he destroyed the Horites before them and they dispossessed them and settled in their place even to this day. As for the Avvim, who lived in villages as far as Gaza, the Caphtorim, who came from Caphtor, destroyed them and settled in their place.)

King Og of Bashan is described as one of the last of "the remnant of the Rephaim" whose bed was over 13 feet long and made of iron (Deut. 3:11). That is no kingly bed alone; that was a large strong iron bed to hold a giant of about 11 feet tall.

The Rephaim have an interesting Biblical history that connects them literarily to the Nephilim in the Bible. First, the Nephilim are described as *gibborim*, or "mighty men," "men of renown" in Genesis 6:4. This word *gibborim* is used extensively throughout the Old Testament of warriors such as David's "mighty men" (2 Sam. 16:6) and even of the giant Goliath (1Sam. 17:51) and many others.[18] The Nephilim were mighty warriors. The Rephaim were mighty warrior kings.

In the Bible, *Rephaim* were Anakim giants, descendants of the Nephilim (Deut. 2:11; Num. 13:33), who were so significant they even had a valley named after them ("Valley of the Rephaim," Josh. 15:8). But there is more to the Rephaim than that. Og, king of Bashan, was a Rephaim giant, and all his portion of the land of Bashan was called "the land of the Rephaim" (Deut. 3:13), an ambiguous wording that could equally be translated as "the 'hell' of the Rephaim."[19] Bashan was a deeply significant spiritual location to the Canaanites and the Hebrews. And as the *Dictionary of Deities and Demons in the Bible* puts it, Biblical geographical tradition agrees with the mythological and cultic data of the Canaanites of Ugarit that "the Bashan region, or a part of it, clearly represented 'Hell', the celestial and infernal abode of their deified dead kings," the Rephaim.[20]

---

[18] Josh. 1:14; 6:2; 8:3; 10:2, 7; Judges 11:1, 1Sam. 2:4; 14:52; 2Sam.23:16-17, 22; 2King 5:1; 24:14; 1Chr. 7:5, 7, 11, 40, and many others. Nimrod was noted as being the first Gibborim mighty warrior on earth after the flood: Gen. 10:8; 1Chr. 5:24.

[19] K. van der Toorn, Bob Becking and Pieter Willem van der Horst, *Dictionary of Deities and Demons in the Bible DDD*, 2nd extensively rev. ed., 162 (Leiden; Boston; Grand Rapids, Mich.: Brill; Eerdmans, 1999).

[20] "Bashan," *DDD*, p 161-162. "According to *KTU* 1.108:1–3, the abode of the dead and deified king, and his place of enthronement as *[Rephaim]* was in *[Ashtarot and Edrei]*, in amazing correspondence with the Biblical tradition about the seat of king Og of Bashan, "one of the survivors of the Rephaim, who lived in Ashtarot and Edrei" (Josh 12:4)."

Mount Hermon was in Bashan, and Mount Hermon was a location in the Bible that was linked to the Rephaim (Josh. 12:1-5), but was also the legendary location where the sons of God were considered to have come to earth and have sexual union with the daughters of men to produce the giant Nephilim.[21]

There are two places in the Bible that hint at the Rephaim being warrior kings brought down to Sheol in similar language to the Ugaritic notion of the Rephaim warrior kings in the underworld:

> Is. 14:9
> Sheol beneath is stirred up to meet you when you come;
> it rouses the [*Rephaim*] to greet you,
> all who were leaders of the earth;
> it raises from their thrones
> all who were kings of the nations.
>
> Ezek. 32:21
> They shall fall amid those who are slain by the sword… The mighty [*Rephaim*] shall speak of them, with their helpers, out of the midst of Sheol: "They have come down, they lie still, the uncircumcised, slain by the sword."

Scholar Michael S. Heiser concludes about this connection of Rephaim with dead warrior kings in Sheol and Bashan:

> That the Israelites and the biblical writers considered the spirits of the dead giant warrior kings to be demonic is evident from the fearful aura attached to the geographical location of Bashan. As noted above, Bashan is the region of the cities Ashtaroth and Edrei, which both the Bible and the Ugaritic texts mention as abodes of the Rephaim. What's even more fascinating is that in the Ugaritic language, this region was known not as Bashan, but *Bathan*—the Semitic people of Ugarit pronounced the Hebrew "sh" as "th" in their dialect. Why is that of interest? Because "Bathan" is a common word across all the Semitic languages, biblical Hebrew included, for "serpent." The region of Bashan was known as "the place of the serpent." It was ground zero for the Rephaim giant clan and,

[21] The non-canonical book of Enoch supports this same interpretation: "Enoch 6:6 And they were in all two hundred [sons of God]; who descended in the days of Jared on the summit of Mount Hermon, and they called it Mount Hermon, because they had sworn and bound themselves by mutual imprecations upon it."

spiritually speaking, the gateway to the abode of the infernal deified Rephaim spirits.[22]

List of Giants

The Bible reveals that there are many different clans that either were giants or had giants among them that were ultimately related in a line all the way back to the Nephilim of Genesis:

Nephilim (Gen. 6:1-4; Num. 13:33)
Anakim (Num. 13:28-33; Deut. 1:28; 2:10-11, 21; 9:2; Josh. 14:12)
Amorites (Amos 2:9-10)
Emim (Deut. 2:10-11)
Rephaim (Deut. 2:10-11, 20; 3:11)
Zamzummim (Deut. 2:20)
Zuzim (Gen. 14:5)
Perizzites (Gen. 15:20; Josh. 17:15)
Philistines (2 Sam. 21:18-22)
Horites/Horim (Deut. 2:21-22)
Avvim (Deut. 2:23)
Caphtorim (Deut. 2:23)

The following are implied as including giants by their connection to the descendants of Anak in Numbers 13:28-29:

Amalekites
Hittites
Jebusites—The word means "Those who trample"
Amorites (Amos 2:9-10 links the Amorites as giant in size and strength)
Hivites (Has the same consonants as a Hebrew name for snake)

Here were the towns, cities or locations that were said to have had giants in them:

Gob (2 Sam. 21:18)
Hebron/Kiriath-arba (Num. 13:22; Josh. 14:15)
Ar (Deut. 2:9)

---

[22] Michael S. Heiser *The Myth That is True*, p 169. Available online at www.michaelsheiser.com.

Seir (Deut. 2:21-22)
Debir/ Kiriath-sepher (Josh. 11:21-22)
Anab (Josh. 11:21-22)
Gaza (Josh. 11:21-22)
Gath (Josh. 11:21-22)
Ashdod (Josh. 11:21-22)
Bashan (Deut. 3:10-11)
Ashteroth-karnaim (Gen. 14:5)
Ham (Gen. 14:5)
Shaveh-kiriathaim (Gen. 14:5)
Valley of the Rephaim (Josh. 15:8)
Moab (1 Chron. 11:22)

Many significant individuals are described in the Bible implicitly or explicitly as giants being struck down in war against Israel:

Goliath (1 Sam. 17)
Lahmi, Goliath's brother (1 Chron. 20:5; 2 Sam. 21:19)
Ishbi-benob (2 Sam. 21:16)
Saph/Sippai (2 Sam. 21:17; 1 Chron. 20:4)
Arba (Josh. 14:15)
Sheshai (Josh.15:14, Num. 13:22)
Ahiman (Josh. 15:14, Num. 13:22)
Talmai (Josh. 15:14, Num. 13:22)
An unnamed warrior giant (1 Chron. 20:6)
And unnamed Egyptian giant (1 Chron. 11:23)
Og of Bashan (Deut. 3:10-11)

The ubiquitous presence of giants throughout the narrative of the Old Testament is no small matter. When God commanded the people of Israel to enter Canaan and devote certain of those peoples to complete destruction (Deut. 20:16-17), it is no coincidence that most of these peoples we have already seen were connected in some way to the Anakim giants, and Joshua's campaign explicitly included the elimination of the Anakim/Sons of Anak giants.

War of the Seed

We see that the cursed giants in the Promised Land of Canaan are theologically and genetically tied to the original Nephilim before the flood. And these Nephilim were the giant hybrid offspring of the angelic Watchers mating with human women. The natural question becomes, why is this act and its fruit so abominable? What is *really* going on?

The answer to that question begins right after Genesis 6 introduces the Sons of God pursuing their unholy union and producing their cursed Nephilim seed, we read:

> Genesis 6:5–6, 11-14
> The LORD saw that the wickedness of man was great in the earth, and that every intention of the thoughts of his heart was only evil continually…Noah was a righteous man, blameless in his generation. Noah walked with God… Now the earth was corrupt in God's sight, and the earth was filled with violence. And God saw the earth, and behold, it was corrupt, for all flesh had corrupted their way on the earth. And God said to Noah, "I have determined to make an end of all flesh, for the earth is filled with violence through them. Behold, I will destroy them with the earth.

Right after these intermarriages, mankind is spoken of as thoroughly evil, which is deserving of judgment in itself. All flesh is corrupt and filled with violence. Notice "corruption" is mentioned three times, making it a very important concept for the writer. (Saying "the earth was corrupt" is not a statement about environmentalism, it is a way of saying "the inhabited world of humanity," or "all people on earth.")

Now if the writer had intended to say that all mankind was merely corrupted spiritually he would have only used the word for mankind (*adam*), as he had used everywhere else in the chapter — but he did not. He used the word for "flesh" (*basar*) – "all flesh was corrupted" — which distinctly points to the physical body. So there is a corruption of flesh going on by the angels mating with humans. This is the first sign that the intermingling is unholy.

This corruption is highlighted even more when we see that Noah is described as a "righteous man, blameless in his generation." (v. 9). Noah walked with God which is an expression of his righteousness. But the Hebrew word used for "blameless" (*tamim*) is the same word that is used everywhere else in the Old Testament of the physically unblemished animal for ritual sacrifice (38 times). God seemed to be requiring physical perfection in sacrifices that symbolized the obligation of purity for atonement. Genesis 6 is making the point that Noah's flesh, or his genetics, were pure and undefiled by the lineage of the Nephilim, the tainted genetic "seed" (Seed of the Serpent).

So the Sons of God (Watchers) were mating with human women and giving birth to a corrupted bloodline of giants called the Nephilim. This corruption was most likely the Watchers' attempt to defile and desecrate God's created order of separation between humanity and divinity. Since man was created as God's image (Gen. 1:26-27), they were seeking to corrupt that image of God.

The immoral weight of this act can be understood through God's provision of capital punishment. After the Flood, God gives Noah a primary command, "Whoever sheds the blood of man, by man shall his blood be shed, for God made man in his own image" (Gen. 9:6). So the violation of God's image in a single human requires the judgment of death. How much more the attempt to defile all of humanity.

But more than that, I believe the Sons of God were seeking to pollute the human bloodline in order to stop the coming Messiah. As we pointed out, Noah was uncorrupted in his flesh. And guess who came from Noah's bloodline? Jesus, the Messiah (Luke 3:23-38).

So how did these Sons of God know about the Messiah so early in the primeval history? Because when God cursed the Serpent in the Garden (and that serpent is Satan, a fallen angelic being – Revelation 12:9), he said, "I will put enmity between you and the woman, and between your Seed and her Seed; he shall bruise your head, and you shall bruise his heel" (Genesis 3:15).

"Seed" means "offspring." God here is prophesying a cosmic War of the Seed, where the "offspring of the Serpent" or Seed of the Serpent will war with the Seed of Eve. And Messiah is the ultimate Seed who would crush the head of the Serpent (Revelation 12:10; Luke 10:17-20). In the New Testament, Jesus is called "the Seed" to whom God made his promises, the Seed of Abraham (Galatians 3:16), the seed of David (Rom. 1:3).

So since the fallen angels knew about this prophecy through Satan, who was one of them, it would make sense that they would seek to corrupt that Seedline of Eve with their own seed to stop Messiah from coming, by corrupting God's image.

A High Priest

In Judaism, the high priest was the one who mediated between men and God. But there was a problem with this system. The high priests were also sinners who needed to atone for their sins as well, over and over. The sacrificial system of atonement was imperfect. It needed a perfect sinless high priest to atone for sins once and for all. It needed a God-man hybrid.

Think about it. The whole point of the Messiah was that he needed to be fully human, but also fully God. This is why the Virgin Birth is so necessary. If Messiah's human flesh was tainted by fallen angelic seed, then he could not be fully human. But the mediator between God and man must be fully human, uncorrupted flesh like Noah, or he cannot mediate for humans.

In the same way, the mediator had to be fully God or he could not mediate on God's behalf. The "seed" that united with Mary's egg in her womb had to be from God himself, not an angel, which is a finite created being.

Look at this New Testament passage and see that reality expressed through Jesus being a sinless "high priest" who sacrifices for our forgiveness or atonement:

> Hebrews 7:26–28
> For it was indeed fitting that we should have such a high priest [Jesus], holy, innocent, unstained, separated from sinners, and exalted above the heavens. He has no need, like those high priests, to offer sacrifices daily, first for his own sins and then for those of the people, since he did this once for all when he offered up himself. For the law appoints men in their weakness as high priests, but the word of the oath, which came later than the law, appoints a Son who has been made perfect forever.

The fallen Watchers were trying to corrupt the bloodline of Messiah with their own pre-emptive tainting of the Seed of Eve with the Seed of the Serpent. Their sexual union with human beings was a mockery of demigods versus the fully enfleshed God-man (John 1:14). But they did not win this War of the Seed. As we will see later, Jesus would triumph over them through his death, resurrection and ascension into heaven as the enthroned Son of Man, Son of God, Yahweh incarnate.

Chapter 4
Leviathan

In my novel *Noah Primeval*, I have a sea dragon called "Leviathan" that is crucial to the plot of the story. While it is a monster of the waters, a symbol of chaos, it nevertheless is providentially used by Elohim and tamed for his own purposes. I found this character in the pages of the Bible itself and had always been befuddled by its presence. It kept popping up in strange places like the book of Job and the Psalms. Was this a mythical creature in holy writ? Was God's power over Leviathan as described in Job, just a poetic way of saying God is in control and nothing is too powerful for him? I would soon find out that this recurring sea dragon was so much more.

Job 41 is devoted to this strange creature. Here is that chapter in its entirety:

> "Can you draw out Leviathan with a fishhook
> or press down his tongue with a cord?
> Can you put a rope in his nose
> or pierce his jaw with a hook?
> Will he make many pleas to you?
> Will he speak to you soft words?
> Will he make a covenant with you
> to take him for your servant forever?
> Will you play with him as with a bird,
> or will you put him on a leash for your girls?
> Will traders bargain over him?
> Will they divide him up among the merchants?
> Can you fill his skin with harpoons
> or his head with fishing spears?
> Lay your hands on him;
> remember the battle—you will not do it again!
> Behold, the hope of a man is false;

he is laid low even at the sight of him.
No one is so fierce that he dares to stir him up.
Who then is he who can stand before me?
Who has first given to me, that I should repay him?
Whatever is under the whole heaven is mine.
I will not keep silence concerning his limbs,
or his mighty strength, or his goodly frame.
Who can strip off his outer garment?
Who would come near him with a bridle?
Who can open the doors of his face?
Around his teeth is terror.
His back is made of rows of shields,
shut up closely as with a seal.
One is so near to another
that no air can come between them.
They are joined one to another;
they clasp each other and cannot be separated.
His sneezings flash forth light,
and his eyes are like the eyelids of the dawn.
Out of his mouth go flaming torches;
sparks of fire leap forth.
Out of his nostrils comes forth smoke,
as from a boiling pot and burning rushes.
His breath kindles coals,
and a flame comes forth from his mouth.
In his neck abides strength,
and terror dances before him.
The folds of his flesh stick together,
firmly cast on him and immovable.
His heart is hard as a stone,
hard as the lower millstone.
When he raises himself up the mighty are afraid;
At the crashing they are beside themselves.
Though the sword reaches him, it does not avail,
nor the spear, the dart, or the javelin.
He counts iron as straw,
and bronze as rotten wood.
The arrow cannot make him flee;
for him sling stones are turned to stubble.
Clubs are counted as stubble;
he laughs at the rattle of javelins.
His underparts are like sharp potsherds;

he spreads himself like a threshing sledge on the mire.
He makes the deep boil like a pot;
he makes the sea like a pot of ointment.
Behind him he leaves a shining wake;
one would think the deep to be white-haired.
On earth there is not his like,
a creature without fear.
He sees everything that is high;
he is king over all the sons of pride."

As this chapter describes, this is no known species on earth. From the smoke and fire out of its mouth to the armor plating on back and belly, this monster of the abyss was more than a mere example of showcasing God's omnipotent power over the mightiest of creatures, it was symbolic of something much more. And that much more can be found by understanding Leviathan in its ancient Near Eastern (ANE) and Biblical covenantal background.

In ANE religious mythologies, the sea and the sea dragon were symbols of chaos that had to be overcome to bring order to the universe, or more exactly, the political world order of the myth's originating culture. Some scholars call this battle *Chaoskampf*—the divine struggle to create order out of chaos.

Hermann Gunkel first suggested in *Creation and Chaos* (1895) that some ANE creation myths contained a cosmic conflict between deity and sea, as well as sea dragons or serpents that expressed the creation of order out of chaos.[1] Gunkel argued that Genesis borrowed this idea from the Babylonian tale of Marduk battling the goddess Tiamat, serpent of chaos, whom he vanquished, and out of whose body he created the heavens and earth.[2] After this victory, Marduk ascended to power in the Mesopotamian pantheon. This creation story gave mythical justification to the rise of Babylon as an ancient world power most likely in the First Babylonian Dynasty under Hammurabi (1792-1750 B.C.).[3] As the prologue of the Code of Hammurabi explains, "Anu, the majestic, King of the Anunnaki, and Bel, the Lord of Heaven and Earth, who established the fate of the land, had given to Marduk, the ruling son of Ea, dominion over mankind, and called Babylon by his great name;

[1] Hermann Gunkel, Heinrich Zimmern; K. William Whitney Jr., trans., *Creation And Chaos in the Primeval Era And the Eschaton: A Religio-historical Study of Genesis 1 and Revelation 12* (Grand Rapids: MI: Erdmans, 1895, 1921, 2006), xvi.

[2] "He cast down her carcass and stood upon it.
After he had slain Tiamat, the leader…He split her open like a mussel into two parts; Half of her he set in place and formed the sky… And a great structure, its counterpart, he established, namely Esharra [earth]." (Enuma Elish, Tablet IV, lines 104-105, 137-138, 144 from Heidel, *Babylonian Genesis*, 41-42)

[3] Heidel, *Babylonian Genesis*, 14.

when they made it great upon the earth by founding therein an eternal kingdom, whose foundations are as firmly grounded as are those of heaven and earth."[4] The foundation of Hammurabi's "eternal kingdom" is literarily linked to Marduk's foundational creation of heaven and earth.

Later, John Day argued in light of the discovery of the Ugarit tablets in 1928, that Canaan, not Babylonia is the source of the combat motif in Genesis,[5] reflected in Yahweh's own complaint that Israel had become polluted by Canaanite culture.[6] In the Baal cycle, Baal battles Yam (Sea) and conquers it, along with "the dragon," "the twisting serpent," to be enthroned as chief deity of the Canaanite pantheon.[7]

Creation accounts were often veiled polemics for the establishment of a king or kingdom's claim to sovereignty.[8] Richard Clifford quotes, "In Mesopotamia, Ugarit, and Israel the *Chaoskampf* appears not only in cosmological contexts but just as frequently—and this was fundamentally true right from the first—in political contexts. The repulsion and the destruction of the enemy, and thereby the maintenance of political order, always constitute one of the major dimensions of the battle against chaos."[9]

The Sumerians had three stories where the gods Enki, Ninurta, and Inanna all destroy sea monsters in their pursuit of establishing order. The sea monster in two of those versions, according to Sumerian expert Samuel Noah Kramer, is "conceived as a large serpent which lived in the bottom of the "great below" where the latter came in contact with the primeval waters."[10] The prophet Amos uses this same mythopoeic reference to a serpent at the bottom of the sea as God's tool of judgment: "If they hide from my sight at the bottom of the sea, there I will command the serpent, and it shall bite them" (Amos 9:3). One Sumerian text, *The Return of Ninurta to Nippur*, refers to

---

[4] W.W. Davies, The Codes of Hammurabi and Moses: With Copious Comments, Index, and Bible References (Berkeley, CA: Apocryphile Press, 1905, 2006), 17.

[5] John Day, *God's Conflict with the Dragon*. Day argues that the Canaanite Baal cycle implies a connection with creation, since it is a ritual fertility festival (cyclical creation) falling on the New Year, traditionally understood as the date of creation. But his strongest appeal is the argument in reverse that the Canaanite myth makes a connection between creation and *Chaoskampf* because the Old Testament does so.

[6] "Then the word of the LORD came to me, saying, "Son of man, make known to Jerusalem her abominations and say, 'Thus says the Lord GOD to Jerusalem, "Your origin and your birth are from the land of the Canaanite, your father was an Amorite and your mother a Hittite." (Ezek. 16:1-3)

[7] Most recently, David Tsumura has argued against any connection of such mythic struggle in the Biblical text in favor of mere poetic flair: David Toshio Tsumura, *Creation And Destruction: A Reappraisal of the Chaoskampf Theory in the Old Testament* (Winona Lake, IN: Eisenbrauns, 2006).

[8] Bruce R. Reichenbach. "Genesis 1 as a Theological-Political Narrative of Kingdom Establishment." *Bulletin for Biblical Research* 13.1 (2003).

[9] Clifford. *Creation Accounts*; footnote 13 p 8.

[10] Samuel Noah Kramer. *Sumerian Mythology: A Study of Spiritual and Literary Achievement in the Third Millennium B.C.* Philadelphia, PA: University of Pennsylvania Press, 1944, 1961, 1972; p 77-78.

"the seven-headed serpent" that must be defeated by the divine Ninurta to illustrate his power to overcome chaos.[11]

Perhaps the closest comparison with the Biblical Leviathan comes from Canaanite texts at Ugarit as John Day argued. In 1929, an archeological excavation at a mound in northern Syria called Ras Shamra unearthed the remains of a significant port city called Ugarit whose developed culture reaches back as far as 3000 B.C.[12] Among the important finds were literary tablets written in multiple ancient languages, which opened the door to a deeper understanding of ancient Near Eastern culture and the Bible. Ugaritic language and culture shares much in common with Hebrew that sheds light on the meaning of things such as Leviathan.

A side-by-side comparison of some Ugaritic religious texts about the Canaanite god Baal with Old Testament passages reveals a common narrative: Yahweh, the charioteer of the clouds, metaphorically battles with Sea (Hebrew: *yam*) and River (Hebrew: *nahar*), just as Baal, the charioteer of the clouds, struggled with Yam (sea) and Nahar (river), which is also linked to victory over a sea dragon/serpent.

UGARTIC TEXTS	**OLD TESTAMENT**
'Dry him up. O Valiant Baal! Dry him up, O Charioteer of the Clouds! For our captive is Prince Yam [Sea], for our captive is Ruler Nahar [River]!' (KTU 1.2:4.8-9)[13] What manner of enemy has arisen against Baal, of foe against the Charioteer of the Clouds? Surely I smote the Beloved of El, Yam [Sea]? Surely I exterminated Nahar [River], the mighty god? Surely I lifted up the dragon, I overpowered him? I smote the writhing serpent, Encircler-with-seven-heads! (KTU 1.3:3.38-41)[14]	Did Yahweh rage against the rivers, Or was Your anger against the rivers (*nahar*), Or was Your wrath against the sea (*yam*), That You rode on Your horses, On Your chariots of salvation? (Hab. 3:8) In that day Yahweh will punish Leviathan the fleeing serpent, With His fierce and great and mighty sword, Even Leviathan the twisted serpent; And He will kill the dragon who lives in the sea. (Isa 27:1) "You divided the sea by your might; you broke the heads of the sea monsters on the waters. You crushed the heads of Leviathan. (Psa 74:13-14)

[11] *The Return of Ninurta to Nippur*, Black, J.A., Cunningham, G., Robson, E., and Zólyomi, G., The Electronic Text Corpus of Sumerian Literature, Oxford 1998-. <http://www.gatewaystobabylon.com/myths/texts/ninurta/nippurninurta.htm>

[12] "Ugarit," Avraham Negev, *The Archaeological Encyclopedia of the Holy Land.* 3rd ed. New York: Prentice Hall Press, 1996.

[13] Wyatt, *RTU2*, pp 69-70.

[14] In Wyatt, *RTU2*, pp 79. Charioteer of the Clouds also appears in these texts: KTU 1.3:4:4, 6, 26; 1.4:3:10, 18; 1.4:5:7, 60; 1.10:1:7; 1.10:3:21, 36; 1.19:1:43; 1.92:37, 39.

Baal fights Sea and River to establish his sovereignty. He wins by drinking up Sea and River, draining them dry, which results in Baal's supremacy over the pantheon and the Canaanite world order.[15] In the second passage, Baal's battle with Sea and River is retold in other words as a battle with a "dragon," the "writhing serpent" with seven heads.[16] Another Baal text calls this same dragon, "*Lotan*, the wriggling serpent."[17] The Hebrew equivalents of the Ugaritic words *tannin* (dragon) and *lotan* are *tannin* (dragon) and *liwyatan* (Leviathan) respectively.[18] The words are etymologically equivalent. Not only that, but so are the Ugaritic words describing the serpent as "wriggling" and "writhing" in the Ugaritic text (*brh* and '*qltn*) with the words Isaiah 27 uses of Leviathan as "fleeing" and "twisting" (*bariah* and '*aqalaton*).[19] Notice the last Scripture in the chart that refers to Leviathan as having multiple heads *just like the Canaanite Leviathan*. Bible scholar Mitchell Dahood argued that in that passage of Psalm 74:12-17 the author implied the seven heads by using seven "you" references to God's powerful activities surrounding this mythopoeic defeat of Leviathan.[20]

The Apostle John adapted this seven-headed dragon into his Revelation as a symbol of Satan as well as a chaotic demonic empire (Rev 12:3; 13:1; 17:3). Jewish Christians in the first century carried on this motif in texts such as the *Odes of Solomon* that explain Christ as overthrowing "the dragon with seven heads… that I might destroy his seed."[21]

Thus, the Canaanite narrative of Lotan (Leviathan) the sea dragon or serpent is undeniably employed in Old Testament Scriptures and carried over into the New Testament as well.[22]

And notice as well the reference to the Red Sea event also associated with Leviathan in the Biblical text. In Psalm 74 above, God's parting of the waters is connected to the motif of the Mosaic covenant as the creation of a new world order in the same way that Baal's victory over the waters and the dragon are emblematic of his establishment of authority in the Canaanite pantheon. This

---

[15] KTU 1.2:4:27-32.

[16] Though this verse is spoken by the goddess Anat, Baal's sister, as if she accomplished these exploits, it is described as Baal's actions in other texts (KTU 1.5:1:1-35) that lead scholars to conclude that Anat's claims are a kind of sympathetic unity of action between her and Baal.

[17] KTU 1.5:1:1-4. Wyatt *RTU2*, p 115.

[18] Walter C. Kaiser, Jr. *The Ugaritic Pantheon* (dissertation). Ann Arbor, Mich: Brandeis University, 1973, p 212.

[19] Michael Fishbane, *Biblical Myth and Mythmaking*, Oxford University Press, 2003, 39.

[20] Mitchell Dahood S.J., *Psalms II 51-100 The Anchor Yale Bible* (Yale University Press, 1995) 24.

[21] Odes of Solomon 22:5. James H. Charlesworth, *The Old Testament Pseudepigrapha and the New Testament, Volume 2: Expansions of the "Old Testament" and Legends, Wisdom, and Philosophical Literature, Prayers, Psalms and Odes, Fragments of Lost Judeo-Hellenistic Works* (New Haven; London: Yale University Press, 1985).

[22] See also Isa 51:9; Ezek 32:2; Rev 12:9, 16, 17;

covenant motif is described as a *Chaoskampf* battle with the Sea and Leviathan (sometimes called *Rahab*[23]) in this and other Biblical references.

> Psa. 74:12-17
> You broke the heads of the sea monsters in the waters.
> You crushed the heads of Leviathan;...
> You have prepared the light and the sun.
> You have established all the boundaries of the earth;
>
> Psa. 89:9-10
> You [Yahweh] rule the raging of the sea;
> when its waves rise, you still them.
> You crushed Rahab like a carcass;
> you scattered your enemies with your mighty arm.
>
> Isa. 51:9-10
> Awake, awake, put on strength, O arm of Yahweh;
> Awake as in the days of old, the generations of long ago.
> Was it not You who cut Rahab in pieces,
> Who pierced the dragon?
> Was it not You who dried up the sea,
> The waters of the great deep;
> Who made the depths of the sea a pathway
> For the redeemed to cross over?
>
> Isa. 27:1
> In that day the LORD with his hard and great and strong sword will punish Leviathan the fleeing serpent, Leviathan the twisting serpent, and he will slay the dragon that is in the sea.

The story of deity battling the river, the sea, and the sea dragon Leviathan/Rahab is clearly a common covenant motif in the Old Testament and its surrounding ancient Near Eastern cultures.[24] The fact that Hebrew Scripture shares common words, concepts, and stories with Ugaritic scripture does not mean that Israel is affirming the same mythology or pantheon of deities, but rather that Israel lives within a common cultural environment, and

[23] An Akkadian equivalent of "Rabu" can be found on the Babylonian Map of the World describing a sea serpent. Wayne Horowitz, *Mesopotamian Cosmic Geography*, Winona Lake; IN: Eisenbrauns, 1998, 35; "Rahab," *DDD*, 684.

[24] Psalm 18, 29, 24, 29, 65, 74, 77, 89, 93, and 104 all reflect *Chaoskampf*. See also Exodus 15, Job 9, 26, 38, and Isa 51:14-16; 2Sam 22.

God uses that cultural connection to subvert those words, concepts and stories with his own poetic meaning and purpose.

Chaoskampf and creation language are used as word pictures for God's covenant activity in the Bible. For God, describing the creation of the heavens and earth was a way of saying he has established his covenant with his people through exodus into the Promised Land,[25] reaffirming that covenant with the kingly line of David, and finalizing the covenant by bringing them out of exile. The reader should understand that the Scriptures listed above, exemplary of *Chaoskampf,* were deliberately abbreviated to make a further point below. I will now add the missing text in those passages in underline to reveal a deeper motif at play in the text—a motif of creation language as covenantal formation.

> Psa. 74:12-17
> Yet God my King is from of old,
> working salvation in the midst of the earth.
> You divided the sea by your might;
> [A reference to the Exodus deliverance of the covenant at Sinai]
> You broke the heads of the sea monsters in the waters.
> You crushed the heads of Leviathan;...
> You have prepared the light and the sun.
> You have established all the boundaries of the earth;
>
> Psa. 89:9-12; 19-29
> You rule the raging of the sea;
> when its waves rise, you still them.
> You crushed Rahab like a carcass;
> you scattered your enemies with your mighty arm.
> The heavens are yours; the earth also is yours;
> the world and all that is in it, you have founded them.
> The north and the south, you have created them...
> I have found David, my servant;
> with my holy oil I have anointed him,
> so that my hand shall be established with him...
> and in my name shall his horn be exalted.
> I will set his hand on the sea
> and his right hand on the rivers...
> My steadfast love I will keep for him forever,
> and my covenant will stand firm for him.

[25] John Owen, *Works*, 16 vols. (London: The Banner of Truth Trust, 1965-1968), Vol. 9 134.

I will establish his offspring forever
and his throne as the days of the heavens.

Isa 51:9-16
Was it not You who cut Rahab in pieces,
Who pierced the dragon?
Was it not You who dried up the sea,
The waters of the great deep;
Who made the depths of the sea a pathway
For the redeemed to cross over?...
[Y]ou have forgotten the LORD your Maker,
Who stretched out the heavens
And laid the foundations of the earth…
"For I am the LORD your God, who stirs up the sea and its waves roar (the LORD of hosts is His name). "I have put My words in your mouth and have covered you with the shadow of My hand, to establish the heavens, to found the earth, and to say to Zion, 'You are My people.'"
[a reaffirmation of the Sinai covenant through Moses]

Isa. 27:1; 6-13
In that day the LORD with his hard and great and strong sword will punish Leviathan the fleeing serpent, Leviathan the twisting serpent, and he will slay the dragon that is in the sea…
In days to come Jacob shall take root,
Israel shall blossom and put forth shoots
and fill the whole world with fruit…
And in that day a great trumpet will be blown, and those who were lost in the land of Assyria and those who were driven out to the land of Egypt will come and worship the LORD on the holy mountain at Jerusalem. *[the future consummation of the Mosaic and Davidic covenant in the New Covenant of Messiah]*

In these texts, and others,[26] God does not merely appeal to his power of creation as justification for the authority of his covenant. More importantly, God uses the creation of the heavens and earth, involving subjugation of rivers, seas, and dragon (Leviathan), as poetic descriptions of his covenant with his people, rooted in the Exodus story, and reiterated in the Davidic

[26] See also Psa. 77:16-20; 136:1-22.

covenant. The creation of the covenant is the creation of the heavens and the earth which includes a subjugation of chaos by the new order. The covenant is a cosmos—not a material one centered in astronomical location and abstract impersonal forces as modern worldview demands, but a theological one, centered in the sacred space of land, temple, and cult as the ancient Near Eastern worldview demands.[27]

It has been noted by scholars that the motif of *Chaoskampf* is absent from Genesis 1 where God creates the heavens and the earth, painting a very different picture of the Hebrew creation story than its ANE neighbors. However, its very absence in that text is most likely a part of the covenantal polemic in the text. For a close look at the original Hebrew shows us that the word for dragon that we have been talking about (*tannin*) is in fact used of the "great sea creatures" (*tanninim*) that God created on Day five:

> Gen. 1:21-22
> So God created the great sea creatures (*tanninim*) and every living creature that moves, with which the waters swarm… And God saw that it was good. And God blessed them, saying, "Be fruitful and multiply and fill the waters in the seas, and let birds multiply on the earth."

The ancient Near Eastern audience would read this text and know full well what was being implied against their cultural familiarity with the sea dragon. Apparently, the ANE notion of struggle against the dragon is subverted in this text by depicting God creating the dragon by the mere words of his mouth, rather than wrestling with a preexistent monster for control over the sea. And then God blesses that dragon as one of the many "good" creations that he commands to reproduce. This picture amounts to the reduction of the dragon to a mere domesticated pet in the language of Genesis 1.

In this text, the conspicuous absence of the struggle of *Chaoskampf* is evidence of its subversion to the greater purposes of the Hebrew creation story. Sometimes Leviathan is used as a covenantal expression for the establishment of God's world order out of chaos, and sometimes, it is used as a symbol of God's authority over pagan religious expressions. In any case, its Biblical meaning is connected to its ancient Near Eastern symbolic context, not to a modern interpretation of a merely physical sea monster.

---

[27] N.T. Wright, *The New Testament and the People of God* (Minneapolis, MN: Fortress Press, 1992), 306-307.

Chapter 5
Mesopotamian Cosmic Geography in the Bible

In my novel, *Noah Primeval*, I depict the universe as it was thought to be through the eyes of ancient Mesopotamians, as a three-tiered universe with a flat disc earth, surrounded by waters, which includes the watery Abyss and beneath that, the underworld of Sheol. Above the earth is a solid dome of the heavens, beyond which is the waters of the "heaven of heavens" where God's throne sits on the waters. A generic illustration of this cosmography is the old public domain image depicted below. I decided to use this cosmic geography as creative literary license to capture the way the ancients saw and experienced the world. This essay explains the Scriptural expression of this worldview as held by the Biblical writers.

Cosmography is a technical term that means a theory that describes and maps the main features of the heavens and the earth. A Cosmography or "cosmic geography" can be a complex picture of the universe that includes elements like astronomy, geology, and geography; and those elements can include theological implications as well. Throughout history, all civilizations and peoples have operated under the assumption of a cosmography or picture of the universe. We are most familiar with the historical change that science went through from a Ptolemaic cosmography of the earth at the center of the universe (geocentrism) to a Copernican cosmography of the sun at the center of a solar system (heliocentrism).

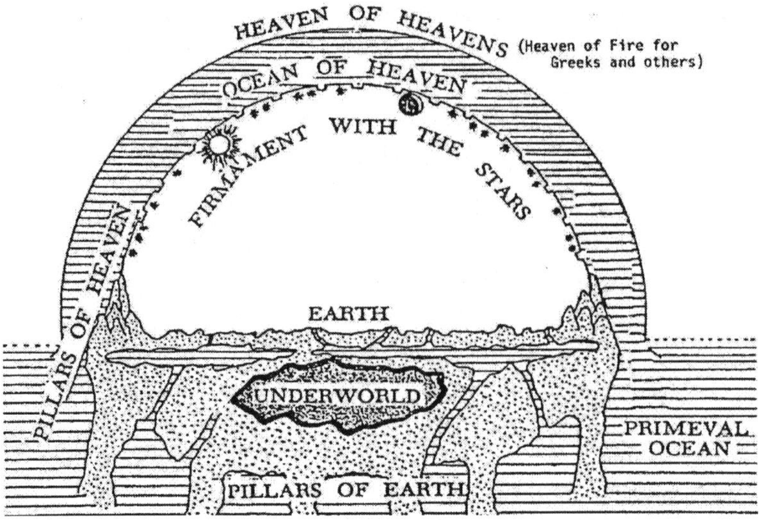

This antique drawing represents the Mesopotamian picture of the universe used in this story.

Some ancient mythologies maintained that the earth was a flat disc on the back of a giant turtle; animistic cultures believe that spirits inhabit natural objects and cause them to behave in certain ways; modern westerners believe in a space-time continuum where everything is relative to its frame of reference in relation to the speed of light. Ancients tended to believe that the gods caused the weather; moderns tend to believe that impersonal physical processes cause weather. All these different beliefs are elements of a cosmography or picture of what the universe is really like and how it operates. Even though "pre-scientific" cultures like the Hebrews did not have the same notions of science that we moderns have, they still observed the world around them and made interpretations as to the structure and operations of the heavens and earth.

A common ancient understanding of the cosmos is expressed in the visions of 1 Enoch, used in the novel *Noah Primeval*. In this Second Temple Jewish writing, codified around the third to fourth century B.C., and probably originally written much earlier, Enoch is taken on a journey through heaven and hell and describes the cosmic workings as they understood them in that day. Here is just a short glimpse into the elaborate construction of this ANE author:

> 1 Enoch 18:1-5
> And I saw the storerooms of all the winds and saw how with them he has embroidered all creation as well as the foundations of the earth. I saw the cornerstone of the earth; I

> saw the four winds which bear the earth as well as the firmament of heaven. I saw how the winds ride the heights of heaven and stand between heaven and earth: These are the very pillars of heaven. I saw the winds which turn the heaven and cause the star to set—the sun as well as all the stars. I saw the souls carried by the clouds. I saw the path of the angels in the ultimate end of the earth, and the firmament of the heaven above.[1]

The Bible also contains a picture of the universe that its stories inhabit. It uses cosmic geographical language in common with other ancient Near Eastern (ANE) cultures that shared its situated time and location. Believers in today's world use the language of Relativity when we write, even in our non-scientific discourse; because Einstein has affected the way we see the universe. Believers before the 17th century used Ptolemaic language because they too were children of their time. It should be no surprise to anyone that believers in ancient Israel would use the language of ANE cosmography because it was the mental construct within which they lived and thought.[2]

The Three-Tiered Universe

Othmar Keel, leading expert on ANE art has argued that there was no singular technical physical description of the cosmos in the ancient Near East, but rather patterns of thinking, similarity of images, and repetition of motifs.[3] A common simplification of these images and motifs is expressed in the three-tiered universe of the heavens, the earth, and the underworld.

Wayne Horowitz has chronicled Mesopotamian texts that illustrate this multi-leveled universe among the successive civilizations of Sumer, Akkad, Babylonia, and Assyria. The heavens above were subdivided into "the heaven of Anu (or chief god)" at the very top, the "middle heavens" below him and the sky. In the middle was the earth's surface, and below that was the third level that was further divided into the waters of the abyss and the underworld.[4]

Let's take a look at the Scriptures that appear to reinforce this three-tiered universe so different from our modern understanding of physical expanding galaxies of warped space-time, where the notion of heaven and hell are

---

[1] James H. Charlesworth, *The Old Testament Pseudepigrapha: Volume 1*, 1 En 18 (New York; London: Yale University Press, 1983).

[2] The book that opened my mind to the Mesopotamian cosmography in the Bible was *Evolutionary Creation: A Christian Approach to Evolution* by Denis O. Lamoureux, Eugene; OR, Wipf & Stock, 2008. I owe much of the material in this essay to Mr. Lamoureux's meticulous research on the ancient science in the Bible. But one need not accept his evolutionary presuppositions to agree with his Biblical scholarship.

[3] Othmar Keel, *The Symbolism of the Biblical World*, Winona Lake; IN: Eisenbrauns, 1972, 1997, 16-59.

[4] Wayne Horowitz, *Mesopotamian Cosmic Geography*, Winona Lake; IN: Eisenbrauns, 1998, xii-xiii.

without physical location. Though the focus of this essay will be on Old Testament context, I want to start with the New Testament to make the point that their cosmography did not necessarily change with the change of covenants.

> Phil. 2:10
> That at the name of Jesus every knee should bow, of those who are in heaven, and on earth, and under the earth.
>
> Rev. 5:3, 13
> And no one in heaven, or on earth, or under the earth, was able to open the scroll, or to look into it… And every creature in heaven and on the earth and under the earth and in the sea…
>
> Ex. 20:4
> "You shall not make for yourself a carved image, or any likeness of anything that is in heaven above, or that is in the earth beneath, or that is in the water under the earth.
>
> Matt. 11:23
> Jesus said, "Capernaum, will you be exalted to heaven? You will be brought down to Hades. [the underworld].

Both apostles Paul and John were writing about the totality of creation being subject to the authority of Jesus on his throne. So this word picture of "heaven, earth, and under the earth" was used as the description of the total known universe—which they conceived of spatially as heaven above, the earth below, and the underworld below the earth. And not only did the inspired human authors write of the universe in this three-tiered fashion but so did God Himself, the author and finisher of our faith, when giving the commandments on Sinai.

One may naturally wonder if this notion of "heaven above" may merely be a symbolic or figurative expression for the exalted spiritual nature of heaven. Since we cannot see where heaven is, God would use physical analogies to express spiritual truths. This explanation would be easier to stomach if the three-tiered notion were not so rooted in a cosmic geography that clearly was their understanding of the universe (as proven below). A figurative expression would also jeopardize the doctrine of the ascension of Jesus into heaven which also affirms the spatial location of heaven above and the earth below, in very literal terms.

Acts 1:9-11
He was lifted up, and a cloud took him out of their sight. And while they were gazing into heaven as he went, behold, two men stood by them in white robes, and said, "Men of Galilee, why do you stand looking into heaven? This Jesus, who was taken up from you into heaven, will come in the same way as you saw him go into heaven."

John 3:13
No one has ascended into heaven except he who descended from heaven, the Son of Man.

John 6:62
Then what if you were to see the Son of Man ascending to where he was before?

John 20:17
Jesus said to her, "Do not cling to me, for I have not yet ascended to the Father; but go to my brothers and say to them, 'I am ascending to my Father and your Father, to my God and your God.'"

Eph. 4:8-10
Therefore it says, "When he ascended on high he led a host of captives, and he gave gifts to men." (In saying, "He ascended," what does it mean but that he had also descended into the lower regions, the earth? He who descended is the one who also ascended far above all the heavens, that he might fill all things.)

The location of heaven being above us may be figurative to our modern cosmology, but it was not figurative to the Biblical writers. To suggest that they understood it figuratively would be to impose our own modern cultural bias on the Bible.

Now let's take a closer look at each of these tiers or domains of the cosmos through the eyes of Scripture in their ANE context.

Flat Earth Surrounded by Waters

I want to start with the earth because the Scriptures start with the earth. That is, the Bible is geocentric in its picture of a flat earth founded on immovable pillars at the center of the universe. Over a hundred years ago, a

Babylonian map of the world was discovered that dated back to approximately the ninth century B.C. As seen below, this map was unique from other Mesopotamian maps because it was not merely local but international in its scale, and contained features that appeared to indicate cosmological interpretation.[5] That map and a translated interpretation are reproduced below.[6]

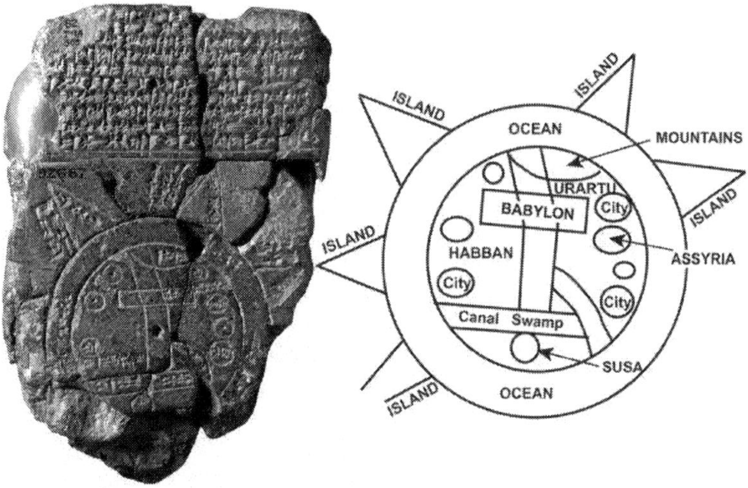

The geography of the Babylonian map portrayed a flat disc of earth with Babylon in the center and extending out to the known regions of its empire, whose perimeters were surrounded by cosmic waters and islands out in those waters. Of the earliest Sumerian and Akkadian texts with geographical information, only the Babylonian map of the world and another text, *The Sargon Geography,* describe the earth's surface, and they both picture a central circular continent surrounded by cosmic waters, often referred to as "the circle of the earth."[7] Other texts like the Akkadian *Epic of Gilgamesh,* and Egyptian, and Sumerian works share in common with the Babylonian map the notion of mountains at the edge of the earth beyond which is the cosmic

---

[5] Horowitz, *Mesopotamian Cosmic Geography*, 25-27.
[6] Photo is public domain (Courtesy of the British Museum). Illustration is my own based on Horowitz, *Mesopotamian Cosmic Geography*, 21.
[7] Horowitz, *Mesopotamian Cosmic Geography*, 320, 334. This interpretation continued to maintain influence even into the Greek period of the 6th century B.C. (41).

sea and the unknown,[8] and from which come "the circle of the four winds" that blow upon the four corners of the earth (a reference to compass points).[9]

The Biblical picture of the earth is remarkably similar to this Mesopotamian cosmic geography. When Daniel had his dream *from God in Babylon*, of a tree "in the middle of the earth" whose height reached so high that "it was visible to the end of the whole earth," (Dan. 4:10) it reflected this very Babylonian map of the culture that educated Daniel. One cannot see the end of the whole earth on a globe, but one can do so on a circular continent embodying the known world of Babylon as the center of the earth.

"The ends of the earth" is a common phrase, occurring over fifty times throughout the Scriptures that means more than just "remote lands," but rather includes the notion of the very physical end of the whole earth all around before the cosmic waters that hem it in. Here are just a few of the verses that indicate this circular land mass bounded by seas as the entire earth:

> Isa. 41:9
> You whom I took from the ends of the earth, and called from its farthest corners
>
> Psa. 65:5
> O God of our salvation, the hope of all the ends of the earth and of the farthest seas
>
> Zech. 9:10
> His rule shall be from sea to sea, and from the River to the ends of the earth.
>
> Mark 13:27
> And then he will send out the angels and gather his elect from the four winds, from the ends of the earth to the ends of heaven.

---

[8] A Sumerian hymn to the god Enlil, Lord of the Wind, represents these ends of the earth within the context of the god's rule over all the earth: "Lord, as far as the edge of heaven, lord as far as the edge of earth, from the mountain of sunrise to the mountain of sunset. In the mountain/land, no (other) lord resides, you exercise lordship. Enlil, in the lands no (other) lady resides, your wife, exercises ladyship." Horowitz, *Mesopotamian Cosmic Geography*, 331.
"Circle of the earth" in Egyptian understanding meant the disc of the earth unto the horizon: "(These) lands were united, and they laid their hands upon the land as far as the Circle of the Earth." "Inscription on the second pylon at Medinet Habu," J.H. Breasted, *Ancient Records of Egypt*, Part Four, University of Chicago, 1906, p 64.

[9] Horowitz, *Mesopotamian Cosmic Geography*, 195-97, 334.

Acts 13:47
'I have made you a light for the Gentiles, that you may bring salvation to the ends of the earth.'

Job 28:24
For he looks to the ends of the earth and sees everything under the heavens.

Remember that Mesopotamian phrase, "circle of the earth" that meant a flat disc terra firma? Well, it's in the Bible, too. "It is he who sits above the circle of the earth, and its inhabitants are like grasshoppers" (Isa. 40:22). Some have tried to say that the Hebrew word for "circle" could mean *sphere*, but it does not. The Hebrew word used here (*ḥûg*) could however refer to a vaulted dome that covers the visible circular horizon, which would be more accurate to say, "above the vault of the earth."[10] If Isaiah had wanted to say the earth was a sphere he would have used another word that he used in a previous chapter (22:18) for a ball (*kaddur*), but he did not.[11]

Two further Scriptures use this "circle of the earth" in reference to God's original creation of the land out of the waters and extend it outward to include the circumferential ocean with its own mysterious boundary:

Prov. 8:27, 29
When he established the heavens, I was there; when he drew a circle on the face of the deep… when he assigned to the sea its limit, so that the waters might not transgress his command, when he marked out the foundations of the earth.

Job 26:10
He has inscribed a circle on the face of the waters at the boundary between light and darkness [where the sun rises and sets].

Even when the Old Testament writers are deliberately using metaphors for the earth, they use metaphors for a flat earth spread out like a flat blanket.

---

[10] "*ḥûg*" Harris, R. Laird, Robert Laird Harris, Gleason Leonard Archer, and Bruce K. Waltke. *Theological Wordbook of the Old Testament*. electronic ed. Chicago: Moody Press, 1999, p 266-67.

[11] Even the Septuagint (LXX) does not translate the Hebrew word into the Greek word for sphere. "Isaiah 40:22," Randall Tan, David A. deSilva, and Logos Bible Software. *The Lexham Greek-English Interlinear Septuagint*. Logos Bible Software, 2009.

Job 38:13
Take hold of the skirts of the earth, and the wicked be shaken out of it.

Job 38:18
Have you comprehended the expanse of the earth?

Psa. 136:6
To him who spreads out the earth above the waters.

Isa. 44:24
"I am the LORD, who spread out the earth by myself."

Geocentricity

In the Bible, the earth is not merely a flat disk surrounded by cosmic waters under the heavens; it was also the center of the universe. To the ANE mindset, including that of the Hebrews, the earth did not move (except for earthquakes) and the sun revolved around that immovable earth. They did not know that the earth was spinning one thousand miles an hour and flying through space at 65,000 miles an hour. Evidently, God did not consider it important enough to correct this primitive inaccurate understanding. Here are the passages that caused such trouble with Christians who took the text too literally because it did not seem to be figurative to them:

Psa. 19:4-6
Their voice goes out through all the earth,
and their words to the end of the world.
In them he has set a tent for the sun,
which comes out like a bridegroom leaving his chamber,
and, like a strong man, runs its course with joy.
Its rising is from the end of the heavens,
and its circuit to the end of them.

Psa. 50:1
The Mighty One, God, the LORD, speaks and summons the earth from the rising of the sun to its setting.

Eccl. 1:5
The sun rises, and the sun goes down,
and hastens to the place where it rises.

Josh. 10:13
And the sun stood still, and the moon stopped,
until the nation took vengeance on their enemies…
The sun stopped in the midst of heaven and did not hurry to set for about a whole day.

Matt. 5:45
Jesus said, "For he makes his sun rise on the evil and on the good."

Two objections are often raised when considering these passages. First, that they use phenomenal language. That is, they describe simply what the viewer observes and makes no cosmological claims beyond simply description of what one sees. We even use these terms of the sun rising and setting today and we know the earth moves around the sun. Fair enough. The only problem is that the ancient writers were pre-scientific and did not know the earth went around the sun, so when they said the sun was moving from one end of the heavens to the other they believed reality was exactly as they observed it. They had absolutely no reason to believe in a "phenomenal distinction" between their observation and reality.[12]

The second objection is that some of the language is obvious metaphor. David painted the sun as a bridegroom coming out of his chamber or of being summoned by God and responding like a human. This is called anthropomorphism and is obviously poetic. But the problem here is that the metaphors still reinforce the sun doing all the moving around a stationary immobile earth.

1Chr. 16:30
Tremble before him, all the earth; yes, the world is established; it shall never be moved.

Psa. 93:1
Yes, the world is established; it shall never be moved.

Psa. 96:10
Yes, the world is established; it shall never be moved."

Understandably, these texts have been thought to indicate that the Bible is explicitly saying the earth does not move. But the case is not so strong for

[12] "The Firmament And The Water Above: Part I: The Meaning Of Raqia In Gen 1:6-8," Paul H. Seely, *The Westminster Theological Journal* 53 (1991) 227-40.

these examples because the Hebrew word used in these passages for "the world" is not the word for *earth* (*erets*), but the word that is sometimes used for the inhabited world (*tebel*). So it is possible that these verses are talking about the "world order" as does the poetry of 2Sam. 22:16.

But the problem that then arises is that the broader chapter context of these verses describe the earth's physical aspects such as oceans, trees, and in the case of 1Chron. 16:30, even the "earth" (*erets*) in redundant context with the "world" (*tebel*), which would seem to indicate that "world" may refer to the physical earth.

Lastly, *world* can be interchangeable with *earth* as it is in 1Sam. 2:8, "For the pillars of the earth are the LORD'S, And He set the world on them."

And this adds a new element to the conversation of a stationary earth: *A foundation of pillars.*

Pillars of the Earth

The notion of an immovable earth is not a mere description of observational experience by earth dwellers; it is based upon another cosmographical notion that the earth is on a foundation of pillars that hold it firmly in place.

> Psa. 104:5
> He set the earth on its foundations, so that it should never be moved.
>
> Job 38:4
> "Where were you when I laid the foundation of the earth? Tell Me, if you have understanding, Who set its measurements, since you know? Or who stretched the line on it? "On what were its bases sunk? Or who laid its cornerstone,
>
> 2Sam. 22:16
> "Then the channels of the sea were seen; the foundations of the world were laid bare.
>
> 1Sam. 2:8
> For the pillars of the earth are the LORD's, and on them, he has set the world.
>
> Psa. 75:3
> "When the earth totters, and all its inhabitants,
> it is I who keep steady its pillars.

> Zech. 12:1
> Thus declares the LORD who stretches out the heavens, and founded the earth.

Ancient man such as the Babylonians believed that mountains and important ziggurat temples had foundations that went below the earth into the abyss (*apsu*) or the underworld.[13] But even if one would argue that the notion of foundations and pillars of the earth are only intended to be symbolic, they are still symbolic *of a stationary earth that does not move.*

Some have pointed out the single verse that seems to mitigate this notion of a solid foundation of pillars, Job 26:6-7: "Sheol is naked before God, and Abaddon has no covering. He stretches out the north over the void and hangs the earth on nothing." They suggest that this is a revelation of the earth in space before ancient man even knew about the spatial location of the earth in a galaxy. But the reason I do not believe this is because of the context of the verse.

Within chapter 26 Job affirms the three-tiered universe of waters of the Abyss below him (v. 5) and under that Sheol (v. 6), with pillars holding up the heavens (v. 11). Later in the same book, God himself speaks about the earth laid on foundations (38:4), sinking its bases and cornerstone like a building (38:5-6). Ancient peoples believed the earth was on top of some other object like the back of a turtle, and that it was too heavy to float on the waters. So in context, Job 26 appears to be saying that the earth is over the waters of the abyss and Sheol, on its foundations, but there is nothing under *those pillars* but God himself holding it all up. This is not the suggestion of a planet hanging in space, but rather the negative claim of an earth that is *not* on top of an ancient object.

Sheol Below

Before we ascend to the heavens, let's take a look at the underworld below the earth. The underworld was a common location of extensive stories about gods and departed souls of men journeying to the depths of the earth through special gates of some kind into a geographic location that might also be accessed through cracks in the earth above.[14] Entire Mesopotamian stories engage the location of the subterranean netherworld in their narrative such as *The Descent of Inanna, The Descent of Ishtar*, *Nergal and Ereshkigal*, and many others.

---

[13] Horowitz, *Mesopotamian Cosmic Geography*, 98, 124, 308-12, 336-37.
[14] Horowitz, *Mesopotamian Cosmic Geography*, p 348-362

Sheol was the Hebrew word for the underworld.[15] Though the Bible does not contain any narratives of experiences in Sheol, it was nevertheless described as the abode of the dead that was below the earth. Though Sheol was sometimes used interchangeably with "Abaddon" as the place of destruction of the body (Prov. 15:11; 27:20),[16] and "the grave" (*qibrah*) as a reference to the state of being dead and buried in the earth (Psa. 88:11; Isa. 14:9-11), it was also considered to be *physically* located beneath the earth in the same way as other ANE worldviews.

When the sons of Korah are swallowed up by the earth for their rebellion against God, Numbers chapter 16 says that "they went down alive into Sheol, and the earth closed over them, and they perished from the midst of the assembly (v. 33)." People would not "fall alive" into death or the grave and then perish if Sheol was not a location. But they would die after they fall down into a location (Sheol) and the earth closes over them in that order.

The divine being (*elohim*), known as the departed spirit of Samuel, "came up out of the earth" for the witch of Endor's necromancy with Saul (1Sam. 28:13). This was not a reference to a body coming out of a grave, but a spirit of the dead coming from the underworld beneath the earth.

When Isaiah writes about Sheol in Isaiah 14, he combines the notion of the physical location of the dead body in the earth (v. 11) with the location beneath the earth of the spirits of the dead (v. 9). It's really a both/and proposition.

Here is a list of some verses that speak of Sheol geographically as a spiritual underworld in contrast with heaven as a spiritual overworld.

> Amos 9:2
> "If they dig into Sheol, from there shall my hand take them;
> if they climb up to heaven, from there I will bring them down.
>
> Job 11:8
> It is higher than heaven—what can you do? Deeper than Sheol—what can you know?
>
> Psa. 16:10
> For you will not abandon my soul to Sheol, or let your holy one see corruption.

---

[15] "Sheol," *DDD*, p 768.
[16] "Abaddon," *DDD*, p 1.

Psa. 139:8
If I ascend to heaven, you are there! If I make my bed in Sheol, you are there!

Isa. 7:11
"Ask a sign of the LORD your God; let it be deep as Sheol or high as heaven."

These are not mere references to the body in the grave, but to locations of the spiritual soul as well. Sheol is a combined term that describes both the grave for the body and the underworld location of the departed souls of the dead.

In the New Testament, the word *Hades* is used for the underworld, which was the Greek equivalent of Sheol.[17] Jesus himself used the term Hades as the location of damned spirits in contrast with heaven as the location of redeemed spirits when he talked of Capernaum rejecting miracles, "And you, Capernaum, will you be exalted to heaven? You will be brought down to Hades" (Matt. 11:23). Hades was also the location of departed spirits in his parable of Lazarus and the rich man in Hades (Luke 16:19-31).

In Greek mythology, Tartarus was another term for a location beneath the "roots of the earth" and beneath the waters where the warring giants called "Titans" were bound in chains because of their rebellion against the gods.[18] Peter uses a derivative of that very Greek word Tartarus to describe a similar location and scenario of angels being bound during the time of Noah and the warring Titans called "Nephilim."[19]

2Pet. 2:4-5
For if God did not spare angels when they sinned, but cast them into hell [*tartaroo*] and committed them to chains of gloomy darkness to be kept until the judgment; if he did not spare the ancient world, but preserved Noah.

---

[17] "Hades," *DDD*, p 382.

[18] "They then conducted them [the Titans] under the highways of the earth as far below the ground as the ground is below the sky, and tied them with cruel chains. So far down below the ground is gloomy Tartarus...Tartarus is surrounded by a bronze moat...above which the roots of earth and barren sea are planted. In that gloomy underground region the Titans were imprisoned by the decree of Zeus." Norman Brown, Trans. *Theogony: Hesiod*. New York: Bobbs-Merrill Co., 1953, p 73-4.

[19] 1.25 ταρταρόω [*tartaroo*] Louw, Johannes P., and Eugene Albert Nida. *Greek-English Lexicon of the New Testament : Based on Semantic Domains*. electronic ed. of the 2nd edition. New York: United Bible societies, 1996. Bauckham, Richard J. Vol. 50, *Word Biblical Commentary : 2 Peter, Jude*. Word Biblical Commentary. Dallas: Word, Incorporated, 2002, p 248-249.

The Watery Abyss

In Mesopotamian cosmography, the Abyss (*Apsu* in Akkadian) was a cosmic subterranean lake or body of water that was between the earth and the underworld (Sheol), and was the source of the waters above such as oceans, rivers, and springs or fountains.[20] In *The Epic of Gilgamesh*, Utnapishtim, the Babylonian Noah, tells his fellow citizens that he is building his boat and will abandon the earth of Enlil to join Ea in the waters of the Abyss that would soon fill the land.[21] Even bitumen pools used to make pitch were thought to rise up from the "underground waters," or the Abyss.[22]

Similarly, in the Bible the earth also rests on the seas or "the deep" (*tehom*) that produces the springs and waters from its subterranean waters below the earth.

> Psa. 24:1-2
> The world, and those who dwell therein, for he has founded it upon the seas, and established it upon the rivers.
>
> Psa. 136:6
> To him who spread out the earth above the waters.
>
> Gen. 49: 25
> The Almighty who will bless you with blessings of heaven above, Blessings of the deep that crouches beneath.
>
> Ex. 20:4
> You shall not make for yourself a carved image, or any likeness of anything that is in heaven above, or that is in the earth beneath, or that is in the water under the earth.

Leviathan is even said to dwell in the Abyss in Job 41:34 (LXX)[23]. When God brings the flood, part of the waters are from "the fountains of the great deep" bursting open (Gen. 7:11; 8:2).

---

[20] Horowitz, *Mesopotamian Cosmic Geography*, p 334-348.

[21] *The Epic of Gilgamesh* XI:40-44. *The Ancient Near East an Anthology of Texts and Pictures.* Edited by James Bennett Pritchard. Princeton: Princeton University Press, 1958, p 93.

[22] Horowitz, *Mesopotamian Cosmic Geography*, p 337.

[23] "[Leviathan] regards the netherworld [Tartauros] of the deep [Abyss] like a prisoner. He regards the deep [Abyss] as a walk." Job 41:34, Tan, Randall, David A. deSilva, and Logos Bible Software. *The Lexham Greek-English Interlinear Septuagint*. Logos Bible Software, 2009.

The Firmament

If we move upward in the registers of cosmography, we find another ancient paradigm of the heavens covering the earth like a solid dome or vault with the sun, moon, and stars embedded in the firmament yet still somehow able to go around the earth. Reformed scholar Paul Seely has done key research on this notion.[24]

> Gen. 1:6-8
> And God said, "Let there be an expanse [firmament] in the midst of the waters, and let it separate the waters from the waters." And God made the expanse [firmament] and separated the waters that were under the expanse [firmament] from the waters that were above the expanse [firmament]. And it was so. And God called the expanse [firmament] Heaven.

I used to think, what is that all about? Waters below separated from waters above by the sky? Some try to explain those waters above as a water canopy above the earth that came down at Noah's flood. But that doesn't make sense Biblically because birds are said to "fly over the face of the firmament" (Gen. 1:20) with the same Hebrew grammar as God's Spirit hovering "over the face of the waters" (Gen. 1:2). But the firmament cannot be the "water canopy" because the firmament is not the waters, *but the object that is separating and holding back the waters*. If the firmament is an "expanse" or the sky itself, then the birds would be flying *within* the firmament, not *over the face of* the firmament as the text states. So the firmament cannot be a water canopy and it cannot be the sky itself.

The T.K.O. of the canopy theory is the fact that according to the Bible those "waters above" and the firmament that holds them back were still considered in place during the time of King David long after the flood:

> Psa. 104:2-3
> Stretching out the heavens like a tent. He lays the beams of his chambers on the waters;

---

[24] "The Firmament And The Water Above: Part I: The Meaning Of Raqia In Gen 1:6-8," Paul H. Seely, *The Westminster Theological Journal* 53 (1991) 227-40. http://faculty.gordon.edu/hu/bi/ted_hildebrandt/OTeSources/01-Genesis/Text/Articles-Books/Seely-Firmament-WTJ.pdf

> Psa. 148:4
> Praise him, you highest heavens, and you waters above the heavens!

Seely shows how the modern scientific bias has guided the translators to render the word for "firmament" (*raqia*) as "expanse." *Raqia* in the Bible consistently means a solid material such as a metal that is hammered out by a craftsman (Ex. 39:3; Isa. 40:19). And when *raqia* is used elsewhere in the Bible for the heavens, it clearly refers to a solid material, sometimes even metal!

> Job 37:18
> Can you, like him, spread out [*raqia*] the skies, hard as a cast metal mirror?

> Ex. 24:10
> And they saw the God of Israel. There was under his feet as it were a pavement [*raqia*] of sapphire stone, like the very heaven for clearness.

> Ezek. 1:22-23
> Over the heads of the living creatures there was the likeness of an expanse [*raqia*], shining like awe-inspiring crystal, spread out above their heads. And under the expanse [*raqia*] their wings were stretched out straight.

> Prov. 8:27-28
> When he established the heavens… when he made firm the skies above.

> Job 22:14
> He walks on the vault of heaven.

> Amos 9:6
> [God] builds his upper chambers in the heavens and founds his vault upon the earth.

Not only did the ancient translators of the Septuagint (LXX) translate *raqia* into the Latin equivalent for a hard firm solid surface (*firmamentum*), but also the Jews of the Second Temple period consistently understood the word *raqia* to mean a solid surface that covered the earth like a dome.

3Bar. 3:6-8
And the Lord appeared to them and confused their speech, when they had built the tower… And they took a gimlet, and sought to pierce the heaven, saying, Let us see (whether) the heaven is made of clay, or of brass, or of iron.

2Apoc. Bar. 21:4
'O you that have made the earth, hear me, that have fixed the firmament by the word, and have made firm the height of the heaven.

Josephus, *Antiquities* 1:30 (1.1.1.30)
On the second day, he placed the heaven over the whole world... He also placed a crystalline [firmament] round it.

The Talmud describes rabbis debating over which remains fixed and which revolves, the constellations or the solid sky (Pesachim 94b),[25] as well as how to calculate the thickness of the firmament scientifically (Pesab. 49a) and Biblically (Genesis Rabbah 4.5.2).[26] While the Talmud is not the definitive interpretation of the Bible, it certainly illustrates how ancient Jews of that time period understood the term, which can be helpful in learning the Hebrew cultural context.

When the Scriptures talk poetically of this vault of heaven it uses the same terminology of stretching out the solid surface of the heavens over the earth *as it does of stretching out an ANE desert tent over the flat ground* (Isa. 54:2; Jer. 10:20)—not like an expanding Einsteinian time-space atmosphere.

Psa. 19:4
He has set a tent for the sun.

Psa. 104:2
Stretching out the heavens like a tent.

Isa. 45:12
It was my hands that stretched out the heavens,

---

[25] Quoted in *The Science in Torah: the Scientific Knowledge of the Talmudic* Sages By Leo Levi, page 90-91.
[26] Seely, "The Firmament," p 236.

Isa. 51:13
The LORD... who stretched out the heavens and laid the foundations of the earth.

Jer. 10:12
It is he who established the world by his wisdom, and by his understanding stretched out the heavens.

Jer. 51:15
"It is he who established the world by his wisdom, and by his understanding stretched out the heavens.

Keeping this tent-like vault over the earth in mind, when God prophesies about the physical destruction he will bring upon a nation, he uses the symbolism of rolling up that firmament like the tent he originally stretched out (or a scroll), along with the shaking of the pillars of the earth and the pillars of heaven which results in the stars falling from the heavens because they were embedded within it.

Isa. 34:4
All the host of heaven shall rot away, and the skies roll up like a scroll. All their host shall fall, as leaves fall from the vine.

Rev. 6:13-14
[An earthquake occurs] and the stars of the sky fell to the earth as the fig tree sheds its winter fruit when shaken by a gale. The sky vanished like a scroll that is being rolled up, and every mountain and island was removed from its place.

Matt. 24:29
"The stars will fall from heaven, and the powers of the heavens will be shaken."

Job 26:11
"The pillars of heaven tremble, and are astounded at His rebuke.

2Sam. 22:8
Then the earth reeled and rocked; the foundations of the heavens trembled and quaked.

Is. 13:13
Therefore I shall make the heavens tremble, and the earth will be shaken out of its place at the wrath of the LORD of hosts.

Joel 2:10
The earth quakes before them, the heavens tremble.

Waters Above the Heavens

Now on to the highest point of the Mesopotamian cosmography, the "highest heavens," or "heaven of heavens," where God has established his temple and throne (Deut. 26:15; Psa. 11:4; 33:13; 103:19). But God's throne also happens to be in the midst of a sea of waters that reside there. These are the waters that are above the firmament, that the firmament holds back from falling to earth (Gen. 1:6-8).

Psa. 148:4
Praise him, you highest heavens, and you waters above the heavens!

Psa. 104:2-3
Stretching out the heavens like a tent. He lays the beams of his chambers on the waters.

Psa. 29:3, 10
The voice of the LORD is over the waters... the LORD, over many waters… The LORD sits enthroned over the flood [not a reference to the flood of Noah, but to these waters above the heavens][27] the LORD sits enthroned as king forever.

Jer. 10:13
When he utters his voice, there is a tumult of waters in the heavens,

Ezek. 28:2
"I sit in the seat of the gods, in the heart of the seas."

[27] Robert G. Bratcher, and William David Reyburn. *A Translator's Handbook on the Book of Psalms*. Helps for translators. New York: United Bible Societies, 1991, p 280. Psalm 29 takes place in heaven amidst God's heavenly host around his throne.

The solid firmament that holds back the heavenly waters has "windows of the heavens" ("floodgates" in the NASB) that let the water through to rain upon the earth.

> Gen. 7:11
> All the fountains of the great deep burst forth, and the windows of the heavens were opened.
>
> Gen. 8:2
> The fountains of the deep and the windows of the heavens were closed, and the rain from the heavens was restrained.
>
> Isa. 24:18
> For the windows of heaven are opened, and the foundations of the earth tremble.

So, What's Wrong With the Bible?

The sheer volume of passages throughout both Testaments illustrating the parallels with Mesopotamian cosmography seem to prove a deeply rooted ancient pre-scientific worldview that permeates the Scriptures, and that worldview consists of a three-tiered universe with God on a heavenly throne above a heavenly sea, underneath which is a solid vaulted dome with the sun, moon, and stars connected to it, covering the flat disc earth, founded immovably firm on pillars, surrounded by a circular sea, on top of a watery abyss, beneath which is the underworld of Sheol.

Some well-intentioned Evangelicals seek to maintain their particular definition of Biblical inerrancy by denying that the Bible contains this ancient Near Eastern cosmography. They try to explain it away as phenomenal language or poetic license. Phenomenal language is the act of describing what one sees subjectively from one's perspective without further claiming objective reality. So when the writer says the sun stood still, or that the sun rises and sets within the solid dome of heaven, he is only describing his observation, not cosmic reality. The claim of observation from a personal frame of reference is certainly true as far as it goes. Of course the observer describes what they are observing. But the distinction between appearance and reality is an imposition of our alien modern understanding onto theirs. As Seely explains,

> It is precisely because ancient peoples were scientifically naive that they did not distinguish between the appearance of the sky and their scientific concept of the sky. They had no

> reason to doubt what their eyes told them was true, namely, that the stars above them were fixed in a solid dome and that the sky literally touched the earth at the horizon. So, they equated appearance with reality and concluded that the sky must be a solid physical part of the universe just as much as the earth itself.[28]

If the ancients did not know the earth was a sphere in space, they could not know that their observations of appearances were anything other than reality. It would be easy enough to relegate one or two examples of Scripture to the notion of phenomenal language, but when dozens of those phenomenal descriptions reflect the same complex integrated picture of the universe that Israel's neighbors shared, and when that picture included many elements that were *not* phenomenally observable, such as the Abyss, Sheol, or the pillars of earth and heaven, it strains credulity to suggest these were merely phenomenal descriptions intentionally unrelated to reality. If it walks like a Mesopotamian duck and talks like a Mesopotamian duck, then chances are they thought it was a Mesopotamian duck, not just the "appearance" of one having no reality.

It would be a mistake to claim that there is a single monolithic Mesopotamian cosmography.[29] There are varieties of stories with overlapping imagery, and some contradictory notions. But there are certainly enough commonalities to affirm a generic yet mysterious picture of the universe. And that picture in Scripture undeniably includes poetic language. The Hebrew culture was imaginative. They integrated poetry into everything, including their observational descriptions of nature. Thus a hymn of creation such as Psalm 19 tells of the heavens declaring God's glory as if using speech, and then describes the operations of the sun in terms of a bridegroom in his chamber or a man running a race. Metaphor is inescapable and ubiquitous.

And herein lies a potential solution for the dilemma of the scientific inaccuracy of the Mesopotamian cosmic geography in Scripture: *The Israelite culture, being pre-scientific, thought more in terms of function and purpose than material structure.* Even if their picture of the heavens and earth as a three-tiered geocentric cosmology, was scientifically "false" from our modern perspective, it nevertheless still accurately describes the teleological purpose and meaning of creation that they were intending to communicate.

Othmar Keel, one of the leading scholars on Ancient Near Eastern art has argued that even though modern depictions of the ancient worldview like the illustration of the three-tiered universe above are helpful, they are

---

[28] Seely, "The Firmament," p 228.

[29] Horowitz, *Mesopotamian Cosmic Geography.*

fundamentally flawed because they depict a "profane, lifeless, virtually closed mechanical system," which reflects our own modern bias. To the ancient Near East "rather, the world was an entity open at every side. The powers which determine the world are of more interest to the ancient Near East than the structure of the cosmic system. A wide variety of diverse, uncoordinated notions regarding the cosmic structure were advanced from various points of departure."[30]

John Walton has written recently of this ANE concern with powers over structure in direct relation to the creation story of Genesis. He argues that in the ancient world existence was understood more in terms of function within a god-created *purposeful order* than in terms of material status within a natural physical structure.[31] This is not to say that the physical world was denied or ignored, but rather that the priority and interests were different from our own. We should therefore be careful in judging their purpose-driven cosmography too strictly in light of our own material-driven cosmography. And in this sense, modern material descriptions of reality are more "false" than ancient pictures because they do not include the immaterial aspect of reality: Meaning and purpose.

Biblical writers did not *teach* their cosmography as scientific doctrine revealed by God about the way the physical universe was materially structured, they *assumed* the popular cosmography to teach their doctrine about God's *purposes and meaning*. To critique the cosmic model carrying the message is to miss the meaning altogether, which is the message. God's throne may not be physically above us in waters held back by a solid firmament, but he truly does rule "over" us and is king and sustainer of creation in whatever model man uses to depict that creation. The phrase "every created thing which is in heaven and on the earth and under the earth" (Rev. 5:13) is equivalent in meaning to the modern concept of every particle and wave in every dimension of the Big Bang space-time continuum, as well as every person dead or alive.

The geocentric picture in Scripture is a depiction through man's ancient perspective of God's purpose and humankind's significance. For a modern heliocentrist to attack that picture as falsifying the theology would be cultural imperialism. Reducing significance to physical location is simply a prejudice of material priority over spiritual purpose. One of the humorous ironies of this debate is that if the history of science is any judge, a thousand years from now, scientists will no doubt consider our current paradigm with which we judge the ancients to be itself fatally flawed. This is not to reduce reality to

[30] Othmar Keel, *The Symbolism of the Biblical World*, Winona Lake; IN: Eisenbrauns, 1972, 1997, 56-57.
[31] John H. Walton, *The Lost World of Genesis One: Ancient Cosmology and the Origins Debate* (Downers Grove: IL, InterVarsity Press, 2009), 23-36.

relativism, but rather to illustrate that all claims of empirical knowledge contain an inescapable element of human fallibility and finitude. A proper response should be a bit more humility and a bit less hubris regarding the use of our own scientific models as standards in judging theological meaning or purpose.

Enoch Primordial

Appendix

Chapter 6
Retelling Biblical Stories and the Mythic Imagination in *Enoch Primordial*

In my novel, *Noah Primeval*, I retell the story of the Biblical Noah as a nomadic tribal warrior. He refuses to worship the divine council of gods in Mesopotamia and is subsequently hunted down by assassin giants, leading the chase through Sheol, and ending in a climactic battle involving Leviathan and other hybrid monsters. In my novel, *Enoch Primordial*, I creatively imagine the untold story of the Biblical Enoch as a bounty hunter, a holy monk with a mission to kill giants who travels through a fantastic world of chimeras, gods, monsters and men.

"What?" you may say. *That's* not in the Bible! That sounds more like the non-canonical book of Enoch or the fantasy world of *The Lord of the Rings* than *Holy* Scripture. Isn't that mythologizing the Bible?

It is hard enough to get some religious believers to appreciate the imagination of the fantasy genre. But when it comes to retelling a story from the Bible, don't even think of putting those two things together; Bible and fantasy. That borders on tampering with the Word of God worthy of the curse in Revelation 21 on those who "add or take away from the words of the book." Or at least that's what some well-meaning believers think.

I think this negative impulse comes from an essentially good intent; the desire to avoid denigrating their sacred stories or reducing them to the level of false pagan myths. But such good intent does not necessarily produce the good result of a well thought out Biblical understanding of story.[1]

---

[1] The curse of Revelation 21, is not a reference to the entire Bible, but the prophecy of the particular book of Revelation. The context is not about taking away individual words but about taking away or adding to the *content* of the prophecy. If it were words, then we are all condemned because we do not have the original words, but only English translations based on many different copied manuscripts with lots of different textual variations. In other words our English translation of Revelation contains added words and taken away words.

What would surprise many of these concerned believers is the fact that the same ancient Hebrews who championed the Scriptures as their sacred text containing the very words of God, were also the holy ones who wrote those Scriptures utilizing pagan imagination and motifs. And they were also the same devout ancient believers who wrote many other non-canonical texts that retold Biblical stories with fantastic embellishments worthy of mythopoeic mastery.

Retelling Bible Stories and Non-Bible Stories

The ancient Jews loved to retell their Bible stories with embellishments in literature we now call apocrypha and pseudepigrapha. And they did so, not with a disdain for "the facts of history," but rather with deep respect for the original theological *meaning* as they understood it. As scholar George Nickelsburg explains, they wanted to "expound sacred tradition so that it speaks to contemporary times and issues."[2] Biblical scholar Peter Enns adds, "It is a characteristic of ancient retellings of Scripture that the exegetical traditions incorporated in to these retellings are not clearly (if at all) marked off from the Biblical texts. The line between text and comment was often blurred, so much so that the two often went hand in hand."[3]

Thanks to manuscript discoveries in recent centuries, we now have access to many of these Jewish retellings of Bible narratives, some of which include Jubilees, The Genesis Apocryphon, The Testament of Moses, The Testaments of the Twelve Patriarchs, and the Books of Adam and Eve and others. In these non-canonical texts we are retold, with creative embellishments, various episodes in Biblical history, from Adam and Eve, to Noah, through Abraham, Isaac, and Jacob, to Moses and more. I have used some of these Second Temple texts and other Jewish legends to embellish the Biblical narrative in *The Chronicles of the Nephilim*.

Not only do non-canonical Second Temple texts retell Bible stories, but the Bible itself uses some of these non-Biblical manuscripts as source texts for holy writ.

The orthodox doctrine of the Inspiration of Scripture is "God-breathed" human-written words (2Tim. 3:16). Human men wrote from God, moved by the Holy Spirit (2Pet. 1:20-21). The Bible was not dictated directly by God to the authors, nor was it written by God's direct "hand" (except for the tablets on Sinai), nor does it claim to be an automatic writing scenario where God

---

[2] George W. E. Nickelsburg and Klaus Baltzer, *1 Enoch : A Commentary on the Book of 1 Enoch*, (Minneapolis, Minn.: Fortress, 2001) 29.

[3] Peter Enns, *Exodus Retold: Ancient Exegesis of the Departure from Egypt in Wisdom 15-21 and 19:1-9*, (Atlanta, GA: Scholars Press, 1997), 35.

uses the hands of writers as puppets to do his bidding. Scripture itself attests to human authors compiling, editing, and drawing from other source texts to achieve their authoritative canon, all under the *providential oversight* of God.

There are well over fifty references in the Scriptures to just over twenty non-canonical source texts used by Biblical authors that are lost to history. Some of them are *The Book of the Wars of Yahweh* (Num. 21:14), *The Book of Jasher* (Josh. 10:12-13; 2Sam. 1:19-27), *The Acts of Solomon* (1Kings 11:41), *Acts of Gad the Seer* (1Chron. 29:29), *Acts of Nathan the Prophet* (2Chron 9:29), *Prophesy of Ahijah the Shilonite* (2Chron. 9:29), *Visions of Iddo the Seer* (2Chron. 9:29), *Acts of Jehu Son of Hanani* (2Chron. 20:34), *Acts of the Seers* (2Chron. 33:19) and others.[4]

One of these source texts quoted by Joshua and Samuel, *the Book of Jasher (or Jashar)*, is believed by some to be extant in a medieval copy of a Hebrew manuscript[5] (which I incidentally used as a source for *Enoch Primordial* and *Noah Primeval*).

The New Testament continues this tradition of non-canonical sources in Scripture. In 2Tim. 3:8 Paul refers to "Jannes and Jambres" who opposed Moses, a reference to Pharaoh's magicians in Exodus 7-9 attempting to reproduce God's miracles and plagues. But there is no mention of the names Jannes and Jambres in the entire Old Testament. So how did Paul know the names of the two magicians? The ancient church fathers, Origen[6] and Ambrose claimed these names were drawn by Paul from the Jewish pseudepigraphal work entitled *Jannes and Jambres* that describes the Exodus episode from the perspective of these two magicians, one repentant, the other unrepentant.[7] There is also a long Jewish tradition recorded in the *Targum Jonathan* of these two names.[8]

The New Testament book of Jude tells us of Michael the Archangel disputing with the devil over the body of Moses (Jude 9), an incident that is

---

[4] For a closer examination of these non-canonical source text references, see Duane Christensen, (1998), "Lost Books of the Bible," *Bible Review*, 14[5]:24-31, October.

[5] Ken Johnson, ThD., *Ancient Book of Jasher: A New Annotated Edition*, (Lexington, KY: BibleFacts Ministry, 2008), p 4.

[6] Origen, *Commentary* on Matthew 27:8. *The International Standard Bible Encyclopedia, Revised.* Edited by Geoffrey W. Bromiley. Wm. B. Eerdmans, 1988, 966.

[7] James H. Charlesworth, ed., *The Old Testament Pseudepigrapha: Vol. 2* (New York, NY.: Doubleday, 1983), pp. 427-442.

[8] "Jewish tradition makes them sons of Balaam. *Targum of Jonathan* on Num. xxii. 22), and places their rise at the time the Pharaoh gave command to kill the first-born of Israel (Sanhedrin, f. 106a; *Sotah* 11a), and supposes them to have been teachers of Moses, the makers of the golden calf (*Midrash Tanhuma*, f. 115b)." "Jannes and Jambres," Philip Schaff , *The New Schaff-Herzog Encyclopedia of Religious Knowledge*, Vol. VI, p. 95, accessed from Christian Classics Ethereal Library online, February 4, 2008, at < http://www.ccel.org/ccel/schaff/encyc06/Page_95.html>.

spoken of nowhere else in Scripture, but appears, according to some ancient Church fathers, in a lost Jewish book called *The Assumption of Moses.*[9]

Scholar Pete Enns explains that the Apostle Paul assumes a non-Biblical tradition when writing about the Hebrew wilderness sojourn.

> 1 Cor. 10:3–5
> and all ate the same spiritual food, and all drank the same spiritual drink. For they drank from the spiritual Rock that followed them, and the Rock was Christ.

In context, Paul makes an object lesson for the New Covenant community by way of analogy with the Old Covenant experience. There's only one problem, the "movable rock" (or "well" as a possible interpretation) is not in the Old Testament.

Enns exegetes the origin of this moveable well as deriving from an "extra-Biblical tradition found in a variety of Jewish sources dating roughly from the New Testament era to medieval rabbinic compilations" (namely, *Pseudo-Philo, Tosephta Sukka* and *Targum Onqelos*, among others).[10]

Hebrews 2:2 claims that the Law on Sinai was "spoken through angels" to Moses, another reference to the intimate involvement of the divine council of sons of God *that is not revealed in the Old Testament as we have it.*

In 2Pet. 2:5, Noah is called a "Preacher of righteousness," a description found only outside the Old Testament (*Sibylline Oracles* 1.125-31).

The Fascinating Case of the Book of Enoch

One of the most fascinating cases of Biblical appropriation of non-canonical texts is the New Testament references to the book of *1 Enoch.* Written sometime around the third to second century B.C., this text has both haunted and been cherished by the Christian Church through its history. It is apocalyptic in genre; cloaking warnings of judgment in dream visions, parables, and complex allegorical imagery. But it is most well-known for its detailed elaboration of the Genesis 6 story about the Sons of God (called "Watchers") and their intimate involvement in the cause of the Noachian Flood. There it describes in much detail the Watchers as fallen angels revealing occultic secrets to mankind, having intercourse with human women, and birthing giants who

---

[9] Richard J. Bauckham, *Word Biblical Commentary Vol. 50, 2 Peter, Jude* (Waco, TX., Word, 1983), pp. 73-74.

[10] Peter E. Enns, "The 'Moveable Well"' in 1 Cor 10:4: An Extrabiblical Tradition in an Apostolic Text," *Bulletin for Biblical Research* (1996) 23-38 [© 1996 Institute for Biblical Research] 6.

cause terror across the land.[11] Here is just a sample of passages that tell that story in much more vivid detail than Genesis 6:

> Enoch 6:1-2
> In those days, when the children of man had multiplied, it happened that there were born unto them handsome and beautiful daughters. And the angels, the children of heaven, [the Watchers] saw them and desired them; and they said to one another, "Come, let us choose wives for ourselves from among the daughters of man and beget us children."
>
> Enoch 7:1-8:3, 19:1
> And they took wives unto themselves, and everyone respectively chose one woman for himself, and they began to go unto them… And the women became pregnant and gave birth to great giants.
>
> These giants consumed the produce of all the people until the people detested feeding them. So the giants turned against the people in order to eat them. And they began to sin against birds, wild beasts, reptiles, and fish. And their flesh was devoured the one by the other, and they drank blood. And then the earth brought an accusation against the oppressors.
>
> And Azaz'el [the Watcher] taught the people the art of making swords and knives, and shields, and breastplates… and alchemy…[or *transmutation*: Ancient Ethiopian commentators explain this phrase as "changing a man into a horse or mule or vice versa, or transferring an embryo from one womb to another."] Amasras taught incantation and the cutting of roots; and Armaros the resolving of incantations; and Baraqiyal astrology, and Kokarer'el the knowledge of the signs, and Tam'el taught the seeing of the stars…
>
> The angels which have united themselves with women. They have defiled the people and will lead them into error so that they will offer sacrifices to the demons as unto gods.

[11] 1 Enoch chapters 1-36 is called the "Book of the Watchers" and deals with this material. The book of *Jubilees* is another respected text that contains a detailed retelling of the Noah story with Watchers cohabiting with women, and birthing giants. See Jubilees 4-10 and 20:4-5.

> Enoch 10:4, 11-12; 54:6
> the Lord said to Raphael, "Bind Azaz'el hand and foot and throw him into the darkness!" And he made a hole in the desert which was in Duda'el and cast him there...And to Michael [the archangel] God said, "Make known to Semyaza [the Watcher] and the others who are with him, who fornicated with the women, that they will die together with them in all their defilement...bind them for seventy generations underneath the rocks of the ground until the day of their judgment and of their consummation, until the eternal judgment is concluded... on account of their oppressive deeds which (they performed) as messengers of Satan, leading astray those who dwell upon the earth."[12]

Just what contemporary situation is Enoch referring to in his apocalyptic prose of fallen Watchers, carnal giants, and coming judgment? Some scholars think its origin around the time of the Maccabean revolt in 167 B.C. makes it a prophetic denunciation of the religious corruption of the Jewish world by its Hellenistic occupiers.[13] This pagan occupation would soon be overthrown by the victorious exploits of Judas Maccabeus and his brothers, returning Judaism to its purity and inspiring the origins of the festival of Hanukkah.

So the author of 1 Enoch was engaging in a rich tradition of retelling a Biblical story of judgment on a corrupted and compromised world as a moral warning for those of his own time. It was also part of this tradition to attribute their manuscripts to such historical luminaries as Enoch himself, not as a lie but as a literary technique that reinforces the significance of the message. However, it is entirely possible that sections of 1 Enoch were copied from much older manuscripts.

Though 1 Enoch is not in the Western canon of Scriptures, it is in the Eastern Ethiopic canon, and was respected by Christian scholars and authorities throughout the early church. It was never considered heretical by church authorities. But the real kicker is that the New Testament even refers favorably to the book of Enoch and its tradition of fallen angels cohabiting with humans which results in their punishment of binding (1Pet. 3:19-20; 2Pet. 2:4-10; Jude 6-14).

First, Jude quotes the book of 1 Enoch outright when he writes of false teachers corrupting the church:

---

[12] James H. Charlesworth, *The Old Testament Pseudepigrapha: Volume 1*, (New York; London: Yale University Press, 1983) 16-18, 38.

[13] Charlesworth, James H. *The Old Testament Pseudepigrapha: Volume 1*. New York; London: Yale University Press, 1983, 8.

Jude 14-15
It was also about these that Enoch, the seventh from Adam, prophesied, saying, "Behold, the Lord comes with ten thousands of his holy ones, to execute judgment on all and to convict all the ungodly of all their deeds of ungodliness that they have committed in such an ungodly way, and of all the harsh things that ungodly sinners have spoken against him."

Here is the text from the actual book of 1 Enoch that Jude is quoting:

1 Enoch 1:9
"And behold! He cometh with ten thousands of His holy ones to execute judgement upon all, and to destroy all the ungodly: And to convict all flesh of all the works of their ungodliness which they have ungodly committed, and of all the hard things which ungodly sinners have spoken against Him."[14]

But not only does Jude explicitly quote a passage out of 1 Enoch regarding God coming with the judgment of his divine council of holy ones (Sons of God), but *all three texts* refer to the Enochian notion of the angelic Watchers' punishment for co-habiting with humans as a violation of the divine/human separation; another main theme of 1 Enoch.

1Pet. 3:18–20
[Christ], being put to death in the flesh but made alive in the spirit, in which he went and proclaimed to the spirits in prison, because they formerly did not obey, when God's patience waited in the days of Noah.

Jude 6-7
And angels who did not keep their own domain, but abandoned their proper abode, He has kept in eternal bonds under darkness for the judgment of the great day, just as Sodom and Gomorrah and the cities around them, since they in the same way as these indulged in gross immorality and went after strange flesh, are exhibited as an example in undergoing the punishment of eternal fire.

[14] *Pseudepigrapha of the Old Testament*, ed. Robert Henry Charles, Enoch 1:9 (Bellingham, WA: Logos Research Systems, Inc., 2004) 14.

2Pet. 2:4-10
For if God did not spare angels when they sinned, but cast them into hell [*Tartarus*] and committed them to pits of darkness, reserved for judgment; and did not spare the ancient world, but preserved Noah...and if He condemned the cities of Sodom and Gomorrah to destruction by reducing them to ashes, having made them an example to those who would live ungodly lives thereafter... then the Lord knows how to...keep the unrighteous under punishment for the day of judgment, and especially those who indulge the flesh in its corrupt desires and despise authority.

Just in case anyone would question this fantastical interpretation of the carnal sin of the angels, Peter and Jude quote a common doublet that linked the sexual violation of the angelic Watchers (and their giant progeny) with the sexual violation of the inhabitants of Sodom who sought sexual intercourse with angels. The common theme of both instances was the transgression of heavenly and earthly separation of flesh.

There's just one big problem: This doublet of the sin of Sodom and the sin of the Watchers in the days of Noah "made as an example" is not found anywhere in the Old Testament, but only in non-canonical ancient Jewish texts.[15]

Here is the list of some of those extra-Biblical texts containing this doublet of connection, and we see clearly that the angelic sexual sin is usually connected to the judgment on giants as well:

Sirach 16:7-8
He forgave not the giants of old,
Who revolted in their might.
He spared not the place where Lot sojourned,
Who were arrogant in their pride.[16]

---

[15] There is one other New Testament passage that links Sodom with the days of Noah: Luke 17:26-34. Here, Jesus is prophecying about his coming in judgment upon Jerusalem and the Temple. He says that his coming will be as "the days or Noah" and "the days of Lot." But rather than referring to the sin of the angels here, he refers to the deception of normalcy that would blind sinners to coming judgment. People were "eating and drinking and marrying and being given in marriage" as well as "buying and selling, planting and building" until judgment came and "destroyed them all." The reference then is to the nature of surprise judgment upon clueless sinners, not about the sin of angels and their giant progeny.
[16] *Apocrypha of the Old Testament, Volume 1,* ed. Robert Henry Charles, Sir 16:7–8. Bellingham, WA: Logos Research Systems, Inc., 2004, 372.

Testament of Naphtali 3:4-5
[D]iscern the Lord who made all things, so that you do not become like Sodom, which departed from the order of nature. Likewise the Watchers departed from nature's order; the Lord pronounced a curse on them at the Flood.[17]

3 Maccabees 2:4-5
Thou didst destroy those who aforetime did iniquity, among whom were giants trusting in their strength and boldness, bringing upon them a boundless flood of water. Thou didst burn up with fire and brimstone the men of Sodom, workers of arrogance, who had become known of all for their crimes, and didst make them an example to those who should come after. [18]

Jubilees 20:4-5
[L]et them not take to themselves wives from the daughters of Canaan; for the seed of Canaan will be rooted out of the land. And he told them of the judgment of the giants, and the judgment of the Sodomites, how they had been judged on account of their wickedness, and had died on account of their fornication, and uncleanness, and mutual corruption through fornication.[19]

2 Enoch 34
God convicts the persons who are idol worshipers and sodomite fornicators, and for this reason he brings down the flood upon them.[20]

The New Testament literary reference to non-canonical sources does not mean those sources are the inspired Word of God, nor that everything in them is true; but it certainly does illustrate that the Bible itself draws meaningfully and favorably from interpretive traditions that engage in imaginative embellishment of Biblical stories. Unlike some Christians, God *does appreciate* creative imagination.

---

[17] Charlesworth, James H. *The Old Testament Pseudepigrapha: Volume 1*. New York; London: Yale University Press, 1983, 812.
[18] *Apocrypha of the Old Testament, Volume 1.* ed. Robert Henry Charles, 3 Mac 2:5. Bellingham, WA: Logos Research Systems, Inc., 2004, 164.
[19] *Pseudepigrapha of the Old Testament Volume 1.* ed. Robert Henry Charles. Bellingham, WA: Logos Research Systems, Inc., 2004, 42.
[20] James H. Charlesworth, *The Old Testament Pseudepigrapha: Volume 1* (New York; London: Yale University Press, 1983) 158.

Jude's references to the book of Enoch are not limited to material citations. He uses the same poetic phraseology throughout his letter that indicates an intimate interaction with the entirety of 1 Enoch on the incident of the Watchers and their condemnation. Researcher Douglas Van Dorn has put together a helpful chart of these linguistic comparisons.[21]

SOME OF JUDE'S ALLUSIONS TO 1 ENOCH			
JUDE		1 ENOCH	
Jude 6	"The angels that did not keep their own position but left their proper dwelling"	"[The angels] have abandoned the high heaven, the holy eternal place"	1 En 12:4
	"until the judgment of the great day"	"preserved for the day of suffering"	1 En 45:2 (1 En 10:6)
	"angels…kept in eternal chains under gloomy darkness"	"this is the prison of the angels, and here they will be imprisoned forever"	1 En 21:10 (1 En 10:4)
Jude 12	"waterless clouds"	"every cloud…rain shall be withheld"	1 En 100:11
	"raging waves"	"ships tossed to and fro by the waves"	1 En 101:2
	"fruitless trees"	"fruit of the trees shall be withheld"	1 En 80:3
Jude 13	"wandering stars"	"stars that transgress the order"	1 En 80:6
	"the gloom of utter darkness has been reserved forever"	"darkness shall be their dwelling"	1 En 46:6
Jude 14	"Enoch the seventh from Adam"	"my grandfather [Enoch]… seventh from Adam	1 En 60:8

1 Peter 3:18-20 speaks of Christ going down into Sheol to proclaim his triumph to the "spirits imprisoned" at the time of the flood. This act appears to be a typological replay of Enoch's own vision journey into Sheol to see the "prison house of the angels" who disobeyed at the flood (1 Enoch 21:9-10).

But the story does not yet end there. You will notice that the location of punishment and binding of the fallen angels that we have already seen in 2 Peter is *Tartarus* in the Greek.

> 2Pet. 2:4
> For if God did not spare angels when they sinned, but cast them into hell [*tartarus*] and committed them to pits of darkness, reserved for judgment.

[21] Douglas Van Dorn, (2013-01-21). *Giants: Sons of the Gods* (Kindle Location 4850). Waters of Creation. Kindle Edition.

What is important to realize is that the Greek word translated as "hell" in this English translation is not one of the usual New Testament Greek words for hell, *gehenna* or *hades*, but *tartarus*.

The Greek poet Hesiod, writing around 700 B.C., described this commonly known underworld called Tartarus as the pit of darkness and gloom where the Olympian Titan giants were banished following their war with Zeus.

> Hesiod, *Theogony* lines 720-739
> as far beneath the earth as heaven is above earth; for so far is it from earth to Tartarus...There by the counsel of Zeus who drives the clouds the Titan gods are hidden under misty gloom, in a dank place where are the ends of the huge earth. And they may not go out; for Poseidon fixed gates of bronze upon it, and a wall runs all round it on every side.[22]

Obviously, Peter does not affirm Greco-Roman polytheism by referring to Tartarus, but he is alluding to a Hellenistic myth that his readers, believer and unbeliever alike, would be very familiar with, subverting it with the Jewish traditional interpretation.

Extra-Biblical Second Temple Jewish legends connected this legend of gods and bound Titans in Tartarus to the bound angelic Watchers and punished giants of Genesis 6.

> Sibylline Oracles 1:97-104, 119
> enterprising Watchers, who received this appellation because they had a sleepless mind in their hearts and an insatiable personality. They were mighty, of great form, but nevertheless they went under the dread house of Tartarus guarded by unbreakable bonds, to make retribution, to Gehenna of terrible, raging, undying fire...draping them around with great Tartarus, under the base of the earth. [23]

Other well-known Second Temple literature reiterated this binding in the heart of the earth until judgment day:

---

[22] Hesiod, *The Homeric Hymns and Homerica With an English Translation by Hugh G. Evelyn-White. Theogony*. (Medford, MA: Cambridge, MA.,Harvard University Press; London, William Heinemann Ltd., 1914).

[23] James H. Charlesworth, The Old Testament Pseudepigrapha: Volume 1 (New York; London: Yale University Press, 1983), 337.

> Jubilees 4:22; 5:10
> And he wrote everything, and bore witness to the Watchers, the ones who sinned with the daughters of men because they began to mingle themselves with the daughters of men so that they might be polluted…
> And subsequently they [the Watchers] were bound in the depths of the earth forever, until the day of great judgment in order for judgment to be executed upon all of those who corrupted their ways and their deeds before the LORD.[24]

This "binding" or imprisoning of supernatural beings in the earth is expressed in 2 Peter's "cast into pits of darkness reserved for judgment" (3:19), 1 Peter's "disobedient spirits in prison" (v. 6), and Jude's "eternal bonds under darkness for the judgment of the great day" (2:4). But it is not altogether unheard of in the Old Testament.

> Isa. 24:21–23
> On that day the LORD will punish
> the host of heaven, in heaven,
> and the kings of the earth, on the earth.
> They will be gathered together
> as prisoners in a pit;
> they will be shut up in a prison,
> and after many days they will be punished.

Isaiah here is speaking of judgment upon Israel by the Babylonians around 600 B.C., but he evokes the same Enochian imagery of the angelic host of heaven (often linked to the astronomical heavenly bodies *and* earthly rulers) being overthrown and imprisoned in the earth until judgment day.

Robert Newman notes that the Qumran Hebrew of the Isaiah scroll of this passage refers to a past event as its reference point: "They *were* gathered together as prisoners in a pit" (past tense). [25] This past event could very well be the antediluvian binding of the fallen host of heaven (*bene ha Elohim*) as an analogy for the future captivity of Israel.

So what shall we make of all this wild exploration of Biblical stories, pagan myths, and Jewish legends? Does this mean that Biblical writers tried

---

[24] James H. Charlesworth, *The Old Testament Pseudepigrapha and the New Testament, Volume 2: Expansions of the "Old Testament" and Legends, Wisdom, and Philosophical Literature, Prayers, Psalms and Odes, Fragments of Lost Judeo-Hellenistic Works* (New Haven; London: Yale University Press, 1985), 62, 65.

[25] Robert C. Newman, "The Ancient Exegesis of Genesis 6:2, 4," *Grace Theological Journal* 5,1 (1984) 13-36.

to integrate their theology with pagan mythology (syncretism)? Is the Bible just an unoriginal adaptation of other religious myths?

Subverted Pagan Imagination

Some Bible believers are fearful of the Bible's adaptation of mythopoetic imagery and seek to ignore it by literalizing everything in the Bible into their modern understanding. They point to New Testament commands of Paul to "have nothing to do with irreverent silly myths" (1Tim. 4:7), to avoid devotion "to myths and endless genealogies, which promote speculations" (1Tim. 1:4), "Jewish myths and the commands of people who turn away from the truth" (Titus 1:14). They even think that it is a sign of the end times that some teachers "will turn away from listening to the truth and wander off into myths" (1Tim. 4:4).

But are these texts denigrating the literary genres of myth and speculative fantasy that employ the imagination in understanding God? A closer look at their context reveals that not all mythology is created equal.

In 1 Timothy and Titus, Paul is not comparing doctrinal teaching with mythical genre, he is comparing *true* doctrine with *false* doctrine that was being taught by the prevailing myths of his Jewish opponents who denied the Gospel.[26] It is the *content* that is damnable heresy to Paul, not the *genre* of mythic storytelling itself. Of this heretical mythology, scholar William Mounce writes,

> It appears to have been a form of aberrant Judaism with Hellenistic/gnostic tendencies that overemphasized the law and underemphasized Christ and faith, taught dualism (asceticism, denial of a physical resurrection), was unduly interested in the minutiae of the OT, produced sinful lifestyles and irrelevant quibbling about words, and was destroying the reputation of the church in Ephesus.[27]

The New Testament does not command against using mythical storytelling, but against its misuse for false doctrine. Put positively, we should devote ourselves to myths that "promote stewardship from God that is by faith" (1Tim. 1:4), myths that "turn people to the truth" (Titus 1:14);

---

[26] "The use is, to be sure, not specifically literary. "Myth" is used here, as is frequently the case elsewhere, to denote false and foolish stories." Martin Dibelius and Hans Conzelmann, *The Pastoral Epistles a Commentary on the Pastoral Epistles, Hermeneia--a critical and historical commentary on the Bible*, (Philadelphia: Fortress Press, 1972) 16.

[27] William D. Mounce, vol. 46, Word Biblical Commentary : Pastoral Epistles, Word Biblical Commentary, (Dallas: Word, Incorporated, 2002) 19.

"reverent, sober myths" of "faith, good doctrine" and "godliness" (1Tim. 4:6-7); myths that "turn toward the truth" (2Tim. 4:4).

But it is equally interesting to see how the Bible itself redeems pagan mythopoeic imagination.

I have written elsewhere about the extensive use of Canaanite poetry and imagination by Bible authors to express God's own imagination.[28] The Bible redeems pagan imagination by using its motifs and baptizing them with altered subversive definitions that support Yahweh, the God of the Jewish Scriptures against Baal, the god of Canaan, and other pagan deities in the ancient Near East.

Two examples of this redemptive subversion that show up in *Noah Primeval* and *Enoch Primordial* are Leviathan and the divine council of the Sons of God. It appears that Yahweh was not only interested in dispossessing the Canaanite people from the Promised Land, he was interested in dispossessing their narrative, because the Bible embodies a subversion of Canaanite imagination within its own narrative.

Baal, the storm god, was the chief deity of the land of Canaan in the time of the Israelite conquest. Canaanite myths depict Baal as a "cloud rider" who defeats the River and the Sea, as well as the seven-headed Sea Dragon called "Leviathan," (a symbol of chaos), in order to claim his eternal dominion.[29]

In polemical response to this mythology, the Biblical writers describe Yahweh as a "cloud rider" (Isa. 19:1; Psa. 104:3-4), who defeats the River and Sea (Hab. 3:8), as well as the Sea Dragon, "Leviathan," (Isa. 89:6-12) or "Rahab" (Psa. 89:9-11) in order to establish his eternal dominion (Psa. 89:19-29). It appears that Yahweh, in consort with the human authors of the Bible, is subversively using the pagan cultural motifs and thought-forms of the day to say, "Baal is not God, Yahweh is God."

In Psalm 74 and 89, and Isaiah 27 and 51 the story of the Exodus crossing of the Red Sea is described with the imaginative terms of creating the heavens and earth, crushing the heads of Leviathan, and binding the chaos waters of the sea in order to establish Yahweh's covenantal dominion on the earth in his people. This is history mixed in with mythopoeic imagination to describe the theological significance of what is taking place — just like other ancient Near Eastern religions did.[30]

Another aspect of Canaanite pagan mythology that is redeemed in the Scriptures is the divine council of the Sons of God. In the sacred Baal texts we

[28] http://godawa.com/Writing/Articles_And_Essays.html

[29] See Wyatt, N. Religious Texts from Ugarit. 2nd ed. Biblical seminar, 53. (London; New York: Sheffield Academic Press, 2002). Also, Brian Godawa, "Old Testament Storytelling Apologetics," http://godawa.com/Writing/Articles/OTStoryApologetics-CRJournal.pdf

[30] See Brian Godawa, "Biblical Creation and Storytelling: Cosmogony, Combat and Covenant" for a detailed explanation of this ANE technique:
http://godawa.com/Writing/Articles/BiblicalCreationStorytelling-Godawa.pdf

read about an assembly of the "Sons of El," the father deity of the pantheon. Baal is a vice regent who ascends to the throne of El and rules over the other gods of the council, who then do his bidding.[31]

In the Bible, God (called "El" or "Elohim") presides over a divine council or assembly of the "Sons of God" (Psa. 82:1; 89:5-7), who also give advice in judicial decisions of Yahweh (Psa. 82), and carry out his bidding as well (Job 1:6-12; 1Kings 22:19-22). A deified figure called the Son of Man is a vice regent who ascends to God's throne surrounded by those "holy ones" who do his bidding (Dan. 7:9-14).[32]

Of course, there are significant differences that separate the monotheistic Biblical divine council and the polytheistic pagan Canaanite divine council. As one example illustrates, the Biblical divine council are not to be worshipped, as God is, while the Canaanite divine council were worshipped.[33] Big similarities, but bigger differences. Biblical imagination does not engage in syncretism (blending opposing views), but in subversion (infiltrating and overthrowing an opposing view). The commonalities show a clear cultural connection that is subversively redeemed and redefined in the Biblical understanding of the concept. God incorporates pagan imagination and motifs into his own narrative and subverts them through redefinition and poetic usage.

Eden

The novel *Enoch Primordial* includes the Garden of Eden as a location important to the plot of the story. For those who believe it was an historical place, there are as many suggestions for its location as there are Bible commentators. We just don't know. The strongest hints are found in one passage, Genesis 2:10-14 that speaks of Eden at the headwaters of four rivers, The Pishon (in the land of Havilah), the Gihon (in the land of Cush), the Tigris, and the Euphrates.

The Tigris and Euphrates we know, but the Pishon and Gihon we do not. And if the flood was historical, whether global or local, then the terrain affected by that cataclysm would be significantly altered to derail all speculation. However, it's still fun to try.

---

[31] See Michael S. Heiser, *The Divine Council In Late Canonical And Non-Canonical Second Temple Jewish Literature* (Madison, WI: University of Wisconsin, 2004) 34-41: http://digitalcommons.liberty.edu/fac_dis/93/; Patrick D. Miller, "Cosmology And World Order In The Old Testament The Divine Council As Cosmic-Political Symbol" *Israelite Religion and Biblical Theology: Collected Essays by Patrick D. Miller*, (NY: Sheffield Academic Press, 2000).

[32] See Michael Heiser's writings on the divine council in the Bible at http://thedivinecouncil.com/.

[33] For more differences explained, see Gerald Cooke, "The Sons of (the) God(s)," *Zeitschrift für die alttestamentliche Wissenschaft*, n.s.:35:1 (1964), p 45-46.

Archaeologist David Rohl takes the Bible as basically truthful about the people and events it speaks of in history. He has looked at geographical, linguistic, and archaeological evidence of the ancient and modern Near East, and has made a persuasive argument that the land of Eden was in the mountainous valley area known to us as Armenia, where modern Turkey, Iran, Syria, and Iraq all meet.[34]

Bible readers often mistake the *Garden* of Eden for Eden itself. But Genesis speaks of "the Lord God planting a garden *in* Eden in the east" (Gen 2:8). So the Garden was in the eastern part of a land called "Eden."

Rohl places the Garden in the Adji Chay valley adjacent to Lake Urmia and nestled in the volcanic mountainous ranges of the Savalan in the north and the Sahand in the south. He shows how that area is at the headwaters of the Tigris and Euphrates as well as two other rivers he suggests are the Pishon (Araxes) and Gihon (Kezel Uzun).

The interesting variety of environments of volcanoes, mountains, lakes and forests were an inspiring setting to tell my story, so the map I've provided in the novel shows that I have followed Rohl's scholarship on the location of that most elusive Paradise.

Enoch

Enoch Primordial is a story that takes place in the primeval ages before the flood. It follows the Biblical hero Enoch on his journey through the "world that then was," as a holy man who preached judgment upon the Watchers and their progeny the giants. As discussed above, the book of 1 Enoch was used as a reference for the story of the novel. The Bible itself says almost nothing about Enoch. Apart from genealogical references, all Genesis has to say about him is this:

> Genesis 5:21–24
> When Enoch had lived 65 years, he fathered Methuselah. Enoch walked with God after he fathered Methuselah 300 years and had other sons and daughters. Thus all the days of Enoch were 365 years. Enoch walked with God, and he was not, for God took him.

In the New Testament, we have three references: A genealogical reference, the quotation from 1 Enoch in Jude about God coming with judgment against the fornicating angels referenced earlier, and this passage from the writer of Hebrews reminding us of Enoch's faith:

---

[34] David Rohl, *Legend: A Test of Time Vol. 2* (London: Random House 1998) 43-70.

> Hebrews 11:5
> By faith Enoch was taken up so that he should not see death, and he was not found, because God had taken him. Now before he was taken he was commended as having pleased God.

Archaeologist David Rohl theorizes that if such important people of the Faith really did exist, then they are likely to show up in other ancient literature of the same geographic location or time period. They may have a different name in a different language and culture, which was common, or they may be distorted vestiges of the real person.

In his book *Legend*, Rohl sifts through extant Sumerian literature to find who he believes is a "distant Sumerian memory" of this antediluvian patriarch Enoch. He uncovers Mesopotamian literature that refers to seven sages called *apkallus*, or wise men who are regarded as the originators of the arts and skills of civilization. By removing the mythological veil covering these advisors to ancient kings whose kingship "descended from heaven," he reveals a fascinating correlation. The seventh sage, Utuabzu, apkallu to King Enmeduranki of Sippar, is described as having "ascended to heaven," just like Enoch, the seventh patriarch, did in the Bible.[35] So I decided to follow this possible connecting point for defining Enoch's character in *Enoch Primordial* as being the apkallu to Enmeduranki of Sippar.

Cain

The infamous first murderer Cain, son of Adam, shows up in *Enoch Primordial*. He has a wolf companion and eventually we find that the curse/mark on Cain that the Bible does not explain is vampirism. Cain is an undead being who must feed on the blood of the living to maintain his wretched life. It reminds one of the fact that sometimes the greatest punishment is not death but living with the disastrous consequences of one's actions.

> Gen 4:11, 15
> And now you are cursed from the ground, which has opened its mouth to receive your brother's blood from your hand…And the LORD put a mark on Cain, lest any who found him should attack him.

---

[35] Rohl, *Legend,* 201-202. Also, Hess, Richard S. "Enoch (Person)". In *The Anchor Yale Bible Dictionary*, edited by David Noel Freedman. New York: Doubleday, 1992.

I drew from Jewish legends for this creative license. The rabbinic *Genesis Rabbah* 22:12 interpreted the "sign" that deterred others from attacking him as a protective dog (domesticated wolf), thus my lycanthropic connection.[36] The Pseudepigraphic *Life of Adam and Eve* paints a vampiric dream of Eve for her son Cain:

> The Life of Adam and Eve 2:1-3:2
> After these things Adam and Eve were together and when they were lying down to sleep, Eve said to her lord Adam, "My lord, I saw in a dream this night the blood of my son Amilabes, called Abel, being thrust into the mouth of Cain his brother, and he drank it mercilessly. He begged him to allow him a little of it, but he did not listen to him but swallowed all of it. And it did not stay in his stomach but came out of his mouth."...
> And God said to Michael the archangel, "Say to Adam, 'The mystery which you know do not report to your son Cain, for he is a son of wrath.[37]

The notion of vampirism is not new to *Enoch Primordial*. We have seen the Watchers drink blood from sacrifices as a means of their sustaining life in *Noah Primeval* as well. Biblical theology links atonement to blood sacrifice because "life is in the blood."

> Leviticus 17:11–12
> For the life of the flesh is in the blood, and I have given it for you on the altar to make atonement for your souls, for it is the blood that makes atonement by the life. Therefore I have said to the people of Israel, No person among you shall eat blood, neither shall any stranger who sojourns among you eat blood.

This is not to make God into a vampire, but it does make vampirism into a reflection of the curse of seeking to be gods or "like god." The notion of blood sacrifice was near universal in the ancient world because the *imago dei*

[36] Gordon J. Wenham, Vol. 1, *Genesis 1–15*. Word Biblical Commentary. Dallas: Word, Incorporated, 1998, 109. See http://www.sacred-texts.com/jud/mhl/mhl05.htm (page 55).
[37] James H. Charlesworth, *The Old Testament Pseudepigrapha and the New Testament, Volume 2: Expansions of the "Old Testament" and Legends, Wisdom, and Philosophical Literature, Prayers, Psalms and Odes, Fragments of Lost Judeo-Hellenistic Works* (New Haven; London: Yale University Press, 1985) 267.

in man, though distorted, is inescapable and thus finds its way into humankind's distortions of God-created reality.

Azazel

Baal is of course, not the only pagan entity that is subverted in the Bible. Remember the fallen Watcher Azazel who, in the Enoch passages above, was bound into the earth in the desert? Azazel makes his appearance in *Enoch Primordial* in this same way as one of the two lead Watchers who instigate the rebellion of the Watchers and the revelation of occultic knowledge to humanity. There is a much debated Scripture where this Azazel tradition may be influencing the Hebrew understanding of atonement. In Leviticus 16, the high priest Aaron is instructed in sin offerings for the people of Israel. One of those offerings is to be a scapegoat.

> Leviticus 16:7–10
> Then he shall take the two goats and set them before the LORD at the entrance of the tent of meeting. And Aaron shall cast lots over the two goats, one lot for the LORD and the other lot for Azazel. And Aaron shall present the goat on which the lot fell for the LORD and use it as a sin offering, but the goat on which the lot fell for Azazel shall be presented alive before the LORD to make atonement over it, that it may be sent away into the wilderness to Azazel.

Scholarly opinion is not unanimous (is it ever?) over just what "Azazel" refers to, but knowing the Enochian tradition of the angelic Azazel bound in the desert, there is strong warrant for the thesis that it refers to a "desert demon"[38] who happens to have the name of the demonic fallen angel who was bound in the desert in 1 Enoch.

Another demonized pagan deity appears in the Old Testament that may shed more light on this desert "goat-demon" Azazel. The Hebrew word, *seirim* is translated in several Old Testament passages as the pagan "satyr" or "hairy goat-demon." In two places it refers to the goat idols to whom some Canaanites made sacrifices (Lev. 17:7; 2Chron. 11:15) and in others to demonic entities that haunt the desert (Isa. 13:21; 34:14).[39] The Hebrews saw these pagan deities as the same thing: Demons.

---

[38] "Azazel", Karel van der Toorn, Bob Becking and Pieter Willem van der Horst, *Dictionary of Deities and Demons in the Bible*, (*DDD*) 2nd extensively rev. ed., (Leiden; Boston; Köln; Grand Rapids, MI; Cambridge: Brill; Eerdmans, 1999) 129.

[39] van der Toorn, Becking, *DDD*, 129.

Banias in ancient northern Canaan/Israel near Caesarea Philippi eventually became the center of worship for Pan, the hybrid goat-man deity. And this temple was near the base of Mount Hermon. To the Old Testament Jew, Azazel was an analog or incarnation of the desert goat-demon.[40]

Lilith

Another Mesopotamian deity subverted in the Old Testament narrative is Lilith, the she-demon. Regarding this monster, the *Dictionary of Deities and Demons in the Bible* says its Mesopotamian narrative reaches back to the third millennium B.C.

> Here we find Inanna who plants a tree later hoping to cut from its wood a throne and a bed for herself. But as the tree grows, a snake [Ningishzida] makes its nest at its roots, Anzu settled in the top and in the trunk the demon makes her lair... Of greater importance, however, is the sexual aspect of the mainly—female demons lilitu and lili. Thus the texts refer to them as the ones who have no husband, or as the ones who stroll about searching for men in order to ensnare them.[41]

Lilith was also known as the demon who stole away newborn babies to suck their blood, eat their bone marrow and consume their flesh.[42] In Jewish legends, she was described as having long hair and wings, and claimed to have been the first wife of Adam who was banished because of Adam's unwillingness to accept her as his equal.[43] Lilith and her offspring make their appearance in *Enoch Primordial* as temptresses guarding the World Tree in the desert with the snake god Ningishzida in the roots and the Anzu bird in its high branches.

Lilith the "night hag" makes her appearance in the Bible in Isaiah 34 along with that other pagan mythical creature, the satyr, a demonized interpretation of the goat-like god Pan. In this chapter, prophetic judgment upon Edom involves turning it into a desert wasteland that is inhabited by all kinds of demons; ravens, jackals, hyenas, satyrs — and Lilith.

---

[40] Judd H. Burton, *Interview With the Giant: Ethnohistorical Notes on the Nephilim*, (Burton Beyond Press, 2009), 19-20.

[41] "Lilith," *DDD*, 520.

[42] Handy, Lowell K. "Lilith (Deity)". In *The Anchor Yale Bible Dictionary*, edited by David Noel Freedman. New York: Doubleday, 1992, 324-325.

[43] Ginzberg, Louis; Szold, Henrietta (2011-01-13). *Legends of the Jews*, all four volumes in a single file, improved 1/13/2011 (Kindle Locations 1016-1028). B&R Samizdat Express. Kindle Edition.

Isaiah 34:13–15 (RSV)
It shall be the haunt of jackals... And wild beasts shall meet with hyenas, the satyr shall cry to his fellow; yea, there shall the night hag [*Lilith*] alight, and find for herself a resting place.

Resheph and Qeteb

Two other "demonized deities" that show up in the Bible are Resheph and Qeteb. In the song of Moses, Yahweh describes how he will punish those Israelites who enter the Promised Land but do not obey him:

Deut. 32:23-24
And I will heap disasters upon them;
I will spend my arrows on them;
they shall be wasted with hunger,
and devoured by plague (*Resheph*)
and poisonous pestilence (*Qetab*)

Resheph and Qeteb were Canaanite gods of plague and pestilence. Similar to this Deuteronomy passage, Resheph was described in Phoenicia as using his arrow of flaming judgment.[44] This curse is a poetic expression of Yahweh handing the rebellious Israelites over to the Canaanite gods for punishment.[45] As the *Dictionary of Deities and Demons in the Bible* concludes, "Qeteb is more than a literary figure, living as a spiritual, and highly dangerous, reality in the minds of poets and readers,"[46] and "in the OT Resheph is a demonized version of an ancient Canaanite god, now submitted to Yahweh."[47]

Rahab

One of the mythopoeic creatures that shows up in *Enoch Primordial* is Rahab, the Sea Dragon of chaos. In the appendix of *Noah Primeval*, I explained the mythological origins of the seven-headed Sea Dragon called

---

[44] Ronald S. Hendel, "The Flame of the Whirling Sword: A Note on Genesis 3:24," *Journal of Biblical Literature*, Vol. 104, No. 4 (Dec., 1985), pp. 673

[45] "Resheph," *DDD*, 703. Resheph is also referenced in Ps 78:48, 1 Chr 7:25, Ps 91:5, and Sir 43:17.

[46] Qeteb," *DDD*, 703, 673-74. Qeteb also makes an appearance in Psa 91:5–6, Hos 13:14 and Isa 28:2.

[47] "[Resheph] appears as a cosmic force, whose powers are great and terrible: he is particularly conceived of as bringing epidemics and death. The Hebrew Bible shows different levels of demythologization: sometimes it describes Resheph as a personalized figure, more or less faded, sometimes the name is used as a pure metaphor. At any rate it is possible to perceive aspects of the personality of an ancient chthonic god, whichs fits the image of Resheph found in the other Semitic cultures."
van der Toorn, Becking van der Horst, *DDD*, 703-704.

Leviathan and its appropriation in the Bible. Though the Old Testament seems to indicate Rahab as simply another name for this sea monster,[48] I decided to separate the two and make Leviathan the offspring of Rahab. But in the big war scene, we see that Rahab has other "helpers" with her, other monsters of the deep. This was also taken from a mythic motif that shows up in Babylonian, Ugaritic, and Biblical texts.

In the Ugaritic texts, the gods Baal and Anat defeat Leviathan along with her divine allies Yam, Nahar, Arsh, Atik, and others.[49] In the Babylonian Enuma Elish, the god Marduk defeats the sea dragon Tiamat and her monster helpers.[50]

> Tiamat assembled her creatures,
> Drew up for battle against the gods her brood [offspring]...[51]
> She has set up the Viper, the Dragon, and the Sphinx, the Great-Lion, the Mad-Dog, and the Scorpion-Man, Mighty lion-demons, the Dragon-Fly, the Centaur…[52]

So, we also see Rahab, the sea monster in Biblical texts being crushed and her "helpers" the enemies of God being "bowed" and "scattered."

> Job 9:13
> God will not turn back his anger;
> beneath him bowed <u>the helpers of Rahab</u>.

> Psalm 89:10
> You <u>crushed Rahab</u> like a carcass;
> you <u>scattered your enemies</u> with your mighty arm.

Behemoth

Speaking of Rahab's monstrous "helpers" of chaos, we come to Behemoth, another creature who finds his way into *Enoch Primordial* and *Noah Primeval*. The one place in Scripture where this huge beast shows up is

---

[48] See Rahab's equivocation with Leviathan in Psalm 89:10; Job 26:12; Isa 51:9-10 with Psa 74:13-14; Isa 27:1.

[49] KTU 1.3:3:35–47: N. Wyatt, *Religious Texts from Ugarit*, 2nd ed., Biblical seminar, 53, 79-80 (London ; New York: Sheffield Academic Press, 2002).

[50] "The Creation Epic," Tablet II lines 1-2, 27-29; IV, lines 107-108: *The Ancient Near East an Anthology of Texts and Pictures*., ed. James Bennett Pritchard, (Princeton: Princeton University Press, 1958) 67.

[51] "The Creation Epic," Tablet II lines 1-2, William W. Hallo and K. Lawson Younger, The Context of Scripture, 393 (Leiden; New York: Brill, 1997-) 393.

[52] "The Creation Epic," Tablet II lines 27-29; *The Ancient Near East an Anthology of Texts and Pictures*., ed. James Bennett Pritchard, (Princeton: Princeton University Press, 1958) 64.

in God's discourse with Job about God's unapproachable incomparable powers of creation:

> Job 40:15–24
> "Behold, Behemoth,
> which I made as I made you;
> he eats grass like an ox.
> Behold, his strength in his loins,
> and his power in the muscles of his belly.
> He makes his tail stiff like a cedar;
> the sinews of his thighs are knit together.
> His bones are tubes of bronze,
> his limbs like bars of iron.
> "He is the first of the works of God;
> let him who made him bring near his sword!
> For the mountains yield food for him
> where all the wild beasts play.
> Under the lotus plants he lies,
> in the shelter of the reeds and in the marsh.
> For his shade the lotus trees cover him;
> the willows of the brook surround him.
> Behold, if the river is turbulent he is not frightened;
> he is confident though Jordan rushes against his mouth.
> Can one take him by his eyes,
> or pierce his nose with a snare?

The most common interpretations of the identity of this monster by Biblical scholars is a hippopotamus, a crocodile, or a water buffalo. Young earth creationists argue that it is a sauropod dinosaur.[53] All of these seek to understand the creature as a real beast that existed in Bible times. Ancient Near Eastern scholar John Day dismisses these naturalistic interpretations in favor of a mythological picture of a chaos monster. There is no paleontological evidence of dinosaurs coexisting with humans. Hippopotamuses and water buffalos do not have strong bones, sinewy muscles, or tails like a cedar. Crocodiles are carnivores and do not eat grass.[54] But more importantly, unlike Behemoth, all of these animals are easily caught by man in contrast with Job's

[53] http://www.answersingenesis.org/articles/tj/v15/n2/behemoth

[54] Day ignores the dinosaur hypothesis. There remains no paleontological evidence of dinosaurs coexisting with humankind. And young earth creationists admit there is no known species of sauropods that fits all the details of Job 40.

emphasis that only God can do so. And lastly, none of them hold pride of status as “the first of the works of God.”[55]

Day argues that Behemoth is a mythological chaos monster that represents the Jewish demonization of pagan deities and symbolizes the subjugation of creation by God. He points out that Behemoth in this Job passage is coupled with the mythical chaos monster Leviathan in the verses following Behemoth (Job 41).

Later Jewish texts also understood Behemoth to be coupled with Leviathan as chaos monsters of creation with eschatological references to future judgment:

> 1 Enoch 60:7-8, 24
> On that day, two monsters will be parted—one monster, a female named Leviathan, in order to dwell in the abyss of the ocean over the fountains of water; and (the other), a male called Behemoth, which holds his chest in an invisible desert whose name is Dundayin, east of the garden of Eden...“These two monsters are prepared for the great day of the Lord (when) they shall turn into food.[56]

God is using these symbols of creative power over Chaos to close the mouth of Job’s complaints. Leviathan and Behemoth were “the first of the works of God” (40:19) and “the king over all the sons of pride” (41:34) because “the powers of chaos were primeval in origin.”[57] But fear not, God created them, God subjugated them, and God will turn them into a feast at the end of time.

Day then shows where this coupling of Leviathan and Behemoth has its origin, in two Canaanite texts of Ugarit where the goddess Anat is described as defeating Leviathan, “the dragon,” “the crooked serpent, the tyrant with seven heads,” and “El’s calf Atik” also called *Ars* (the ox-like Behemoth of Job 40:15).[58] Kenneth Whitney shows an established 2nd Temple Rabbinic

---

[55] John Day, *God's Conflict with the Dragon and the Sea: Echoes of a Canaanite Myth in the Old Testament* (University of Cambridge Press, 1985) 62-87.

[56] James H. Charlesworth, *The Old Testament Pseudepigrapha: Volume 1,* (New York; London: Yale University Press, 1983) 40-42. See also 2 Bar. 29:4; 4 Ez. 6:49, 5.

[57] Day, *God’s Conflict*, 80.

[58] Day, *God’s Conflict*, 80-81.
KTU I.3.III.43-4
Surely I lifted up the dragon...
(and) smote the crooked serpent,
the tyrant with the seven heads.
I smote Ars beloved of El,
I put an end to El's calf Atik.

tradition of Leviathan and Behemoth as companions of destruction in this same manner, thus the bovine nature of the amphibious creature in the *Chronicles of the Nephilim*.[59]

Day then concludes, "The reason for the inclusion of the sections on Behemoth and Leviathan in Job 40-1 is to drive home the point that, since Job is unable to overcome them, how much less can he hope to overcome in argument the God who defeated them."[60]

In *Enoch Primordial*, I took liberties to alter this monster's description somewhat in order to make him more ferociously carnivorous, but he remains a monster of chaos that is held at bay by the mountainous gates of a hidden valley of God's creation.

Mushussu

Another mythological creature that shows up in *Enoch Primordial* is the mushussu chimera that is well known from its tiled depiction on the Babylonian Ishtar Gate and many other seals discovered throughout Mesopotamia. It was a lion's body with a dragon's head, taloned back feet, and a tail that was a snake.

Robert Koldeway, an amateur archeologist of the 19th century, wrote a book about the Gate of Ishtar and noted that this mythical creature, called a *sirrush* at the time, was one of the few animals that were depicted remarkably consistent in Babylonian art over time. He thought that this might be because they had actual specimens of them. His thoughts were that they were dinosaurs misinterpreted as dragons. Ancient astronaut authors like Joseph Farrell suggest they were examples of actual genetic splicing by extraterrestrial aliens.[61] I used it as the first hint of the dark arts that the Watchers were just beginning to perfect in their own miscegenation project. We would see their advancements in *Noah Primeval*, but it represented the notion of the violation of the natural order of separation that seemed to be an important element of God's creation.

Scholar Theodore Lewis explains regarding the mushussu genetic combination of lion and dragon, "The common denominator for associating these two creatures seems to be that they could both inspire paralyzing, heart-

---

KTU 1.6.VI.51-3
In the sea are Ars and the dragon,
May Kothar-and-Hasis drive (them) away,
May Kothar-and-Hasis cut (them) off.

[59] Kenneth William Whitney, Jr., *Two Strange Beasts: A Study of Traditions Concerning Leviathan and Behemoth in Second Temple and Early Rabbinic Judaism*, Cambridge, Massachusetts: Harvard University, 1992.

[60] Day, *God's Conflict*, 87.

[61] Joseph P. Farrell, *Genes, Giants, Monsters, and Men: The Surviving Elites of the Cosmic War and Their Hidden Agenda* (2011-05-09). Perseus Books Group. Kindle Edition 1-9.

stopping fear when encountered."[62] He concludes that this is the creature used as a metaphor for the Pharaoh who had oppressed Judah rather than the "crocodile of outdated scholarship."[63] Yahweh was going to capture and cast that beast of a ruler onto the ground for the nations to gorge on its flesh.

> Ezekiel 32:2
> You are like a lion among the nations,
> You are like a dragon in the seas.

The literary pairing of a lion and serpent also occurs in Psalm 91:13; Isaiah 30:6; and Amos 5:19 and may come from the cultural awareness of this mythopoeic creature the mushussu.

Cherubim

Some of the critical characters that come to play in the narratives of *Noah Primeval* and *Enoch Primordial* are the Cherubim. The Mesopotamian version of this creature is the *aladlammu*, the bull-man and lion-man who guarded the thrones of Anu and Inanna. These large sphinx-like monsters were made famous by their presence on the huge stone Ishtar Gate of Babylon and other statues in museums around the world. But they are also ubiquitous in artifacts all around the ancient Near East, from Phoenicia to Syria to Egypt.[64] They were chimeras, hybrid creatures with the body of a lion or bull, the head of a man, and the wings of an eagle, and they protected the thrones of royalty and divinity throughout the Ancient Near East.[65]

It is not surprising then, to discover that they were also the creatures that guarded the throne of Yahweh, a throne that some explain was a commonplace Mesopotamian motif of a divine "throne chariot."[66]

---

[62] Theodore J. Lewis, "CT 13.33-34 and Ezekiel 32: Lion-Dragon Myths," *Journal of the American Oriental Society*, Vol. 116, No. 1 (Jan. - Mar., 1996), 35.
[63] Lewis, "Lion-Dragon Myths," 39. He also points out that Ezekiel was in Babylon under Nebuchadnezzar, who rebuilt the Gate of Ishtar. So it is likely the prophet draws from this imagery rather than from Egyptian.
[64] Ronald S. Hendel, "The Flame of the Whirling Sword: A Note on Genesis 3:24," *Journal of Biblical Literature*, Vol. 104, No. 4 (Dec., 1985), pp. 671-674.
[65] William F. Albright, "What Were the Cherubim?" *The Biblical Archaeologist*, Vol. 1, No. 1 (Feb., 1938), 1-3.
[66] "Assyrian art portrays the god Aššur riding into battle on behalf of the king. The god Baal is described in Ugaritic texts as one who rides the clouds mounted on a chariot (see 68:4; 104:3). This image dates as far back as the Old Akkadian period (ca. 2400 B.C.), from which a cylinder seal depicts the storm god riding a chariot drawn by a winged lion."
John H Walton, *Zondervan Illustrated Bible Backgrounds Commentary (Old Testament) Volume 5: The Minor Prophets, Job, Psalms, Proverbs, Ecclesiastes, Song of Songs*, (Grand Rapids, MI: Zondervan, 2009) 333.

Psalm 80:1
You who are enthroned upon the cherubim.

Psalm 99:1
The LORD reigns; let the peoples tremble!
He sits enthroned upon the cherubim!

Psalm 18:10
He rode on a cherub and flew;
he came swiftly on the wings of the wind.

When Ezekiel has his vision of the cherubim in chapters 1 and 10 as "living creatures," their usual sphinx-like morphology is expanded into a multiplicity of four wings, and four faces of human, lion, eagle and ox. But its essential nature remains the same.

The cherubim guarding the ark of the covenant with their outspread wings was crafted by pagan Phoenician artistry for Solomon (1Kings 8:6-7), and an ivory artifact discovered in Megiddo, Israel shows an Israelite king, possibly Solomon, seated on his throne guarded by a lion-bodied, eagle-winged, human-headed sphinx cherubim.[67]

In contrast with this imaginative art, the living cherubim guarding the way to the Tree of Life in the Garden of Eden were no sedentary statues (Gen 3:24), *but they were the sphinx-like cherubim.*

Genesis 3:24 says that these cherubim guard the Tree of Life with "the flame of the whirling sword." Scholar Ronald Hendel has argued that "the 'flame' is an animate divine being, a member of Yahweh's divine host, similar in status to the cherubim; the 'whirling sword' is its appropriate weapon, ever-moving, like the flame itself."[68]

Scholar P.D. Miller appeals to passages such as Psalm 104:4 where "fire and flame" are described as "Yahweh's ministers" to conclude a convergence of imagery with ancient Ugaritic texts that describe "fire and flame" as armed deities with flashing swords. He writes that "the cherubim and the flaming sword are probably to be recognized as a reflection of the Canaanite fiery messengers."[69] Thus the Biblically strange, yet strangely Biblical presence in *Enoch Primordial* of the Cherubim and their divine fiery beings beside them brandishing whirling swords of flashing lightning.

---

[67] Walton, John H. *Zondervan Illustrated Bible Backgrounds Commentary (Old Testament) Volume 5: The Minor Prophets, Job, Psalms, Proverbs, Ecclesiastes, Song of Songs*. Grand Rapids, MI: Zondervan, 2009, 405.

[68] Ronald S. Hendel, "'The Flame of the Whirling Sword': A Note on Genesis 3:24," *Journal of Biblical Literature*, Vol. 104, No. 4 (Dec., 1985), pp. 671-674.

[69] Patrick D. Miller, "Fire in the Mythology of Canaan and Israel," *Catholic Biblical Quarterly*, 27 no 3 Jl 1965, p 256-261.

Whence all this commonality between pagan and Hebrew cosmology? Did the Biblical writers draw from their ancient Near Eastern neighbors for their concepts of the cherubim or were pagan depictions distorted memories of the "myth that was true"?

Archaeologist David Rohl argues that the cherubim may have been a mythological spiritualization of a very human tribe of sentinels called the Kheruba who guarded the Edenic paradise.[70] I decided to incorporate all these interpretations into *Enoch Primordial.* How subversive of me.

Seraphim

The prophet Isaiah had an exalted vision of the Lord sitting on his heavenly throne high and lifted up with the glorious train of his robe filling the temple. But there were also some other chimeric creatures in his presence:

> Isaiah 6:2–7
> Above him stood the seraphim. Each had six wings: with two he covered his face, and with two he covered his feet, and with two he flew. And one called to another and said: "Holy, holy, holy is the LORD of hosts; the whole earth is full of his glory!"… Then one of the seraphim flew to me, having in his hand a burning coal.

The meaning of the Hebrew word for *seraphim* is "fiery serpent."[71] It was used to describe the fiery serpents in the wilderness whose poisonous burning venom was God's punishment for Israel's grumbling and complaining (Num. 21:6). God's balm of healing forgiveness was obtained by looking to a brass serpent (*seraph*) image raised on a pole called Nehushtan (Num. 21:8).

But this is not the only use of *seraph* that sheds light on the meaning of the angelic seraphim. The Brown-Driver-Briggs Hebrew Lexicon points out that Isaiah 14:29 and 30:6 refer to a "flying fiery serpent" (*seraph*) in the wilderness that originated in mythically conceived winged serpent deities.[72] The term is unavoidably serpentine in all its cognates.

Some deny this serpentine essence by pointing out that the Isaianic seraphim are described as having human heads, wings, hands and feet. But Karen Randolph Joines has persuasively argued that the Egyptian winged

---

[70] David Rohl, *From Eden to Exile: The 5000-Year History of the People of the Bible,* (Lebanon, TN: Greenleaf Press, 2002), 31-32.

[71] Harris, R. Laird. "2292 שָׂרָף". In *Theological Wordbook of the Old Testament*, edited by R. Laird Harris, Gleason L. Archer, Jr. and Bruce K. Waltke. electronic ed. Chicago: Moody Press, 1999.

[72] Brown, Francis, Samuel Rolles Driver, and Charles Augustus Briggs. *Enhanced Brown-Driver-Briggs Hebrew and English Lexicon.* electronic ed. Oak Harbor, WA: Logos Research Systems, 2000.

ureus (upright cobra) that guarded the Pharaoh's tombs and thrones with its "fiery" venom is demonstrably the equivalent of the Hebrew seraph. Like the seraphim in Isaiah, the ureus was also commonly described as having a human face, wings, hands and feet when it was necessary for it to accomplish tasks like those of Isaiah 6.[73] But it remained a winged serpent.

ANE scholar Michael S. Heiser goes one step further and provisionally considers a literary overlapping of all these elements of fiery serpents, flying, humanoid features, and divinity to be variations of descriptions for the "Watcher paradigm":

> "Seraphim, then, are reptilian/serpentine beings – they are the Watchers (the "watchful ones" who diligently guard God's throne, which is carried [cf. Ezekiel 1, 10] by the cherubim, who may also serve as guardians). There are "good" serpentine beings (seraphim) who guard God's throne (so Isaiah 6's seraphim), and there are fallen, wicked serpentine beings (seraphim) who rebelled against the Most High at various times, and who became the pagan gods of the other nations."[74]

He supports his view from Isaiah 14:29, a prophecy about Philistia (the city of Goliath and other giants) that references the messianic war of the seed of the serpent (*nachash*) that brings forth the fruit of the flying fiery serpent (*seraph*).

> Isaiah 14:29
> 29 Rejoice not, O Philistia… for from the serpent's [*nachash*] root will come forth an adder, and its fruit will be a flying fiery serpent [seraph].

Could this be a literary reference to the Watcher paradigm?

A text fragment from the Dead Sea Scrolls affirms the ancient Jewish understanding of Watchers having this reptilian presence and ruling over specific peoples:

> 4QAmram (4Q544) lines 10-14
> [I saw Watchers] in my vision, the dream-vision. Two men were fighting over me…I asked them, "Who are you, that you

---

[73] Karen Randolph Joines, "Winged serpents in Isaiah's inaugural vision," *Journal of Biblical Literature*, 86 no 4 D 1967, p 414-415.

[74] Michael S. Heiser, "Serpentine / Reptilian Divine Beings in the Hebrew Bible: A Preliminary Investigation" 4.

> are thus empowered over me?" They answered me, "We have been empowered and rule over mankind," They said to me, "Which of us do you choose to rule you?" I raised my eyes and looked. One of them was terrifying in his appearance, like a serpent, his cloak many-colored yet very dark... And I looked again and... in his appearance, his visage was like a viper.[75]

Rephaim

The Rephaim that appear in *the Chronicles of the Nephilim* are based upon Biblical and ancient Near Eastern references to giants or deified kings that ended up in the underworld. A buried library of cuneiform tablets was excavated at Ras Shamra from the ancient city of Ugarit during the years 1940-47. They yielded tablets that have been crucial to understanding the development of Syrian and Canaanite religion. One of the corpus of texts unearthed there was what came to be known as the Rephaim Texts. These texts and others talked about a *marzih* feast, like that in *Enoch Primordial,* that involved royalty traveling distances in their chariots to participate in this feast, wherein the "most ancient Rephaim of the netherworld" are summoned to assemble as the "council of the Ditanu, (or Didanu)."[76] Some names of these deified royal ancestors were given as Ulkan, Taruman, Sidan-and-Radan, and Thar, the eternal one.[77] This is where I drew the names for my council of Didanu that meets in Baalbek for a diabolical plan. The names of the infamous Rephaim Thamaq and Yahipan, the Rephaim targets of Methuselah's revenge in *Enoch Primordial*, were drawn from these ancient texts as well.[78]

As Ugaritic scholars Levine and Tarragon sum up, "the Rephaim are long departed kings (and heroes) who dwell in the netherworld, which is located deep beneath the mountains of that far-away eastern region where the Ugaritians originated."[79]

---

[75] Robert H. Eisenman, Michael Wise, *The Dead Sea Scrolls Uncovered: The First Complete Translation and Interpretation of 50 Key Documents withheld for Over 35 Years*, (Rockport, MA: Element Books, 1992) 55-56.

[76] William W. Hallo and K. Lawson Younger, *The Context of Scripture*, (Leiden; New York: Brill, 1997-) 356-58.

[77] N. Wyatt, *Religious Texts from Ugarit, 2nd ed.*, Biblical seminar, 53, 431-34 (London ; New York: Sheffield Academic Press, 2002).

[78] N. Wyatt, *Religious Texts from Ugarit, 2nd ed.*, Biblical seminar, 53, 321 (London ; New York: Sheffield Academic Press, 2002).

[79] Baruch A. Levine and Jean-Michel de Tarragon, "Dead Kings and Rephaim: The Patrons of the Ugaritic Dynasty," *Journal of the American Oriental Society*, Vol. 104, No. 4 (Oct. - Dec., 1984), pp. 649-659

While creative license and speculation drives *Enoch Primordial*, even the names of the Nephilim brothers, Ohyah and Hahyah, as well as the giant General Mahawai, were taken from the ancient manuscript *The Book of Giants* that was part of the Dead Sea Scrolls found at Qumran.[80] In these texts the giant brothers are described as the giant offspring of Semjaza, one of the Watchers, and they have dreams of God's judgment coming upon them in the form of tablets being drowned in water and a garden being uprooted. As in the novel, so they seek out Enoch to explain their dreams and allow them repentance.[81]

The Bible also reinforces this ancient Ugaritic understanding of Rephaim as dead royal or heroic ancestors who reside in the underworld, but with a twist. In Isaiah 14, the prophet pronounces an oracle of judgment upon the king of Babylon whose arrogance leads him to consider himself a god (v. 13-14). Isaiah concludes with an ironic mockery of the Rephaim, these exalted dead kings and heroes, including The Babylonian king in their ultimate impotence.

> Isaiah 14:9–11
> Sheol beneath is stirred up
> to meet you when you come;
> it rouses the shades (*Rephaim*) to greet you,
> all who were leaders of the earth;
> it raises from their thrones
> all who were kings of the nations.
> All of them will answer
> and say to you:
> 'You too have become as weak as we!
> You have become like us!'
> Your pomp is brought down to Sheol.

To the Hebrew prophet, these proud kings were humiliated in the underworld of Sheol. Their glory became as "shades" in the light of God.[82] Apparently, the prophet transforms ancient Canaanite mythology into a polemical emasculation of pagan pride.[83]

---

[80] 4Q203 and 6Q8, Florentino García Martínez and Eibert J. C. Tigchelaar, *The Dead Sea Scrolls Study Edition* (Translations) (Leiden; New York: Brill, 1997-1998) 410.

[81] 4Q539, García Martínez, Florentino, and Eibert J. C. Tigchelaar. *The Dead Sea Scrolls Study Edition* (Translations). Leiden; New York: Brill, 1997-1998, 1064-65.

[82] See also Proverbs 2:18-19; 9:18; 21:16; Psa 88:10; Job 26:5-6; where the Hebrew word Rephaim is translated variously as "departed," "the dead" and "shades."

[83] For a good exegesis of Rephaim from the Ugaritic and Biblical texts, see Conrad L'Heureux, "The Ugaritic and Biblical Rephaim," *The Harvard Theological Review*, Vol. 67, No. 3 (Jul., 1974), pp. 265-274.

But there is another element that the Biblical text adds to these royal "divinized" Rephaim: Gigantism. The very land of Canaan around Mount Hermon that was called Bashan was described as the "land of the Rephaim" (Deut. 3:13), whose inhabitants were described as tall giants like the Anakim (Deut. 2:11, 20) and were related to Goliath the giant (1Chron. 20:4-8). When Joshua was wiping out the tribes and cities of giants in Canaan, one of the last ones to go was the mighty Og of Bashan, the "last of the Rephaim" (Joshua 12:4) whose bed (or sarcophagus) was thirteen and a half feet long (Deut. 3:11). The reader will learn more about Og's exploits later in the series *The Chronicles of the Nephilim.*

The satan

A familiar character that shows up in *Enoch Primordial* but not in a familiar way is Satan — or rather, *the satan.* The typical Evangelical mythology surrounding Satan is that he was the highest cherub in God's heavenly host, a worship leader with the name of Lucifer, who before the Garden of Eden, rebelled by trying to usurp God's seat of authority in heaven. He wanted to be "like God." He was then cast out of heaven with a third of the angels and fell to earth, where he tempted Eve in the Garden as a snake, and now he is "Lord of the air" over the earth.

I have no problem utilizing *lesser known* extra-Biblical mythology or legends in *the Chronicles of the Nephilim* in order to bring a fresh perspective to the Biblical story. But I also have no problem dismantling other *well-known* extra-Biblical mythology and legends in order to support that same goal of fresh perspective. The Satan legend as I described it above is one of those accepted myths that I decided to avoid because, well, it really isn't in the Bible.

I am going to follow David Lowe's strategy and "deconstruct Lucifer" in order to rediscover Satan in a new and more Biblical light.[84] First, let me affirm that the New Testament does equate Satan with the Serpent in the Garden (2Cor. 11:3; Rev. 12:9; 20:2) so I have no quarrel with that notion. But let's take a look at the rest of the Lucifer/Satan mythology to see if it really has Biblical merit.

The two passages that are most often used as source material for this myth are Isaiah 14:12-15 and Ezekiel 28:12-16. Let's look first at the Isaiah passage:

> Isaiah 14:12–15
> "How you are fallen from heaven,
> O Day Star (Lucifer), son of Dawn!

---

[84] David W. Lowe, *Deconstructing Lucifer: Reexamining the Ancient Origins of the Fallen Angel of Light*, (Seismos Publishing 2011).

How you are cut down to the ground,
you who laid the nations low!
You said in your heart,
'I will ascend to heaven;
above the stars of God
I will set my throne on high;
I will sit on the mount of assembly
in the far reaches of the north;
I will ascend above the heights of the clouds;
I will make myself like the Most High.'
But you are brought down to Sheol,
to the far reaches of the pit.

The context of the entire passage of Isaiah 14 is that the prophet is making a prophesy of judgment upon the king of Babylon who existed in Isaiah's own day during the Jewish Babylonian exile. Well-meaning Christians interpret this text as a mythopoeic allusion or analogy of pride between Satan, called Lucifer, and the Babylonian tyrant.

To start with, the name *Satan* is nowhere in the story, but *Lucifer* is. The problem with this name is that we have come to consider it a proper name of a demonic entity only by tradition. As author David Lowe points out, Lucifer was actually the Latin translation for the Hebrew words *Helel ben shahar*, which means "Morningstar," known to the ancients as the planet Venus.[85] In the ancient Near East, planets and stars were equated with deities and the heavenly host, so this is indeed a mythopoeic reference. But scholars have uncovered a very different narrative being referenced than the Garden of Eden. It is in fact a pagan Canaanite myth that Isaiah used to mock the pagan king of Babylon.

Scholar Michael S. Heiser definitively explains the linguistic and narrative referent of Helel ben Shahar as being the Ugaritic god Athtar from the epic Baal Cycle of myths at Ugarit. Heiser reveals that Athtar was equated with the planet Venus. Athtar sought to raise himself above "the stars of El," a reference to the divine council or heavenly host that surrounded the high god of the Canaanite pantheon. He tried to do so by seeking to sit on the throne of Baal, referred to as "the Most High," upon the "mount of assembly" in the north called Saphon. But Athtar was not powerful enough for the position of power and was cast to earth/Sheol.[86]

---

[85] Lowe, *Deconstructing Lucifer*, 39-40.
[86] Michael Heiser, "The Mythological Provenance of Isaiah 14:12-15: A Reconsideration of the Ugaritic Material" Liberty University <http://digitalcommons.liberty.edu/lts fac pubs/280>

There are no versions of this Isaianic narrative applying to Satan anywhere in the Bible but there sure is one of Athtar in the Canaanite context in which ancient Jews like Isaiah lived and breathed. Isaiah was declaring judgment upon the Babylonian tyrant by using pagan myths against the pagan king as mockery.

As Norman Habel put it,

> The presence of this archaic mythological imagery to describe the dwelling place of God does not imply that the Israelite writers thereby espoused the crass mythological view of reality current in the ancient Near Eastern world. Polemical and poetical considerations governed the Israelite writers' use of imagery taken from their pagan environment.[87]

The second passage that well-intentioned Christians use to justify their belief in the Satan/Lucifer mythology is Ezekiel 28:12-15. I will focus in on the most important elements to keep this as short as possible. Similar to Isaiah, Ezekiel prophesied about the hubris and fall of the king of Tyre. Also like Isaiah, Ezekiel makes a mythopoeic reference to some narrative. In this case, I would argue it *is* the Garden of Eden narrative being referenced. But the difference is that whereas many Christians assume Ezekiel is equating the fall of the king of Tyre with the fall of Satan, the truth is that the prophet is actually equating it with the fall of *Adam*![88]

> Ezekiel 28:12–16
> You were the signet of perfection…
> You were in Eden, the garden of God…
> You were an anointed guardian cherub…
> I placed you; you were on the holy mountain of God;
> in the midst of the stones of fire you walked.
> You were blameless in your ways
> from the day you were created,
> till unrighteousness was found in you…
> so I cast you as a profane thing from the mountain of God,
> and I destroyed you, O guardian cherub,

It was Adam who was in Eden and was blameless in his ways, not Satan. According to the Evangelical Satan legend, Satan already fell *before* the

---

[87] Norman C. Habel, "Ezekiel 28 and the fall of the first man." *Concordia Theological Monthly*, 1967, 38 (8),. 520.

[88] For an excellent explanation of this view, see Norman C. Habel, "Ezekiel 28 and the fall of the first man." *Concordia Theological Monthly*, 1967, 38 (8),. 516-524.

Garden. It was Adam who was created blameless and fell into sin and was cast out of Eden, not Satan. Satan's name is nowhere to be found in this passage.[89]

One possible reason to presume the Satan connection here is the description of the character as an "anointed guardian cherub." But there is a problem with this translation. Many commentators make the point that this is based upon the Masoretic text (MT) of the Bible. But the Septuagint (LXX), another authoritative Greek text of the Old Testament that is quoted by the New Testament authors and Jesus, renders those phrases "From the day that thou wast created thou *wast with* the cherub"[90] and "the cherub has brought thee out of the midst of the stones."[91] Being "with the cherub" is a very different meaning than "being a cherub." Though this is not unanimously conclusive, an increasing number of Bible scholars point to this ambiguity and likelihood of the Septuagint being the superior textual tradition here.[92] Adam was not a cherub, he was with the cherubim.

Lastly, in Revelation 12, we see the origin of the notion that one third of the angels fell to earth with Satan at his fall. The only problem is that this event did not occur before the garden of Eden in a cosmic rebellion, *it happened at the birth of Jesus Christ*! Revelation 12:1-6 describes an apocalyptic parable of the cosmic war of the Seed of the Serpent (a dragon of chaos) and the Seed of the Woman (Israel/the Church).[93] It describes one third of the angelic stars (Watchers?) joining Satan with the swipe of his serpentine tail. The dragon and his minions seek to devour the male seed (offspring) of the woman, but they fail and the child becomes king. And then the passage tells of a heavenly war:

> Revelation 12:7–10
> 7 Now war arose in heaven, Michael and his angels fighting against the dragon. And the dragon and his angels fought back, 8 but he was defeated, and there was no longer any place for them in heaven. 9 And the great dragon was thrown down, that ancient serpent, who is called the devil and Satan, the deceiver of the whole world—he was thrown down to the

---

[89] Scholar H.J. van Dijk makes an interesting grammatical and linguistic argument that "You were the signet of perfection" is better translated, "You were the serpent of perfection" because the Hebrew word translated *signet* remains obscure. In Phoenician and Aramaic, however it means *serpent*. This would provide serious evidence for a link to the Serpent of the Garden. H. J. van Dijk, vol. 20, *Ezekiel's Prophecy on Tyre (Ez. 26:1–28:19): A New Approach* (Biblica et orientalia; Rome: Pontifical Biblical Institute, 1968).

[90] Lancelot Charles Lee Brenton, *The Septuagint Version of the Old Testament: English Translation*, Eze 28:14 (London: Samuel Bagster and Sons, 1870).

[91] Lancelot Charles Lee Brenton, *The Septuagint Version of the Old Testament: English Translation*, Eze 28:16 (London: Samuel Bagster and Sons, 1870).

[92] Notes on Ezekiel 28:14, Biblical Studies Press. *The NET Bible First Edition Notes*. Biblical Studies Press, 2006. Also see Lowe, *Deconstructing Lucifer*, 118-131.

[93] The woman's crown of twelve stars is a symbol of the twelve tribes of Israel.

> earth, and his angels were thrown down with him. [10] And I heard a loud voice in heaven, saying, "Now the salvation and the power and the kingdom of our God and the authority of his Christ have come, for the accuser of our brothers has been thrown down, who accuses them day and night before our God.

Most Christians believe this is a reference to Satan's fall before the Garden of Eden incident, where he takes one third of the angels in heaven with him. But a closer look at the context reveals that this is not the case at all, but rather the opposite. The war in heaven *does not* happen before the Garden, it happens at the time of the incarnation of Messiah on earth! The woman (Israel) gives birth to a male child (Messiah, v. 5), who the dragon (Satan) seeks to devour (from Herod's slaughter of the innocents all the way to the Cross). That Messiah ascends to the throne in authority after his resurrection (v. 5; Eph 1:20-22), during which time that woman (Israel) flees to the wilderness (time of tribulation under the Roman Empire).

The war in heaven we see cannot be before the Garden because it says that the throwing down of Satan occurs with the coming of the kingdom of Christ! (v. 10). He is thrown down to earth and then seeks to kill the Christ (v. 13). Satan then seeks to make war with the rest of her offspring (God's people) which we see in history.

Revelation 12 is an apocalyptic parable that is describing the incarnation of Messiah, his ascension to the throne of authority over all principalities and powers, and his suppression of Satan's power as the Gospel goes forth into the world.

But our problems with Satan do not end there. In *Enoch Primordial*, I do not call Satan, Satan, but *the satan*, lowercase, or the Accuser. Why? Because the Hebrew word is not an individual's name, but a *legal role* meaning "accuser" or "adversary." The satan/accuser depicted in Job 1 and 2 is one of the divine council of heavenly host (1Kings 22) who engages in legal accusations against God and his people and sometimes carries out God's intentions. In short, he is a kind of manipulative prosecutor whose purpose is to challenge God and his perfect law.

In Hebrew, *satan* is prefixed by the definite article *ha* which makes it translate more accurately as *the satan*, or *the accuser*. In the New Testament Greek, Satan is prefixed by the definite article *ho*, carrying the same result of *the satan* as the adversary (Rev. 12:9) or the accuser (Rev. 12:10).

So the most we can know of the satan's work in the Old Testament is that he was the Serpent in the Garden, and he *may have been* a prosecuting attorney-like accuser of God's heavenly court. I say *may have been* because the satan was more a role or state of being than an individual. The avenging angel who was going to strike down Balaam was described as *the satan* in Numbers 22:22 and verse 32 ("adversary" and "oppose"); the political opponents of king David were defined as *the satan* to him (2Sam. 19:22); David himself was described as a potential *satan* to the Philistines (1Sam. 29:4); Hadad the Edomite and Reznon, son of Eliada are both described as *satans* to Israel (1Kings 11:14, 23); and even God himself is described as *the satan* (adversary) when he incites David to take a census (1Chron. 21:1; 2 Sam. 24:1). In the Old Testament, *the satan* was not always the same individual, but more likely the legal office of prosecutor.

This short excursion into deconstructing Satan is the foundation for why I portrayed him as I did in *Enoch Primordial*, as the prosecutorial Seraph, the Serpent of the Garden, whose purpose became accusing God's people and bringing lawsuits to God's throne to try to foil his plans.

Covenant Lawsuit

In *Enoch Primordial*, the satan prosecutes a "covenant lawsuit" against Yahweh Elohim in order to buy time for the Watchers to accomplish their nefarious plans of world domination. The satan and most of the Watchers "present themselves" before the heavenly court, along with "ten thousand times ten thousand of God's holy ones," the divine council. God is seated on his chariot throne above the Cherubim and beneath the Seraphim, and the satan engages in his arguments against God with Enoch, the translated holy man, as defense attorney.

At first blush this may seem to the modern "enlightened" religious mind like an artificial modern construct imposed upon the ancient story. But in fact, it is organically derived from the Bible itself, which drew from the ancient suzerain vassal treaties of the ancient Near East (most likely Hittite in origin).

Whenever "the satan" is named in the Bible (meaning "the accuser," a legal term), it is usually in the legal context of a heavenly lawsuit. In the *Noah Primeval* appendices, I examined the divine council in the Scriptures in detail. In passages such as Job 1 and 2, and 1Kings 22 we are told that "the sons of God came to present themselves before Yahweh,"[94] "all the host of heaven standing beside him on his right and on his left."[95] God then asks counsel and recommendation from this multitude on what to do regarding a specific

---

[94] Job 1:6; 2:1.
[95] 1Kings 22:19.

situation.[96] The heavenly beings give their opinions, God renders his verdict, and directs some of the host to carry out the sentence.[97]

The context in these passages is that of a legal body of divine beings counseling with God over justice and the satan is one of these divine beings whose role is to accuse.[98] In Zechariah 3:1-4, Joshua the High Priest stands in this divine council before God. The satan stands beside him "to accuse him" before Elohim in good legal form.

While some of these scenes are the satan initiating legal accusations against God's people, others are litigation against pagan rulers for their own defiance of God's universal sovereignty. In Daniel 7:9-14, we see "the Ancient of Days" seated on his throne, "and ten thousand times ten thousand stood before him; the court sat in judgment" over the nations of the earth (Dan. 7:10). And in Psalm 82, God renders legal judgment upon the members of the divine council who failed to carry out justice for God upon the gentile nations they had inherited.[99] We read this Psalmic phrase used in *Enoch Primordial*, "God has taken his place in the divine council; in the midst of the gods he holds judgment" (v. 1-2).

Another kind of Biblical lawsuit saw Old Testament prophets as Yahweh's prosecuting attorneys indicting Israel for breaking her covenant with God. The prophet would stand before God's divine council and make the summons and charges against Israel before calling her to respond to the charges. Then Yahweh as judge would pronounce his verdict. One of the qualifications of a prophet's authority to speak for God was that he had stood in this divine council (Jer. 23:18, 22).

Herbert Huffmon has pointed out examples of covenant lawsuits in Jeremiah, Isaiah, Micah, and other prophets carried out in God's courtroom against Israel that illustrated a Biblical pattern of legal procedure:

> A description of the scene of judgment
> II. The speech of the plaintiff
> A. Heaven and earth are appointed judges
> B. Summons to the defendant (or judges)

---

[96] Job 1:8; 1King 22:20, 22; Isa 6:8. Scholar Frank Moore Cross shows that the divine council is implied in other passages such as Isaiah 40:1-6 and 48:20-21 where God is heard asking a question to an "unknown" plural audience. "Comfort my people," "a voice says, 'Cry!'" and "declare this with a shout" are all plural imperatives as if spoken to a multitude surrounding God's throne. Frank M. Cross, Jr., "The Council of Yahweh in Second Isaiah," *Journal of Near Eastern Studies*, Vol. 12, No. 4 (Oct., 1953), pp. 274-277.

[97] Job 1:12; 2:6; 1King 22:22-23.

[98] Lowell K. Handy, "The Authorization of Divine Power and the Guilt of God in the Book of Job: Useful Ugaritic Parallels," *Journal for the Study of the Old Testament* (60) December 1993, 108-109: Min Sue Kee, "The Heavenly Council and its Type-scene," *Journal for the Study of the Old Testament*, Vol 31.3(2007): 259-273.

[99] See Appendix A "The Sons of God" in *Noah Primeval* for a detailed explanation of this Biblical concept of the sons of God inheriting the pagan nations.

C. Address in the second person to the defendant
1. Accusation in question form to the defendant
2. Refutation of the defendant's possible arguments
3. Specific indictment[100]

I used this basic scenario in *Enoch Primordial* when the satan accuses Elohim of being unjust in his own covenantal relationship with man. But I also used the ancient Near Eastern covenant formula for the document under attack in the satan's lawsuit. This ancient formula can be seen in the form of the Biblical covenant as well. Biblical scholars have shown how God's covenants with Israel displayed the same five or six point structure that their neighboring Hittite nation used during the Late Bronze or Early Iron Ages (1400-1200 B.C.).

It is commonly understood now that covenant texts occupy a significant proportion of Biblical composition. As Biblical scholar Eugene Merrill states,

> The Covenant Code of Exodus 20-23 and the entire Book of Deuteronomy are the most outstanding examples of this type. It is quite apparent that Moses undoubtedly utilized already existing treaty formulas in the construction of biblical treaty contracts between God and individuals or God and Israel.[101]

The chart below summarizes how the book of Deuteronomy reflects five key elements of the ancient Hittite suzerain treaty as currently attested by scholarship:

[100] Herbert B. Huffmon, "The Covenant Lawsuit in the Prophets," *JBL* 78 (1959): 7. 285–95.
[101] Eugene Merrill, "Covenant and the Kingdom : Genesis 1- 3 As Foundation for Biblical Theology." Criswell Theological Review 1 (1987) 296-7.

Parallels Between Hittite Suzerainty Treaties and the Book of Deuteronomy[102]	
Structure of Hittite Suzerainty Treaties (14th Century B.C.)	Structure of Deuteronomy, a Hebrew "Covenant Document"
1. Preamble: "These are the words of the Great King..."	**1. Preamble**: (1:1–6). "These are the words which Moses spoke..."
2. Historical Prologue: The events leading up to the treaty.	**2. Historical Prologue:** (1:7–4:49). Events leading up to the making and renewing of the covenant.
3. Ethical Stipulations: Laws relating to the vassal's obedience to the suzerain.	**3. Ethical Stipulations:** (5–26). The loyalty due to God.
4. Curses and Blessings: Contingent upon disobedience or obedience.	**4. Curses and Blessings:** (27, 28). Contingent upon disobedience or obedience.
5. Divine Witnesses: Called to witness the making of the treaty ("heaven and earth").[103]	**5. Divine Witnesses:** (32). The witness of "heaven and earth" (30:19; 32:1).

Whether the majority of the Pentateuch (first five books of the Bible) was written by Moses or compiled and edited in the centuries that followed him, some scholars such as Meredith Kline have argued that the entire Bible, including the early chapters of Genesis, is formulated on the model of an extended ancient Near Eastern covenant.[104]

Another well established "Tablet Theory" by D.J. Wiseman suggests that the early portions of Genesis may have even found their sources in clay tablets inscribed by those closest to the primeval events.[105] So maybe the notion of the satan referring to "discovery documents" of genealogies in *Enoch Primordial* is not so far fetched after all.

---

[102] Adapted and modified from Walter A. Elwell and Barry J. Beitzel, *Baker Encyclopedia of the Bible*, 535 (Grand Rapids, Mich.: Baker Book House, 1988). See also Meredith Kline, *Treaty of the Great King* (Overland Park: KS, 2000); Walton, John H. *Zondervan Illustrated Bible Backgrounds Commentary (Old Testament) Volume 1: Genesis, Exodus, Leviticus, Numbers, Deuteronomy*. Grand Rapids, MI: Zondervan, 2009 420-515.

[103] The *DDD* has this to say about the divine witness duo of heaven and earth: "'Olden gods' frequently occur in pairs in the ancient theogonies and often represent elements of the natural order. In texts of diverse origins in the ancient world, these pairs of deities are invoked to serve as witnesses to treaties and covenants. We find analogous petitions made in OT covenant lawsuit formulas used by the prophets. Isaiah (Isa 1:2) invokes the Heavens and the Earth to act as witnesses against Israel for breaking the covenant with Yahweh. The prophet Micah makes a similar appeal (Mic 6:2; cf. Jer 2:12). While these elements were by no means considered divine by the prophets, their use in covenant lawsuit formulas indicates a common rhetorical form whose origins may be traced back to originally mythological conceptions." Karel van der Toorn, Bob Becking and Pieter Willem van der Horst, *Dictionary of Deities and Demons in the Bible*, 2nd extensively rev. ed., (Leiden; Boston; Köln; Grand Rapids, MI; Cambridge: Brill; Eerdmans, 1999) 644-45.

[104] M.G. Kline, *The Treaty of the Great King* (Grand Rapids: Eerdmans, 1963); *The Structure of Biblical Authority* (Grand Rapids: Eerdmans,1972).

[105] P.J. Wiseman and D. J. Wiseman, *Ancient Records and the Structure of Genesis* (Nashville: Thomas Nelson, Inc., 1985). Online, see: Curt Sewell, "The Tablet Theory of Genesis Authorship," *Bible and Spade*, Winter 1994, Vol. 7, No. 1. http://www.biblearchaeology.org/post/2010/10/11/the-tablet-theory-of-genesis-authorship.aspx

In conclusion, even the legal procedures and divine council found in the Bible reflect the covenant treaty structures, and city-state bureaucracy of Israel's ancient Near Eastern pagan neighbors redeemed and applied to God's purposes.

The Chronicles of the Nephilim

So that's what I did in *Noah Primeval* and *Enoch Primordial*. I retold the story of these two heroes of faith, incorporating the respected Enochian tradition of the Watchers and giants, Ancient Near Eastern imagery of Azazel, Lilith, Leviathan and Rahab, cherubim and seraphim, speculation on the divine council of the Sons of God, along with other Mesopotamian mythopoeia and Biblical imagination, in order to give a theological explanation for the true origins and "partial truth" of pagan mythology. It's all positively primeval.

Gilgamesh Immortal

Appendix

Chapter 7
Gilgamesh and the Bible

The Biblical fantasy novel *Gilgamesh Immortal* is a retelling of the ancient Babylonian *Epic of Gilgamesh*. This narrative of the heroic journey of its protagonist, is a myth imagined around a supposedly historical figure, King Gilgamesh of Uruk, the fourth king of the first Dynasty of Uruk. His name is mentioned in an ancient *Sumerian King List* as reigning after "the flood swept over" the land, and scholars place him in the third millennium B.C. But the truth is, even this is not sure, and nothing much is known about this great hero except what we have in the epic, which was first uncovered in 1849 by Austen Henry Layard in the library of Ashurbanipal at the excavations at Nineveh in modern Iraq.

Since that time, many other older fragments have been discovered in other locations around the Middle East that seem to indicate that the epic had been pieced together and rewritten from much earlier unconnected individual Gilgamesh episodes from Sumer. Jeffrey Tigay documented this editorial process from the extant clay tablets in *The Evolution of the Gilgamesh Epic.*[1] Tzvi Abusch concluded that at least three major versions of the epic can be documented as retellings of the story that embody the social, political, and religious concerns of the ever-changing national identity of Babylonia, from the older heroic age of individualistic kings into the more "civilized" existence of the state-governed city.[2]

Gilgamesh Immortal was drawn from the various versions of the epic narrative as well as the original Sumerian Gilgamesh episodes now found in several published editions of the poem.[3] Upon first blush, some readers may

---

[1] Jeffrey H. Tigay, *The Epic of Gilgamesh*, Wauconda, IL: Bolchazy-Carducci, 1982, 2002.
[2] Tzvi Abusch, "The Development and Meaning of the Epic of Gilgamesh: An Interpretive Essay, *Journal of the American Oriental Society*, Vol. 121, No. 4 (Oct. - Dec., 2001), pp. 614-622.
[3] The three I found most helpful in studying the epic were A.R. George, *The Babylonian Gilgamesh Epic: Introduction, Critical Edition and Cuneiform Texts*, Vol. 1, Oxford University Press, 2003; Benjamin Foster, transl. ed., *The Epic of Gilgamesh: A Norton Critical Edition*, New York: W.W. Norton, 2001;

question a novel about a non-Biblical character in a saga of Biblical heroes. But patient reading yields a powerful revelation of interconnectedness of these ancient Near Eastern narratives. When I was researching for the novel, I was amazed at how many elements of the epic fit within the storyline of the *Chronicles of the Nephilim*, so much so that very little was altered in terms of story structure, characters, and plot of the original Gilgamesh story. Of course, the context and meaning is reinterpreted through the Biblical paradigm, but readers of *Gilgamesh Immortal* will nevertheless be introduced to a prose edition of the epic poem that is fairly representative of the original plotline.

The epic is relevant for the primeval history of *Genesis* because it sets the stage for a lost and rebellious Mesopotamian world in which God chooses his lineage to bring about the promised Seed. The time after the Flood before the Tower of Babel seemed to be a time where God was distant from humanity, "giving up" the pagans who did not honor God "over to their lusts," "foolish hearts," and "futile thinking," to "worship and serve the creature instead of the Creator" (Romans 1). What better way to capture that hiddenness of God than to tell a pagan story that embodies the hiddenness?

The Gilgamesh epic was a national story that embodied the worldview and spirit of Babylonia which would be the ultimate enemy of God's chosen seedline. As readers of the novel discover, it depicts the origin of a very important character who embodies that rebellion against God which would ultimately lead to the scattering of the nations and their allotment ("giving over") to the sovereignty of the rebellious Sons of God (Deut. 32:8-9).

Death and the Meaning of Life

The *Epic of Gilgamesh* is the oldest extant hero story excavated from ancient archaeological mounds in the Middle East, yet it reads like a modern novel or movie in its story structure and hero's journey. Moderns fancy themselves as more intellectually sophisticated than ancient man, yet they are often ignorant of the fact that their notions of existential angst and individual identity that they think is the erudite offerings of modern existentialist philosophers like Kierkegaard, Sartre, and Nietzsche, were wrestled with millennia before the chaotic narcissistic spasm of the modern period.

Gilgamesh is a ruler who is two thirds god, one third human, yet that humanity means he is ultimately mortal. He seeks significance and immortality because of the dread of death and its apparent blanket of meaninglessness on a world without a clear vision of the afterlife. He begins as a godlike oppressive king who lives in debauchery of power, only to discover his equal in the tamed

---

and the Maureen Gallery Kovacs Translation at http://king-of-heroes.co.uk/the-epic-of-gilgamesh/maureen-gallery-kovacs-translation/

"Wild-Born" Enkidu. He makes a friend of this champion and proceeds to pursue acts of heroism in the killing of Humbaba, the ogre guardian of the cedar forest of the mountain of the gods in Lebanon.

With the aid of his loyal Enkidu, he brings back the head of the monster with such hubris that he defies the goddess Ishtar's proposal of marriage. He spurns her promise of deification because he knows it will only lead to slavery in the Netherworld, not glorious immortality. When he overcomes the Bull of Heaven sent by the vengeful Ishtar, he becomes even more filled with pride, until his mighty equal Enkidu is struck dead with sickness from the gods. This brings him face to face with the fact that no matter how heroic or powerful he becomes, he too will die like all men. Death is both the great equalizer and the great destroyer of significance and meaning. The age of heroes does not bring lasting glory after all.

So he seeks an audience with Utnapishtim the Faraway (Noah), the survivor of the Flood and the only human granted immortality along with his wife, who are now far removed from normal humans in a distant mystical island. Gilgamesh figures he might wrest from Utnapishtim his secret of eternal life from the gods. But when he discovers that death is intrinsic to human existence and the special gift will never be granted to another human being, he returns to his beloved city of Uruk and finds his final fame in building the mighty walls and city, which will continue after he is long dead. In the end, man can only find lasting glory in being a part of something bigger than himself that continues on when he is gone. For Gilgamesh that something bigger is the city-state.

Gilgamesh's ruminations of death, meaninglessness, and despair will be familiar to Bible readers in the similar ruminations of another king in the book of Ecclesiastes. Called *Qoheleth* or "the Preacher," this king of Jerusalem writes about all of life being a vapor because death destroys all human pursuits. He tells of seeking pleasure, wealth, and wisdom, only to conclude that none of it brings lasting meaning because death turns it all upside down. The Preacher speaks of enjoying the simple pleasures of life like a wife, good food, and hard work because the pursuit of power and glory is ultimately worthless and defeating, the equivalent of striving after wind.

A side by side comparison of passages from the Gilgamesh Epic and the book of Ecclesiastes illustrates a profound congruity between the wisdom writings of the Old Testament and Babylonia.

GILGAMESH EPIC	ECCLESIASTES
Do we build a house for ever? Do we seal (contracts) for ever? Do brothers divide shares for ever? Does hatred persist for ever in [the land]? Does the river for ever raise up (and) bring on floods? [4]	There is no remembrance of former things, nor will there be any remembrance of later things yet to be among those who come after. (Ecclesiastes 1:11) A generation goes, and a generation comes, but the earth remains forever. All streams run to the sea, but the sea is not full… (Ecclesiastes 1:4–7)
Since the days of yore there has been no permanence; The *resting* and the dead, how alike they are! Do they not compose a picture of death, The commoner and the noble, Once they are near to [their fate]?[5]	For of the wise as of the fool there is no enduring remembrance, seeing that in the days to come all will have been long forgotten. How the wise dies just like the fool! (Ecclesiastes 2:16)
[You,] kept toiling sleepless (and) what did you get? You are exhausting [yourself with] ceaseless toil, you are filling your sinews with pain, bringing nearer the end of your life. (Tablet X:297-300)[6]	And what gain is there to him who toils for the wind? Moreover, all his days he eats in darkness in much vexation and sickness and anger. (Ecclesiastes 5:16–17)
Man is one whose progeny is snapped off like a reed in the canebrake: (Tablet X:301)[7]	For who knows what is good for man while he lives the few days of his vain life, which he passes like a shadow? (Ecclesiastes 6:12)
the comely young man, the pretty young woman, all [too soon in] their very [prime] death abducts (them). (Tablet X:302-303)[8]	The wise person has his eyes in his head, but the fool walks in darkness. And yet I perceived that the same event happens to all of them. (Ecclesiastes 2:14)
No one sees death, no one sees the face [of death,] no one [hears] the voice of death:	For man does not know his time… so the children of man are snared at an evil time, when it suddenly falls upon them.

---

[4] *The Ancient Near East an Anthology of Texts and Pictures.*, ed. James Bennett Pritchard, 92-93 (Princeton: Princeton University Press, 1958).
[5] *The Ancient Near East an Anthology of Texts and Pictures.*, ed. James Bennett Pritchard, 92-93 (Princeton: Princeton University Press, 1958).
[6] A.R. George, *The Babylonian Gilgamesh Epic: Introduction, Critical Edition and Cuneiform Texts*, Vol. 1, Oxford University Press, 2003, p. 697.
[7] George, *The Babylonian Gilgamesh Epic*, p. 697.
[8] George, *The Babylonian Gilgamesh Epic*, p. 697.

(yet) savage death is the one who hacks man down. (Tablet X:304-307)[9]	(Ecclesiastes 9:12)
At some time we build a household, at some time we start a family, at some time the brothers divide, at some time feuds arise in the land. At some time the river rose (and) brought the flood, the mayfly floating on the river. Its countenance was gazing on the face of the sun, then all of a sudden nothing was there![10] (Tablet X:308-315)[11]	For everything there is a season, and a time for every matter under heaven: a time to be born, and a time to die;... a time to love, and a time to hate;... a time for war, and a time for peace. (Ecclesiastes 3:1–8) Vapor of vapors, says the Preacher, ...All is mist and vapor. (Ecclesiastes 1:2)
Oh, Enkidu, a team of two will not perish. He who is lashed to a boat will not sink, No one can tear asunder a three-ply cloth.[12] (Gilgamesh and Humbaba A)	Two are better than one, ...For if they fall, one will lift up his fellow...a threefold cord is not quickly broken. (Ecclesiastes 4:9–12)
Thou, Gilgamesh, let full be thy belly, Make thou merry by day and by night. Of each day make thou a feast of rejoicing, Day and night dance thou and play! Let thy garments be sparkling fresh, Thy head be washed; bathe thou in water. Pay heed to the little one that holds on to thy hand, Let thy spouse delight in thy bosom! For this is the task of [mankind]!"[13] (Tablet XI)	Go, eat your bread with joy, and drink your wine with a merry heart, for God has already approved what you do. Let your garments be always white. Let not oil be lacking on your head. Enjoy life with the wife whom you love, all the days of your vain life that he has given you under the sun, because that is your portion in life. (Ecclesiastes 9:7–10)

The natural question that arises is whether or not the Biblical author got his ideas from Babylonia, or the reverse, or whether they both used a common source background. Regardless of which way the influence flows, the Gilgamesh Epic and Ecclesiastes certainly display a striking exchange of ideas. The last verses of Gilgamesh Tablet XI and Ecclesiastes 9:7-10 show a thought for thought progress of thinking that surely suggests a deliberate cultural exchange of ideas.

---

[9] George, *The Babylonian Gilgamesh Epic*, p. 697.

[10] George, *The Babylonian Gilgamesh Epic*, p. 697.

[11] George, *The Babylonian Gilgamesh Epic*, p. 697.

[12] v. 130-133, Benjamin R. Foster, Ed., *The Epic of Gilgamesh: A Norton Critical Edition*, New York: Norton and Company, 2001, p. 109.

[13] *The Ancient Near East an Anthology of Texts and Pictures.*, ed. James Bennett Pritchard, 90 (Princeton: Princeton University Press, 1958).

But the differences are perhaps just as profound and striking as the similarities. First and foremost is of course the polytheism of Gilgamesh that is dutifully overturned by the monotheism of Ecclesiastes. Jewish ethical monotheism was a hostile unbridgeable chasm between the worldviews of Israel and her surrounding pagan neighbors, a chasm between Abraham's bosom and Hades.

But an equally profound separation lies in the anthropocentric (human-centered) paganism of Gilgamesh versus the theocentric (God-centered) optimism of Qoheleth. While both affirm a kind of meaningless despair that death brings to the human condition, Gilgamesh concludes with resignation that the best one can do is a substitute immortality of glory in the perpetual life of the state, a rather modern humanistic proposition for an ancient.

But the Preacher argues that we are to eat, drink, and be merry, not merely because tomorrow we die (9:10), but because it is a gift from God (3:13), and that "for all these things God will bring you into judgment (11:9)," because "whatever God does endures forever" (3:14). So eternal life *is* found in connection with God in Ecclesiastes because not even the *polis* or city of the ancient world lasts forever like God does, and the individual life rooted in God is a life rooted in transcendence.

> Ecclesiastes 12:13–14
> The end of the matter; all has been heard. Fear God and keep his commandments, for this is the whole duty of man. For God will bring every deed into judgment, with every secret thing, whether good or evil.

Echoes of Eden

The thematic existential pursuit of meaning and transcendence is not the only thing in common between the Babylonian epic and Biblical Scriptures. Echoes of Eden resound in the journey of Gilgamesh that scholars have long pointed out reflect a literary correspondence with the Bible.

When Enkidu enters the Gilgamesh story, he is a "Wild-Born" untamed man who lives as an animal in the steppe with a hairy naked body, wandering the hills, feeding on grass and upsetting traps set by the hunter for his mammalian kin. He was in fact created by the goddess Aruru as a foil to the "civilized" oppression and "fierce arrogance" of king Gilgamesh over the city of Uruk.[14] Theirs is the perennial conflict between rural and urban human identity. The city dweller may be "civilized," yet he can be barbaric and cruel

[14] George, *The Babylonian Gilgamesh Epic*, pp. 543-544.

compared to the "noble savage" who is the only redemption for such oppression.

In the Standard version of the Babylonian epic, a hunter tries to stop Enkidu from ruining his traps by seducing him with a harlot named Shamhat. Enkidu is drawn to her with instinctual lust and he is ultimately tamed by his sexual satisfaction with the female, who then civilizes him with clothes and human etiquette.[15] It is the ancient classical paradigm of human nature: The sensuality of Woman tames the savagery of Man.

But this civilizing of human nature is also depicted as a loss of innocence required for human maturity. Suddenly, Enkidu's eyes are opened, "he had reason, he was wide of understanding." His psychic link with the animals is broken, and Shamhat says to Enkidu, "You are just like a god."[16]

This little episode and its mythic metaphor of human growth and separation from the animals through loss of innocence has obvious parallels with the Garden of Eden in *Genesis* 3. Eve, seduced by the serpent, influences Adam to eat of the fruit of the tree of the knowledge of good and evil which "opens their eyes" and they "become like God" losing their innocence.

Critical scholarship has noted these parallels and has prioritized the Babylonian account, which results in twisting the Biblical account into a humanistic parable that subverts Original Sin into Original Wisdom, where it was a good thing to disobey God and take control of human destiny. God becomes the villain and the serpent becomes the hero of this interpretation in that the serpent helps mankind escape dependency on a jealous deity fearful of man taking his place and making him unnecessary. Liberal scholar James Charlesworth, quoting another liberal scholar suggests that to "characterize him [God] as villain is not impossible, in view of 3:8 (the Garden is for his own enjoyment), and vs. 23 (where he feels 'threatened' by the man!) As villain, he is the opponent of the main program."[17]

Charlesworth then concludes that,

> "The story of the serpent in our culture is a tale of how the most beautiful creature [the serpent] became seen as ugly, the admired became despised, the good was misrepresented as the bad, and a god was dethroned and recast as Satan. Why? It is perhaps because we modern humans have moved farther and farther away from nature, cutting the umbilical cord with our mother earth?"[18]

---

[15] Tablets I and II, George, *The Babylonian Gilgamesh Epic*, pp. 549-561.
[16] Tablet I: 202, 207, George, *The Babylonian Gilgamesh Epic*, pp. 551
[17] James Charlesworth, *The Good and Evil Serpent: How a Universal Symbol Became Christianized*, New Haven: Yale University Press, p. 309.
[18] Charlesworth, *The Good and Evil Serpent*, p. 419.

But this critical hermeneutic is autobiographical projection of fashionable modern prejudice against the Judeo-Christian depersonalization of nature. It completely misunderstands the polemical nature of most Biblical interaction with its pagan environment, and misunderstands the Gilgamesh story as well. Similarities in stories illustrate a common subject, but differences express a contrast of meaning.

Charlesworth surveys iconography on archaeological artifacts in Bronze Age Canaan to accurately describe ancient Canaan as a "serpent cult civilization."[19] Canaan was the land promised to the Israelites by God. They were commanded to devote all the giant clans and their cities to complete destruction because of the connection of the giant Anakim clans to the antediluvian Nephilim (Numb 13:32-33).[20]

> Joshua 11:21–22
> And Joshua came at that time and cut off the Anakim [giants] from the hill country... Joshua devoted them to destruction with their cities. There was none of the Anakim left in the land of the people of Israel.

I have explained elsewhere that the creation story of Genesis follows the ancient Near Eastern paradigm of justifying territorial and governmental control over a region. When a kingdom would assert its authority or power, it told a creation story of how its deity established order out of the primordial chaos and laid claim on the land.[21] The Babylonian creation story Enuma Elish does this with its ascendency of the Babylonian patron deity Marduk as king over the assembly of gods, and the Genesis account does this for Yahweh's people as inheritors of the Promised Land. "The earth" in Genesis 1, is better translated as "the land" in Hebrew and, as John Sailhamer has pointed out, is most likely a literary reference to the Promised Land of Canaan.[22] Since the Old Testament is filled with a history of Israel constantly falling away from Yahweh and worshipping the false gods of Canaan, it makes perfect theological sense that the Tempter in the Garden that draws Israel's forebear Adam away from obedience is the symbol of Canaan, the serpent.

---

[19] Charlesworth, *The Good and Evil Serpent*, p. 100.

[20] See the appendix "The Nephilim" in *Noah Primeval* for the explanation of the expulsion of the giant clans from the Holy Land. They are essentially the Seed of the Serpent at war with the Seed of Eve. Brian Godawa, *Noah Primeval*, Los Angeles, CA: Embedded Pictures Publishing, 2012, pp. 307-326.

[21] Brian Godawa, "Biblical Creation and Storytelling: Cosmogony, Combat and Covenant," http://godawa.com/Writing/Articles/BiblicalCreationStorytelling-Godawa.pdf.

[22] Bruce R. Reichenbach, "Genesis 1 as a Theological-Political Narrative of Kingdom Establishment," *Bulletin for Biblical Research* 13.1 (2003), pp. 47-69. See also, John Sailhamer, *Genesis Unbound: A Provocative New Look at the Creation Account* (Sisters, OR: Multnomah, 1996).

There is no meaningful way that serpents could be interpreted as a hero or positive symbol in Genesis 2-3 in context with the Israelite worldview. And the serpent is not a positive symbol in Gilgamesh either.

Another episode in the Epic of Gilgamesh that carries overtones of the Genesis creation story is on Tablet XI. After Gilgamesh encounters Utnapishtim (Noah) and discovers he cannot attain eternal life, he leaves dejected. But Utnapishtim feels sorry for him and decides to tell him about the location of a magic plant that is able to make one young again. Gilgamesh journeys to find the plant, and then see what happens next:

> At thirty leagues they pitched camp.
> Gilgamesh found a pool whose water was cool,
> he went down into it to bathe in the water.
> A snake smelled the fragrance of the plant,
> [silently] it came up and bore the plant off;
> as it turned away it sloughed a skin.[23]

The notion of a plant that rejuvenates and a serpent "stealing" the opportunity of renewed youth has long been connected to the Genesis account of the rejuvenating effect of the Tree of Life being withheld from Adam due to the serpent's deception. But they also both contain etiological explanations of snake biology, Genesis for the serpent crawling on its belly, and Gilgamesh for the snake shedding its skin. These echoes of Eden reaffirm the negative character of the serpent as one who spoils the opportunity for renewed life, not the positive agent of human maturity.

Noah and the Flood in the Epic of Gilgamesh

Perhaps the most fascinating connection that the Epic of Gilgamesh has to the Bible is in the presence of a Noah character and his story of the Great Deluge. Scholars have written endlessly on this topic ever since the first translations of the account were available in the late nineteenth century. A comparison of the two stories yields, yet again, some significant similarities that indicate a common origin, yet some even more significant differences that indicate divergent meaning.

As mentioned earlier, extant tablets prove that the Gilgamesh epic had gone through a literary evolution. One very distinct change involves the addition of the Flood story that probably did not exist in the oldest Babylonian version of the epic poem, but does exist in a later Babylonian version. This has prompted Tigay to suggest, and most scholars now agree, that an

---

[23] Tablet XI:302-307, George, *The Babylonian Gilgamesh Epic*, p. 723.

additional Akkadian story of the Flood called Atrahasis was used as a source to add to the Gilgamesh cycle. And a third and older Sumerian version called The Deluge may also have had some influence on Gilgamesh.[24]

But what about the Genesis story of Noah's ark? While it is virtually unanimous among scholars that Genesis was written and edited over time using multiple sources, the more extreme view of this has been adopted by the scholarly establishment that has sought to divide the Old Testament, and in particular the Flood story, into contradictory sources that have been woven together from an older "Yahwist" source and a newer "Priestly" source, all with opposing agendas.

This radical view is falling from favor with the advent of literary and form criticism and because of the complete absence of manuscript evidence to support the remote speculation of such radical redaction.[25] What is coming more to light is the genius of composition that exists in the final canonical literary form that virtually defies categorizing of specific sources. For example, Gordon Wenham has pointed out the complex literary poetic form of "chiasmus" used in the Flood narrative. Chiasmus is a kind of mirroring literary structure that builds the plot with increasing succession, to the middle of the story, where the thematic message is highlighted, only to conclude the second half of the story in a reflective reversal of the first half.

At the risk of overwhelming the reader, here is the literary structure of the Genesis Flood narrative as detailed by Wenham, emphasizing the superior originality of authorship over alleged source material.[26]

---

[24] Tigay, *The Epic of Gilgamesh*, pp. 214-240.

[25] See Umberto Cassuto, *The Documentary Hypothesis and the Composition of the Pentateuch,* Skokie, IL: Varda Books, 1941, 2005; Duane A. Garrett, *Rethinking Genesis: The Sources and Authorship of the First Book of the Pentateuch*, Baker, 1991; John H. Sailhamer, *The Meaning of the Pentateuch: Revelation, Composition and Interpretation,* Downers Grove, IL: Intervarsity, 2009; "The New Literary Criticism," Gordon J. Wenham, Vol. 1, *Genesis 1–15*. Word Biblical Commentary. Dallas: Word, Incorporated, 1998, pp. xxxii-xlii; Victor P. Hamilton, *The Book of Genesis, Chapters 1–17*. The New International Commentary on the Old Testament. Grand Rapids, MI: Wm. B. Eerdmans Publishing Co., 1990, pp. 12-38.

[26] Gordon J. Wenham, "The Coherence of the Flood Narrative," *Vetus Testamentum* 28, no. 3 (1978), p. 338.

Genesis vi 10-ix 19

A Noah (vi 10a)
B Shem, Ham and Japheth (10b)
C Ark to be built (14-16)
D Flood announced (17)
E Covenant with Noah (18-20)
F Food in the ark (21)
G Command to enter ark (vii 1-3)
H 7 days waiting for flood (4-5)
I 7 days waiting for flood (7-10)
J Entry to ark (11-15)
K Yahweh shuts Noah in (16)
L 40 days flood (17a)
M Waters increase (17b-18)
N Mountains covered (19-20)
O 150 days waters prevail ((21)-24)
P GOD REMEMBERS NOAH (viii 1)
O′ 150 days waters abate (3)
N′ Mountain tops visible (4-5)
M′ Waters abate (5)
L′ 40 days (end of) (6a)
K′ Noah opens window of ark (6b)
J′ Raven and dove leave ark (7-9)
I′ 7 days waiting for waters to subside (10-11)
H′ 7 days waiting for waters to subside (12-13)
G′ Command to leave ark (15-17(22))
F′ Food outside ark (ix 1-4)
E′ Covenant with all flesh (8-10)
D′ No flood in future (11-17)
C′ Ark (18a)
B′ Shem, Ham and Japheth (18b)
A′ Noah (19)

Early Biblical criticism tried to reduce the Biblical Flood narrative to a derivative of the Babylonian version, but that theory is now thoroughly discredited.[27] Archaeologist P.J. Wiseman uncovered the existence of a "toledoth" formula in the repeated Genesis phrase, "these are the generations of," that indicates original source material of inscribed clay tablets rather than a hodgepodge of Yahwist, Priestly, and other contrary sources.[28] Whatever narrative congruity exists between the Bible and the Gilgamesh Epic, their genetic ties are not found in being a derivative of one another.

In *Gilgamesh Immortal*, while I do write of Gilgamesh visiting Noah and his wife on a distant island, and I do have Noah tell Gilgamesh the story of the Flood, just as he does in the Epic of Gilgamesh, I bring a subversive twist to the scenario. The story that Gilgamesh inscribes onto clay and stone is not the one that Noah told him. Why? Because Gilgamesh is not a repentant follower

---

[27] Bill T. Arnold and David B. Weisberg, "A Centennial Review of Friedrich Delitzsch's 'Babel und Bibel' Lectures," *Journal of Biblical Literature*, Vol. 121, No. 3 (Autumn, 2002), pp. 441-457.
[28] P. J. Wiseman, D. J. Wiseman, Ed., *Ancient Records and the Structure of Genesis: A Case for Literary Unity* Thomas Nelson, 1985.

of Noah's god, Yahweh Elohim, the God of the Bible. So it would make sense that if he rejects the living God, he would reject the living God's metanarrative and replace it with his own that would exalt himself or his biased religious construction. So the version we read in the Epic of Gilgamesh today is the deliberately fabricated version of a rebel against Yahweh. This is the nature of all subversive storytelling as I have indicated in previous appendices of the *Chronicles of the Nephilim*.[29]

So what is the storyline of the Flood in the original Gilgamesh Epic?

In Tablet XI of the epic poem, Utnapishtim, the Gilgamesh Noah, explains that because of some unexplained sin of man, the pantheon of gods decide to send a Deluge to kill all of mankind. But the god of the waters of the Abyss, Enki (or Ea) defies the decision and sneaks away to give a dream to Utnapishtim, a wealthy man who lives in the city of Shuruppak in Mesopotamia. Through the dream, he tells him to tear down his house and build a large boat to save "the seed of all living creatures." He gives him the dimensions of the boat and instructions of how to build it.

Utnapishtim is to lie to his neighbors when asked about the large boat by explaining that he is going to move downstream to the city of Eridu. When he finishes the boat, he loads on it all kinds of animals as well as all his extended family members and some skilled craftsman.

The gods then start a storm of wind and rain, led by the storm god Adad, that devastates the land with such force, even the gods get scared and hide up in heaven like frightened dogs with their tails between their legs. The blowing wind and gale force downpour lasts six days and seven nights until "all the people are turned to clay."

The boat finally runs aground on Mount Nimush, and after seven days, Utnapishtim lets out a dove to see if it can find a perch, but it does not and returns to him. He waits and sends a swallow, and then finally a raven that does not return, indicating enough dry land to get out of the boat.

Utnapishtim then offers a sacrifice to the gods, who "smell the sweet savour" and "gather like flies around the sacrificer." But when the great god Enlil arrives, he is angry to discover Utnapishtim survived the destruction. When he finds out that Enki had leaked the plan to Utnapishtim, they quarrel. But the crafty Enki denies violating the will of the gods because he did not tell Utnapishtim *directly*, but through a dream.

---

[29] One of the major premises of *Chronicles of the Nephilim* is that pagans replace the narrative of the Biblical God with their own mythical constructs that justify their prejudices and protect their consciences from moral repentance. Their accusations that Biblical religion is a fairy tale concocted to control others is a projection of their own hubris to control others by negating transcendent authority.

Enlil resigns himself to the trickery and decides to bestow immortality on Utnapishtim and his wife, so they would be like the gods, but placing them "at the mouth of the rivers" to dwell faraway from normal mankind.

Utnapishtim then explains to Gilgamesh that the gods will not assemble for his benefit to bestow upon him eternal life. He is destined to die like all humanity. To prove the impossibility, Utnapishtim tells Gilgamesh to stay awake for six days and seven nights to prove his worthiness of becoming immortal by exercising power over the stepchild of death: sleep. Gilgamesh cannot do so and he is sent on his way with the consolation prize of finding a magic plant that will restore his youth. As stated before, the serpent then steals that plant away from him.

Wenham has listed seventeen major correlations between the *Genesis* Flood and the *Gilgamesh* Deluge that indicate a strong genetic connection between the two narratives:

1. Divine decision to destroy
2. Warning to flood hero
3. Command to build ark
4. Hero's obedience
5. Command to enter
6. Entry
7. Closing door
8. Description of flood
9. Destruction of life
10. End of rain, etc.
11. Ark grounding on mountain
12. Hero opens window
13. Birds' reconnaissance
14. Exit
15. Sacrifice
16. Divine smelling of sacrifice
17. Blessing on flood hero[30]

But Alexander Heidel's classic *The Gilgamesh Epic and Old Testament Parallels* has teased out the differences between the two that shed light on their radically divergent meanings.

To begin with, the name for the Flood hero in Gilgamesh is Utnapishtim, which means, "he saw life," an apparent free rendering of the Sumerian

[30] Wenham, "The Coherence of the Flood Narrative," p. 346.

Ziusudra, that meant "he found everlasting life." In the Flood story most likely borrowed for the Gilgamesh Epic, his name is Atrahasis which means "exceedingly wise." In Genesis, Noah means, "rest."[31]

The Sumerian Noah, Ziusudra, was a priestly king of the city of Shuruppak, the tenth in line of the prediluvian Babylonian kings. In Gilgamesh, Utnapishtim is not a king, but a wealthy citizen of Shuruppak. The Biblical Noah is the tenth prediluvian patriarch, but beyond this, we only know he was pious in that he "walked with God" and found favor in his sight.[32] In Genesis, only eight people were in the ark with the animals; Noah, his three sons, and all their wives. In the Sumerian Deluge and Gilgamesh, Noah's extended family also came along with some craftsmen, and a boatman.

Heidel then points out the theological differences between the narratives regarding the cause of the Flood and the possibility of redemption for humanity.[33] In Atrahasis, the "noise" of man's overpopulation and "cries of rebellion" awaken Enlil from his sleep to send several plagues and famines without satisfying results before he conspires to send a flood to drown out their rebellious noise.[34] In Gilgamesh, the gods send the Deluge because of an undefined sin of mankind (Tablet XI:180). Utnapishtim lies to his neighbors about the ark because the gods do not want man to know what they are about to do.

Contrarily, in Genesis, the Flood is very clearly a righteous judgment upon an earth that was "corrupted and filled with violence." "The LORD saw that the wickedness of man was great in the earth, and that every intention of the thoughts of his heart was only evil continually." God gives man a "period of grace" of one hundred and twenty years with which to repent and obey God (Gen 6:5-6). Though this purpose is not stated explicitly in Genesis, two other passages in the New Testament seem to indicate this notion of God providing such opportunity.

> 1 Peter 3:19–20
> [In the spirit] he went and proclaimed to the spirits in prison, because <u>they formerly did not obey, when God's patience waited in the days of Noah, while the ark was being prepared</u>,

---

[31] Alexander Heidel, *The Gilgamesh Epic and Old Testament Parallels*, Chicago, IL: University of Chicago, 1946, 1963, p. 227.
[32] Heidel, *The Gilgamesh Epic*, p. 228.
[33] Heidel, *The Gilgamesh Epic*, p. 230-232.
[34] Bernard Batto points out this distinction that is often missed by scholars. The noise and din "indicate the cries of rebellion of humankind against the authority of the deity. In the prior revolt by the lesser gods Enlil's sleep was also interrupted by a similar outcry from the rebel gods. The humans are thus portrayed as carrying on in the spirit of the slain rebel god out of whose flesh and blood they were created." Bernard Batto, "The Sleeping God: An Ancient Near Eastern Motif of Divine Sovereignty," *Biblica* 68 (1987), p. 160.

> in which a few, that is, eight persons, were brought safely through water.
>
> 2 Peter 2:5–6
> if he did not spare the ancient world, but preserved Noah, a herald of righteousness, with seven others, when he brought a flood upon the world of the ungodly... making them an example of what is going to happen to the ungodly;

Surely, there is an assumption, sometimes explicit, but always implicit throughout the Old Testament that if man repents, God will stay his hand of planned judgment. But the notion that Noah actually "preached" words to the condemned is not necessarily in the text. Some Evangelicals assume that Noah as "herald of righteousness" means he preached sermons like the Apostles in Acts. But this assumes too much. For the context of the New Testament passages are about Noah's *example to us* "of what is going to happen to the ungodly" of Peter's current era.

Jesus in his Olivet sermon uses Noah's *example* as a sermon illustration for his coming judgment as well.

> Matt. 24:37–39
> For as in those days before the flood they were eating and drinking, marrying and giving in marriage, until the day when Noah entered the ark, and they were unaware until the flood came and swept them all away, so will be the coming of the Son of Man.

Noah's preparation for the Flood was a *declaratory action* that spoke louder than words, and apparently, it was not understood by those who were "unaware until the flood came and swept them all away."

Another passage sheds light on the notion that Noah's *act* of building the boat in anticipation of the Flood was itself the "proclamation."

> Hebrews 11:7
> By faith Noah, being warned by God concerning events as yet unseen, in reverent fear constructed an ark for the saving of his household. By this he condemned the world and became an heir of the righteousness that comes by faith.

Though God always seems to give a generation under condemnation an opportunity to repent, he does not always do so with sermons of words, but certainly with examples of actions.

The ark also provides an example of significant difference between the narratives. The length of Noah's ark was 450 feet long, 75 feet wide, and 45 feet high, with a displacement of approximately 43,300 tons. It had three levels to contain the animals, that on the surface of the account is structurally feasible. Utnapishtim's vessel however, was not so amiable to reality. According to Babylonian measurements, it was supposed to be a square cube of 200 feet on all sides and was divided into seven levels, displacing approximately 228,500 tons, making it a rather questionable sea worthy craft.[35]

In the Biblical story, it is well known that the flood began with rain coming down from the heavens and waters coming up from the deep. The rain storm lasted 40 days and 40 nights, and then after 150 days, the waters began to abate until the earth was dry enough to leave the ark about 360 days or 1 year after the start of the flood. In the Babylonian versions, the flood storm lasts only 7 days and 7 nights, followed by an unspecified number of days for the waters to dry up before Noah leaves the ark.

Upon leaving the boat, Ziusudra, Utnapishtim, and Noah all build altars and offer sacrifices of thanksgiving and appeasement unto their gods. But the theological incongruity between the accounts is spelled out in the divine reactions. In Gilgamesh, "The gods smelled the savour, the gods smelled the sweet savour, the gods gathered like flies around the sacrificer" (Tablet XI:161-163). Of this passage, Andrew George writes,

> The simile used to describe the gods' arrival is famously the image of hungry flies buzzing around a piece of food. This imagery implies a somewhat cynical view of gods, even more disrespectful than the earlier simile likening them to cowering dogs.[36]

Heidel adds a dimension to this zoomorphic (animal-like) denigration of the gods when he suggests that the gods had been without food sacrifice from humans for so long that they were hungry like a bunch of flies dependent on parasitic hosts. Enlil then starts to quarrel with Enki for revealing the secret to Utnapishtim, wherein Enki defends himself with trickery by arguing that he did not reveal it directly to Utnapishtim, but through a dream, thus freeing him from blame.

Contrary to the Babylonian zoomorphic simile of the gods, the Bible engages in anthropomorphism (human-like) in that man is created in the image of God and thus sacrifice is understood in the priestly terms of atonement for

---

[35] Heidel, *The Gilgamesh Epic*, pp. 232-236.

[36] George, *The Babylonian Gilgamesh Epic*, pp. 518.

sin (Lev. 1:9). God "smelled the pleasing aroma, the LORD said in his heart, 'I will never again curse the ground because of man (Gen. 8:21).'" Heidel explains

> The propitiatory character of the sacrifice is brought out quite clearly in the biblical narrative, where the ascending essence of the burnt-offerings is called a "soothing odor," or, literally, an "odor of tranquilization." One purpose of Noah's sacrifice, as seems to be indicated by what follows, probably was to appease the wrath of God which had been kindled by the sins of mankind and which Noah had just witnessed. But at the same time it was undoubtedly an offering for the expiation of his own sins and those of his family.[37]

Whereas the Babylonian anthropomorphic descriptions of their deities tended to reflect human weaknesses (hunger) and sin (quarreling), the Biblical account depicts the human-like character traits of God in terms of relationship (propitiation and atonement).

In the Babylonian versions, Noah and his wife are blessed with eternal life after Enlil gives in to Enki's defensive arguments. They are then taken to a distant place, "at the mouth of the rivers," probably referring to the Persian Gulf, into which the Euphrates and Tigris rivers opened up. In Gilgamesh, this was the mythical and distant "place where the sun rises," in the Sumerian version it was the island of Dilmun, now considered by most scholars to be in the area of the Bahrain islands.

The Biblical version is theologically motivated by God's covenantal nature. God blesses Noah, and then grants him the original charge given to Adam to multiply and fill the earth, and to exercise dominion over the creatures (Gen 9:1-3). As the flood was a return to the chaos waters before creation, so the world of Noah is a new creation with a new Adam. And God reinforces his value of the created image of God in man, by bringing special attention to capital punishment for murdering man, made in the image of God.

The rainbow becomes God's covenant promise to stay his hand from Deluge judgment, unlike the Gilgamesh Epic, that has a secondary mother goddess claim that a necklace strung with flies will, "remind her of the hungry gods buzzing around [Utnapishtim's] sacrifice, and ultimately of her special responsibility to her human children"[38] (Tablet XI:165-169).

---

[37] Heidel, *The Gilgamesh Epic*, p. 255.
[38] George, *The Babylonian Gilgamesh Epic*, pp. 518.

Comparison and Contrast

The value of comparative religion lies in achieving a better understanding of the historical and cultural context of ancient writings like the Bible. Too often, both religious believers and unbelievers approach the text with their own preconceived modern worldview or political agenda that they project upon the text in order to "use" it for their own purposes, positive or negative. Christians have been guilty of forcing poetic passages into the straightjacket of a hyper-literalistic hermeneutic, or imposing our notions of historical accounting or scientific accuracy upon ancient writers who just did not write with our post-Enlightenment modern scientific or historical worldview.

I addressed the Mesopotamian cosmology in the Bible in an appendix of *Noah Primeval* to make the point that the Biblical authors were men of their times that could not have possibly been writing Genesis as a scientific treatise on the origin of the material universe, simply because they did not write creation texts with that intent. They wrote them as theological/political documents. When we impose our own modern categories upon the Bible, we are engaging in the worst sort of cultural imperialism, denying the human side of the divinely inspired text.

But it works the other way as well. Modern notions of literary evolution get imposed upon the Bible by detractors who wish to discredit the narrative by reducing it to one of a variety of myths that evolve over time. This modern prejudice also ignores the polemical thrust of much ancient literature that interpreted historical events with divergent meanings, or engaged in retelling narratives through contrary theological lenses. This is not the syncretism of evolutionary plagiarism, but the subversion of worldview polemics.

Another aspect of storytelling where this subversion occurs is in the changing names of characters and locations in ancient narratives. As indicated earlier, the Flood hero has different names depending on which era and culture is composing the text. Some of this comes down to simple translation between languages. *Utnapishtim* in Akkadian may simply be the Babylonian translation of the Sumerian *Ziusudra*, which both mean "finding long life" or something similar. Others may be derivative. Some scholars argue that the name *Noah* can possibly be derived from the middle element of *Utnapishtim*, as one rendering has it: Ut**n'ah**pishtim.

Other cases illustrate outright changes of names to fit the story to the culture's paradigm and differing deities. An important Sumerian text, *The Descent of Inanna into the Underworld*, was literally rewritten by the Babylonians as *the Descent of Ishtar into the Underworld* to accommodate their goddess Ishtar.[39] The Babylonian creation epic, Enuma Elish tells the story of the Babylonian deity Marduk, and his ascendancy to power in the Mesopotamian pantheon, giving mythical justification to the rise of Babylon as an ancient world power in the early 18th century B.C.[40] And then when King Sennacherib of Assyria conquered Babylon around 689 B.C., Assyrian scribes rewrote the Enuma Elish and replaced the name of Marduk with Assur the name of the Assyrian chief god.[41]

The Bible contains the renaming of people that often occurred in the ancient Near East with the intent of expressing destiny or identity. Faithful readers are familiar with Abram's name changed to Abraham to become the "father of many," or Jacob ("supplanter") to Israel ("striving with God"), or Saul of Tarsus being changed to Paul, as a possible Romanizing of his mission to the Gentiles.

But the Hebrew writers of the Bible also engaged in the renaming of enemies for polemical purposes. Thus *Baalzebul*, the god of Ekron, whose name meant "lord of the heavenly dwelling," was renamed *Baalzebub* by the author of 2 Kings 1:2-6, which means the derogatory, "lord of the flies."[42] The wicked queen of Tyre, whose name *Izebul* meant "where is the Prince Baal?" was renamed by the Jews as *Jezebel*, which is a slurring wordplay on dung (2 Kings 9:37).[43] Genesis 11:9 even explains its polemical renaming of the city of Babylon ("Gateway of the Gods") to Babel ("Confusion of Tongues") .

I sought to capture this historical environment of changing names and concepts throughout the series of *Chronicles of the Nephilim* by having characters, locations and measurements change in ways that reflected history. Thus, locations like Erech, Aratta, and Shinar in *Enoch Primordial* (and the Bible) become the later known Uruk, Ararat, and Sumer in *Gilgamesh Immortal*. The Watchers change their names to Mesopotamian deities, Inanna changes her name to Ishtar, Ninurta to Marduk, and Gilgamesh changes his name, reflecting an important historical theory of the origins of Babylon. Even measurements begin as ancient calibrations like cubits and leagues in *Noah Primeval*, but eventually become the more modern familiar measurements of

---

[39] Stephanie Dalley, trans., *Myths from Mesopotamia: Creation, The Flood, Gilgamesh and Others*. New York: Oxford University Press, 1989, 2000, 2008, p 154-162. The Sumerian version can be found in Jeremy Black, trans., *The Literature of Ancient Sumer*. New York: Oxford university Press, p 65-76.
[40] Alexander Heidel, trans., *The Babylonian Genesis*. Chicago, Ill: University of Chicago, 1942, 1951, 1963; 14.
[41] C. Jouco Bleeker and Geo Widengren, eds., *Historia Religium I: Religions of the Past*. Netherlands; E.J. Brill, 1969; p 134. Richard J. Clifford. *Creation Accounts in the Ancient Near East and in the Bible*, Catholic Biblical Quarterly Monograph Series 26. Washington D.C.: Catholic Biblical Association of America, 1994; p 7-8.
[42] "Baalzebub," *The International Standard Bible Encyclopedia, Revised*. (*ISBE*) Edited by Geoffrey W. Bromiley. Wm. B. Eerdmans, 1988.
[43] "Jezebel," *ISBE*.

feet and miles by *Gilgamesh Immortal*. I wanted to give the reader the same experience of real world changing identities, times, and cultures.

There is both continuity and discontinuity within comparative religion, that captures both the common understanding as well as the polemical differences that separate and change meaning. A comparison of the Gilgamesh Epic with the Bible bears this out as Heidel concludes,

> As in the case of the creation stories, we still do not know how the biblical and Babylonian narratives of the Deluge are related historically. The available evidence proves nothing beyond the point that there is a genetic relationship between Genesis and the Babylonian versions. The skeleton is the same in both cases, but the flesh and blood and, above all, the animating spirit are different.[44]

Uncovering Noah's Nakedness

One additional significant element of *Gilgamesh Immortal* requires explanation. In the novel, Noah's son Ham rapes his own mother Emzara that results in the curse of the fruit of that maternal incest: the child Canaan. This brutal scene is not mere voyeurism of depravity, it is the very theological foundation upon which the rest of the *Chronicles of the Nephilim* are based. And that foundation is not imagined fantasy, it is the actual Biblical basis of the Jewish claim on the Promised Land of Canaan, as odd and controversial as it may seem. But as previous discussions have shown, Genesis is no stranger to odd and controversial stories.

Here is the text from the Bible:

> Genesis 9:20–27
> 20 Noah began to be a man of the soil, and he planted a
> vineyard. 21 He drank of the wine and became drunk and lay
> uncovered in his tent. 22 And Ham, the father of Canaan, saw
> the nakedness of his father and told his two brothers outside.
> 23 Then Shem and Japheth took a garment, laid it on both their
> shoulders, and walked backward and covered the nakedness
> of their father. Their faces were turned backward, and they
> did not see their father's nakedness. 24 When Noah awoke
> from his wine and knew what his youngest son had done to
> him, 25 he said, "Cursed be Canaan; a servant of servants shall
> he be to his brothers." 26 He also said, "Blessed be the LORD,

[44] Heidel, *The Gilgamesh Epic*, p. 268.

> the God of Shem; and let Canaan be his servant. [27] May God enlarge Japheth, and let him dwell in the tents of Shem, and let Canaan be his servant."

Literalists have a difficult time with this passage for several reasons. They do not like to admit the fact that Noah becomes a drunk after being the worlds' greatest Bible hero of that time. They read Genesis 6:9 that says Noah was a righteous man, blameless in his generation, and that he walked with God as being a description of Noah as some kind of moral perfectionist one level less than Jesus. But as explained in the appendix of *Noah Primeval*, they miss the fact that righteousness was having faith, not moral perfection. Secondly, having faith was not perfect faith because all Biblical heroes falter in their faith. Thirdly, "blameless" was a physical Levitical reference to genetic purity (as in "spotless" lamb) that was most likely a reference to being uncorrupted by the fallen Sons of God. Fourthly, walking with God did not mean being sinless. Noah was a sinner with imperfect faith and obedience as every believer is. His broken humanity is how we identify with him and draw our inspiration.

The real problem for literalists who do not consider the ancient Near Eastern poetic language of Genesis is in concluding that an entire nation was cursed simply because one of its forefathers saw his dad without clothes on! While it is certainly possible that ancient Mesopotamians had some holy taboo about a parent's nakedness that we are simply unfamiliar with, there is nowhere else in the Bible that affirms the absurdity of such a taboo.

There are however, several places that explain the concept of "uncovering a father's nakedness" as a figurative idiom for having sexual intercourse with his wife.

Bergsma and Hahn's masterful article "Noah's Nakedness and the Curse of Canaan (Genesis 9:20-27)" elucidated for me the notion that I used in my novel that Ham had forced maternal incest with his mother, Noah's wife.[45] They explore the different scholarly explanations of "uncovering Noah's nakedness" and disprove them: voyeurism, castration, and homosexual paternal incest. There are simply no references in the Bible anywhere that reinforce any of these interpretations.

The only one that is reaffirmed and makes sense is that Ham's uncovering his father's nakedness was an idiom or euphemism for maternal incest.

They explain that the definitions of uncovering nakedness in Leviticus 18 are tied to the practices of the Canaanites (sound familiar? Canaan is cursed?).

---

[45] John Sietze Bergsma, Scott Walker Hahn, "Noah's Nakedness and the Curse on Canaan (Genesis 9:20–27)", *Journal of Biblical Literature* 124 (2005): 25, ed. Gail R. O'Day, 25 (Decatur, GA: Society of Biblical Literature, 2005)..

And the Biblical text itself explains that in a patriarchal culture, uncovering a man's nakedness was an expression that actually meant uncovering his wife's nakedness.

> Leviticus 18:7–8
> You shall not uncover the nakedness of your father, which is the nakedness of your mother; she is your mother, you shall not uncover her nakedness. You shall not uncover the nakedness of your father's wife; it is your father's nakedness.

Likewise, they explain, "Lev 18:14, 16; 20:11, 13, 21 all describe a woman's nakedness as the nakedness of her husband."

They then prove that "seeing nakedness" and "uncovering nakedness" are equivalent phrases and are the usual expressions of sexual intercourse in the Holiness Code of Leviticus (18:6; 20:17). It could not be more explicit than Deuteronomy 27:20:

> Deuteronomy 27:20
> 'Cursed be anyone who lies with his father's wife, because he has uncovered his father's nakedness.'

Biblically, "uncovering a man's nakedness" was an idiom for having sexual intercourse with his wife. What then of Shem and Japheth walking backward so as not to see Noah's nakedness? Surely, this is not a reference to avoiding maternal incest, but a literal covering of Noah's body with a cloak? In that case, the literal and the figurative collide in a metaphor of meaning. The authors explain the apparent incongruity this way:

> *The brothers' actions play on the broader meaning of the phrase.* Not only did the brothers not "see their father's nakedness" in the sense of having intercourse with him, but also they did not even dare to "see their father's nakedness" in a literal sense. Where Ham's act was exceedingly evil, their gesture was exceedingly pious and noble.[46]

The final clincher to making sense of this bizarre passage is the curse of the son Canaan. Throughout Genesis 9, Ham is oddly and repeatedly referred to as the father of Canaan. It is a strange repetition that draws attention to itself and is finally climaxed with Canaan being cursed instead of Ham for Ham's

[46] *Journal of Biblical Literature* 124 (2005): 33, ed. Gail R. O'Day, 33 (Decatur, GA: Society *of* Biblical Literature, 2005).

dirty deed. Well, if Canaan was the fruit of that illicit union of maternal incest between Ham and Emzara, it makes perfect sense within that culture that he is cursed. It may not sound kind to our modern ears, but it is perfectly consistent with that Biblical time period. Ham sought to usurp his father's patriarchal authority through maternal incest which was "uncovering his nakedness." The fruit of that action, the son Canaan, is a cursed man. And that cursed man is the forefather of a cursed nation.

The writer of Genesis, whether Moses or a later editor, was clearly showing the origins of the evil curse on the land of Canaan that they were about to take from the Canaanites. Canaan was cursed to be a servant of the Shemites, or Semites of Israel, and that is a justification of their conquest of the Promised Land.

In short, the Canaanites are the Seed of the Serpent at war with the Israelites, the Seed of the Woman, and they deserve to be dispossessed of their land by the God whom their ancestors rejected and by whom they were cursed. Of course, there is much more to the story than that, for there were giants in the land of Canaan as well, giants that were the descendants of the Nephilim, the original Seed of the Serpent. But you will have to wait for the novels *Joshua Valiant* and *Caleb Vigilant* to see how that all fits together.

Abraham Allegiant

Appendix

Chapter 8
Between the Lines:
In Defense of Ancient Traditions

There is a danger for any author who shares the research behind his fictionalized storytelling. If he reveals "what really happened" as different from his story, then readers may have their story spoiled much like a child who is told the true story behind Santa Claus. If he shares the choices he makes of which evidence he chose over others, then the magic and mystery is ruined for those who prefer their imagination to the "historic details." But since I have established a kind of tradition by providing appendices in each of the books of the *Chronicles of the Nephilim*, I have decided to continue that dangerous tradition with the hopes of inspiring readers to go deeper in their study of the Bible than daily devotions and inspirational readings.

Retelling the story of the Tower of Babel and the life of Abraham is a particularly difficult task. The problem is that the further back in history one goes, the murkier are the waters, and anything in the fourth millennium B.C. Mesopotamia is complete guesswork. Biblically speaking, anything before the Davidic monarchy around 1000 B.C. is being increasingly contested by archaeological interpretations of the Near East.

The Biblical scholarly consensus is that Abraham lived around 2000 B.C. in Mesopotamia. But the evidence for this is thin and largely anecdotal. The best that can be offered is that there are some customs discovered in second millennium archives like Ebla and Mari that are similar to some customs in the Patriarchal narratives. Famous Egyptologist Kenneth Kitchen elucidates these similar customs such as treaty types, patriarchal proper names, patriarchal religion, slave prices, the use of camels, and other cultural customs.[1]

---

[1] Kenneth A. Kitchen, *On the Reliability of the Old Testament* (Grand Rapids, MI: Eerdmans, 2003), 353-355.

But David Noel Freedman points out that such cultural connections are not very reliable in establishing dates because "The Middle Bronze pattern of social custom and practice survived basically unchanged for centuries in certain localities in the Near East."[2]

Of all the events that occur in the Abraham narrative, none of them correspond with any known external historical or archaeological sources we have. This is not to say Abraham was made up, but merely to point out that scholars simply do not know for sure when Abraham's story took place in history because they do not have corroboration.

With the release of *Centuries of Darkness* in 1991 by Peter James, a dirty little secret of historiography was let out of the bag: There is a period of several centuries of historical "darkness" at the end of the Late Bronze Age in the received historical chronology of the ancient world. James argued that this period of darkness was an artifact of improper chronological accounting of the texts. A chronological revolution was established that began to rewrite ancient world chronology with a three hundred year shift.

Much of ancient history is anchored in Egyptian chronology that is notoriously ambiguous and imprecise and creates problems for all kinds of historical anchoring of events. Donovan Courville in the 1970s, and more recently David Rohl, has explored the Egyptian problems to offer a "New Chronology" of the ancient world that roots Biblical history in new contexts significantly different from the conventional chronology.[3] They too have shaken up the establishment by uncovering the significant chronological problems of the conventional view.

In more recent years, Gerald Aardsma, has offered the Biblical theory that the Exodus occurred in 2450 B.C., *nearly one thousand years earlier* than the conventional dates of 1445 B.C. or 1225 B.C.[4] This would place Abraham in Mesopotamia around 3000 B.C. instead of 2000 B.C. A radical reconsideration.

But the reason why this is all so important is because the standard interpretation of Biblical archaeology is increasingly that the events of the Bible did not happen because they do not line up with the artifactual evidence of archaeology. There is simply no current evidence of a crushing defeat of Egypt or the resultant wandering of the Jews in the desert around the critical

---

[2] David Noel Freedman. "The chronology of Israel and the Ancient Near East," *The Bible and the Ancient Near East* (Winona Lake, IN: Eisenbrauns, 1961) 208.

[33] Donovan Courville, *The Exodus Problem and Its Ramifications: A Critical Examination of the Chronological Relationships Between Israel and the Contemporary Peoples of Antiquity* (Loma Linda, CA: Challenge Books, 1971); David Rohl, *A Test of Time* (London, Random House, 1995); *From Eden to Exile: The Five Thousand Year History of the People of the Bible* (Lebanon, TN: Greenlead Press, 2003).

[4] Gerald E. Aardsma, Ph.D., *A New Approach to the Chronology of Biblical History from Abraham to Samuel* (Loda, IL: Aardsma Publishing, 2003, 2005); Aardsma, *The Exodus Happened 2450 B.C.* (Loda, IL: Aardsma Publishing, 2008).

late date of 1275 B.C. There is no current evidence of the cities of Ai or Jericho being inhabited, much less destroyed around the dates that critical Biblical scholars say they must have happened. Rohl and the New Chronology shows that there is however archaeological evidence of all of the above occurring hundreds of years earlier in the fifteenth century B.C. With a few centuries shift backwards, all the Biblical history falls into place with known external evidence.

I write this because in my fictionalized novel, *Abraham Allegiant*, I used the interpretation of ancient Jewish texts and legends as my paradigm to place Abraham back during the time of the Tower of Babel, an event that would be considered about a thousand years before Abraham under the conventional chronology. While this supposition is largely rejected now, it has a long venerable tradition in 2nd Temple Jewish literature and Talmudic interpretation and shows up in Ginzberg's famous *Legends of the Jews*.[5] It is that interpretation that I found interesting enough to present within the pages of the novel because I have used these ancient Jewish sources throughout the entire series of *Chronicles of the Nephilim* to bring to life such characters as Enoch, Noah, Adam, Cain, the archangels Mikael, Gabriel and Uriel, and others.

The Book of Jasher

One of the dominant references I used in retelling this tale of Abraham and the Tower of Babel was the ancient *Book of Jasher*. *Jasher* is said to be one of the historical sources used by the Bible writers for their own texts (Josh. 10:13; 2Sam. 1:18). The only copy we have of this text is a medieval manuscript that most believe is a forgery. But Bible researcher Ken Johnson has argued for its authenticity based on the caliber of its writing, its possible transmission, its inclusion of the Biblically quoted material, as well as other missing details. Johnson fearlessly confronts some of the strange things in the book as indications of why it is not Scripture, while maintaining it as a solid historical reference used by the Bible writers. He argues that it was one of the texts brought from Jerusalem to Spain at the fall of Jerusalem in A.D. 70.[6]

In the *Book of Jasher*, we read about the story of Nimrod building the Tower of Babel and hearing an astrological prophecy about the birth of Abram whose seed would rule over kings. Nimrod confronts Abram by throwing him in a furnace of fire, and Abram survives it by a miracle. It is also in this text that Amraphel, the king of Shinar who joined the four-nation confederation of

---

[5] Louis Ginzberg; trans. Henrietta Szold, (2011-01-13). *Legends of the Jews*, all four volumes in a single file, improved 1/13/2011 B&R Samizdat Express. Kindle Edition.
[6] Ken Johnson, *The Ancient Book of Jasher: Referenced in Joshua 10:13, 2 Samuel 1:18, and 2 Timothy 3:8* (Biblefacts Ministries, 2008) 4-6, 188-190.

Chedorlaomer that invaded Canaan, is explained as Nimrod under a new name.

What's in a Name

The idea of individuals changing their names is nothing new in the ancient world. We know that Abram's name which meant "exalted father" was changed to Abraham to mean "father of many nations" (Gen 17:5) based on the historical events of God's covenant with him. Later in the Bible, Jacob ("usurper") was changed to Israel ("struggles with God") as the ancestor of the people of God. Even ancient gods changed names based on locales. Inanna of Sumer became Ishtar of Babylonia, and then Ashtart of Canaan. Ninurta of Sumer was probably the basis for Marduk of Babylon, and then Ba'al of Canaan.

While it is a cardinal rule not to change a character's names in a modern story in order to avoid confusion, I have utilized this technique of changing names and identities as a foundational element in the *Chronicles of the Nephilim* storyline in order to incarnate the living cultural zeitgeist of the ancient world. Names were more than mere shallow title references to a person; they were believed to incarnate the person's very essence or identity, as well as mark significant moments in their lives.

Yahweh

Even God himself is referred to by many different names in Scripture. Critical scholars use this fact to concoct a conspiracy theory that these different names were different gods that Israel worshipped in their own pantheon. As years went by elitist Jewish religious leaders became more intolerant. They finally recorded their zealous monotheist demands to worship one God instead of the others, but somehow foolishly left the residue of polytheism in the text of the Bible by neglecting to edit out the names from their source texts.

Apart from the fact that there is not a single scrap of actual historical or archeological evidence for this theorizing, it also reeks of modern imperialism by projecting stupidity onto the writers of some of the most intelligent and poetic literature in history. Such arrogance is easily dismissed when one studies the ancient cultural context of divine names as expressing character traits related to specific situations.

The text that illustrates this most suitably is Exodus 6:3-4 where God speaking to Moses says, "I am Yahweh. I appeared to Abraham, to Isaac, and to Jacob, as El Shaddai, but by my name Yahweh I did not make myself known to them."

Unfortunately, English translations obscure the meaning of the text by painting over the Hebrew names with bastardized generic terms. Thus, Yahweh is translated as "the LORD," and El Shaddai, as "God Almighty," which drains them of their rich cultural context and meaning. They further this offensive activity by translating El Elyon as "God Most High," and Elohim as "God," and on and on. We have reduced the names of the living God to nameless generic references to a "supreme being." This *de-naming* of Yahweh Elohim is more a reflection of the Greek impersonal "Prime Mover" than the Hebrew personal "Named One."

But when one researches the meaning behind the original Hebrew words, their truer fuller meaning comes to light. Elohim is revealed as a more generic plural reference to the Creator as all humankind can know through general revelation.[7] El Elyon has a linguistic affinity to the Ugaritic "Elyon Ba'al" a name for the Most High God of Canaan, and therefore a polemical stance against him. Ba'al is not the Most High, the God of Israel is.[8] El Shaddai, carries with it a possible derivation of "God of the mountain," a common understanding of deities in the ancient Near East as revealed in power on mountains (Mount Sinai and Mount Zion are God's locations of self-disclosure).[9] Finally, Yahweh is the "eternally self-existent one" who is the unique covenantal name of Israel's deity in opposition to the nations.[10]

When Yahweh told Moses he revealed himself to the forefathers as El Shaddai, but not as Yahweh, he was saying that they only knew him in a limited sense that was not as full as he was about to reveal. The Mosaic revelation of Yahweh on Sinai would be a dramatic world changing self-disclosure of God's unique character through his Law, a new revelation of God. This is what would separate them from the nations as a holy people of God's own choosing.

In the section below on Babel Inheritance, Deuteronomy 32:9 is shown to describe Yahweh as dividing the nations up at Babel and allotting the peoples under the authority of other gods, while keeping Israel as his own people. Yahweh would be the name he would use to mark the strong demarcation between his people and the people in slavery to other gods.

---

[7] Names of God: Elohim, vol. 2, *The International Standard Bible Encyclopedia, Revised*, ed. Geoffrey W. Bromiley, 505 (Wm. B. Eerdmans, 1988).

[8] E. E. Elnes and P. D. Miller, "Elyon", in *Dictionary of Deities and Demons in the Bible*, ed. Karel van der Toorn, Bob Becking and Pieter W. van der Horst, 2nd extensively rev. ed., 295 (Leiden; Boston; Köln; Grand Rapids, MI; Cambridge: Brill; Eerdmans, 1999).

[9] Gordon J. Wenham, "The Religion of the Patriarchs," A.R. Millard & D.J. Wiseman, eds., *Essays on the Patriarchal Narratives*. Leicester: IVP, 1980, pp.157-188.

[10] Names of God: Yahweh, vol. 2, *The International Standard Bible Encyclopedia, Revised*, ed. Geoffrey W. Bromiley, 507 (Wm. B. Eerdmans, 1988).

Gilgamesh

This ancient Near Eastern obsession with changing names was also why I made Gilgamesh change his name and identity into Nimrod. This was not mere fancy or fabrication. There are some scholars who believe that Gilgamesh was the person behind the Nimrod of the Bible. But again, because of its antiquity, there are as many theories of who Nimrod really was as there are scholars.

W.H. Gispen listed just a few options of theories for the true historical identity of Nimrod by other scholars:

1. Gilgamesh, king of Uruk (2750 – 2600 B.C.)
2. Ninurta, the Sumerian deity
3. Marduk, the Babylonian deity
4. Tikulti-Ninurta, king of Assyria (1242-1206 B.C.)
5. Naram-Sin, king of Akkad (approx. 2300 B.C.)
6. Sargon, king of Akkad (2350 – 2294 B.C.)[11]
7. Enmerkar, king of Eridu in Sumer (approx. 2850 B.C.)[12]

As the reader can see, the theories are as widespread and diverse in their possibilities as a deity or a king, with a space of about one thousand years difference of possible fulfillment. The conclusion is pretty clear: Nobody really knows who Nimrod *really was*, but the name of Nimrod was most likely a Hebrew play on words that demonized the leader, because Nimrod in Hebrew means "to revolt." One hardly thinks a person would make his name with such negative connotations, since such kings often considered themselves like the gods — Unless a king did so as a defiant gesture "in the face of" a deity he hated. Thus the motivation behind the Nimrod of the *Chronicles*.

Scholars van der Toorn and van der Horst suggest that Nimrod was most likely a deliberately distorted Hebrew version of Ninurta as the hunter god of Mesopotamia. They argue that the reign of Nimrod was most likely a symbolic synopsis of the history of Mesopotamia embodied in one character, a deity deliberately dethroned by the Jewish writer to a hunter king.

> The cities [of Nimrod] mentioned in Gen 10:9-12 are given in a more or less chronological sequence. The list reads as a condensed resume of Mesopotamian history. Akkad, though still in use as a cult-center in the first millennium, had its *floruit* under the Sargonic dynasty. Kalhu had its heyday in

[11] W. H. Gispen, "Who Was Nimrod," in *The Law and the Prophets*, ed. J. H. Skilton (Philadelphia: Presbyterian & Reformed, 1974), 207–14.
[12] Rohl, *From Eden to Exile*, 58-77.

> the first half of the first millennium BCE, some fifteen hundred years later. If Nimrod is not a god, he must at least have enjoyed a divine longevity, his reign embracing both cities.[13]

Babel

The Tower of Babel incident is also an event that has a long history of as many interpretive possibilities as there are scholars. The standard ancient interpretation was that Babel and its tower were simply the city of Babylon in mid-Mesopotamia that had been started, then stopped by the confusion of tongues, only to be reborn a thousand years later under Hammurabi's predecessors.

Contrarily, Anne Habermehl has argued that it was in the far northeastern part of Syria;[14] David Rohl argued that Babel was actually the oldest known city of Eridu in the southernmost region of Sumeria on the gulf, and its tower was the famous ziggurat called *Nunki*.[15]

Again, with so many different interpretations possible, spanning thousands of miles of geography, no one really knows. But I went with the traditional interpretation on this one because it was still a sensible option. Unfortunately, because the water table is so high in the modern region of the ruins of Babylon, we will never be able to excavate any layers of sediment below to discover its more ancient past.

Abraham and the Giants

The picture of Abraham as a warrior fits very well with the warrior motif of *Chronicles of the Nephilim*. But even this is not as much fiction as it is Biblical fact because in Genesis 14 we read about Abram leading 318 warriors trained in his household on a rescue mission of his nephew Lot. Not only did he and his men, along with an unspecified group of allies from three friendly Amorite tribes, bring back the Sodomite captives and their booty, but they overtook a four-city coalition army that had just swept through Canaan. Abraham and his men were no mere pastoral shepherds. They were warriors.

But Genesis 14 is a particularly peculiar Biblical passage because it speaks of that four-city coalition, led by Chedorlaomer, as specifically coming to Canaan to punish Sodom and Gomorrah and the five cities of the Plain for rebelling against them as their vassals (v. 4). But before Chedorlaomer goes

---

[13] K. van der Toorn and P. W. van der Horst, "Nimrod before and after the Bible," *Harvard Theological Review* 83 (1990): 1–29.

[14] Anne Habermehl, "Where in the World Is the Tower of Babel?" *Answers Research Journal* 4 (2011) 25–53.

[15] Rohl, *From Eden to Exile*, 65.

to Sodom and Gomorrah, he goes out of his way to wipe out giant clans throughout Canaan.

> Genesis 14:5–7
> Chedorlaomer and the kings who were with him came and defeated the Rephaim in Ashteroth-karnaim, the Zuzim in Ham, the Emim in Shaveh-kiriathaim, 6 and the Horites in their hill country of Seir… 7 Then they turned back and came to En-mishpat (that is, Kadesh) and defeated all the country of the Amalekites, and also the Amorites who were dwelling in Hazazon-tamar.

All these named tribes are elsewhere in the Bible described as giant clans as listed below.

> Rephaim (Deut. 2:10-11, 20; 3:11)
> Zuzim, short for "Zamzummim" (Deut. 2:20)
> Emim (Deut. 2:10-11)
> Horites/Horim (Deut. 2:21-22)
> Amalekites (Numbers 13:28-29)
> Amorites (Amos 2:9-10)

Chedorlaomer and his armies were targeting the giant clans before returning home to Mesopotamia. After this genocide, we do not hear much at all about the giants again until over 400 years later when the Israelites are entering Canaan. So the remnant of giants must have taken all that time to rebuild their population numbers.

Semiramis

Another tradition that shows up in ancient legends surrounding Nimrod and Babylon is that of Queen Semiramis. The most well known ancient reference to this queen of Babylon comes from the Greek historian Diodorus Siculus who wrote of the mythical romance of Semiramis with King Ninus, around 2189 B.C.[16] Since Ninus was the reputed founder of Nineveh, it was a simple connection to be made with Nimrod who was the founder of Nineveh in the Bible.

Later in 1853, Protestant minister Alexander Hislop expanded on the relationship of Nimrod and Semiramis in *The Two Babylons*. Hislop's

[16] Diodorus Siculus, Library of History, Book II, (Loeb Classical Library Edition, 1933) Online: < http://penelope.uchicago.edu/Thayer/E/Roman/Texts/Diodorus_Siculus/2A*.html>

mythmaking became very influential though it was entirely fabricated by the writer to serve his anti-Catholic polemic.[17]

The closest historical personage that can be said to be the source of the Semiramis legends was Queen Shammuramat of Assyria, who reigned with King Shamshi-Adad V around 824-811 B.C., and whose Neo-Assyrian empire included Babylonia. There was a legend that she had once been a brothel keeper in Uruk, thus her connection with Shamhat the harlot from *Gilgamesh Immortal*.

Arba

The giant king Arba makes his appearance in *Abraham Allegiant*. But this is not a character of the author's imagination. There was a giant named Arba after whose name the city of Kiriath-Arba (later called Hebron) was named. He was of such significance to the author of Joshua, that he wrote of him, "Arba was the greatest man among the Anakim" (Joshua 14:15), and that "he was the father of Anak" (15:13). The Anakim were the giant descendants of the Nephilim who seemed to dominate southern Canaan when Israel arrived for conquest. Joshua's campaign in the hill country was focused on eliminating these Anakim as mortal enemies (Joshua 11:21-22).

Since Arba was the father of the giant Anak who birthed the people devoted to destruction much later in history, and since Abraham was said to live only two miles from the city founded by Arba (Gen 13:18; 23:2), it is not too much to speculate that Arba may have met Abraham, foreshadowing the providential rivalry these two people groups would have over that territory.

The Destroyer

"The Destroyer" is a translation of the Hebrew word used of the angel who entered the houses of the Egyptians and killed their first born as God's last plague on the Hebrews' oppressors (Ex 12:23). The *Dictionary of Deities and Demons in the Bible* says of this peculiar angel,

> "'Destroyer' is the designation of a supernatural envoy from God assigned the task of annihilating large numbers of people, typically by means of a plague… there was originally a distinction between the angel of death who comes to an individual at the time appointed for him to die and the Destroyer who massacres entire populations with premature

[17] Ralph Woodrow, *The Babylon Connection?* (Ralph Woodrow Evangelistic Association, 1997, 2004).

and violent deaths. Later traditions, however, fuse the two conceptions.[18]

In 1 Chronicles 21:14-16 we see a poignant picture of God sending the Destroyer to wipe out Jerusalem with a plague, but changing his mind from the calamity. One wonders if this is not also what happened at Babel.

Babel Inheritance

Another key element of the storyline of *Chronicles of the Nephilim* is the allotment of nations to the sons of God as punishment for humanity's rebellion. While I wrote a bit about this in the appendices of *Noah Primeval*, *Abraham Allegiant* is where this fascinating Biblical theological legal concept takes place at the Tower of Babel incident.

A brief look at the original full text of the Tower of Babel pericope in the Bible will help set the stage for a closer look at the theological ramifications of what it was all about.

> Genesis 11:1–9
> 1 Now the whole earth had one language and the same words.
> 2 And as people migrated from the east, they found a plain in the land of Shinar and settled there. 3 And they said to one another, "Come, let us make bricks, and burn them thoroughly." And they had brick for stone, and bitumen for mortar. 4 Then they said, "Come, let us build ourselves a city and a tower with its top in the heavens, and let us make a name for ourselves, lest we be dispersed over the face of the whole earth." 5 And the LORD came down to see the city and the tower, which the children of man had built. 6 And the LORD said, "Behold, they are one people, and they have all one language, and this is only the beginning of what they will do. And nothing that they propose to do will now be impossible for them. 7 Come, let us go down and there confuse their language, so that they may not understand one another's speech." 8 So the LORD dispersed them from there over the face of all the earth, and they left off building the city. 9 Therefore its name was called Babel, because there the LORD confused the language of all the earth. And from there the LORD dispersed them over the face of all the earth.

---

[18] S. A. Meier, "Destroyer", in *Dictionary of Deities and Demons in the Bible*, ed. Karel van der Toorn, Bob Becking and Pieter W. van der Horst, 2nd extensively rev. ed., 240 (Leiden; Boston; Köln; Grand Rapids, MI; Cambridge: Brill; Eerdmans, 1999).

So we see that within a short time after the Flood, mankind had proven to be corrupt once again in seeking to unite in a headlong pursuit of self-deification. They decidedly used kiln-burned brick with bitumen for mortar most likely because of their memory of the Flood wiping away their mud brick buildings and temples. This waterproofing technique was the first expression of their devious attempt to circumvent God's future judgment.

Then they seek to build a city and a tower "with its top in the heavens." The Hebrew word for tower no doubt referred to the ziggurat temple-tower at the heart of every Mesopotamian city. To discover the idolatrous meaning of this reference, John Walton explains that the function of the ziggurats came from the names given to them:

> For instance, the name of the ziggurat at Babylon, *Etemenanki*, means "temple of the foundation of heaven and earth." One at Larsa means "temple that links heaven and earth." Most significant is the name of the ziggurat at Sippar, "temple of the stairway to pure heaven." The word translated "stairway" in this last example is used in the mythology as the means by which the messenger of the gods moved between heaven, earth, and the netherworld.[19]

So the temple-tower of Babylon was a religious incarnation of their attempt to create a forbidden link between heaven and earth by building their own stairway to heaven for the gods, a violation of God's monarchic authority.

Then they seek to "make a name for themselves," which is a common Biblical and ancient Near Eastern idiom for greatness. By uniting together, their pride was so great that there would be no limit to their hubris. This blasphemous self-deification would be a real threat because, remember, mankind was God's image, his representative ruler over creation. So, if man would unite in this kind of rebellion, imagine the evil that would result, an evil that might rival what happened before the Flood.

So the confusion of tongues and dispersion of mankind breaks apart the tyrannical potential of this global one world government.

We are told twice that God "dispersed them over the face of the earth" in order to stop the megalomaniacal and totalitarian potential of mankind unified in rebellion against God.

The seventy nations described in Genesis 10 are the resultant new boundaries allotted to mankind that came from this Dispersion.

---

[19] John H Walton, *Zondervan Illustrated Bible Backgrounds Commentary (Old Testament) Volume 1: Genesis, Exodus, Leviticus, Numbers, Deuteronomy*, (Grand Rapids, MI: Zondervan, 2009) 62.

Sons of God Over the Nations

But this Dispersion is not the whole picture. There is something else that happens at this dividing of mankind, something spiritual and legal in the heavenly courtroom of God. God actually divides up the seventy nations and apportions them under the authority of the *Bene ha Elohim*, the sons of God, those divine beings that surround his heavenly throne.

Let's take a look at some of the Biblical passages that reveal this allotment of nations.

> Deut. 32:8–9
> When the Most High gave to the nations their inheritance, when he divided mankind, he fixed the borders of the peoples according to the number of the sons of God. But the LORD's portion is his people, Jacob his allotted heritage.

In this passage, the Scripture refers to the "dividing of mankind," which happened in the Dispersion at the Tower of Babel that we already looked at. God separated the nations by giving them different languages so they can no longer unite in blasphemous self-deification. And he divides up the borders of their dwelling. But he does so *according to the number of the sons of God.*

God put the seventy divided nations under the authority of these sons of God to whom they were "allotted." But he allotted the people of Jacob to himself as his heritage. The question then arises, what kind of authority do these sons of God have over the nations? Are they good or evil host of heaven? A look at other Biblical passages reveals that these sons of God are fallen beings and they are to become the false deities that own and rule over the pagan nations as Yahweh owns and rules over his people.

> Deut. 4:19-20
> And beware lest you raise your eyes to heaven, and when you see the sun and the moon and the stars, all the host of heaven, you be drawn away and bow down to them and serve them, things that the LORD your God has allotted to all the peoples under the whole heaven. But the LORD has taken you and brought you out of the iron furnace, out of Egypt, to be a people of his own inheritance, as you are this day.

> Deut. 29:24-26
> Then men will say, 'Because they forsook the covenant of the LORD, the God of their fathers, which He made with them when He brought them out of the land of Egypt. They went

> and served other gods and worshiped them, gods whom they have not known and whom He had not allotted to them.

Here again, we see a description of the "allotment" of the host of heaven to the pagan nations along with the allotment of Israel to Yahweh as his inheritance. The gentile nations are allotted to the sons of God/heavenly host/false gods of the land, while Israel is allotted to Yahweh and Yahweh allotted to Israel.

But notice in this passage, there is an equivalency of the sun, moon and stars with the host of heaven, a term used interchangeably with the Sons of God.[20] The sun, moon, and stars were worshipped as gods, and Yahweh is saying that these gods are the ones allotted to the nations. So, this is not a holy host of heaven, but an unholy host of heaven. These sons of God are not in God's heavenly court, they are evil fallen beings from that divine council.

The demonic reality of pagan gods is expressed further down in the same Deuteronomy chapter 32. The false gods were demons, real spiritual beings that had fallen from God's divine council:

> Deut. 32:16-17
> They stirred him to jealousy with strange gods; with abominations they provoked him to anger. They sacrificed to demons that were no gods, to gods they had never known, to new gods that had come recently, whom your fathers had never dreaded.

Second Temple Jewish literature and legend is not Scripture, but it certainly shows a paradigm that lines up with this Biblical notion of God allotting pagan nations to geographical territories ruled over by Sons of God as their deities. A perusal of some of these passages sheds more light on this paradigm:

> Ginzberg's Legends of the Jews
> It was on this occasion that God and the seventy angels that surround His throne cast lots concerning the various nations. Each angel received a nation, and Israel fell to the lot of God.

---

[20] H. Niehr, "Host of Heaven," Toorn, K. van der, Bob Becking, and Pieter Willem van der Horst. *Dictionary of Deities and Demons in the Bible DDD*. 2nd extensively rev. ed. Leiden; Boston; Grand Rapids, Mich.: Brill; Eerdmans, 1999., 428-29; I. Zatelli, "Astrology and the Worship of the Stars in the Bible," *ZAW* 103 (1991): 86-99.

To every nation a peculiar language was assigned, Hebrew being reserved for Israel.[21]

Jubilees 15:30-32
(There are) many nations and many people, and they all belong to him, but over all of them he caused spirits to rule so that they might lead them astray from following him. But over Israel he did not cause any angel or spirit to rule because he alone is their ruler and he will protect them and he will seek for them at the hand of his angels and at the hand of his spirits and at the hand of all of his authorities so that he might guard them and bless them and they might be his and he might be theirs henceforth and forever.[22]

Targum Jonathan, Deuteronomy 32, Section LIII
When the Most High made allotment of the world unto the nations which proceeded from the sons of Noach [Noah], in the separation of the writings and languages of the children of men at the time of the division, He cast the lot among the seventy angels, the princes of the nations with whom is the revelation to oversee the city.[23]

Philo, On the Posterity of Cain and His Exile 25.89
The Most High, when he divided the nations, dispersed the sons of Adam, and fixed the boundaries of the nations according to the number of the angels of God. And the portion of the Lord was his people Jacob, the limitation of the inheritance of Israel."[24]

Now, when we take a look at Psalm 82, an otherwise confusing passage becomes crystal clear in its context of the Tower of Babel, the Dispersion, and the Allotment of gods and nations.

---

[21] Ginzberg, Louis; Szold, Henrietta (2011-01-13). Legends of the Jews, all four volumes in a single file, improved 1/13/2011 (Kindle Locations 2586-2588). B&R Samizdat Express. Kindle Edition.
[22] James H. Charlesworth, *vol. 2, The Old Testament Pseudepigrapha and the New Testament, Volume 2: Expansions of the "Old Testament" and Legends, Wisdom, and Philosophical Literature, Prayers, Psalms and Odes, Fragments of Lost Judeo-Hellenistic Works*, (New Haven; London: Yale University Press, 1985) 87.
[23] See also *Targum Jonathan, Genesis 11*, Section II; *Concerning Noah's Work as a Planter* 14.59; *On the Migration of Abraham* 36.202; *1 Clement 29*; Origen, *First Principles* 1.5.1. Thanks to Don Enevoldsen for some of these passages.
[24] Philo of Alexandria and Charles Duke Yonge, *The Works of Philo: Complete and Unabridged*, 140 (Peabody, MA: Hendrickson, 1995).

Psalm 82:1–8
1 God has taken his place in the divine council;
in the midst of the gods he holds judgment:
2 "How long will you judge unjustly
and show partiality to the wicked? Selah
3 Give justice to the weak and the fatherless;
maintain the right of the afflicted and the destitute.
4 Rescue the weak and the needy;
deliver them from the hand of the wicked."

5 They have neither knowledge nor understanding,
they walk about in darkness;
all the foundations of the earth are shaken.

6 I said, "You are gods,
sons of the Most High, all of you;
7 nevertheless, like men you shall die,
and fall like any prince."

8 Arise, O God, judge the earth;
for you shall inherit all the nations!

Many Christians try to interpret this passage as if it were talking about human judges over Israel being punished for not meting out justice. But in its ancient Near Eastern context we can see that God is talking to the supernatural Sons of God ("sons of the Most High"), who were allotted the gentile nations to rule over them being judged for their failure to rule justly. And then the writer says that Yahweh will inherit those nations, a reference to the Gospel where all the pagan nations would be allowed to come under God's rule through faith in Jesus Christ.

In a very real sense, the Gospel breaks the power of false gods over the gentile nations and brings them into the fold of God's people along with believing Jews. God will inherit the nations who were once under the allotment and inheritance of the pagan gods.

The event of Pentecost that occurs in Acts 2, where a diversity of gentile tongues proclaimed "the mighty works of God," is a theological reversal of Babel by the Holy Spirit. At Babel, God confused their languages, and dispersed the peoples, placing them under the authority of Sons of God as their deities. God "gave them over" to their wickedness. With the arrival of Messiah, the Gospel liberates those gentile nations from their bondage to be drawn back and become united as one in Christ through faith. The power of the false gods over the gentile nations is broken.

Thus the apostle Paul can preach to his gentile pagans,

> Acts 17:26–31
> "And he made from one man every nation of mankind to live on all the face of the earth, having determined allotted periods and the boundaries of their dwelling place, that they should seek God, and perhaps feel their way toward him and find him. Yet he is actually not far from each one of us… The times of ignorance God overlooked, but now he commands all people everywhere to repent, because he has fixed a day on which he will judge the world in righteousness by a man whom he has appointed; and of this he has given assurance to all by raising him from the dead."

Joshua Valiant

Appendix

Chapter 9
Mythical Monsters in the Bible

Perhaps one of the most unique creative elements of the *Chronicles of the Nephilim* series is its ability to interact with pagan mythologies within the context of retelling Biblical stories in such a way as to bring out universal and shared meanings. But it does so within the context of a Biblical worldview. So famous and infamous giants, monsters, and other creatures from pagan myths show up in the stories of Enoch, Noah, Abraham and others: The sea dragon of chaos, Gilgamesh the ancient Babylonian hero, the chimeric mushussu lion dragon, The demoness Lilith, and others all make their appearances in this theological Biblical fantasy.

Rather than being a syncretistic blending of all religions into heretical oneness, this technique more accurately is described in Narnian terms as a subversive submission of all stories under the lordship of Aslan.

But this is not a new phenomenon created by innovative Christian geniuses like Lewis and Tolkien; it is in fact a storytelling technique common to much ancient literature of imagination—including the Bible!

Leviathan and Behemoth

I have already written much about Leviathan and Behemoth as monsters of chaos in the Bible in appendices of previous Chronicles. In those essays, I exegeted the Biblical texts where these monsters occurred. I debunked the notions that they are ancient descriptions of dinosaurs or other naturally occurring creatures, only to conclude that they bear the same characteristics of other ancient Near Eastern chaos monsters such as the Canaanite Leviathan and the Babylonian Tiamat. In passages such as Psalm 74 and Psalm 89, the historical event of the Exodus is mythopoeically presented as Yahweh fighting the waters and crushing the multiple heads of Leviathan or Rahab (another name for the same creature) in order to establish a new heavens and earth, his covenant order with Israel.

It is not that the Jews "copied" or "borrowed" such imagery from their pagan neighbors; but rather that, just as today, everyone of that time period used a common vocabulary of imagination to describe their worldviews. The Sumerians, Akkadians, Babylonians, Canaanites, Jews, and other ancient Near Easterners all described their gods' supremacy in terms of battling and overcoming the sea dragon of chaos so they could create order out of the chaos.

But this is just the tip of the ziggurat of other examples of Biblical authors poetically incorporating mythical elements into their writings about real people, places, and times of history.

Now things start to get hairy.

Satyrs and Centaurs and Demons, Oh My!

In my novels, *Joshua Valiant* and *Caleb Vigilant*, I write about a tribe called the Seirim people of Banias at Mount Hermon. They live in caves at the foot of the mountains and are led by satyrs; chimeric beings with the lower body of a goat and the upper body of a human. But this mythopoeic imagery is not a mere assimilation of ancient Greek myths about Pan, the satyr deity of nature and shepherding. The notion of satyrs or goat deities predates Greek myth and finds a place in Canaanite lore, and therefore, in the Bible as well.

Take a look at these prophecies of Isaiah referencing the destruction of Edom and Babylon.

> Isaiah 34:11–15 (The destruction of Edom)
> 11But the hawk and the porcupine shall possess it, the owl and the raven shall dwell in it… 13Thorns shall grow over its strongholds, nettles and thistles in its fortresses. It shall be the haunt of jackals, an abode for ostriches. 14And wild animals shall meet with hyenas; the wild goat (*seirim*) shall cry to his fellow; indeed, there the night bird settles and finds for herself a resting place. 15There the owl nests and lays and hatches and gathers her young in her shadow; indeed, there the hawks are gathered, each one with her mate.

> Isaiah 13:21–22 (The destruction of Babylon)
> 21But wild animals will lie down there, and their houses will be full of howling creatures; there ostriches will dwell, and there wild goats (*seirim*) will dance. 22Hyenas will cry in its towers, and jackals in the pleasant palaces; its time is close at hand and its days will not be prolonged.

The passages above speak of God's judgment upon the nations of Babylon and Edom (symbols of all that is against Israel and Yahweh). A cursory reading of the texts seem to indicate a common word picture of Yahweh destroying these nations so thoroughly that they end up a desert wasteland with wild animals and birds inhabiting them because the evil people will be no more.

Nothing about mythical monsters like satyrs there, right?

Wrong. Because the English translation of the Hebrew word *seirim* as "wild goats," obscures the full ancient meaning. If we look closer into the original Hebrew, we find a more expanded mythopoeic reference to pagan deities.

A look at the Septuagint (LXX) translation into Greek made by ancient Jews in the second century before Christ, reveals the hint of that different picture.

> Isaiah 34:13-14 (LXX)
> 11 and for a long time birds and hedgehogs, and ibises and ravens shall dwell in it: and the measuring line of desolation shall be cast over it, and satyrs shall dwell in it… 13 And thorns shall spring up in their cities, and in her strong holds: and they shall be habitations of monsters, and a court for ostriches. 14 And devils shall meet with satyrs, and they shall cry one to the other: there shall satyrs rest, having found for themselves *a place of* rest.[1]
>
> Isaiah 13:21-22 (LXX)
> But wild beasts shall rest there; and the houses shall be filled with howling; and monsters shall rest there, and devils shall dance there, 22 and satyrs shall dwell there.[2]

Wow, what a dramatic difference, huh? Of course, the LXX passages above are not in Greek, but are English translations, which adds a layer of complication that we will unravel shortly to reveal even more mythopoeic elements. But the point is made that ancient translators understood those words within their ancient context much differently than the modern bias of more recent interpreters. Of course, this does not necessarily make the ancient translators right all the time, but it warrants a closer look at our own blinding biases.

The LXX translates the word for "satyrs" that appears in these Isaiah passages as *onokentaurois* or "donkey-centaurs," from which we get our word

[1] Lancelot Charles Lee Brenton, *The Septuagint Version of the Old Testament: English Translation*, Is 34:13–14 (London: Samuel Bagster and Sons, 1870).
[2] Lancelot Charles Lee Brenton, *The Septuagint Version of the Old Testament: English Translation*, Is 13:21–22 (London: Samuel Bagster and Sons, 1870).

"centaur." The *Greek-English Lexicon of the Septuagint* defines this word as "donkey-centaur, mythic creature (a centaur resembling a donkey rather than a horse)."[3]

In Isaiah 34:14 of the ESV we read of "the wild goat crying to his fellow," and in 13:21, "there wild goats will dance." But the underlying Hebrew (*seirim*) is not about wild goats, but satyrs, that were prevalent in Canaanite religion. Scholar Judd Burton points out that Banias or Panias at the base of Mount Hermon in Bashan was a key worship site for the Greek goat-god Pan as early as the third century B.C. and earlier connections to the goat-idol Azazel (see *Azazel* below).[4]

Satyrs were well known for their satyrical dance, the *Sikinnis*, consisting of music, lascivious dance, licentious poetry and sarcastic critique of culture.[5] This reflects the mockery of the "goats" dancing on the ruins of Edom and Babylon in Isaiah, and the Sikinnis finds its way also into *Joshua Valiant* of the Chronicles.

The Bible writers considered these pagan *seirim* deities to be demons and thus called them "goat demons." So prevalent and influential were these satyr gods that Yahweh would have trouble with Israel worshipping them as idols.

> Leviticus 17:7
> [7] So they shall no more sacrifice their sacrifices to goat demons (*seirim*), after whom they whore. This shall be a statute forever for them throughout their generations.

> 2 Chronicles 11:15
> [15] [Jeroboam] appointed his own priests for the high places and for the goat idols (*seirim*) and for the calves that he had made.

Not only did Israel fall into worshipping the *seirim* in Canaan, they were even committing spiritual adultery with them while in the wilderness! It is no wonder Yahweh considered them demons, a declaration reiterated in Moses' own prophecy that after Israel would be brought into Canaan by the hand of God, she would betray Yahweh by turning aside to other gods, redefined as demons.

---

[3] Johan Lust, Erik Eynikel and Katrin Hauspie, *A Greek-English Lexicon of the Septuagint: Revised Edition* (Deutsche Bibelgesellschaft: Stuttgart, 2003).

[4] Judd H. Burton, *Interview With the Giant: Ethnohistorical Notes on the Nephilim* (Burton Beyond Press, 2009) 19-21. "Regardless of his [Azazle's] origins—in pre-Israelite practice he was surely a true demon, perhaps a satyr, who ruled in the wilderness." Jacob Milgrom, *A Continental Commentary: Leviticus: a Book of Ritual and Ethics* (Minneapolis, MN: Fortress Press, 2004), 169.

[5] Gaston Vuillier, trans. Joseph Grego, *A History Of Dancing From The Earliest Ages To Our Own Times* (New York, NY: D. Appleton and Co., 1848), 27-28.

Deuteronomy 32:17
17 They sacrificed to demons that were no gods, to gods they had never known, to new gods that had come recently, whom your fathers had never dreaded.[6]

Demons and Goblins

Moving back to the prophecies of Isaiah 13 and 34 we find additional spiritual creatures of chaos that are connected to the satyrs. We read of hawks, ostriches, owls, and ravens was well as other unknown animals. But the English translations make it look like they are just more natural animals.

Not so in the Hebrew.

Let's take a closer look at the Hebrew words behind two more of these strange creatures, "wild animals" and "hyenas."

Isaiah 13:21–22
21 But wild animals *(siyyim)* will lie down there, and their houses will be full of howling creatures; there ostriches will dwell, and there wild goats will dance. 22 Hyenas *(iyyim)* will cry in its towers, and jackals in the pleasant palaces; its time is close at hand and its days will not be prolonged.

Isaiah 34:14
14 And wild animals *(siyyim)* shall meet with hyenas; *(iyyim)* the wild goat shall cry to his fellow; indeed, there the night bird settles and finds for herself a resting place.

The Hebrew for the words "wild animals" and "hyenas" are not readily identifiable,[7] so the ESV translators simply guessed according to their anti-mythical bias and filled in their translations with naturalistic words like "wild animals" and "hyenas." But of these words, Bible commentator Hans Wildberger says,

> "Whereas (jackals) and (ostriches), mentioned in v. 13, are certainly well-known animals, the creatures that are mentioned in v. 14 cannot be identified zoologically, not

[6] The Psalmist also casts the gods of Canaan; Molech, Asherah, Ashtart, Ba'al, and others as demons as well in Psalm 106:37–38: "They sacrificed their sons and their daughters to the demons; they poured out innocent blood, the blood of their sons and daughters, whom they sacrificed to the idols of Canaan, and the land was polluted with blood."

[7] "Siyyim," Francis Brown, Samuel Rolles Driver, and Charles Augustus Briggs, *Enhanced Brown-Driver-Briggs Hebrew and English Lexicon* (Oak Harbor, WA: Logos Research Systems, 2000), 850.

> because we are not provided with enough information, but because they refer to fairy tale and mythical beings. *Siyyim* are demons, the kind that do their mischief by the ruins of Babylon, according to [Isaiah] 13:21. They are mentioned along with the *iyyim* (goblins) in this passage.[8]

The demons and goblins that Wildberger makes reference to in Isaiah 13:21-22 and 34:14 are the Hebrew words *siyyim* and *iyyim*, a phonetic play on words that is echoed in Jeremiah's prophecy against Babylon as well:

> Jeremiah 50:39
> 39 "Therefore wild beasts (*siyyim*) shall dwell with hyenas (*iyyim*) in Babylon, and ostriches shall dwell in her. She shall never again have people, nor be inhabited for all generations.

The Dictionary of Biblical Languages (*DBL*) admits that another interpretation of *iyyim* other than howling desert animals is "spirit, ghost, goblin, i.e., a night demon or dead spirit (Isa. 13:22; 34:14; Jer. 50:39), note: this would be one from the distant lands, i.e., referring to the nether worlds."[9] One could say that *siyyim and iyyim* are similar to our own play on words, "ghosts and goblins."

The proof of this demon interpretation is in the Apostle John's inspired reuse of the *same exact language* when pronouncing judgment upon first century Israel as a symbolic "Mystery Babylon."

> Revelation 18:2
> 2"Fallen, fallen is Babylon the great! She has become a dwelling place for demons, a haunt for every unclean spirit, a haunt for every unclean bird, a haunt for every unclean and detestable beast."[10]

Because of the exile under the Babylonians, Jews would use Babylon as the ultimate symbol of evil. So when John attacks his contemporaries in Israel for rejecting Messiah, he describes them as demonic Babylon worthy of the same judgment as that ultimate evil nation.

---

[8] Hans Wildberger, *A Continental Commentary: Isaiah 28–39* (Minneapolis, MN: Fortress Press, 2002).
[9] James Swanson, *Dictionary of Biblical Languages With Semantic Domains : Hebrew (Old Testament)*, electronic ed. (Oak Harbor: Logos Research Systems, Inc., 1997).
[10] Special thanks to Doug Van Dorn for this "revelation." Van Dorn, Douglas (2013-01-21). *Giants: Sons of the Gods* (Kindle Locations 3922-3925). Waters of Creation. Kindle Edition. In fact, his "Chapter 13: Chimeras" was helpful for more than one insight in this appendix.

But regardless of one's eschatological interpretation, the "wild beasts" or "monsters" and "hyenas" of Isaiah and Jeremiah are interpreted as demons, unclean spirits and detestable beasts, along with the unclean animals that will scavenge over the ruins of the judged nation. The Old Testament "haunt of jackals" is the New Testament equivalent of the "haunt of demons." The "dwelling of hyenas and ostriches" is the "dwelling of demons."

In fact, even the Hebrew for "ostriches" is a word that is not all it seems. The actual Hebrew is *benot yaanah,* "daughters of ostriches," not merely "ostriches." Of course, this odd adjective did not make the translators comfortable because it pointed to something that may be other than ostriches, so they left it out.

The DBL says this Hebrew word phrase is "formally, daughter of greed, or daughter of wilderness... a kind of owl."[11] So they are not even sure it means an ostrich. Owls are connected to the underworld and spirits through all of ancient literature. But since there is no conclusive scholarship available on what this term really means, we will leave it as another possible reference to a strange creature of the demonic wilderness in a passage of much debated strange demonic references.

Lilith

Another strange creature that occurs in Isaiah 34:14 is the "night hag," or "night bird" that "settles and finds for herself a resting place." The Hebrew word is actually *Lilith*, which the *Dictionary of Deities and Demons in the Bible* explains is a Mesopotamian demoness residing in a tree that reaches back to the third millennium BC.

> Here we find Inanna (Ishtar) who plants a tree later hoping to cut from its wood a throne and a bed for herself. But as the tree grows, a snake makes its nest at its roots, Anzu settled in the top and in the trunk the demon ki-sikil-líl-lá [Lilith] makes her lair.[12]

I've already written about Lilith in the appendix of *Enoch Primordial*,[13] but it is important that she shows up in this Biblical context connected with the satyrs and Azazel. The very next verse (Isa. 34:15) talks about the owl that nests and lays and hatches her young in its shadow. But lexicons such as the

---

[11] James Swanson, *Dictionary of Biblical Languages With Semantic Domains : Hebrew (Old Testament)*, electronic ed. (Oak Harbor: Logos Research Systems, Inc., 1997).

[12] M. Hutter, "Lilith", in *Dictionary of Deities and Demons in the Bible*, ed. Karel van der Toorn, Bob Becking and Pieter W. van der Horst, 2nd extensively rev. ed., 520 (Leiden; Boston; Köln; Grand Rapids, MI; Cambridge: Brill; Eerdmans, 1999).

[13] Brian Godawa, *Enoch Primordial* (Los Angeles: Embedded Pictures Publishing, 2013), 349.

Theological Wordbook of the Old Testament and *Brown, Driver, Briggs Hebrew Lexicon* contest this Hebrew word for owl (*qippoz*) with more ancient interpretations of an "arrow snake."[14] If they are correct, then the poetry of the passage would be more complete as the NASB indicates.

> Isaiah 34:14–15 (NASB95)
> [14] Yes, the night monster (*Lilith*) will settle there And will find herself a resting place. [15] The tree snake (*qippoz*) will make its nest and lay *eggs* there, And it will hatch and gather *them* under its protection.

The snake of verse 15 would match the Lilith myth (v. 14) with the snake in the roots making its nest. The correlation is too close to deny that this is another Biblical reference to a popular mythic creature that the Bible writers refer to in demonic terms.

The Dead Sea Scrolls of Qumran evidence a preoccupation with demonology that includes reference to this very Isaianic passage. In *The Songs of the Sage*, we read an exorcism incantation,

> "And I, the Instructor, proclaim His glorious splendor so as to frighten and to terrify all the spirits of the destroying angels, spirits of the bastards, demons, Lilith, howlers, and [desert dwellers…] and those which fall upon men without warning to lead them astray[15]

Note the reference to "spirits of the bastards," a euphemism for demons as the spirits of dead Nephilim who were not born of human fathers, but of angels.[16]

---

[14] 2050a, קִפּוֹז *Theological Wordbook of the Old Testament*, ed. R. Laird Harris, Gleason L. Archer, Jr. and Bruce K. Waltke, electronic ed., 806 (Chicago: Moody Press, 1999). קִפּוֹז Brown, Francis, Samuel Rolles Driver, and Charles Augustus Briggs. *Enhanced Brown-Driver-Briggs Hebrew and English Lexicon.* electronic ed. Oak Harbor, WA: Logos Research Systems, 2000.

[15] 4Q510 Frag. 1. Michael O. Wise, Martin G. Abegg Jr., and Edward M. Cook, *The Dead Sea Scrolls: A New Translation* (New York: HarperOne, 2005), 527. Janet Howe Gaines, "Lilith: Seductress, Heroine or Murderer?" Bible History Daily, 08/11/2014, http://www.biblicalarchaeology.org/daily/people-cultures-in-the-bible/people-in-the-bible/lilith/, accessed 9/8/14.

[16] Loren T. Stuckenbruck, "The 'Angels' and 'Giants' of Genesis 6:1-4 in Second and Third Century BCE Jewish Interpretation: Reflections on the Posture of Early Apocalyptic Traditions," Dead Sea Discoveries, Vol. 7, No. 3, *Angels and Demons* (2000), pp. 354-37; Ida Fröhlich,"Theology and Demonology in Qumran Texts," *Henoch*; Vol. 32 Issue 1, June 2010, 101-129.

Lion Men of Moab

As a side note, one other possible chimeric creature appears in the story of David's mighty men in 2Sam. 23:20. There it says that Benaiah, a valiant warrior, "struck down two *ariels* of Moab." The word "ariel" is a transliteration because scholars are not sure what it means. Lexicons explain the most likely meaning as "lion of god,"[17] which is why the King James and Young's Bibles translate these opponents of Benaiah as "lion-like men of Moab."

The ancient understanding of ariel as a lion-like hybrid humanoid finds support in a later Nag Hammadi text that speaks of a gnostic deity, Yaldabaoth, who was an ariel (spelled slightly different): "Ariael is what the perfect call him, for he was like a lion."[18]

The Lion Men of Moab will make their entrance in the coming Chronicle, *David Ascendant.*

But there is still more behind this hybrid creature concept of goat demons or satyrs than meets a cursory reading of the text. And it is something that ties in with *Chronicles of the Nephilim* with peculiar interest.

Azazel

In Leviticus 16, we read of the sacrificial offering on the Day of Atonement. Among other sacrifices, the high priest would take two goats for atonement of the people. One, he would kill as blood sacrifice on the altar, and the other, he would transfer the sins of the people onto the goat by confession and the laying on of his hands. This action of transferring the bloodguilt onto the "other" is where we got the concept of "scapegoat."

But that is not the most fascinating piece of this puzzle. For in verses 8–10 and 26, the priest is told to send the goat "away into the wilderness to Azazel" (v. 10)! You read that right: *Azazel.*

> Leviticus 16:7-10
> Then he shall take the two goats and set them before the Lord at the entrance of the Tent of Meeting. And Aaron shall cast lots over the two goats, one lot for the Lord and the other lot <u>for Azazel</u>.And Aaron shall present the goat on which the lot fell for the Lord and use it as a sin offering, but the goat on which the lot fell <u>for Azazel</u> shall be presented alive before

[17] Francis Brown, Samuel Rolles Driver and Charles Augustus Briggs, *Enhanced Brown-Driver-Briggs Hebrew and English Lexicon*, electronic ed., 72 (Oak Harbor, WA: Logos Research Systems, 2000).
[18] James McConkey Robinson, Richard Smith and Coptic Gnostic Library Project, *The Nag Hammadi Library in English*, 4th rev. ed., 173 (Leiden; New York: E. J. Brill, 1996).

> the Lord to make atonement over it, that it may be sent away into the wilderness to Azazel.

The name Azazel is not explained anywhere in the Old Testament, but we've heard that name before in the book of 1Enoch.[19] Azazel was one of the lead Watchers who led the rebellion of 200 Watchers to mate with the daughters of men. And that Watcher was considered bound in the desert of Dudael.

The natural question arises whether this is the same sacrifice to goat demons that Yahweh condemns in the very Leviticus and Isaiah passages we already looked at. But a closer look dispels such concerns.

The first goat was "for Yahweh" and the second "for Azazel" (v. 8). But whereas the first goat was a sacrifice, the second was not. As commentator Jacob Milgrom claims, "In pre-Israelite practice [Azazel] was surely a true demon, perhaps a satyr, who ruled in the wilderness—in the Priestly ritual he is no longer a personality but just a name, designating the place to which impurities and sins are banished."[20]

Milgrom then explains that in the ancient world, purgation and elimination rites went together. The sending out of the scapegoat to Azazel in the wilderness was a way of banishing evil to its place of origin which was described as the netherworld of chaos, where its malevolent powers could no longer do harm to the sender.[21] This wilderness of "tohu and wabohu" or emptiness and wasteland was precisely the chaos that Yahweh pushed back to establish his covenantal order of the heavens and earth, so it was where all demonic entities were considered to reside.

So Azazel could very well have been considered the father or leader of the goat demons. In the book of 1Enoch, Azazel is imprisoned in an opening in the desert of Dudael (1Enoch 13:4–8). But scholar Judd Burton argues that this unknown location might very well be connected to Mount Hermon, the original home of the Watchers when they came down to the earth (1Enoch 6:6). He points out that a very important "opening" existed near Hermon in the Grotto of Pan at the site called Banias. In the Hellenistic period (200 B.C.) the Greeks established a shrine to Pan, the satyr god of nature and shepherding, that became quite influential in the worship of Pan in the Greco-Roman period.

Judd then speculates that the shrine was originally to Azazel in antediluvian days because of the close similarities between Azazel and Pan. Firstly, both deities were associated with the goat. Secondly, Pan was driven

[19] 1 Enoch 8:1; 9:6; 10:4–8; 13:1–2; 54:5; 55:4; 69:2.

[20] Jacob Milgrom, A Continental Commentary: Leviticus: A Book of Ritual and Ethics, 169 (Minneapolis, MN: Fortress Press, 2004).

[21] Jacob Milgrom, *A Continental Commentary: Leviticus: A Book of Ritual and Ethics*, 169, 166 (Minneapolis, MN: Fortress Press, 2004).

by primal sexual lusts, just as Azazel lusted after human women and led the Watchers to mate with them. Thirdly, both Pan and Azazel were adept at war craft. The victory at Marathon in 490 BC was attributed to Pan, just as the art of making weapons and waging war was attributed to Azazel. And lastly, "with regard to the mystical, Pan and Azazel are also kindred spirits. The Greeks associated Pan with divination and prophecy, and Azazel himself took an active role in revealing the mystical knowledge of heaven to humanity."[22]

It was this cave grotto at Banias near Hermon that may be the mysterious Dudael location or the memorial to Azazel's imprisonment. The Seirim clan of Banias in *Joshua Valiant* and *Caleb Vigilant* embodies this spiritual and theological reality. And this is how I appropriated Azazel's original binding at the Flood in *Noah Primeval*, by having him bound in a desert called Dudael, but his final binding occurred at Mount Hermon in *Joshua Valiant*. It was a both/and theological unity.

The Serpent Clan of Gilgal Rephaim

Throughout the *Chronicles of the Nephilim*, Bashan, "the place of the serpent," plays an important part of the storyline of the Watchers because it seems to have an important role in the spiritual history of the region. Bashan is where Mount Hermon, the touch point for the Watchers, resides (1Enoch 6:6), as well as the Seirim tribe of satyrs at Banias. The very land of Canaan around Mount Hermon that was called Bashan was described as the "land of the Rephaim" (Deut. 3:13), whose inhabitants were described as tall giants like the Anakim (Deut. 2:11, 20) and were related to Goliath the giant (1Chron. 20:4–8). It was also the domain of the mighty giant, Og of Bashan, the "last of the Rephaim" (Josh. 12:4; Deut. 3:11), who was Joshua's last impediment to entering the Promised Land. The ancient Jewish book of Jubilees adds some more details about these giant Rephaim ("Raphaim") and their territory to corroborate the Biblical record:

> Jubilees 29:9–10
> [9] But formerly the land of Gilead was called "the land of Raphaim" because it was the land of the Raphaim. And the Raphaim were born as giants whose height was ten cubits (15 ft.), nine cubits (13.5 ft.), eight cubits (12 ft.), or down to seven cubits (10.5 ft.). [10] And their dwelling was from the land of the Ammonites to Mount Hermon and their royal palaces

[22] Judd H. Burton, *Interview With the Giant: Ethnohistorical Notes on the Nephilim* (Burton Beyond Press, 2009) 20.

were in Qarnaim, and Ashtaroth, and Edrei, and Misur, and Beon.[23]

But there is more to this region that has been unearthed in recent decades. The Hivites, one of the seven Canaanite peoples marked out for annihilation (Ex. 23:23), resided "under Hermon" (Josh. 11:3) "on Mount Lebanon, from Mount Baal-hermon as far as Lebo-hamath (Jdg. 3:3). Though the Bible tells us no particulars about these people, there are some interesting factoids that illuminate some possibilities.

The Hebrew word for Hivite has the same consonants as another common word for snake,[24] and they are descendants of the cursed line of Canaan, son of Ham (Gen. 10:17; 1Chron. 1:15).

About 20 miles south of Mount Hermon is a serpentine ravine about a mile long bearing the marks of manmade engraving that do not match its surrounding natural formations. It's like a huge snake cut into the earth. And then about seven miles southwest of there lies a large serpentine mound that may date back to ancient days.[25]

And right near that serpentine mound lays Gilgal Rephaim.

Gilgal Rephaim is a large monument of megalithic stones set in concentric circles with a tomb ("tumulus") at the center and an outer diameter of about 520 feet. The ruins are anywhere between eight and fifteen feet tall and amount to forty thousand tons of stone. The name means, "Circle of Giants," and it lays 25 miles northwest of Edrei, the city of Og of Bashan, in the land of the Rephaim, the territory ruled by Og. Scholars have conjectured that this site, much like other circular megalithic sites around the world, was used for religious astronomical/astrological purposes.[26] Other sites like it include the famous Stonehenge, as well as the newly discovered ancient Gobleki Tepe in Turkey, the world's oldest known religious monument, dating as far back as 9000 B.C.

---

[23] James H. Charlesworth, vol. 2, *The Old Testament Pseudepigrapha and the New Testament, Volume 2: Expansions of the "Old Testament" and Legends, Wisdom, and Philosophical Literature, Prayers, Psalms and Odes, Fragments of Lost Judeo-Hellenistic Works*, 111 (New Haven; London: Yale University Press, 1985).

[24] Michael S. Heiser *The Myth That is True*, p 186. Available online at www.michaelsheiser.com

[25] Van Dorn, Douglas (2013-01-21). *Giants: Sons of the Gods* (Kindle Locations 3074-3076). Waters of Creation. Kindle Edition.

[26] Anthony Aveni and Yonathan Mizrachi, "The Geometry and Astronomy of Rujm el-Hiri, a Megalithic Site in the Southern Levant," *Journal of Field Archaeology*, Vol. 25, No. 4 (Winter, 1998), pp. 475-496.

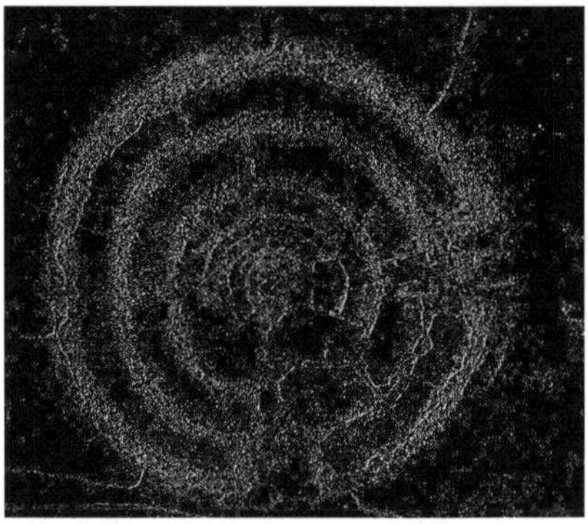

Aerial view of Gilgal Rephaim

But the connections are all there between a cult of the serpent in the land of the Rephaim and Bashan, the place of the serpent. Thus, the Serpent Clan of Gilgal Rephaim, from which Arisha, a key character originates in *Joshua Valiant*.

Winged Fiery Serpents

In *Joshua Valiant* I tell the infamous story of Nehushtan, the bronze serpent, from Numbers 21. As Moses leads the people of Israel through the Negeb desert on their way to enter the Transjordan, the Israelites grumble and complain yet again about their lack of food and water. Yahweh responds by sending serpents to punish them.

> Numbers 21:6–9
> Then the LORD sent fiery serpents among the people, and they bit the people, so that many people of Israel died. 7 And the people came to Moses and said, "We have sinned, for we have spoken against the LORD and against you. Pray to the LORD, that he take away the serpents from us." So Moses prayed for the people. 8 And the LORD said to Moses, "Make a fiery serpent and set it on a pole, and everyone who is bitten, when he sees it, shall live." 9 So Moses made a bronze serpent and set it on a pole. And if a serpent bit anyone, he would look at the bronze serpent and live.

The Hebrew word for "fiery serpents" used in this text is *seraph*, which is the same word used for the winged serpentine guardians of Yahweh's throne in passages like Isaiah 6:2.[27] There are several different Hebrew words that can be used for serpents, so the choice of this word here should clue us into the deliberations of the writer. While the notion of "fiery" can refer to the venomous sting of a desert snake such as a viper or cobra, there may be more going on here than a mere poetic description of snake bites.

The picture of *seraph* snakes having wings shows up in two other passages from Isaiah.

> Isaiah 14:29
> 29 Rejoice not, O Philistia, all of you, that the rod that struck you is broken, for from the serpent's root will come forth an adder, and its fruit will be a flying fiery serpent.
>
> Isaiah 30:6–7
> 6 An oracle on the beasts of the Negeb. Through a land of trouble and anguish, from where come the lioness and the lion, the adder and the flying fiery serpent… 7 Egypt's help is worthless and empty; therefore I have called her "Rahab who sits still."

Both of these prophecies against Philistia and Egypt respectively use the idea of a "flying fiery serpent" as a poetic description of the evil or dangerous nature of those nations. Though they are not required to be literal existing creatures for the prophecy to be legitimate, they nevertheless use the same Hebrew reference to fiery serpents that was used in the more historical passage of Numbers describing the "fiery serpents."

Additionally, the Isaiah 30 passage describes these flying fiery serpents as the beasts of the Negeb, the same location for the fiery serpents of Numbers 21.

Jacob Milgrom argues that the bronze or copper snake that Moses put on the pole was a winged serpent. He concludes this from the link of the Hebrew *seraph* to the Egyptian *uraeus* serpent.

> Egypt is the home for images of winged serpents. For example, the arms on the throne of Tutankhamen consist of two wings of a four-winged snake (uraeus), which rise vertically from the back of the seat. Indeed, the erect cobra, or uraeus, standing on its coil is the symbol of royalty for the pharaoh and the gods throughout Egyptian history. Winged

[27] Timothy R. Ashley, *The Book of Numbers*, The New International Commentary on the Old Testament (Grand Rapids, MI: Wm. B. Eerdmans Publishing Co., 1993), 404–405.

> uraei dating from the Canaanite period have been found, proving that the image of the winged serpent was well known in ancient Israel.[28]

Scholar Karen Randolph Joines adds more to the Egyptian origin of this motif, by explaining that the usage of serpent images to defend against snakes was also an exclusively Egyptian notion without evidence in Canaan or Mesopotamia.[29] And Moses came out of Egypt.

But the important element of these snakes being flying serpents or even dragons with mythical background is reaffirmed in highly respected lexicons such as the *Brown, Driver, Briggs Hebrew Lexicon.*[30]

The final clause in Isaiah 30:7 likening Egypt's punishment to the sea dragon Rahab lying dead in the desert is a further mythical serpentine connection.[31]

But the Bible and Egypt are not the only places where we read of flying serpents in the desert. Hans Wildberger points out Assyrian king Esarhaddon's description of flying serpents in his tenth campaign to Egypt in the seventh century B.C.

> "A distance of 4 double-hours I marched over a territory… (there were) two-headed serpents [whose attack] (spelled) death—but I trampled (upon them) and marched on. A distance of 4 double-hours in a journey of 2 days (there were) green [animals] [Tr.: Borger: "serpents"] whose wings were batting."[32]

---

[28] Jacob Milgrom, *Numbers*, The JPS Torah Commentary (Philadelphia: Jewish Publication Society, 1990), 459.

[29] Karen Randolph Joines, "The Bronze Serpent in the Israelite Cult," *Journal of Biblical Literature*, Vol. 87, No. 3 (Sep., 1968), 251.

[30] Francis Brown, Samuel Rolles Driver, and Charles Augustus Briggs, *Enhanced Brown-Driver-Briggs Hebrew and English Lexicon* (Oak Harbor, WA: Logos Research Systems, 2000), 977. Wilhelm Gesenius and Samuel Prideaux Tregelles, *Gesenius' Hebrew and Chaldee Lexicon to the Old Testament Scriptures* (Bellingham, WA: Logos Bible Software, 2003), 795. See also, James Swanson, *Dictionary of Biblical Languages with Semantic Domains : Hebrew (Old Testament)* (Oak Harbor: Logos Research Systems, Inc., 1997).

[31] "This final clause uses the name Rahab (51:9; Job 9:13; 26:12; Ps 87:4; 89:11), the great sea monster from ancient Near Eastern legends, as a symbol for Egypt. The final cryptic clause, "Rahab the Do-Nothing" (NIV), interprets "Do-Nothing" as a sarcastic name for this supposedly powerful monster. Beuken prefers to interpret this as Rahab "who sits still," meaning that Egypt will not come to assist Judah in her conflict with Assyria.[133] Another possible translation is Rahab the dead one. All these warnings argue for a policy that does not depend on Egypt. It makes no sense to trust in a political policy that is sure to fail. It is futile to follow a plan that God opposes." Gary V. Smith, *Isaiah 1–39*, ed. E. Ray Clendenen, *The New American Commentary* (Nashville: B & H Publishing Group, 2007), 513.

[32] Hans Wildberger, *A Continental Commentary: Isaiah 28-39* (Minneapolis, MN: Fortress Press, 2002), 136. Quoting from James Bennett Pritchard, ed., *The Ancient Near East an Anthology of Texts and Pictures*, 3rd ed. with Supplement (Princeton: Princeton University Press, 1969), 292.

The Greek historian Herodotus wrote of "sacred" winged serpents and their connection to Egypt in his *Histories*:

> There is a place in Arabia not far from the town of Buto where I went to learn about the winged serpents. When I arrived there, I saw innumerable bones and backbones of serpents... This place... adjoins the plain of Egypt. Winged serpents are said to fly from Arabia at the beginning of spring, making for Egypt... The serpents are like water-snakes. Their wings are not feathered but very like the wings of a bat. I have now said enough concerning creatures that are sacred.[33]

The notion of flying serpents as mythical versus real creatures appearing in the Bible is certainly debated among scholars, but this debate gives certain warrant to the imaginative usage of winged flying serpents appearing in *Chronicles of the Nephilim.*[34]

Giants in the Land

There are some monsters that I want to address here that are not as mythical as the ones we have looked at, but they are nevertheless as demonic and worthy of comment. These are the giants of Canaan: the Rephaim and the Anakim.

A cursory reading of the conquest narrative certainly results in the discovery of giants in the land of Canaan, but a closer look at the sacred text brings out just how important they are to the cosmic storyline of the Wars of Yahweh.

In *Joshua Valiant* we see two kings of the Transjordan that must be overcome in order for Israel to secure a safe entry point into the Cisjordan to begin their conquest of the Promised Land: Sihon of Heshbon, and Og of Bashan.

These are not fictional characters. They are from the text. But Sihon is not described as a giant, only as a mighty king of the area whose colonial ambitions were so well known that he had a ballad penned for him about his

---

[33] *Herodotus, Herodotus, With an English Translation* by A. D. Godley, ed. A. D. Godley (Medford, MA: Harvard University Press, 1920) Histories 2:75.1-76.3. Thanks to my editor, Don Enevoldsen, for this reference.

[34] Scholars who acknowledge the evidence for mythical flying serpents, but argue against it: Wilhelm Gesenius and Samuel Prideaux Tregelles, *Gesenius' Hebrew and Chaldee Lexicon to the Old Testament Scriptures* (Bellingham, WA: Logos Bible Software, 2003), 796; R. Laird Harris, "2292 שָׂרָף," ed. R. Laird Harris, Gleason L. Archer Jr., and Bruce K. Waltke, *Theological Wordbook of the Old Testament* (Chicago: Moody Press, 1999), 884.

subduing of the Moabites under his power. A ballad that finds its way into the novel as well.

> Numbers 21:26–29
> For Heshbon was the city of Sihon the king of the Amorites, who had fought against the former king of Moab and taken all his land out of his hand, as far as the Arnon. 27 Therefore the ballad singers say, "Come to Heshbon, let it be built; let the city of Sihon be established. 28 For fire came out from Heshbon, flame from the city of Sihon. It devoured Ar of Moab, and swallowed the heights of the Arnon. 29 Woe to you, O Moab! You are undone, O people of Chemosh! He has made his sons fugitives, and his daughters captives, to an Amorite king, Sihon.

Last of the Rephaim: Og of Bashan

Og of Bashan is another Biblical story in need of a closer look. The Bible says that he reigned in the northern region of the Transjordan and ruled out of Ashtaroth over sixty cities of Bashan (Deut. 3:4; Josh. 9:10).

These two kings, Og and Sihon are depicted in the Bible as the enemies to overthrow in the Transjordan, so God gives Israel their victory over them (Num 32:33; Deut 1:1–8).

But then the text adds an important note about Og. It says that he was the "last of the Rephaim," a species we have seen elsewhere to be giants (Deut. 2:10–11, 20–23). It says that his territory, Bashan was called "The land of the Rephaim" for its population of giants (Deut. 3:13). It says his bed, or sarcophagus was at least 13 1/2 feet long. His size was so impressive that the bed had become a museum trophy piece in Israel years later.

> Deuteronomy 3:11
> 11 (For only Og the king of Bashan was left of the remnant of the Rephaim. Behold, his bed was a bed of iron. Is it not in Rabbah of the Ammonites? Nine cubits (13.5 feet) was its length, and four cubits (6 feet) its breadth, according to the common cubit.)

In the original Hebrew, Og's "land of the Rephaim" is an ambiguous wording that could equally be translated as "the 'hell' of the Rephaim."[35]

---

[35] K. van der Toorn, Bob Becking and Pieter Willem van der Horst, *Dictionary of Deities and Demons in the Bible DDD*, 2nd extensively rev. ed., 162 (Leiden; Boston; Grand Rapids, Mich.: Brill; Eerdmans, 1999).

Bashan was a deeply significant spiritual location to the Canaanites and the Hebrews. And as the *Dictionary of Deities and Demons in the Bible* puts it, Biblical geographical tradition agrees with the mythological and cultic data of the Canaanites of Ugarit that "the Bashan region, or a part of it, clearly represented 'Hell', the celestial and infernal abode of their deified dead kings," the Rephaim.[36]

Mount Hermon was in Bashan, and Mount Hermon was a location in the Bible that was linked to the Rephaim and ruled over by Og (Josh. 12:1–5), but it was also the legendary location where the Sons of God were considered to have come to earth and had sexual union with the daughters of men to produce the giant Nephilim.[37]

As I explained in previous Chronicles' appendices, the Rephaim have an extra-Biblical tradition in Ugarit that is also tied to the land of Canaan. One of the corpus of texts unearthed at Ugarit just north of Canaan within the last century was what came to be known as the Rephaim Texts. These texts and others talked about a *marzih* feast that involved royalty traveling distances in their chariots to participate, wherein the "most ancient Rephaim of the netherworld" are summoned to assemble as the "council of the Ditanu, (or Didanu)."[38]

As Ugaritic scholars Levine and Tarragon sum up, "the Rephaim are long departed kings (and heroes) who dwell in the netherworld, which is located deep beneath the mountains of that far-away eastern region where the Ugaritians originated."[39]

There are two places in the Bible that hint at the Rephaim being warrior kings brought down to Sheol in similar language to the Ugaritic notion of the Rephaim warrior kings in the underworld:

> Is. 14:9
> Sheol beneath is stirred up
> to meet you when you come;
> it rouses the shades [The Hebrew word *Rephaim*]
> to greet you,

---

[36] "Bashan," *DDD*, p 161-162. "According to *KTU* 1.108:1–3, the abode of the dead and deified king, and his place of enthronement as *[Rephaim]* was in *[Ashtarot and Edrei]*, in amazing correspondence with the Biblical tradition about the seat of king Og of Bashan, "one of the survivors of the Rephaim, who lived in Ashtarot and Edrei" (Josh 12:4)."

[37] The non-canonical book of Enoch supports this same interpretation: "Enoch 6:6 And they were in all two hundred [sons of God]; who descended in the days of Jared on the summit of Mount Hermon, and they called it Mount Hermon, because they had sworn and bound themselves by mutual imprecations upon it."

[38] William W. Hallo and K. Lawson Younger, *The Context of Scripture*, (Leiden; New York: Brill, 1997-) 356-58.

[39] Baruch A. Levine and Jean-Michel de Tarragon, "Dead Kings and Rephaim: The Patrons of the Ugaritic Dynasty," *Journal of the American Oriental Society*, Vol. 104, No. 4 (Oct. - Dec., 1984), pp. 649-659

> all who were leaders of the earth;
> it raises from their thrones
> all who were kings of the nations.
>
> Ezek. 32:21
> They shall fall amid those who are slain by the sword… The mighty chiefs [*Rephaim*] shall speak of them, with their helpers, out of the midst of Sheol: "They have come down, they lie still, the uncircumcised, slain by the sword."

Hebrew scholar, Michael S. Heiser concludes about this connection of Rephaim with dead warrior kings in Sheol and Bashan:

> That the Israelites and the biblical writers considered the spirits of the dead giant warrior kings to be demonic is evident from the fearful aura attached to the geographical location of Bashan. As noted above, Bashan is the region of the cities Ashtaroth and Edrei, which both the Bible and the Ugaritic texts mention as abodes of the Rephaim. What's even more fascinating is that in the Ugaritic language, this region was known not as Bashan, but *Bathan*—the Semitic people of Ugarit pronounced the Hebrew "sh" as "th" in their dialect. Why is that of interest? Because "Bathan" is a common word across all the Semitic languages, biblical Hebrew included, for "serpent." The region of Bashan was known as "the place of the serpent." It was ground zero for the Rephaim giant clan and, spiritually speaking, the gateway to the abode of the infernal deified Rephaim spirits.[40]

Sons of Anak: Ahiman, Sheshai and Talmai

But the real enemy to overcome in Canaan was the Anakim, a powerful giant clan that seemed to dominate the southern region of the hill country. In fact, when the spies went on their forty day reconnaissance of the country, they came back with a report that told of the "Sons of Anak," who were giants that apparently had genetic roots in the original Nephilim before the Flood.

[40] Michael S. Heiser *The Myth That is True*, p 169. Available online at www.michaelsheiser.com.

Numbers 13:32–33
"The land, through which we have gone to spy it out, is a land that devours its inhabitants, and all the people that we saw in it are of great height. [33] And there we saw the Nephilim (the sons of Anak, who come from the Nephilim), and we seemed to ourselves like grasshoppers, and so we seemed to them."

These Anakim are referred to as being "of great height" making the Israelites feel "like grasshoppers" (Num. 13:33), their height was a standard of tallness that other giants are compared to (Deut. 2:10, 21), a people "great and tall" who had a reputation for being so mighty that no one could stand before them (Deut. 9:2).

Deuteronomy 9:2–3
[2] a people great and tall, the sons of the Anakim, whom you know, and of whom you have heard it said, 'Who can stand before the sons of Anak?' [3]

Joshua 14:15 adds that the city of Kiriath-arba, (later changed to the name Hebron), was founded by Arba, "the greatest among the Anakim." In Joshua 15:13 we discover that "Arba was the father of Anak," the original descendant of the Anakim. That is why I placed Arba many generations earlier as the founder of Kiriath-arba during the time of Abraham in the previous novel *Abraham Allegiant*. Since Abraham spent many of his years at the Oaks of Mamre, only two miles away from Kiriath-arba (Gen. 35:27), it was not too much of a leap to think that he had some contact with Arba, and maybe that was where a blood feud arose between the two peoples.

But then the Bible says that there were three very important Anakim who Caleb had ousted from Kiriath-arba when he conquered that key Anakite city. (Judg. 1:9–10)

Joshua 15:13–14
[13] He gave to Caleb the son of Jephunneh a portion among the people of Judah, Kiriath-arba, that is, Hebron (Arba was the father of Anak). [14] And Caleb drove out from there the three sons of Anak, Sheshai and Ahiman and Talmai, the descendants of Anak.

But there were also some interesting Jewish legends that added Ahiman as being the mightiest of the three.[41] Rabbinic tradition records Ahiman as challenging passers-by with the taunt, "Whose brother will fight with me?"[42] Sheshai and Talmai were said to make deep furrows or pits in the ground with their footsteps.[43]

I used these names of Sheshai, Ahiman, and Talmai, as brothers of a ruling Anakim family and chief villains in *Joshua Valiant* and *Caleb Vigilant*. These warriors must have been the most difficult to overcome for Israel since they received such a special mention in Scripture several times for their mighty prowess (Josh. 15:13–14; Num. 13:22; Judg. 1:9–10). This was the basis for my focus on these three in the novels as the ones to beat for Joshua and Caleb.

How Tall Were the Giants?

Most of the giants in *Joshua Valiant* and *Caleb Vigilant* are between eight and twelve feet tall. While some writers on the Nephilim have conjectured giants in Canaan to be as tall as thirty feet and higher, I think that is without Biblical, historical, or archaeological justification.[44]

The only sizes of giants that are specified in the Bible are that of Goliath ("6 cubits and a span" or 9 1/2 feet tall),[45] Og of Bashan (his bed of nine cubits long or 13 1/2 feet),[46] and an unnamed Egyptian giant "of great stature, five cubits tall" (7 1/2 feet).[47] These numbers are based on the cubit size in Scripture as being the "common" cubit of Canaan, which most scholars agree is about eighteen inches. But the definition of a cubit in that day was the span of a man's elbow to his forefinger, which was not uniform like we have today.

---

[41] b. Yoma 10A - Jacob Neusner, *The Babylonian Talmud: A Translation and Commentary*, vol. 5a (Peabody, MA: Hendrickson Publishers, 2011), 31.

[42] in Num. R. xvi. and Tan., Shelaḥ, 7, ed. Buber, 11 — Isidore Singer, ed., *The Jewish Encyclopedia: A Descriptive Record of the History, Religion, Literature, and Customs of the Jewish People from the Earliest Times to the Present Day*, 12 Volumes (New York; London: Funk & Wagnalls, 1901–1906), 552.

[43] b. Yoma 1:1, III.20.C-E: "C. Ahiman: the most skilled among the brothers. D. Sheshai: for he made the ground on which he walked into pits. E.Talmai: he made the ground full of ridges."

[44] Some interpreters take the obviously poetic phrase of the giants being "the height of the cedars" quite literally (Amos 2:9), and claim some giants could have been thirty six feet high or so. This kind of literalistic interpretation is naïve.

[45] 1Sam 17:4. Some scholars point out that the Septuagint (LXX), Dead Sea Scrolls and Josephus after them describe Goliath at only four cubits and a span, which would make him more like six feet six inches tall. But scholar Clyde Billington has pointed out that the DSS and Josephus took their cue from the LXX, which was written in Egypt, whose royal cubit was consistently at 20.65 inches. The result would then be over 9 feet tall. So rather than the Bible exaggerating for mythic effect, the later translators adjusted numbers to fit their local Egyptian measurements. Clyde E. Billington, "Goliath and The Exodus Giants: How Tall Were They?" *JETS*, 50/3 (September 2007) 489-508.

[46] Deut. 3:11.

[47] 1Chron. 11:23.

So in reality, those sizes are only approximations and could more likely be a bit larger.[48]

A further complication arises when one considers the fact that Moses had been raised and educated as royalty in Egypt. So he and the Exodus Israelites no doubt used the Egyptian royal cubit in their measurements. The question then is whether or not the Biblical text translated that cubit measurement to the smaller Mesopotamian/Levantine cubit or not. There is an indication in other Biblical texts of the awareness of this cubit difference. The writer of the Chronicles (written much later in Israel's history during the exile) makes this distinction when describing the dimensions of Solomon's temple. He writes that the "the length, in cubits *of the old standard*, was sixty cubits, and the breadth twenty cubits" (2 Chron. 3:3). Ezekiel, describing the measurements of the temple in his vision, also makes this distinction of cubit difference as well when he writes, "the altar by cubits (the cubit being a cubit and a handbreadth)" (Ezek. 43:13). He later calls this a "long cubit" (Ezek. 41:8). So these parentheticals written by authors around the time of the exile indicate that during that time, there was still an awareness of the older and longer Egyptian cubit as if they had been still using it up until that date.[49]

If we apply this longer cubit measurement to Goliath's 6 cubits and a span, we get a height of about 10 1/2 feet tall![50] And the Egyptian warrior that was killed by Benaiah (1 Chron. 11:23) 8 feet 6 inches tall. Remember Og of Bashan, whose bed was 9 cubits long? (Deut. 3:11). That would make his bed approximately 15 1/2 feet long and Og about 13 to 14 feet tall. The longer cubit however is most likely not being used in reference to Og's height since the text says it is measuring "according to the common cubit" as opposed to the longer royal cubit.

A few extra-Biblical sources add some more context to the size of Canaanite giants. The pseudepigraphal *Book of Jubilees*, when speaking of Og's kingdom of Rephaim, measures the giants from the size of 10 feet to 15 feet tall.

> Jubilees 29:9
> But before they used to call the land of Gilead the land of the Rephaim; for it was the land of the Rephaim, and the Rephaim

---

[48] John H. Walton, Zondervan *Illustrated Bible Backgrounds Commentary* (Old Testament): Joshua, Judges, Ruth, 1 & 2 Samuel, vol. 2 (Grand Rapids, MI: Zondervan, 2009), 347.

[49] Conservative scholars claim that Moses wrote the Pentateuch during the time of the Exodus, so that would most likely mean that the older longer cubit was used in those texts. Critical scholars claim that Moses did not write the Pentateuch, but that it was mostly written and/or compiled during the time of the Exile which would mean they most likely used the newer shorter cubit in the Pentateuch, but then made some reference to that older cubit in Chronicles and Ezekiel to remind their readers of the changeover.

[50] If this is the case, then the Septuagint translators misunderstood the cubit of the Hebrew text as being the smaller cubit, when in fact it was the larger Egyptian cubit. They would then be translating the number incorrectly downward.

> were born (there), giants whose height was ten, nine, eight down to seven cubits [10 1/2 feet to 15 feet tall].

One thirteenth-century Egyptian papyrus describes bedouin nomads in Canaan as being "four or five cubits (7 to 9 feet) from their nose to their foot and have fierce faces."[51]

First century Jewish historian Josephus wrote about the giants in Hebron or Kiriath-arba of Canaan as giants

> who had bodies so large, and countenances so entirely different from other men, that they were surprising to the sight, and terrible to the hearing. The bones of these men are still shown to this very day, unlike to any creditable relations of other men.[52]

Josephus also wrote of a Jew named Eleazar during the time of Tiberius who was 7 cubits tall (10 1/2 feet).[53]

Pliny, the Roman historian wrote of a giant during the time of Claudius named Gabbaras, who was over 9 feet tall.[54]

Greek historian Herodotus (ca. 430 B.C.) wrote of ancients finding a coffin ten feet long with human bones in it to match.[55]

A Greek geographer, Pausanias (ca. A.D. 150) wrote of Roman soldiers diverting the river Orontes in Syria finding a coffin more than 16 feet long with a corpse the size of it inside. The Orontes flows through Mount Hermon in the land of Bashan, where the Rephaim king Og ruled.[56]

Scholar Adrienne Mayor analyzes many other ancient accounts of the discovery of coffinless giant bones, some as big as sixty cubits tall, in her book *The First Fossil Hunters: Dinosaurs, Mammoths, and Myth in Greek and Roman Times.* She analyzes them only to reveal that most of them are mammoth and other ancient extinct fossils innocently misinterpreted as buried bones of giants by ancient man unaware of such prehistoric beasts.

---

[51] Edward Frank Wente and Edmund S. Meltzer, vol. 1, *Letters from Ancient Egypt*, Writings from the Ancient World, 108 (Atlanta, GA: Scholars Press, 1990).

[52] Antiquities 5.125. Flavius Josephus and William Whiston, *The Works of Josephus: Complete and Unabridged* (Peabody: Hendrickson, 1987).

[53] Josephus, *Antiquities* 18.4.5.

[54] Pliny the Elder, *The Natural History* 7.16, ed. John Bostock (Medford, MA: Taylor and Francis, Red Lion Court, Fleet Street, 1855), 2157.

[55] Herodotus (ca. 430 B.C.) *The Histories* 1.67–68. Quoted in Mayor, Adrienne (2011-07-27). *The First Fossil Hunters: Dinosaurs, Mammoths, and Myth in Greek and Roman Times* (New in Paper) (Kindle Locations 4672-4678). Princeton University Press. Kindle Edition.

[56] Pausanias, Guide to Greece, 8.29.1-4 referenced in *Mayor, Adrienne (2011-07-27). The First Fossil Hunters: Dinosaurs, Mammoths, and Myth in Greek and Roman Times (New in Paper) (Kindle Locations 4770-4778). Princeton University Press. Kindle Edition.*

In light of these ancient descriptions, I kept my giants within this more realistic range of 7 to 12 feet tall, with Ahiman being an anomaly of 15 feet high.

But the Bible does not merely mention giants as being generic bad guys in the land just because they are tall and mean. Joshua seems to be on a systematic search and destroy mission for the Anakim in particular, which as noted earlier in Numbers 13:33 was because they had direct ancestral ties to the evil Nephilim giants wiped out at the Flood.

> Joshua 11:21–22
> 21 And Joshua came at that time and cut off the Anakim from the hill country, from Hebron, from Debir, from Anab, and from all the hill country of Judah, and from all the hill country of Israel. Joshua devoted them to destruction with their cities.
> 22 There was none of the Anakim left in the land of the people of Israel. Only in Gaza, in Gath, and in Ashdod did some remain.

But since the Anakim were theologically tied to the Nephilim of Genesis 6, whose bloodguilt was partially responsible for the Flood, it makes sense that God would engage in a mop up operation on their giant descendants later. Interestingly, the giants left in Gaza and Gath, the land of the Philistines, would cause much pain for Israel in the time of the Judges and be wiped out finally by David, the symbolic type of Messiah, who would be the ultimate victor over the principalities and powers of this present darkness in the heavenly places. Christus Victor. But that is for the upcoming novels to reveal.

Caleb Vigilant

Appendix

Chapter 10
Canaanite Ba'al and Old Testament Storytelling Polemics

For many Christians, the word *apologetics* conjures a picture of defending the faith with philosophical arguments, archeological evidence, historical inquiry, and other rational and empirical forms of discourse. Apologetics also involves *polemics*, which are aggressive arguments against the opposition. Sometimes a good offense is the best defense. But what is often missed in some apologetic strategies is the Biblical use of imagination. This is illustrative of a distinct imbalance when one considers that the Bible is only about one-third propositional truth and about two-thirds imagination: image, metaphor, poetry, and story.[1]

With the discovery in the nineteenth and twentieth centuries of pagan religious texts from ancient Near Eastern (ANE) cultures such as Babylon, Assyria, and Ugarit, Biblical scholarship has discovered many literary parallels between Scripture and the literature of ancient Israel's enemies. The Hebrews shared many words, images, concepts, metaphors, and narrative genres in common with their neighbors. And those Hebrew authors of Scripture sometimes incorporated similar literary imagination into their text.

With regard to these Biblical and ancient Near Eastern literary parallels, liberal scholarship tends to stress the similarities, downplay the differences, and construct a theory of the evolution of Israel's religion from polytheism to monotheism.[2] In other words, liberal scholarship is anthropocentric, or human-centered.

Conservative scholarship tends to stress the differences, downplay the similarities, and interpret the evidence as indicative of the radical otherness of

[1] I discuss this fact and its ramifications in my book *Word Pictures: Knowing God Through Story and Imagination* (Downers Grove, IL: InterVarsity Press, 2009).
[2] A significant author of this view is Mark S. Smith, *The Origins of Biblical Monotheism: Israel's Polytheistic Background and the Ugaritic Texts* (Oxford: Oxford University, 2003).

Israelite religion.[3] In other words, conservative scholarship is theocentric, or God-centered. Both liberal and conservative hermeneutics err on opposite extremes.

The orthodox doctrine of the inspiration of Scripture states that it is composed of "God-breathed" human-written words (2 Tim. 3:16). Men wrote from God, moved by the Holy Spirit (2 Pet. 1:20-21). This is a "both/and" reality of humanly and heavenly authorship. While I affirm the heavenly side of God's Word, in this essay I will illustrate how the authors of the Old Testament used the imagination of their enemies as a polemic against those enemies' religion and deities. In my book, *Word Pictures: Knowing God through Story and Imagination*, I describe the nature of this subversive storytelling as the act of entering the opposition's cultural narrative, retelling it through their own paradigm, or worldview, and thereby capturing the cultural narrative. God used literary subversion in the Bible as a means of arguing against the false gods and idols of that time.

Baal in Canaan

In 1929, an archeological excavation at a mound in northern Syria called Ras Shamra unearthed the remains of a significant port city called Ugarit, whose developed culture reaches back as far as 3000 BC.[4] Among the important finds were literary tablets that opened the door to a deeper understanding of ancient Near Eastern culture and the Bible. Those tablets included Syro-Canaanite religious texts of pagan deities mentioned in the Old Testament. One of those deities was Baal (alternate spelling of Ba'al).

Though the Semitic noun *baal* means "lord" or "master," it was also used as the proper name of the Canaanite storm god.[5] In the Baal narrative cycle from Ugarit, El was the supreme "father of the gods," who lived on a cosmic mountain. A divine council of gods called "Sons of El" surrounded him, vying for position and power. When Sea is coronated by El and given a palace, Baal rises up and kills Sea, taking Sea's place as "Most High" over the other gods (excepting El). A temple is built and a feast celebrated. Death then insults Baal, who goes down to the underworld, only to be defeated by Death. But Anat, Baal's violent sister, seeks Death and cuts him up into pieces and brings

---

[3] A significant author of this view is Gleason L. Archer, *A Survey of Old Testament Introduction* (Chicago: Moody Press, 2007).

[4] Avraham Negev, "Ugarit," *The Archaeological Encyclopedia of the Holy Land*, 3rd ed. (New York: Prentice Hall Press, 1996).

[5] Karel van der Toorn, Bob Becking, and Pieter Willem van der Horst, *Dictionary of Deities and Demons in the Bible* (*DDD*), 2nd ext. rev. ed. (Grand Rapids: Eerdmans, 1999), 132.

Baal's body back up to earth where he is brought back to life, only to fight Death to a stalemate.[6]

The Dictionary of Deities and Demons in the Bible explains of Baal:

> "His elevated position shows itself in his power over clouds, storm and lightning, and manifests itself in his thundering voice. As the god of wind and weather Baal dispenses dew, rain, and snow and the attendant fertility of the soil. Baal's rule guarantees the annual return of the vegetation; as the god disappears in the underworld and returns in the autumn, so the vegetation dies and resuscitates with him."[7]

Baal in the Bible

In the Bible, Baal is used both as the name of a specific deity[8] and as a generic term for multiple idols worshipped by apostate Israel.[9] It was also used in conjunction with city names and locations, such as Baal-Hermon and Baal-Zaphon, indicating manifestations of the one deity worshipped in a variety of different Canaanite situations.[10] Simply speaking, in Canaan, Baal was all over the place. He was the chief god of the land.

On entering Canaan, Yahweh gave specific instructions to the Israelites to destroy all of the places where the Canaanites worshipped, along with their altars and images (Deut. 12:1-7). They were to "destroy the names" of the foreign idols and replace them with Yahweh's name and habitation (vv. 3-4). God warned them, "Take care lest your heart be deceived, and you turn aside and serve other gods and worship them" (Deut. 11:16).

Yet, turning to other gods in worship is exactly what the Israelites did—over and over again. No sooner had the people settled in Canaan than they began to adopt Baal worship into their culture. The book of Judges describes this cycle of idolatry under successive leaders.[11] In the ninth century BC, Elijah fought against rampant Baal worship throughout Israel (1Kings 18). In the eighth century, Hosea decried the adulterous intimacy that both Judah and Israel had with Baal (Hos. 2:13, 16-17), and in the seventh century, Jeremiah battled with an infestation of it in Judah (Jer. 2:23; 32:35).

Baal worship was so cancerous throughout Israel's history that Yahweh would have to intervene periodically with dramatic displays of authority in

---

[6] N. Wyatt, *Religious Texts from Ugarit*, 2nd ed., The Biblical Seminar, vol. 53 (London: Sheffield Academic Press, 2002), 36-39.
[7] "Baal," *DDD*, 134.
[8] Judges 6; 1 Kings 18; 2 Kings 10.
[9] Judges 2:13; 1 Samuel 12:10; Jeremiah 2:23.
[10] "Baal," *DDD*, 136.
[11] Judges 2:11; 3:7; 8:33.

order to stem the infection that polluted the congregation of the Lord. Gideon's miraculous deliverances from the Baal-loving Midianites (Judges 6-8) and Elijah's encounter with the prophets of Baal (1Kings 18) are just a couple examples of Yahweh's real-world polemic against Baal. But physical battles and miraculous signs and wonders are not the only way God waged war against Baal in ancient Canaan. He also used story, image, and metaphor. He used literary imagination.

Yahweh Vs. Baal

Literary subversion was common in the ancient world to affect the overthrow or overshadowing of one deity and worldview with another. For example, the high goddess Inanna, considered Queen of Heaven in ancient Sumeria, was replaced by her Babylonian counterpart, Ishtar. An important Sumerian text, *The Descent of Inanna into the Underworld*, was rewritten by the Babylonians as *the Descent of Ishtar into the Underworld* to accommodate their goddess Ishtar.[12] The Babylonian creation epic, *Enuma Elish* tells the story of the Babylonian deity Marduk and his ascendancy to power in the Mesopotamian pantheon.[13] And then when King Sennacherib of Assyria conquered Babylon around 689 BC, Assyrian scribes rewrote the *Enuma Elish* and replaced the name of Marduk with Assur, their chief god.[14]

Picture this scenario: The Israelites have left Egypt where Yahweh literally mocked and defeated the gods of Egypt through the ten plagues (Exod. 12:12; Num. 33:4). Pharaoh claimed to be a god, who according to Egyptian texts, was the "possessor of a strong arm" and a "strong hand."[15] So when Yahweh repeatedly hammers home the message that Israel will be delivered by Yahweh's "strong arm" and "strong hand," the polemical irony is not hard to spot. Yahweh used subversive literary imagery, which in effect said, "Pharaoh is not God, I am God." Nothing like an arm wrestling match to show who is stronger.

But now, God is leading Israel into the Promised Land, which is very different from where they came, with very different gods. "For the land that you are entering to take possession of it is not like the land of Egypt, from which you have come, where you sowed your seed and irrigated it, like a garden of vegetables. But the land that you are going over to possess is a land

---

[12] Stephanie Dalley, trans., *Myths from Mesopotamia: Creation, The Flood, Gilgamesh and Others* (New York: Oxford University Press, 1989, 2000, 2008), 154-62. The Sumerian version can be found in Jeremy Black, trans., *The Literature of Ancient Sumer* (New York: Oxford University Press **2004, 2006**), 65-76.

[13] Alexander Heidel, trans., *The Babylonian Genesis* (Chicago: University of Chicago, 1942, 1951, 1963), 14.

[14] C. Jouco Bleeker and Geo Widengren, eds., *Historia Religionum I: Religions of the Past* (Leiden, Netherlands: E. J. Brill, 1969), 134.

[15] John D. Currid, *Ancient Egypt and the Old Testament* (Grand Rapids: Baker; 1997), 83.

of hills and valleys, which drinks water by the rain from heaven" (Deut. 11:10-11). And the god of rain from heaven in this new land was believed to be the storm god, Baal.[16]

Now the Biblical text begins to reflect that storm god language in its reference to Israel's god, Yahweh. Let's take a look at some Ugaritic texts will give us a literary description of the Baal that Israel faced in Canaan. A side-by-side sampling of those Ugaritic texts with Scripture illustrates a strong reflection of Canaanite echoes in the Biblical storytelling.

UGARITIC TEXTS[17]	OLD TESTAMENT
Baal sits... in the midst of his divine mountain, Saphon, in the midst of the mountain of victory. Seven lightning-flashes, eight bundles of thunder, a tree-of-lightning in his right hand. His head is magnificent, His brow is dew-drenched. his feet are eloquent in wrath. (KTU 1.101:1-6)[18]	Yahweh came from Sinai... At His right hand there was flashing lightning... There is none like the God of Jeshurun, Who rides the heavens to your help, And through the clouds in His majesty... And He drove out the enemy from before you, And said, 'Destroy!'... In a land of grain and new wine; His heavens also drop down dew. (Deut. 33:2, 26-28)
The season of his rains may Baal indeed appoint, the season of his storm-chariot. And the sound of his voice from the clouds, his hurling to the earth of lightning-flashes (KTU 1.4:5.5-9) At his holy voice the earth quaked; at the issue of his lips the mountains were afraid... the hills of the earth tottered. (KTU 1.4:7.30-35)	The voice of the LORD is over the waters; the God of glory thunders, the LORD, over many waters... The voice of the LORD breaks the cedars; the LORD breaks the cedars of Lebanon... The voice of the LORD flashes forth flames of fire [lightning]. The voice of the LORD shakes the wilderness...
now your foe, Baal, now your foe the Sea you must smite; now you must destroy your adversary! Take your everlasting kingdom, your eternal dominion! (KTU 1.2:4.9-10)	And in His temple everything says, "Glory!" Yahweh sits enthroned over the flood; Yahweh is enthroned as King forever. (Ps. 29:3-11)

[16] Fred E. Woods, *Water and Storm Polemics against Baalism in the Deuteronomic History*, American University Studies, Series VII, Theology and Religion (New York: Peter Lange Publishing, 1994), 32-35.
[17] The abbreviation *KTU* stands for "Keilalphabetische Texte aus Ugarit", the standard collection of this material from Ugarit.
[18] All these Ugaritic texts can be found in N. Wyatt, *Religious Texts from Ugarit*, 2nd ed., The Biblical Seminar, vol. 53 (London: Sheffield Academic Press, 2002).

Like the usage of Yahweh's "strong arm" to poetically argue against the so-called "strong arm" of Pharaoh, Yahweh inspires His authors to use water and storm language to reflect God's polemic against the so-called storm god, Baal.

Comparing the texts yields identical words, memes, and metaphors that suggest God is engaging in polemics against Baal through scriptural imagery and storytelling. It is not Baal who rides his cloud chariot from his divine mountain Saphon (Sapan), it is Yahweh who rides the clouds as a chariot from mount Sinai. It is not Baal who hurls lightning flashes in wrath; it is Yahweh whose lightning flashes destroy His enemies. It is not Baal whose dew-drenched brow waters the land of Canaan; it is Yahweh who drops dew from heaven to Canaan. It is not Baal's voice that thunders and conquers the waters resulting in his everlasting temple enthronement; it is Yahweh whose voice thunders and conquers the waters resulting in His everlasting temple enthronement.

Psalm 29 (quoted in part above) is so replete with poetry in common with Canaanite poetry that many ANE scholars have concluded it is a Canaanite hymn to Baal that has been rewritten with the name Baal replaced by the name Yahweh.[19] God was not only *physically* dispossessing Canaan of its inhabitants; He was *literarily* dispossessing the Canaanite gods as well. Old Testament appropriation of Canaanite culture is a case of subversion, not syncretism—overthrowing cultural narratives as opposed to blending with them.

A closer look at comparing just two elements of the Baal cycle with Yahweh's story will yield a clearer picture of the literary subversion of the Canaanite narrative that God and the human authors were employing. Those two elements are the epithet of "cloud-rider" and God's conflict with the dragon and the sea.

Cloud-Rider

In the Ugaritic text cited above, we are introduced to Baal as one who rides the heavens in his cloud-chariot dispensing judgment from the heights. "Charioteer (or 'Rider') of the Clouds" was a common epithet ascribed to Baal throughout the Ugaritic texts. Here is another side-by-side comparison of Ugaritic and Biblical texts that illustrate that common motif.

UGARITIC TEXTS	OLD TESTAMENT
'Dry him up. O Valiant Baal! Dry him up, O Charioteer [Rider] of the Clouds! For our captive is Prince Yam [Sea], for our captive is Ruler Nahar [River]!'	"[Yahweh] bowed the heavens also, and came down With thick darkness under His feet. And He rode on a cherub and flew; And He appeared on the wings of the wind.

[19] Aloysius Fitzgerald, "A Note on Psalm 29," *Bulletin of the American Schools of Oriental Research*, no. 215 (October 1974), 62. A more conservative interpretation claims a common Semitic poetic discourse.

(KTU 1.2:4.8-9)	He made darkness canopies around Him, A mass of waters, thick clouds of the sky. (Sam. 22:7-12)
What manner of enemy has arisen against Baal, of foe against the Charioteer of the Clouds? [then, he judges other deities] Surely I smote…Yam [Sea]? Surely I exterminated Nahar [River], the mighty god? Surely I lifted up the dragon, I overpowered him? I smote the writhing serpent, Encircler-with-seven-heads! (KTU 1.3:3.38-41)	[Yahweh] makes the clouds His chariot; He walks upon the wings of the wind; (Ps. 104:3-4) Behold, the LORD is riding on a swift cloud and is about to come to Egypt; The idols of Egypt will tremble at His presence, (Isa. 19:1)

Yahweh is described here with the same exact moniker as Baal, in the same exact context as Baal—revealed in the storm and riding a cloud in judgment on other deities. Baal is subverted by Yahweh.

This correlation of deity with cloud judgment sheds light on the vision of Daniel's Son of Man that Christians understand as a reference to Jesus Christ.[20] The everlasting dominion received by the divine Baal riding the clouds before the throne of the High God El is apologetically ascribed to the divine Son of Man (Jesus Christ) riding the clouds to the throne of "Elyon," the Ancient of Days.[21]

> Dan. 7:13-14
> "I kept looking in the night visions,
> And behold, with the clouds of heaven
> One like a Son of Man was coming,
> And He came up to the Ancient of Days
> And was presented before Him.
> "And to Him was given dominion,
> Glory and a kingdom…
> His dominion is an everlasting dominion.

Yahweh is God, not the Canaanite El. Jesus is Yahweh's son, as opposed to Baal being El's son. And that "Son of Man" is the one who is given a kingdom of everlasting dominion, not Baal.

---

[20] This also sheds light on Jesus' prophecy regarding his coming judgment on Israel at the destruction of the Temple: "and they will see the Son of Man coming on the clouds of heaven with power and great glory" (Matt 24:30).

[21] The Hebrew word for "Highest One" used in Daniel 7 is *Elyon*, which is the Hebrew equivalent of *Aliyan* in Ugaritic - another frequently used epithet of Baal! "Aliyan," *DDD*, p 18.

The Dragon and the Sea

The second narrative element of the Canaanite Baal cycle that I want to address is God's conflict with the dragon and the sea. In ancient Near Eastern religious mythologies, the sea and the sea dragon were symbols of chaos that had to be overcome to bring order to the universe, or more exactly, the political world order of the myth's originating culture. Some scholars call this battle *Chaoskampf*—the divine struggle to create order out of chaos.[22] Creation accounts were often veiled polemics for the establishment of a king or kingdom's claim to sovereignty.[23] Richard Clifford quotes, "In Mesopotamia, Ugarit, and Israel the *Chaoskampf* appears not only in cosmological contexts but just as frequently—and this was fundamentally true right from the first—in political contexts. The repulsion and the destruction of the enemy, and thereby the maintenance of political order, always constitute one of the major dimensions of the battle against chaos."[24]

For example, the Sumerians had three stories where the gods Enki, Ninurta, and Inanna all destroy sea monsters in their pursuit of establishing order. The sea monster in two of those versions, according to Sumerian expert Samuel Noah Kramer, is "conceived as a large serpent which lived in the bottom of the 'great below' where the latter came in contact with the primeval waters."[25] In the Babylonian creation myth, *Enuma Elish*, Marduk battles the sea dragon goddess Tiamat, and splits her body into two parts, creating the heavens and the earth, the world order over which Babylon's deity Marduk ruled.

Another side-by-side comparison of those same Ugaritic passages that we considered above with *other* Old Testament passages reveals another common narrative: Yahweh, the charioteer of the clouds, metaphorically battles with Sea (Hebrew: *yam*) and River (Hebrew: *nahar*), just as Baal struggled with Yam and Nahar, which is also linked to victory over a sea dragon/serpent.

UGARTIC TEXTS	OLD TESTAMENT
'Dry him up. O Valiant Baal! Dry him up, O Charioteer of the Clouds! For our captive is Prince Yam [Sea], for our captive is Ruler Nahar [River]!' (KTU 1.2:4.8-9)[26]	Did Yahweh rage against the rivers (*nahar*) Or was Your anger against the rivers (*nahar*), Or was Your wrath against the sea (*yam*), That You rode on Your horses,

[22] Hermann Gunkel first suggested this theme in *Schöpfung und Chaos in Urzdt und Endzeit* (1895).
[23] Bruce R. Reichenbach, "Genesis 1 as a Theological-Political Narrative of Kingdom Establishment," *Bulletin for Biblical Research* 13, 1 (2003).
[24] Clifford, *Creation Accounts*, 8, n. 13.
[25] Samuel Noah Kramer, *Sumerian Mythology: A Study of Spiritual and Literary Achievement in the Third Millennium B.C.* (Philadelphia: University of Pennsylvania Press, 1944, 1961, 1972), 77-78.
[26] "Charioteer of the Clouds" also appears in these texts: KTU 1.3:4:4, 6, 26; 1.4:3:10, 18; 1.4:5:7, 60; 1.10:1:7; 1.10:3:21, 36; 1.19:1:43; 1.92:37, 39.

What manner of enemy has arisen against Baal, of foe against the Charioteer of the Clouds? Surely I smote the Beloved of El, Yam [Sea]? Surely I exterminated Nahar [River], the mighty god? Surely I lifted up the dragon, I overpowered him? I smote the writhing serpent, Encircler-with-seven-heads! (KTU 1.3:3.38-41)	On Your chariots of salvation? (Hab. 3:8) In that day Yahweh will punish Leviathan the fleeing serpent, With His fierce and great and mighty sword, Even Leviathan the twisted serpent; And He will kill the dragon who lives in the sea. (Isa. 27:1) "You divided the sea by your might; you broke the heads of the sea monsters on the waters. You crushed the heads of Leviathan. (Ps. 74:13-14)

Baal fights Sea and River to establish his sovereignty. He wins by drinking up Sea and River, draining them dry, and thus establishing his supremacy over the pantheon and the Canaanite world order.[27] In the second passage, Baal's battle with Sea and River is retold in other words as a battle with a "dragon," the "writhing serpent" with seven heads.[28] Another Baal text calls this same dragon, "*Lotan*, the wriggling serpent."[29] The Hebrew equivalents of the Ugaritic words *tannin* (dragon) and *lotan* are *tannin* (dragon) and *liwyatan* (Leviathan) respectively.[30] Thus, the Canaanite narrative of Leviathan the sea dragon or serpent is undeniably employed in Old Testament Scriptures.[31] Notice the last Scripture in the chart that refers to Leviathan as having multiple heads *just like the Canaanite Leviathan*.

And notice as well the reference to the Red Sea event also associated with Leviathan in the Biblical text. In Psalm 74 above, God's parting of the waters is connected to the motif of the Mosaic covenant as the creation of a new world order in the same way that Baal's victory over the waters and the dragon are emblematic of his establishment of authority in the Canaanite pantheon. This covenant motif is described as a *Chaoskampf* battle with the Sea and Leviathan (also called *Rahab*) in several other significant Biblical references as well.[32]

---

[27] KTU 1.2:4:27-32.
[28] See KTU 1.5:1:1-35.
[29] KTU 1.5:1:1-4.
[30] Walter C. Kaiser, Jr., *The Ugaritic Pantheon* (dissertation) (Ann Arbor, MI: Brandeis University, 1973), 212.
[31] See also Isaiah 51:9; Ezekiel 32:2; Revelation 12:9, 16, 17.
[32] Psalm 89:9-10; Isaiah 51:9-10; Job 26:12-13. Psalms 18, 29, 24, 29, 65, 74, 77, 89, 93, and 104 all reflect *chaoskampf*. See also Exodus 15, Job 9, 26, 38, and Isaiah 51:14-16; 2 Samuel 22.

Mount Zaphon/Sapan

Another element of Baal's reign that was touched upon is his mountain abode of Mount Sapan or Saphon (*Zaphon* in Hebrew). As illustrated in the passages above, a plethora of Ugaritic texts link Baal with his "divine mountain, Saphon/Sapan" (KTU 1.101:1-9; 1.100:9; 1.3:3:29), that he is buried there (KTU 1.6:1:15-18), in his sanctuary (KTU 1.3:3:30), and mountain of victory (KTU 1.101:1-4). Earlier Hurrian and Hittite traditions of Baal link Mount Zaphon with another mountain, Namni, both in the northern Syrian ranges.[33]

This linking of the two mountains is of particular importance because as the *Dictionary of Deities and Demons in the Bible* explains, the Psalmist asserts Yahweh's authority as creator and therefore owner of all the heavens and the earth by referring to the mountains of pagan mythology as under the lordship of Yahweh.

> Psalm 89:12
> The north (zaphon) and the south (yamin), you have created them; Tabor and Hermon joyously praise your name.

Tabor and Hermon are well-known holy mountains in ANE mythology.[34] But the deliberate linking of *Zaphon* and *Yamin* are most likely Hebrew references to the Saphon and Namni of Ugarit in a symbolic reflection of Tabor and Hermon.

In Isaiah 14:13, Isaiah mocks the arrogance of the king of Babylon by likening him to another mythological figure, Athtar, who sought to take Baal's throne and failed "on the mountain of assembly on the summit of Zaphon [Sapan]."[35]

In the Bible, this Mount Zaphon is subverted by Israel's holy Mount Zion.

> Psalm 48:1–2
> Great is the LORD and greatly to be praised in the city of our God! His holy mountain, beautiful in elevation, is the joy of all the earth, Mount Zion, in the far north [Zaphon], the city of the great King.

---

[33] H. Niehr, "Zaphon", in *Dictionary of Deities and Demons in the Bible*, ed. Karel van der Toorn, Bob Becking and Pieter W. van der Horst, 2nd extensively rev. ed., 927 (Leiden; Boston; Köln; Grand Rapids, MI; Cambridge: Brill; Eerdmans, 1999).

[34] Rami Arav, "Hermon, Mount (Place)," ed. David Noel Freedman, *The Anchor Yale Bible Dictionary* (New York: Doubleday, 1992), 158.

[35] Michael Heiser, "The Mythological Provenance of Isaiah 14:12-15: A Reconsideration of the Ugaritic Material" Liberty University <http://digitalcommons.liberty.edu/lts fac pubs/280>

Note in this Scripture that the holy Mount Zion is described as being in "the far north," the very location of Mount Sapan, but not in fact the actual location of Israel's Mount Zion. So "the far north" is a theological not a geographical designation of Zion replacing Sapan as the divine mountain par excellence.[36]

Subverting Paganism

The story of deity battling the river, the sea, and the sea dragon Leviathan is clearly a common covenant motif in the Old Testament and its surrounding ancient Near Eastern cultures. The fact that Hebrew Scripture shares common words, concepts, and stories with Ugaritic scripture need not mean that Israel is affirming the same mythology or pantheon of deities. The orthodox Christian need not fear literary similarity between Israel and Canaanite imagination. Common imagination springs from what Old Testament scholar John Walton calls a "common cognitive environment" of people in a shared space, time, or culture.

Walton suggests "borrowing is not the issue…Likewise this need not concern whose ideas are derivative. There is simply common ground across the cognitive environment of the cultures of the ancient world."[37]

The story of a cloud-rider controlling the elements and battling the Sea and Leviathan to establish his sovereignty over other gods with a new world order is not a false "myth." It is a narrative shared between Israel and its pagan neighbors that Jewish authors appropriate, under divine authority of Yahweh, as a metaphor within their own discourse. God uses that cultural connection to subvert those words, concepts, and stories with His own poetic meaning and purpose.

Great fathers of the Faith utilized this same subversive storytelling. Curtis Chang, in his book, *Engaging Unbelief*, explains how Augustine wrote his *City of God* to defend the Christian faith in the Roman Empire in terms of urban historical narrative saturated with references, motifs, and themes from classical Roman authors. He subverted that "City of Man" by revealing the destructive pride lurking behind all human social construction. Aquinas, in his *Summa contra Gentiles*, appealed to the Aristotelian story of knowledge because he was addressing a Muslim culture steeped in Aristotle. But he

---

[36] H. Niehr, "Zaphon", in *Dictionary of Deities and Demons in the Bible*, ed. Karel van der Toorn, Bob Becking and Pieter W. van der Horst, 2nd extensively rev. ed., 929 (Leiden; Boston; Köln; Grand Rapids, MI; Cambridge: Brill; Eerdmans, 1999). Also see Job 26:7; 37:22; Ezek. 1:4 where the word "north" is used as a spiritual reference, more allusion to the divine mountain Saphon of Canaanite belief.

[37] John H. Walton, *Ancient Near Eastern Thought and the Old Testament: Introducing the Conceptual World of the Hebrew Bible* (Grand Rapids: Baker, 2006), 21.

subverted that cultural narrative by teasing out the ultimate insufficiency of human reason.

Campus evangelist Curtis Chang explains this rhetorical strategy as threefold: "1. Entering the challenger's story, 2. Retelling the story, 3. Capturing that retold tale with the gospel metanarrative."[38] He writes that the challenge of each epoch in history is a contest in storytelling, a challenge to "overturn and supplant the inherited story of the epoch with its own metanarrative…The one who can tell the best story, in a very real sense, wins the epoch."[39]

The defense of the gospel in this hostile epoch requires muscular Christians to enter into the narratives of our culture and retell those stories with bold fresh perspectives. I have repeatedly used J. R. R. Tolkien and C. S. Lewis as examples of subversive authors who entered into the genres and mythology of pagan worlds to harness them for Christian imagination. Tolkien's Middle Earth abounded with the mythical Norse characters of wizards, dwarves, elves, giants, trolls, and others. Lewis's Narnia is saturated with a plethora of beasts from assorted pagan mythologies, deliberately subjugated to the Lordship of Aslan.

I am a filmmaker, so I think in terms of movies. We need more storytellers to tell vampire stories with a Christian worldview (*The Addiction*); more zombie stories with a Christian worldview (*I Am Legend*); more demonic stories with Christian redemption (M. Night Shyamalan's *Devil*); more post-apocalyptic thrillers that honor God (*The Book of Eli*); more subversion of adultery (*Fatal Attraction*), fornication (*17 Again*), unbelief (*Paranormal Activity*), paganism (*Apocalypto*), humanistic anti-supernaturalism (*The Last Exorcism*), and our "pro-Choice" culture of death (*The Island*).

I will end with a question and a charge. With two exceptions, why were all these movies that subversively incarnate the Christian worldview made by non-Christians instead of Christians? Rise up, O Christian storytellers and subvert ye the world's imagination!

---

[38] Curtis Chang, *Engaging Unbelief: A Captivating Strategy from Augustine to Aquinas* (Downers Grove, IL: InterVarsity Press, 2000), 26.
[39] Ibid., 27.

David Ascendant

Appendix

Chapter 11
Goliath Was Not Alone

David Ascendant tells the story of a league of giant assassins who seek to kill King David during his reign as the ruler of Israel. Goliath is only one of them, and when his brother Lahmi, another giant, discovers David killed his sibling, he sets out to kill the Israelite leader for both revenge and to stop the messiah king from securing victory over the Philistines and ownership over all of Canaan.

As much as I admit creative license in my adaptation of Scriptural story, my goal for the entire saga *Chronicles of the Nephilim* is to faithfully retell those stories of the Bible that touch on the giants and the War of the Seed as expressed in Genesis 3:15 through God's curse upon the Serpent: "I will put enmity between you and the woman, and between your offspring [Seed] and her offspring [Seed]; he shall bruise your head, and you shall bruise his heel."

My goal has been to bring to light all these Biblical references to giants (ala, *Chronicles of the Nephilim*) that hint at that cosmic war of principalities and powers against the Biblical God, Yahweh and his victorious Messiah. My standard for deciding which stories to tell was only those that had explicit or implicit references to the Nephilim giants and their progeny in the Bible. Admittedly, Scriptural references to the giants are sparse, but they are significant and seem to hint at this War of the Seed that I have been writing about.

In *Noah Primeval* and *Enoch Primordial*, I retold the story of the Flood based on Genesis 6 and the book of 1 Enoch that the New Testament uses as source material. In *Gilgamesh Immortal*, I retold the pagan myth about a giant king as a prelude or origin story of the Biblical uber-villain, Nimrod. Then in *Abraham Allegiant*, I expanded on that villain and his building of the Tower of Babel and how it wove into the Divine Council worldview of God allotting territory to fallen Watchers. These were the same Watchers who sought to use the giants as the "Seed of the Serpent" to corrupt the earth and destroy the bloodline of God's people and his Messiah. The giant clans are referenced in

Genesis 14 and the Watcher/human copulation is hinted at in the Sodom and Gomorrah episode in Genesis 19. Abraham settled right near the city of Kiriath-arba, later called Hebron (Gen. 13:18). Kiriath-arba was the city of King Arba, forefather of the Anakim giants that Joshua would battle (Josh. 14:15, 15:13). That is a subtle but critical theological fact that is easily overlooked by less rigorous Bible study. The Sons of Anak and the Sons of Abraham had a history together that went back to Arba and Abraham, their forefathers. Or in other words, the Seed of the Serpent and the Seed of Eve.

In *Joshua Valiant* and *Caleb Vigilant*, I retold the conquest of the Promised Land, where the Bible indicates a deliberate targeting of giant clans by Joshua for eradication (Joshua 11:21-22). We even read about specific giants in Scripture who were mighty opponents of this campaign, such as the Rephaim giant king Og of Bashan (Deut. 3:1-11), and the Anakim giant warriors; Ahiman, Sheshai, and Talmai (Num. 13:22; Josh. 15:14; Judges 1:10). Again, we are not told the details of these giant warriors, so I filled in between the lines of Scripture with story that would be consistent with those lines, making those apparently random historical "factoids" more meaningful in the big picture of God's plans. I connected the dots that our western Christian bias might miss because of our lack of ancient Near Eastern Jewish context.

As much as I assume there had to be giants in Canaan during the time of the book of Judges, none are actually mentioned in that Biblical tome, so my saga must jump from the story of Joshua's conquest of Canaan to the next Scriptural occurrence of giants, which is in the life of David.

Goliath and Giants Galore

In King David's story there are five passages that contain giants in the narrative. The most famous one is 1 Samuel 17 that tells the story of Goliath. In fact, that story is so famous, it seems that some Christians think he's the only giant in the Bible! Others say he wasn't much of a giant at all. That's because there are textual problems with the sources we have for the English text of the Old Testament.

In 1 Samuel 17:4, Goliath is described as being "6 cubits and a span." Scholarly consensus describes the "cubit" as being approximately 18 inches, measured by the distance between an average man's elbow and forefinger. A "span" is about half of that length, which is about the distance of an outstretched hand, or 9 inches. So by these standards, Goliath's "6 cubits and a span" was about 9 feet, 9 inches tall.

But there is a problem with that measurement. The 6 1/2 cubit dimension is taken from the Hebrew Masoretic Texts (MT), which are not always the most reliable in their transmission history. Some scholars point out that the Septuagint (LXX), the Dead Sea Scrolls, and Josephus after them describe Goliath at only "4 cubits and a span," which would make him more like 6 feet, 9 inches tall. According to archeological estimates of discovered remains in Canaan, the average Jew was about 5 feet, 6 inches tall.[1] This shorter version of Goliath would still be a tall man compared to the average ancient Jew, but not at all the supernatural monstrosity of 9 feet, 9 inches tall.

But scholar Clyde Billington has pointed out that the DSS and Josephus took their cue from the LXX, which was translated in Egypt. Egypt's royal cubit was consistently at 20.65 inches.[2] It is entirely reasonable that the LXX translators would adjust the Biblical numbers to coincide with their own definitions of measurement. Using the Egyptian cubit would make Goliath's height from the LXX come out to 7 feet 9 inches, not as tall as the MT, but a giant nonetheless..

A further complication arises when one considers the fact that Moses had been raised and educated as royalty in Egypt. So he and the Exodus Israelites no doubt used the Egyptian royal cubit in their measurements. The question then is whether or not the *original* Hebrew text translated that cubit measurement to the smaller Mesopotamian/Levantine cubit.

There is an indication in other Biblical texts of the awareness of this cubit difference. The writer of the Chronicles (written much later in Israel's history during the exile) makes this distinction when describing the dimensions of Solomon's temple. He writes, "the length, in cubits *of the old standard*, was sixty cubits, and the breadth twenty cubits" (2 Chron. 3:3). Ezekiel describing the measurements of the temple in his vision also makes this distinction of cubit difference as well when he writes, "the altar by cubits (the cubit being a cubit and a handbreadth)" (Ezek. 43:13). He later calls this a "long cubit" (Ezek. 41:8). So these parentheticals written by authors around the time of the exile indicate that during that time, there was still an awareness of the older longer Egyptian cubit as if they had been still using it up until that date.[3]

If we apply this longer cubit measurement to Goliath's 9 cubits and a span, we get a height of about 10 1/2 feet tall![4] Remember Og of Bashan, whose bed

---

[1] G. Ernest Wright, "Troglodytes and Giants in Palestine," *Journal of Biblical Literature* 57:3 (Sept 1938): 305-309.

[2] Clyde E. Billington, "Goliath and The Exodus Giants: How Tall Were They?" *JETS*, 50/3 (September 2007) 489-508.

[3] Conservative scholars claim that Moses wrote the Pentateuch during the time of the Exodus, so that would most likely mean that the older longer cubit was used in those texts. Critical scholars claim that Moses did not write the Pentateuch, but that it was mostly written and/or compiled during the time of the Exile which would mean they most likely used the newer shorter cubit in the Pentateuch, but then made some reference to that older cubit in Chronicles and Ezekiel to remind their readers of the changeover.

[4] If this is the case, then the Septuagint translators misunderstood the cubit of the Hebrew text as being the smaller cubit, when in fact it was the larger Egyptian cubit. They would then be translating the number incorrectly downward.

was 9 cubits long? (Deut. 3:11). That would make his bed approximately 15 1/2 feet long and Og about 13 to 14 feet tall.[5] And the Egyptian warrior that was killed by Benaiah (1 Chron. 11:23) 8 feet 6 inches tall.

Whichever way one measures a cubit, Goliath was a giant. But that is not the only controversy surrounding that rabid Rephaim Gittite of old.

In 2 Samuel 21 we read a description of several giant warriors who were killed by David's Mighty Men (*gibborim*). But verse 19 is a disturbing sentence that seems to contradict David's slaying of Goliath. It says, "And there was again war with the Philistines at Gob, and Elhanan the son of Jaare-oregim, the Bethlehemite, struck down Goliath the Gittite, the shaft of whose spear was like a weaver's beam."

Well, who was it that killed Goliath, then? Was it David or Elhanan? Critical scholars use this single difficult text to justify constructing a complex conspiracy theory that David didn't exist and that Elhanan killed Goliath, but the Jewish writer then attributed it to a fictional "David" but forgot to make that change in this passage.

On the other side of desperate conspiracy theories are desperate hyper-literalist harmonizers who conclude that either Elhanan was another name for David or that there was a second Goliath of Gath who was killed by a different warrior later than David. But the lack of a David/Elhanan connection anywhere else in the Bible and the clear coincidence of redundant language about Goliath are no less biased in their attempts to harmonize.

Desperate conspiracies and harmonies aside, the problem needs a reasonable answer. And there is one. 1 Chronicles 20:4-8 is a rewrite of the same historical information in 2 Sam. 21:16-22. They are passages that have clearly used the same source with some modifications. They talk about the same Israelite warriors killing the same giants. But there are some slight differences. And the biggest difference is where the Chronicler addresses that sentence about Elhanan's victory over the giant. Here are the two passages after one another to make the point:

> 2 Samuel 21:19
> 19 And there was again war with the Philistines at Gob, and Elhanan the son of Jaare-oregim, the Bethlehemite, struck down Goliath the Gittite, the shaft of whose spear was like a weaver's beam.

---

[5] The longer cubit however is most likely not being used in reference to Og's height since the text says it is measuring "according to the common cubit" as opposed to the royal cubit.

> 1 Chronicles 20:5
> [5] And there was again war with the Philistines, and Elhanan the son of Jair struck down Lahmi the brother of Goliath the Gittite, the shaft of whose spear was like a weaver's beam.

1 Chronicles 20 says that Elhanan struck down *Lahmi the brother of Goliath*, not Goliath! So was it Elhanan or David? Did they kill Goliath or his brother Lahmi?

In short, the answer is quite simply that 2 Samuel 21 is the problematic text as the result of scribal error. Michael Heiser, a Biblical language scholar, explains the forensic anatomy of the scribal mishap. He looks at the Hebrew behind the texts and shows how the Hebrew words for "son of Jaare-oregim, the Bethlemite," (1 Sam.) and "Lahmi the brother of" (1 Chron.) contain very similar Hebrew constructions that show the writer of 2 Samuel confusing the word for weaver (oregim) and adding it to Jair, and then misconstruing the Hebrew word for Lahmi as meaning Bethlehemite. The writer of 2 Samuel had a defective text and tried to fix it. In so doing, he created the problem that we now have.

Heiser's conclusion:

> The solution to the contradiction between 2 Sam 21:19 and 1 Chr 20:5 is recognizing that 2 Sam 21:19 is a defective reading since it is the result of a scribe's sincere effort to cope with a problematic manuscript…1 Chr 20:5 should be used to correct 2 Sam 21:19. David killed Goliath as 1 Samuel 17 says, and Elhanan killed Lahmi, the brother of Goliath.[6]

The Other Five

There are two other passages in 1 Chronicles, with parallel passages in 2 Samuel that explain the giants defeated by David and his Mighty Men. I will only reproduce the 1 Chronicles passages and fill out the facts with additional information from 2 Samuel.

> 1 Chronicles 11:22–23
> [22] And Benaiah the son of Jehoiada was a valiant man of Kabzeel… And he struck down an Egyptian, a man of great stature, five cubits tall. [7 1/2 to 8 1/2 feet] The Egyptian had in his hand a spear like a weaver's beam, but Benaiah went

---

[6] Michael Hesier, "Clash of the Manuscripts: Goliath & the Hebrew Text of the Old Testament," *Bible Study Magazine* May/Jun2009, Vol. 1 Issue 4, p33; http://biblestudymagazine.com/interactive/goliath/#

down to him with a staff and snatched the spear out of the Egyptian's hand and killed him with his own spear.

1 Chronicles 20:4–8
[4] And after this there arose war with the Philistines at Gezer. Then Sibbecai the Hushathite struck down Sippai [Saph - 2 Sam. 21:18], who was one of the descendants of the giants, and the Philistines were subdued. [5] And there was again war with the Philistines, and Elhanan the son of Jair struck down Lahmi the brother of Goliath the Gittite, the shaft of whose spear was like a weaver's beam. [6] And there was again war at Gath, where there was a man of great stature, who had six fingers on each hand and six toes on each foot, twenty-four in number, and he also was descended from the giants. [7] And when he taunted Israel, Jonathan the son of Shimea, David's brother, struck him down. [8] These were descended from the giants in Gath, and they fell by the hand of David and by the hand of his servants.

2 Samuel 21:16–22
[16] And Ishbi-benob, one of the descendants of the giants, whose spear weighed three hundred shekels of bronze, and who was armed with a new sword, thought to kill David. [17] But Abishai the son of Zeruiah came to his aid and attacked the Philistine and killed him.

So in all, we have five giants being killed by David's men. 1) Benaiah killed an Egyptian giant, 2) Sibbecai killed the giant Sippai [Saph], 3) Elhanan killed the giant Lahmi, brother of Goliath, 4) Jonathan killed an unnamed giant, and 5) Abishai killed Ishbi-benob the giant.

But these are not mere chronicling of random deaths of a few tall bad guys. There is meaning and deliberation behind these facts. There is deliberate intent by the author to link these giants to the Nephilim of Genesis 6 whose diabolical plan was thwarted by God with the Flood.

Firstly, they are all summarized in the same paragraph, indicating a theological purpose behind combining them together. Secondly, except for the Egyptian, they are all Philistines fighting Israel. In Deut. 3:1-11 we read that Joshua killed Og of Bashan, the last of the Rephaim giants. Then in Joshua 11:21-22 we read that Joshua deliberately sought out the Anakim giants in Canaan and cut them off everywhere in the hill country. But then it gives this qualification: "There was none of the Anakim left in the land of the people of Israel. Only in Gaza, in Gath, and in Ashdod did some remain."

So, some giants were left by Joshua – in the land of Philistia. The very cities from which came the giants David would fight, including Goliath. It was almost as if God was deliberately keeping the last of the giants in order to finally destroy them through his messianic king. They were the leftover giants from Joshua's conquest, and they were linked back to the evil Nephilim before the flood (Num. 13:32-33).

And there is strong indication that the giants were trying to kill David specifically as well. Ishbi-benob is said to explicitly have been trying to kill David (2 Sam. 21:16); another one "taunted Israel" (1Chron 20:7), the same phrasing used of Goliath; and of course, Lahmi, Goliath's brother, would no doubt have revenge against the slayer of his sibling on his mind. But there is still more to this picture.

The English phrase used of the giants in these passages is that they were "descendants of the giants." It is used three times in 1 Chron. 20 and four times in 2 Sam. 21. The authors go out of their way to stress these warriors as connected to that special group of giants that were theologically tied to the Nephilim of Genesis 6.

Excursus on Connecting the Nephilim giants of Genesis 6 to the Rephaim giants of King David's Time

1) The Nephilim offspring of the fallen angelic "Sons of God" were part of God's reason for judgment.

> Genesis 6:1–4
> The Nephilim were on the earth in those days, and also afterward, when the sons of God came in to the daughters of man and they bore children to them. These were the mighty men who were of old, the men of renown.
>
> Genesis 6:11–13
> 11 Now the earth was corrupt in God's sight, and the earth was filled with violence. 12 And God saw the earth, and behold, it was corrupt, for all flesh had corrupted their way on the earth. 13 And God said to Noah, "I have determined to make an end of all flesh, for the earth is

filled with violence through them. Behold, I will destroy them with the earth.

2) The Anakim giant clans that Joshua was to eradicate were theologically connected to the cursed Nephilim before the Flood.

Numbers 13:32–33 (ESV)
32 So they brought to the people of Israel a bad report of the land that they had spied out, saying, "The land, through which we have gone to spy it out, is a land that devours its inhabitants, and all the people that we saw in it are of great height. 33 And there we saw the Nephilim (the sons of Anak, who come from the Nephilim), and we seemed to ourselves like grasshoppers, and so we seemed to them."

3) The giant clans were all considered Rephaim in a generic sense. In this sense, Rephaim can be the catch-all term for all giant warriors.

Deuteronomy 2:10–11
10 (The Emim formerly lived there [in Moab], a people great and many, and tall as the Anakim. 11 Like the Anakim they are also counted as Rephaim, but the Moabites call them Emim.

Deuteronomy 2:20–21
20 (It [Ammon] is also counted as a land of Rephaim. Rephaim formerly lived there—but the Ammonites call them Zamzummim— 21 a people great and many, and tall as the Anakim.

4) The Philistine "Descendants of Giants" ("Sons of Rapha") in David's time were considered descendants or devotees of those cursed Rephaim/Anakim that Joshua had left alive in Philistia (Joshua 11:).

Joshua 11:21–22
21 And Joshua came at that time and cut off the Anakim from the hill country, from Hebron, from Debir, from Anab, and from all the hill country of Judah, and from all the hill country of Israel. Joshua devoted them to destruction with their cities. 22 There was none of the

> Anakim left in the land of the people of Israel. Only in Gaza, in Gath, and in Ashdod did some remain.
>
> 2 Samuel 21:22
> These four [giants warriors] were descended from the giants in Gath, and they fell by the hand of David and by the hand of his servants.

This narrative theological thread of giants from the Nephilim of Noah's day to the Rephaim of David's time conspires to imply a deliberate summary of climactic conflict between the titan Seed of the Serpent in Canaan and the Seed of Abraham from Eve.

But a closer look at the original Hebrew behind the translation "descendants of the giants" in 1 Samuel and 1 Chronicles reveals much more then merely being linked to those oversized warriors left alive by Joshua in Philistia.

Biblical scholar Conrad E. L'Heureux examines this Hebrew phrase, *yalid ha rapha*, that translates as "descendants of the giants." He explains that the word *rapha*, is the specific word for the Rephaim giants and warriors in the Bible. But the word *yalid*, "never refers to genealogical lineage. Rather, the *yalid* was a person of slave status and dedicated to the deity who was head of the social unit into which he was admitted by a consecration."[7]

Because the discoveries of Ugarit shed light on the Rephaim as deified dead giant warriors,[8] this religious devotion indicates that the "descendants of the giants" is really more the giant "devotees of Rapha." L'Heureux concludes that this was probably some kind of reference to an elite fighting force religiously bound to their Rephaim code. What was that code? Was it to hunt down and destroy the Seed of Eve, the messianic king?

He then points out that of the eight times that the Bible speaks of the location of battle called "Valley of the Rephaim," five of them are in these narratives of the Philistines fighting Israel in that valley. This brings him to suggest that "Valley of the Rephaim" may simply be an anachronism that was used in the stories about where that name came from. They called it Valley of the Rephaim because that valley is where David's army defeated these Philistine elite fighting forces.

---

[7] Conrad E. L'Heureux "The yelîdê hārāpā': A Cultic Association of Warriors," *Bulletin of the American Schools of Oriental Research*, No. 221,(Feb., 1976), pp. 83-85.

[8] See Brian Godawa, *Enoch Primordial* Appendix on the Rephaim,(Los Angeles, CA, Embedded Pictures Publishing, 2012), pp 364-366.

Thus, the origin of my elite corps of giants in *David Ascendant* called the *Yalid ha Rapha* or the "Sons of Rapha," bound by oath to their own Seed (of the Serpent) to destroy the Seed of Eve, David.

Were Agag and Saul Giants?

Agag. In 1 Samuel 15 we read that King Saul defeated the Amalekites, ancient enemies of the Israelites. God tells Saul in verse 15 to "devote to destruction, all that they have. Do not spare them, but kill both man and woman, child and infant, ox and sheep, camel and donkey." This was the language of *herem* (devotion to destruction) used for Joshua's conquest of Canaan's Nephilim infestation. It was not used for all of Israel's enemies, only the specific clans that God was focusing on, and those clans all had Nephilim or giants in them.[9]

While 1 Samuel does not tell us that Agag was a giant, there is some indication that he could have been and that the Amalekites also had giants in their midst.

Their history goes all the way back to Genesis 14 and the Giant Wars in the days of Abraham. In that passage, Chedorlaomer leads his alliance of four Mesopotamian kings to wipe out specific giant clans in Canaan. The list of giant clans they take out are the Rephaim, Zuzim, Emim, Horites and Amorites. In *Abraham Allegiant* I explained this campaign and how Abraham fit in with it. But for our purposes now, suffice it to say that mentioned within that list of giant clans is one more people group: The Amalekites.

Though it is not stated explicitly that the Amalekites were a giant clan, it is implied by its inclusion in the list of all the other giant clans. In the Zohar, a 13th century Jewish mystical text, there is a clear reference to the Amalekites as giants among the Nephilim, Anakim, and Rephaim.[10] The Arabs also have legends about Ad, the son of Amalek, being a giant.[11]

Some scholars think that this Genesis 14 reference is just an anachronism in the Bible text, and that the Amalekites did not come in history until later. Genesis 36:12 states that Amalek came later as a son of Esau, father of the Edomites, a tribe that Israel was commanded by God *not* to fight (Deut. 2:4-

---

[9] See Appendix B "The Nephilim," *Noah Primeval* (Los Angeles, Embedded Pictures, 2012), 304-322.

[10] Special thanks to Doug Van Dorn for this bit of research. *Beresheet A,* 20.224, "There are five races of mixed multitude. These are the Nefilim (fallen), the Giborim (mighty), the Anakim (giants), the Refaim (shades) and the Amalekim." Van Dorn, Douglas (2013-01-21). *Giants: Sons of the Gods* (Kindle Locations 2629-2631). Waters of Creation. Kindle Edition. It is important to note however that the Zohar is of questionable origin, so it represents a much later tradition than is preferable for our ancient research.

[11] "A tradition told in the famous Al-Khitat, a history of Egyptian lore compiled by al-Maqrizi (1364-1442 AD), recounts the teaching of one master Ibrahim bin Wasif Shah (d. 1203 AD) who said that King Adim (Ad) was, 'A violent and proud prince, tall in stature.'" Van Dorn, *Giants* (Kindle Locations 2605-2608).

6). But there is a problem here. When the Israelites encounter the Amalekites in the desert during the Exodus, God says, "I will utterly blot out the memory of Amalek from under heaven…The LORD will have war with Amalek from generation to generation" (Ex. 17:15-16). After Israel had taken the Promised Land for an inheritance, God told them again, "You shall blot out the memory of Amalek from under heaven; you shall not forget" (Deut. 25:19). Again, the holy war language used against the Nephilim in Canaan.

So either Genesis 36 is an anachronism and a contradiction or there are two separate lines of Amalekites, one from Esau and one from this earlier giant clan in Abraham's time. Balaam's prophecy, just before the conquest of the Promised Land, seems to blend both clans into one. It indicates that "Amalek was the first among the nations, but its end is utter destruction" (Num. 24:20), thus favoring the earlier Genesis 14 existence. But it also links Amalek to Edom, the favored nation of Seir in verse 18, favoring the Esau lineage. The problem is that the prophecy from God himself then declares that Edom shall be dispossessed by Israel. Why would God change his mind and dispossess the tribe he was protecting? Maybe there was some kind of mixing of two Amalekite clans into one under the name of Amalek. And that people group had giants.[12]

Saul. One more literary reference hints at Agag being a giant. In Balaam's prophecy just quoted, Israel is predicted to overcome her enemies in Canaan.

> Numbers 24:6–8 (NASB95)
> [6] [Israel is planted] <u>like cedars</u> beside the waters. [7] "Water will flow from his buckets, And <u>his seed</u> *will be* by many waters, And <u>his king shall be higher than Agag</u>, And his kingdom shall be exalted… He <u>will devour the nations</u> *who are* his adversaries, And will <u>crush their bones</u> in pieces.

This Scripture uses the language of the giants in an ironic application to Israel. The cedar tree, used in reference to the giants of Canaan (Amos 2:9), is now used of Israel; the nations of giants that "devoured its inhabitants" (Num. 13:32), would be devoured (same Hebrew word) by Israel instead. Like a giant, Israel would crush the bones of his enemies. The seed motif is brought up that reminds us of the Seed of Eve versus the Seed of the Serpent (Gen. 3:15). And then we read that Israel's king shall be "higher than Agag."

---

[12] Like Edom, Moab and Ammon were to be left alone by the Israelites in their conquest because of their descendancy from Lot, Abraham's nephew (Deut. 2:9, 19). But then King David conquers all three of these peoples for his kingdom; Edom, Moab and Ammon (2 Sam. 8; 10). It was as if God was saving their ultimate dispossession for his messiah king.

This reference to height is an obvious metaphor for glory and exaltation of David's house. But of course it also hints at Agag's own stature being a defining trait. An interesting textual gloss appears in some of the Septuagint manuscripts that render Agag as "Gog" or "Og."[13] We've seen Og before: The last of the Rephaim giants in the Transjordan during Israel's approach to Canaan.

Another literary linkage seems to be occurring in the Biblical text. 1 Samuel goes out of its way to point out that Saul was "taller than any of the people from his shoulders upward" (1 Sam. 9:2; 10:23). This would make him at least 6 1/2 to 7 feet tall. Could he have been of Nephilim seed? Verse 2 also says, "There was not a man among the people of Israel more handsome than he." It was customary to describe kings in glorious language as exemplary physical and spiritual specimens to justify their royalty.[14] This description of Saul is used to make a point later that God does not look upon the outward appearance like man does, but upon the heart (1 Sam. 16:7). However, as Bible commentator Bergen points out, it is not a coincidence that "Saul is the only Israelite specifically noted in the Bible as being tall; elsewhere it was only Israel's enemies [the giants] whose height was noted (cf. Num. 13:33; Deut. 1:28; 2:10; 9:2; 1 Sam. 17:4). Israel had asked for a king 'like all the other nations' (8:20), and the Lord was giving them the desires of their heart, even down to the physical details!"[15]

So Saul is likened to the giants of Israel's enemies. This is not to say that he was a Nephilim, but certainly the writer is making a theological comparison with Saul to Israel's enemies. But with Saul at close to 7 feet of height, no doubt some Israelites gossiped to one another about the possibility of such a thing. A double irony occurs in that Saul, the giant's equal, does not kill Israel's perpetual enemy the Amalekite king (a giant?), but David, the ruddy and small youth, does kill Goliath the Rephaim giant who embodied the last of the Serpentine Seed in the Promised Land.

What this all means is that Israel's first encounter with giants may have been when they battled the Amalekites in the exodus (Ex. 17:8-16); Saul may have defiantly failed to kill the Serpentine Seed of Amalek, which resulted in his cursing by God; and David may have faced those giants when he all but wiped them out at Ziklag in 1 Samuel 30, resulting in their ultimate decline.

---

[13] "There shall come a man out of his seed, and he shall rule over many nations; and the kingdom of Gog (or "Og") shall be exalted, and his kingdom shall be increased." Lancelot Charles Lee Brenton, *The Septuagint Version of the Old Testament: English Translation* (London: Samuel Bagster and Sons, 1870), Nu 24:7. For the Og version, see John William Wevers, ed., *Numeri, vol. III, 1, Vetus Testamentum Graecum. Auctoritate Academiae Scientiarum Gottingensis Editum* (Göttingen: Vandenhoeck & Ruprecht, 1982), 289.

[14] John H. Walton, *Zondervan Illustrated Bible Backgrounds Commentary (Old Testament): Joshua, Judges, Ruth, 1 & 2 Samuel, vol. 2* (Grand Rapids, MI: Zondervan, 2009), 311.

[15] Robert D. Bergen, *1, 2 Samuel*, vol. 7, The New American Commentary (Nashville: Broadman & Holman Publishers, 1996), 121.

Yet One More Giant

But there's one more giant hiding out between the lines of sacred writ. The Septuagint (LXX), an earlier Greek translation of the Old Testament that Jesus and the apostles quoted as authoritative, contains additional information about one other giant that was left out in the Masoretic text, or later Hebrew version of the Old Testament.[16]

In 2 Samuel 21, the Gibeonites demand that David release to them all of Saul's sons as justice for their oppression by Saul. David hands over six of them to be hanged by the Gibeonites. But David spared Mephibosheth, because of his oath of loyalty to the crippled son of Saul. One of the mothers, Rizpah, asks for the remains of the victims and spreads out a sackcloth to mourn over them and protect them from the vultures.

The LXX then adds this gloss:

> 2 Samuel 21:11 (LXX)
> 11 And it was told David what Rizpah the daughter of Aia the concubine of Saul had done, and they were faint and Dan the son of Joah of the descendant of the giants overtook them.[17]

Apparently, Dan ben Joah, was a giant. The text is not clear as to who was faint or what it means that Dan "overtook them." Overtook who or what? The *bones*, or the *scavengers* that Rizpah was keeping from the bones? It would not make sense for Dan to overtake the scavengers of the bones, because giants are always in a negative disposition toward Israel in the Bible. Dan would not care to protect Israelite bones. If it was the bones that Dan overtook or "captured" as other translations have it, then David would have had to fight the giant to get them back because in verse 21, David gathers those bones with the bones of Saul and Jonathan to bury them all.[18]

Interestingly, the name Dan has a nefarious heritage in Biblical tradition. He was described in Genesis 49:17 as "a serpent in the way, a viper by the path, that bites the horse's heels so that the rider falls backward." This serpentine connection rings ominously familiar with the Genesis 3:15

---

[16] Special thanks to Douglas Van Dorn for this discovery.

[17] Lancelot Charles Lee Brenton, *The Septuagint Version of the Old Testament: English Translation* (London: Samuel Bagster and Sons, 1870), 2 Kgdms 21:11.

[18] David scholar McCarter suggests "overtook them" may be translated "captured them," as in capturing the bones of the Saulides. (P. Kyle McCarter Jr, *II Samuel: a New Translation with Introduction, Notes, and Commentary, vol. 9, Anchor Yale Bible* (New Haven; London: Yale University Press, 2008), 440.) The Lexham LXX translates that phrase as "took them down," as if to mean that the giant took down the remains of the six hanged descendants of Saul in order for the Gibeonites to release them to Rizpah. But in the Bible, giants are never in a positive disposition toward Israel, so this is most likely not the best translation. Randall Tan and David A. deSilva, Logos Bible Software, *The Lexham Greek-English Interlinear Septuagint* (Logos Bible Software, 2009), 2 Kgdms 21:11–12.

prophetic curse on the Serpent's Seed biting the heels of Eve's Seed. And is it mere coincidence that the tribe of Dan lost their apportioned land in Canaan (Josh. 19:47), leading them to take the territory of the city Laish (Judg. 18) in the far north of Bashan, "place of the serpent," in the foothills of Mount Hermon, the location of the Watchers' fall and the pagan community of Banias that worshipped Azazel?[19]

The text also says that this giant Dan was from the "descendants of the giants." The Greek for this phrase in the LXX is *apoganon ton giganton*, the same Greek translation of the *Yalid ha Rapha* warrior cult of the other four giants in 2 Samuel 21:22 (LXX): "These four were descended from the giants (*apoganoi ton giganton*) in Gath."[20]

Like the other five giants spoken of in 1 and 2 Samuel, we have no personal details spelled out for us beyond the statements of fact. So the storyline of these giants in *David Ascendant* is speculative conjecture, but surely consistent with the explicit facts and implicit connections of the text.

Giant Weapons

Goliath's armor is among the most studied in the Old Testament. The reason for this is because it is the most descriptive of all passages about a soldier's armor anywhere in the entire corpus. It reads like a Homeric description of the heroic warrior in Greece.

> 1 Samuel 17:5–7
> 5 He had a helmet of bronze on his head, and he was armed with a coat of mail, and the weight of the coat was five thousand shekels of bronze [126 pounds]. 6 And he had bronze armor on his legs, and a javelin of bronze slung between his shoulders. 7 The shaft of his spear was like a weaver's beam, and his spear's head weighed six hundred shekels of iron [16 pounds]. And his shield-bearer went before him.

Though the Philistines most likely consisted of Mycenaean and other Sea Peoples who had migrated to Canaan from the Aegean, they nevertheless were highly adaptive and built their own culture through assimilation of others. Thus, scholars indicate that Goliath's armor was not distinctly Mycenaean

---

[19] Brian Godawa, Appendix, *Joshua Valiant*, (Los Angeles, CA: Embedded Pictures Publishing, 2013), 322. See also, Judd H. Burton, *Interview With the Giant: Ethnohistorical Notes on the Nephilim* (Burton Beyond Press, 2009) 20.
[20] Randall Tan and David A. deSilva, Logos Bible Software, *The Lexham Greek-English Interlinear Septuagint* (Logos Bible Software, 2009), 2 Kgdms 21:11, 22.

Greek or even uniquely Philistine but rather a kind of conglomeration of different styles.

His helmet was not the typical feathered headdress of the Philistines, but rather a bronze covering more akin to Greek or Assyrian protection.[21] His bronze cuirass of armored scales was also unlike Aegean style armor, but more like Egyptian styled scales like that seen on Pharaoh Shishak's tenth century engravings.[22] His bronze shin greaves were Greek and his shield bearer before him apparently was carrying a full-bodied shield rather than the small round one of the Philistines and other Sea Peoples. Goliath was a Philistine, but his Rephaim background and his distinct armor indicates he was most likely indigenous to the region, making him either a Canaanite convert or conscript of his Philistine rulers.

In the English translation it says that Goliath had a "javelin of bronze slung between his shoulders." Citing similar language in the War Scroll at Qumran's Dead Sea Scrolls, recent scholars have more accurately translated that phrase as referring to a bronze scimitar sword (curved blade), not the javelin.[23]

Another translation clarified by many scholars is that the shaft of Goliath's spear being "like a weaver's beam" is more accurately a likeness of the shape rather than the size of his dart. A well known form of javelin used in both Egypt and Greece included a loop or leash attached to the missile that could be flung by the fingers of the soldier to facilitate a throw of up to three times the normal velocity and distance.[24] This looped leash is very similar to what the heddle rod on a weaver's beam looks like, thus indicating it as a new weapon in the eyes of the Israelites.

And that "weaver's beam" javelin is the exact same description used of the weapon of another giant, the unnamed Egyptian Rapha (1 Chron. 20:5, 11:23). These giants are linked together by their elite guild connection as well as the weapons they use.

Goliath's iron spearhead weighed 16 pounds. Ishbi-benob's bronze spearhead weighed 7.5 pounds, since bronze is a lighter metal. Ishbi-benob is also described as carrying a "new sword," in 2 Sam. 21:16. But as commentator Robert Bergren points out, the Hebrew word for "sword" is not actually in the text, making the phrase a reference to an unnamed weapon unknown to the writer. Translators assumed it was a sword, but we don't know

[21] David Tsumura, *The First Book of Samuel, The New International Commentary on the Old Testament* (Grand Rapids, MI: Wm. B. Eerdmans Publishing Co., 2007), 442.
[22] Yigal Yadin, *The Art of Warfare in Biblical Lands*, 2 vols. (New York: McGraw-Hill, 1963), I, pp. 196–97; II, p. 354.
[23] Ralph W. Klein, *1 Samuel, vol. 10, Word Biblical Commentary* (Dallas: Word, Incorporated, 1998), 176.
[24] Yadin, Y. 1955. "Goliath's javelin and the menor `orgim", *PEQ* 87:58-69

for sure.[25] Thus, the strange new weapon Ishbi-benob carries in *David Ascendant*. Strange for the Israelites, but not for readers of previous *Chronicles of the Nephilim*

Lastly, the unnamed giant killed by Jonathan in 2 Sam. 21:20 and 1 Chron. 20:6 is described as having six fingers on each hand and six toes on each foot. This is the only place in the Bible where a giant is described with polydactylism, but its genetic connection to the other giants is a strong possibility. While some may not think extra digits on hands and feet are a weapon, they certainly increase the gripping power extent of hands while adding wider balancing skill for feet that are no doubt advantageous in battle. This is the origin of the polydactylism of the giants as read in *Chronicles of the Nephilim*.

The descriptions of the giants and their weapons mentioned in Chronicles and Samuel indicates obvious ties between Goliath and the elite members of the giant warrior guild, the *yalid ha rapha*. And these giants are strongly implied to be part of a deliberate plan on the part of the Seed of the Serpent at war with the Seed of Eve: God's people, king, and messiah.

Lion Men of Moab

Another strange warrior breed shows up in *David Ascendant*: Lion Men of Moab called Ariels. They are effectively werewolves – but more like werelions.

In 2 Sam. 23:20 Benaiah, a valiant warrior, strikes down "two *ariels* of Moab." The word "ariel" is a transliteration because scholars are not sure what it means. The King James and Young's Bibles translate these opponents of Benaiah as "lion-like men of Moab," which captures the strangeness of the creatures but fails to express the religious or supernatural connotation of the word.

Some translators translate the phrase "*ariels* of Moab" as "sons of Ariel of Moab" after the unlikely LXX Greek translation,[26] or "lion-like heroes of Moab." But there is no Hebrew word for "sons of" in the sentence, no indication of *ariel* being a personal name, and no Hebrew word for warrior used in the sentence. The Hebrew word for mighty warrior, *gibborim*, is used

[25] Robert D. Bergen, *1, 2 Samuel, vol. 7, The New American Commentary* (Nashville: Broadman & Holman Publishers, 1996), 448.

[26] "Although the LXX interferes seriously in the text, presupposing a double haplography in the Hebrew text, this reading points into the right direction. As a matter of fact NKH Hiphʿil in the historical books never means to strike upon an object (cf. also E. Jenni, ErIs 24 [1993] 114–118), but to strike down, i.e. to kill somebody... Consequently, Ariel here designates some kind of person, best translated as 'lion of God': S. Münger, "Ariel," ed. Karel van der Toorn, Bob Becking, and Pieter W. van der Horst, *Dictionary of Deities and Demons in the Bible* (Leiden; Boston; Köln; Grand Rapids, MI; Cambridge: Brill; Eerdmans, 1999), 88–89.

frequently throughout David's narrative and that word is not here. The text says "two *ariels* of Moab."

Some suggest it may be a reference to killing two lions. But the very next sentence states that Benaiah, the killer of the *ariels*, then killed a lion in a pit.

> 2 Samuel 23:20
> And Benaiah the son of Jehoiada was a valiant man of Kabzeel, a doer of great deeds. He struck down two ariels of Moab. He also went down and struck down a lion in a pit on a day when snow had fallen.

The Hebrew word for "lion" is not *ariel*, but *aryeh*. Adding the suffix "el" to the word adds a religious dimension of meaning that transcends mere lions. This is why Hebrew lexicons explain the most likely meaning as "lion of god."[27] El was not merely a name used of Yahweh in the Bible, it was the name of the figurehead deity of the Canaanite pantheon as well as a general reference to deity in Mesopotamia.[28]

In 1 Chronicles, some additional warriors from Gad join David when he is at Ziklag, and they are described exactly like *ariels* as "lion-faced warriors" with preternatural skills:

> 1 Chronicles 12:8
> From the Gadites there went over to David at the stronghold in the wilderness mighty and experienced warriors, expert with shield and spear, whose faces were like the faces of lions and who were swift as gazelles upon the mountains:

Though animal-like skills is a common metaphor used to describe extraordinary warrior skills, having faces like the faces of lions could mean more in light of the existence of these a*riels,* or Lion Men of Moab. Since the tribal location of Gad was precisely all the land of Moab across the Jordan, I decided to make the Gadite lion-faced men be those very Lion Men of Moab who converted to Israel and joined David. Two of these hybrid warriors then become the two traitors who face down Benaiah.

Psalm 57 was written when David was on the run and hiding out in a cave from Saul's bounty hunters. Verse 4 says, "My soul is in the midst of lions; I lie down amid fiery beasts— the children of man, whose teeth are spears and

---

[27] Francis Brown, Samuel Rolles Driver and Charles Augustus Briggs, *Enhanced Brown-Driver-Briggs Hebrew and English Lexicon*, electronic ed., 72 (Oak Harbor, WA: Logos Research Systems, 2000).
[28] W. Herrmann, "El," ed. Karel van der Toorn, Bob Becking, and Pieter W. van der Horst, Dictionary of Deities and Demons in the Bible (Leiden; Boston; Köln; Grand Rapids, MI; Cambridge: Brill; Eerdmans, 1999), 275.

arrows, whose tongues are sharp swords." Though a surface reading of this text appears to be an obvious figurative expression of David's enemies, scholar B. Mazar suggests it may be a reference to a mercenary military corps of archers whose emblem was the lion-goddess.[29] Could they have come from Moab?

So what if these *ariels* are hybrid creatures reminiscent of the Watchers' miscegenation in Genesis 6? What if they are elite warriors with hairy bodies and lion-like faces that only one of David's own *gibborim* Mighty Men could slay? After all, the exploits of those Mighty Men in the passages we have been looking at are supernatural slayings of giants and hundreds of soldiers by single warriors. If these *ariels* were mere warriors, then the feat accomplished by Benaiah in slaying them would be the only one in the entire passage that was banal and without significance.

These *ariels* were something more than men, something supernatural.

The ancient understanding of *ariel* as a lion-like hybrid humanoid finds support in a later Nag Hammadi text that speaks of a gnostic deity, Yaldabaoth, who was an *ariel* (spelled slightly different): "Ariael is what the perfect call him, for he was like a lion."[30]

The Dictionary of Deities and Demons in the Bible says of this possible religious mythical interpretation of *ariel*:

> This interpretation could be supported by a recently found bronze-silver figurine from Tell Abū el-Kharaz in Transjordan representing, according to the excavator's opinion a male lion-faced warrior(-god?), which can be viewed, because of its appearance and its attributes, as a male pendant.[31]

The author then reveals that the word *ariel* shows up in the Mesha Stele, a Moabite stone inscription not too long after the time of King David.[32] These are the very Moabites from which 2 Samuel says the *ariels* come. The line of text in question could be translated, "the lion figure [*ariel*] of their beloved (god)' which was dragged before Chemosh after the fall of the Israelite city."[33]

---

[29] B. Mazar, "The Military Élite of King David," *Vetus Testamentum*, Vol. 13, Fasc. 3 (Jul., 1963), 312.

[30] James McConkey Robinson, Richard Smith and Coptic Gnostic Library Project, *The Nag Hammadi Library in English*, 4th rev. ed., 173 (Leiden; New York: E. J. Brill, 1996).

[31] S. Münger, "Ariel," ed. Karel van der Toorn, Bob Becking, and Pieter W. van der Horst, *Dictionary of Deities and Demons in the Bible* (Leiden; Boston; Köln; Grand Rapids, MI; Cambridge: Brill; Eerdmans, 1999), 89. Münger refers to the *Annual of the Department of Antiquities of Jordan* (P. M. Fischer, *ADAJ* 40 [1996] 101–110, esp. 103–104 with figs. 3a-b).

[32] 850 B.C.

[33] S. Münger, *DDD*, 89. Pritchard's *Ancient Near Eastern Texts Relating to the Old Testament* translates *ariel* as the name of the king of the city, and Hallo's Context of Scripture translates it as the more unlikely

Bible scholar B. Mazar notes this Mesha Stele connection and adds that the word *ariel* became a synonym for the lion-headed cherubim at the base of kingly thrones.[34]

So in *David Ascendant*, I created a special unit of these Ariels, lion-headed warriors of Moab, to explore that supernatural dimension with imagination that fit the thread of the cosmic War of the Seed.

The ancient Book of Jasher was a source text for both Joshua and David's stories (Josh. 10:13, 2 Sam. 1:18). The extant version we have of the Book of Jasher, though dubitable, tells of two different stories that contain hybrid creatures that may be similar to the lion-men of Moab or the satyrs of Banias. In Jasher 36:29-35 we read of Anah, one of the sons of Seir the Horite, (remember the Seirites' connection to satyrs) during the days of Abraham. There is a large storm that the writer says caused a group of about 120 "great and terrible animals" to come out of the forest by the seashore to be witnessed by Anah feeding his asses.

> Jasher 36:29-35
> And those animals, from their middle downward, were in the shape of the children of men, and from their middle upward, some had the likeness of bears, and some the likeness of the keephas, with tails behind them from between their shoulders reaching down to the earth, like the tails of the ducheephath, and these animals came and mounted and rode upon these asses, and led them away, and they went away unto this day.[35]

Another chapter in Jasher tells the story during the youth of Balaam son of Beor, about a strange animal that was devouring the cattle of the people of Chittim. A man named Zepho went in search of this creature and…

> Jasher 61:15
> he came into the cave and he looked and behold, a large animal was devouring the ox; from the middle upward it resembled a man, and from the middle downward it resembled an animal, and Zepho rose up against the animal and slew it with his swords.[36]

---

object, *fire hearth*. James Bennett Pritchard, ed., *The Ancient Near East an Anthology of Texts and Pictures, 3rd ed. with Supplement* (Princeton: Princeton University Press, 1969), 320; William W. Hallo and K. Lawson Younger, *Context of Scripture* (Leiden; Boston: Brill, 2000), 137.

[34] B. Mazar, "The Military Élite of King David," *Vetus Testamentum*, Vol. 13, Fasc. 3 (Jul., 1963), pp. 316.

[35] Johnson, Ken (2012-01-09). *Ancient Book Of Jasher* (p. 129). Kindle Edition.

[36] Johnson, *Book Of Jasher* (p. 223).

Were these creatures just legends or were they genetic hybrid remnants of the miscegenation of the Watchers?

Dagon and Asherah

Two new gods take the stage in *David Ascendant* that were not in previous Chronicles: Dagon and Asherah. These are both mysterious deities about whom not much is revealed in the Old Testament or in ancient extra-Biblical sources beyond their names and few details.

Dagon. In the Bible, Dagon is described as the chief god of the Philistines. The story of Samson's death in Judges 16 takes place in the temple of Dagon, god of the Philistines. In 1 Chron. 10:10 the Philistines are said to have hung the decapitated head of King Saul in a temple of Dagon at Beth-shan. 1 Sam. 5 tells the story of Philistines capturing the ark of the covenant and placing it in the temple of Dagon in Ashdod. Two mornings in a row, the statue of Dagon was found flat on its face before the ark, the second time, with its head and hands "cut off." Severing hands and heads was a common tactic of ancient Near Eastern powers, both Mesopotamian and Canaanite.[37] This supernatural "power encounter" between Yahweh and Dagon becomes then a spiritual polemic of warfare and conquest between gods. But beyond these mentions, nothing more is revealed in the Old Testament.

The meaning of the name Dagon is uncertain. Early scholarly interpreters argued that it came from the Hebrew word for "fish," thus one tradition depicts him as a hybrid deity with the upper torso of a man and the lower bottom of a fish. The 1 Samuel passage describing the lower part of the Dagon statue has been interpreted by some as "his fishy part." Later scholars argued the name Dagon came from the Hebrew word for "grain," thus another tradition understands him as a god of fertility or grain. Still others have argued Dagon was a storm god, whose name came from the Arabic word for cloudy rain.[38] No scholarly consensus has been reached on these interpretations, though the earlier ones have fallen out of favor.[39]

---

[37] Steve A. Wiggins, "Old Testament Dagan in the Light of Ugarit," *Vetus Testamentum*, Vol. 43, Fasc. 2 (Apr., 1993), 370.

[38] T. C. Mitchell, "Dagon," ed. Geoffrey W. Bromiley, *The International Standard Bible Encyclopedia*, Revised (Wm. B. Eerdmans, 1979–1988), 851; Lowell K. Handy, "Dagon (Deity)," ed. David Noel Freedman, *The Anchor Yale Bible Dictionary* (New York: Doubleday, 1992), 2.

[39] It is now thought by some that Dagon as a fish-man may have been etiologically influenced by Atargatis, a mermaid goddess of nearby Philistine Ashkelon and by the Sumerian fish-man god Odakon as interpreted by the Babylonian historian Berossus. Frank J.. Montalbano, "Canaanite Dagon: Origin, Nature," *Catholic Biblical Quarterly*, 13 no 4 O 1951, p 395.

Dagon had a strong presence in Mesopotamia and Syria primarily as a storm god, spelled *Dagan,* and likened to the Babylonian weather god Enlil.[40] The Syrians included Dagon in their pantheon at Ugarit, which was in Syria, but nowhere in Canaan. The Canaanite champion deity Ba'al is described throughout the Ugaritic texts as the "Son of Dagon" which made him an outsider to the family of gods ruled over by the high god El and his wife, Athirat (Asherah), the Mother of the Gods.[41]

But since the Philistines were known for adapting customs and gods from their newly conquered lands it is entirely possible that Dagon was imported from Philistine contact with Syria and adapted to the interests of the coastal Sea People.[42] Because of this syncretistic worldview of the Philistines, I combined all three of the major interpretations of Dagon into one in *David Ascendant* as a hybrid fish-man who is a god of both storm and grain. And this is not too different from the nature of the Babylonian Marduk and the Canaanite Ba'al, who were also both gods of storm and vegetation.

Asherah. The name Asherah appears 40 times in the Bible (plural: *Asherim*, *Asheroth, Ashtaroth*). Some of those instances refer directly to the goddess herself (Judg. 3:7; 1 Kgs. 14:13, 18:19; 2 Kgs. 21:7, 23:4) and many others refer to a wooden cult object used in worship to symbolize the goddess (Deut. 16:21; Judg. 6:25-30; 2 Kgs. 18:4; Isa. 17:8; Jer. 17:2). From the time of Judges on into the monarchy and the Josianic reforms, The Asherah poles or sacred pillars are often spoken of in close connection with altars of Ba'al (Judg. 6:25; 1 Kgs. 16:33; 2 Kgs. 17:16; 21:3), which hints at a theological connection between this unseemly pair of idols that exercised an ongoing apostasizing influence on Israel throughout her history. Archeological discoveries of inscriptions in Israel have even confirmed the attempt of Israelites to syncretize Asherah into their religion as Yahweh's consort (Deut. 16:21-22).[43]

Asherah appears extensively in the Ugaritic texts from Ras Shamra. There, she is referred to as *Athirat*. John Day points out that as consort of the high god of the pantheon El, she is called "mother of the gods," whose divine offspring are called the "seventy sons of Athirat." He then concludes, "There is a direct line of connection between this concept and the later Jewish idea of

---

[40] Montalbano "Canaanite Dagon," p 381-397.

[41] Mark S. Smith, *The Ugaritic Baal Cycle: Introduction with Text, Translation and Commentary of KTU 1.1-1.2, vol. 1* (Leiden; New York; Köln: E.J. Brill, 1994), 293.

[42] Wiggins, "Old Testament Dagan," 372.

[43] John Day, "Asherah in the Hebrew Bible and Northwest Semitic Literature," *Journal of Biblical Literature,* Vol. 105, No. 3 (Sep., 1986), 391-92. While the Scriptures are replete with many calls to Israelites to repent from worshipping Ba'al and Asherah, there is no Biblical indication that Israel ever worshipped Dagon, the god of the Philistines.

the seventy guardian angels of the nations (see 1 Enoch 89:59; 90:22-25; Tg. Ps.-J. on Deut 32:8)."[44]

She is a goddess of fertility and connected to sacred prostitution (2 Kgs. 23:7). She is also linked with the host of heaven (2 Kgs. 17:16; 21:3; 23:4), which are acknowledged as deities (Job 38:7), thus supporting her moniker the "mother of the gods."

Here is what the *International Standard Bible Encyclopedia* says of Asherah in the Ugaritic texts:

> In the *Râs* Shamrah texts Asherah is the consort of El, the supreme god. She is mentioned as "creatress of the gods" and as "Lady Asherah of the sea," titles that are given to the most important goddess of the pantheon. In the Ugaritic Keret text Asherah is said to have a shrine in Tyre, which would indicate her supremacy there also. She is the adversary of Baal… As the role of Baal grows in importance and overshadows that of El, Asherah's interest seems to shift more toward Baal. When a house is to be built for Baal, he and Anat, his sister-consort, bribe Asherah with gold and silver in order to persuade her to intervene for them before El, a mission she gladly undertakes. Again, in a myth stemming from the Late Bronze Age, Asherah attempts to seduce Baal.[45]

The Asherah as a wooden cultic object has several explanations without a clear conclusion. The Septuagint translates the word Asherah as "groves" of trees. Thus some earlier scholars argued they were literal groves of trees. But as Day explains, "the OT often refers to the making of Asherim (1 Kgs 14:15; 16:33; 2 Kgs 17:16;21:3, 7; 2 Chr 33:3) and also of the building (1 Kgs 14:23) and erection (2 Kgs 17:10) of Asherim, which does not seem appropriate for trees."[46] He concludes that the most widely held view is that the Asherim were wooden poles sacred to the goddess Asherah. But how they functioned and exactly what they looked like, no evidence can be found.

---

[44] John Day, "Asherah in the Hebrew Bible," 387.

[45] K. G. Jung, "Asherah," ed. Geoffrey W. Bromiley, *The International Standard Bible Encyclopedia, Revised* (Wm. B. Eerdmans, 1979–1988), 317–318.

[46] John Day, "Asherah in the Hebrew Bible," 402.

Jesus Triumphant

Appendices

Chapter 12
Jesus and the Cosmic War

Jesus Triumphant is a dangerous novel. I knew it long before I wrote it. In fact, I had originally not intended to write it because, of all the *Chronicles of the Nephilim*, I thought it would probably be the most scrutinized and criticized with accusations of taking liberties with God's Word. Jesus and his story is the most prized of all Christian narratives—for me as well.

But the more I studied and the more I wrote of the *Chronicles*, I came to realize that I had to write this one because it is the true theological climax of the Biblical cosmic war of Christus Victor against the principalities and powers of this present darkness. Jesus Christ is the Seed which was prophesied in Genesis 3:6 to be at war with the Seed of the Serpent. Jesus Christ is the Seed to whom God made his Promises (Gal. 3:16). So how could I not finish my story with the conclusion I believed was in the Bible?

The premise of the series is to retell only those Scriptural narratives that touch upon the story thread of the Nephilim and the allotment of the Watchers (Sons of God) as described in the Divine Council worldview of the Bible. At first blush readers may legitimately ask the question "Where are there giants or Watchers in the New Testament?" But the reader of the entire series will not be so surprised as he sees key theological elements already established in previous *Chronicles* now show up in the New Testament in a way they had never seen before.

Chronicles of the Nephilim is primarily a theological saga that attempts to communicate a spiritual storyline that is behind the physical events and symbolic motifs and imagination of the Bible. So strap yourself in and get ready for a wild Biblical ride of theological imagination from the depths of Hades to the heights of heaven.

A Giant and Some Zealots

There may not be mention of giants in the Gospels, but I did find a giant placed in the same approximate time and location of Christ's ministry. One of my historical resources has been the ancient Jewish historian Josephus. His rich text, *Wars of the Jews*, is the only detailed source we have of the events that led up to the destruction of Jerusalem and the holy temple in A.D. 70. (this will be the subject of *Jerusalem Judgment*). Josephus is a non-Christian source that confirms Gospel details of Pontius Pilate, the Herods, John the Baptist, the apostle James, and even Jesus Christ.[1] Though his pro-Roman agenda is well-known, he nevertheless provides helpful reliable information for the historical inquirer.

One of those interesting factoids is the reference to a 10 1/2 foot giant Jew named Eleazar who was presented as a gift to Tiberius Caesar in the presence of Herod Antipas, by the king of Parthia, Artabanus III in A.D. 33 or 34.[2]

> When Tiberius had heard of these things, he desired to have a league of friendship made between him and Artabanus… Artabanus and Vitellius went to Euphrates…And when they had agreed upon the terms of peace, Herod the tetrarch erected a rich tent on the midst of the passage, and made them a feast there. Artabanus also, not long afterwards, sent his son Darius as an hostage, with many presents, among which there was a man seven cubits tall, a Jew he was by birth, and his name was Eleazar, who, for his tallness, was called a giant.[3]

Josephus doesn't tell us if the Jewish giant was a servant or a captive, but he was certainly chattel of some kind to be traded as a means of diplomacy between the two empires. It occurred on the shores of the Euphrates in a tent constructed by Herod Antipas, the tetrarch of Galilee at the time. Antipas inserted himself into the negotiations in order to ingratiate himself to Caesar. All this, the reader will recognize occurring in *Jesus Triumphant*.

Vitellius, the king of Syria and representative of Caesar, brought the "gifts" of his son and the giant to Antioch, where they were presumably

---

[1] His infamous paragraph describing Jesus Christ (*Antiquities of the Jews* 18.63-64) is controversial and some have argued that it is a later Christian redaction. But there remains solid scholarship for its legitimacy. For a balanced scholarly assessment see Steve Mason, *Josephus and the New Testament*, (Peabody, MA Hendrickson Publishers, 1992), 163-174.

[2] In *Antiquities* 18.106 Josephus places the trade around the time of the death of Herod's brother, Philip, who died in A.D. 33/34: Flavius Josephus and William Whiston, *The Works of Josephus: Complete and Unabridged* (Peabody: Hendrickson, 1987), footnote C.

[3] Josephus, *Antiquities of the Jews* 18.101-105. Flavius Josephus and William Whiston, *The Works of Josephus: Complete and Unabridged* (Peabody: Hendrickson, 1987).

shipped to Rome.[4] But were they? Josephus doesn't say. So, what if the giant Eleazar escaped? What if he found his short way down to Caesarea Philippi, where Jesus was during that last year of ministry? Thus the creative license of the novel applying to historical characters in a feasible scenario.

But that is not all the novel drew from historical characters. Many Bible readers know the name of Barabbas as the one who the Jews chose to release at Pilate's offer instead of Jesus (Matt. 27:15-26). But what many casual readers of the Bible do not know is that Barabbas was a leader of a failed insurrection around that time in Jerusalem (Luke 2:19). He was no ordinary criminal. He was a zealot warrior, as he is in *Jesus Triumphant.*

The two "thieves on crosses" next to Jesus are another case of commonly misunderstood identity. "Thief" or "robber" makes one think of common criminals or kleptomaniacs caught stealing camels or jewelry. But the Greek word for "thief" used of the two on the cross is *lestai*, the same word used by Josephus to describe the zealous Jewish brigands in revolution against Rome. Crucifixion was the punishment for such organized sedition and insurrection. The "thieves" on the cross were actually revolutionaries in the tradition of the Zealots.[5]

Though the existence of bands of Jewish insurrectionists against Rome at the time of Christ is not in dispute, the exact nature and chronology of the infamous Zealots is. Some have argued they did not come into existence until around the fall of Jerusalem,[6] but others have shown that they originated in Judas of Galilee's failed insurrection of A.D. 6.[7] He made famous the slogan "No king but God," that came to mark the Zealot cause.[8]

Judas of Galilee's sons, James and Simon, went on to be executed as zealous rebels around A.D. 46.[9] Josephus also describes two Zealot-like leaders Eleazar ben Dinai and Amram, who were captured and banished around A.D. 45 by Roman procurator Fadus. Another brigand leader, Tholomy was executed.[10] Eleazar was captured again later and executed in Rome in A.D. 60.[11] This means that James, John, Amram, Tholomy and Eleazar had been rising within the ranks of the newly growing Zealot movement during the time of Christ. Thus, their presence in *Jesus Triumphant.*

---

[4] Josephus, *Antiquities* 18.105.

[5] N. T. Wright, *The New Testament and the People of God, Christian Origins and the Question of God* (London: Society for Promoting Christian Knowledge, 1992), 178–180.

[6] Richard A. Horsley and John S. Hanson, *Bandits, Prophets, and Messiahs: Popular Movements at the Time of Jesus* (New York: NY, Winston Press, 1985).

[7] Martin Hengel, *The Zealots: investigations into the Jewish freedom movement in the period from Herod I until 70 A.D.* (Edinburgh: U.K., T. & T. Clark, 1989).

[8] Hengel, *The Zealots,* 108.

[9] Josephus, *Antiquities* 20.102.

[10] Josephus, *Antiquities* 20.4-5.

[11] Josephus, *Antiquities* 20.161. Under the procurator Felix.

Qumran, Essenes and the Dead Sea Scrolls

In 1946, the famous Dead Sea Scrolls were uncovered in caves near the ancient Essene settlement of Qumran on the northwest shores of the Dead Sea thirteen miles east of Jerusalem. They shed light on the early monastic community that had been previously found nearby, and written about by Josephus. Much discussion and debate surrounds these texts and the people who stored them in libraries.

One of the more interesting elements of their beliefs was the similarity of Messianic hope with what would end up being the New Testament claims for Jesus. Scholar Marvin Pate explains that, like many Jews of Second Temple Judaism, they too sought a Davidic Messiah to deliver Israel from her continuing exile under Roman rule.[12]

A more recent discovery of an ancient text on stone called "Vision of Gabriel," dated to the first century B.C., has revealed a unique correspondence with the New Testament notion of Messiah rising after three days. This is much more explicit than any Old Testament reference to such a thing. I incorporated this prophecy into *Jesus Triumphant* as part of the literature that persuades an Essene character of Christ's fulfillment. Several of the lines from the stone indicate this amazing correspondence.

> *By three days you shall know that, thus said Yahweh of Hosts, the god of Israel,*
> *the evil has been broken by righteousness...*
> *Behold, all the nations gather against Jerusalem...*
> *In just a little while, I will shake the heavens and the earth...*
> *My servant David [Messiah], ask of Ephraim for a sign...*
> *By three days, live/be resurrected, I Gabriel, command you, prince of princes.*[13]

This is not to say that the Vision of Gabriel should be considered Scripture. But it certainly adds outside corroboration to the understanding of the Jewish messianic hope fulfilled in Christ.

The Jewish expectation based on Nebuchadnezzar's dream in Daniel 2 was that Messiah would come and crush the nation of Rome in history. The Qumran community had a document called "The War Scroll" that describes

[12] C. Marvin Pate, *Communities of the Last Days: The Dead Sea Scrolls, The New Testament & The Story of Israel*, (Downers Grove, IL: InterVarsity Press, 2000), 107-132.
[13] Israel Knohl, "By Three Days, Live": Messiahs, Resurrection, and Ascent to Heaven in Hazon Gabriel, *The Journal of Religion*, Vol. 88, No. 2 (April 2008), pp. 147-158

in detail this War of the Sons of Light Against the Sons of Darkness, calling Romans by the symbolic name of *Kittim*.[14]

But as Josephus explains, the time period after Herod the Great's death in 4 B.C. was plagued with various messianic movements and revolutionaries, many that were deeply at odds with each other. They argued over whose interpretation was correct and what marked the true people of God. Pate argues that another element of distinction emerges in the Dead Sea Scrolls: they considered themselves the only true remnant of Israel. And when Messiah came, he would deliver the Essene Community alone, while destroying the rest of Israel with his holy army![15] This is remarkably reminiscent of Jesus' Olivet Discourse that describes God's destructive judgment of Jerusalem and the Temple (Matt. 24), and concurrent rescue of the remnant elect believers (Matt. 24:15-22; Rom. 11:1-10). Those Essenes were so close, and yet, so far.

N.T. Wright sums up this earthly expectation of why the Jews were looking for a physical conquering king rather than a suffering servant.

> Many if not most second-Temple Jews, then, hoped for the new exodus, seen as the final return from exile. The story would reach its climax; the great battle would be fought; Israel would truly 'return' to her land, saved and free; YHWH would return to Zion. This would be, in the metaphorical sense, the end of the world, the ushering in at last of YHWH's promised new age. From the perspective of covenant history, this complex event would be climactic, and not merely a paradigmatic example of a general principle (such as the importance of social justice). Moreover, this whole set of ideas and themes belongs together as a whole, not as a collection of abstract ideas, but precisely as a story.[16]

All this is not to say, as liberal scholars and Bible haters say, that Jesus was wrong in his apocalyptic declarations, but rather that, as the spiritual warfare motif of *Jesus Triumphant* points to, he was both suffering servant *and* mighty conqueror of a spiritual Armageddon, a covenantal "end of the age," for a kingdom not of this world, whose effect would ultimately be seen in history.

---

[14] Michael O. Wise, Martin G. Abegg Jr., and Edward M. Cook, *The Dead Sea Scrolls: A New Translation* (New York: HarperOne, 2005), 146–170.

[15] Pate, *Communities of the Last Days,* 113.

[16] N. T. Wright, *Jesus and the Victory of God, Christian Origins and the Question of God* (London: Society for Promoting Christian Knowledge, 1996), 209. N. T. Wright, Jesus and the Victory of God, Christian Origins and the Question of God (London: Society for Promoting Christian Knowledge, 1996), 209.

Caesar and Christ

But even pagans have their Christ prophecies too. It seems everyone wanted to be God. And the Romans were no exception. The language of Augustus Caesar reflected similar concepts of the divinity of their emperor, as the New Testament did of Jesus Christ. Inscriptions on coins and buildings throughout the empire called Augustus, "God, Son of God, Savior."[17] A famous proclamation of Augustus used phrases such as "savior," "god manifest," and "good news [*gospel*]."

> The most <u>divine Caesar</u>...we should consider equal to the Beginning of all things...; for when everything was falling [into disorder] and tending toward dissolution, he restored it once more and gave to the whole world a new aura...and who being sent to us and our descendants as <u>Savior</u>...and [whereas,] having <u>become [god] manifest</u>, Caesar has fulfilled all the hopes of earlier times... and whereas, finally, the birthday of <u>the god [Augustus]</u> has been for the whole world the beginning of <u>good news</u> concerning him [therefore let a new era begin from his birth].[18]

Early and Medieval Church Fathers were so impressed by classical wisdom, they sought to incorporate great Greek and Roman writers into their revealed wisdom of God. Some claimed that Aristotle or Plato were even saved through natural revelation. Augustine told a story in his *City of God* about a prophecy that was allegedly given by the Erythraean Sibyl to Augustus Caesar, but pointed toward Christ, not Caesar, as the world ruler. As scholar Burke elucidates some of the lines of this prophecy as they appear in *Jesus Triumphant*,

> *"In token of judgment, the earth shall drip with sweat.*
> *A king destined to rule forever will arrive from heaven,*
> *present in mortal flesh, in order to judge the world."*[19]

Though these are fabricated legends by well meaning Christians, reading into Greek sibylline literature to bolster their faith, they point up the fact that

---

[17] Stanley E. Porter, "Paul Confronts Caesar with the Good News," Stanley E. Porter, Cynthia Long Westfall, Ed., *Empire in the New Testament* (Wipf and Stock, 2011), 172-3.
[18] Richard A. Horsley, *Jesus and Empire: The Kingdom of God and the New World Disorder* (Minneapolis, MN: Fortress Press, 2003) 23.
[19] Paul F. Burke, "Augustus and Christianity in Myth and Legend," *New England Classical Journal* 32.3 (2005) 213-220. From Augustine's *City of God* 18.23.1.

sometimes, God does use pagans as instruments of prophecy or judgment (Num. 22:21-39; 1Sam. 19:21-24; Isa. 10).

Nephilim and Demons

Demons are a theological problem. Where do they come from? What are they? Why are they almost entirely absent in the Old Testament, and then all of a sudden, there is a flurry of demonic activity and possessions once Messiah comes to Israel? The casting out or exorcism of demons is so frequently linked with Jesus' proclamation of the Gospel that it seems to be more than a mere symbolic expression of his power over the spiritual world. It is an essential theological component of the New Covenant.

First, just what are demons? We see in the New Testament that they are evil spirits that possess or inhabit the physical bodies of living individuals (Luke 11:24-26), and who are cast out by Jesus and his disciples by the power of the Holy Spirit (Matt. 8:16; Luke 10:17). Their presence sometimes causes physical infirmities like blindness (Matt. 12:22), deafness (Mark 9:17-29), or epilepsy (Matt. 17:15-18), as well as mental insanity (Mark 5:15). Many of them can inhabit one body (Mark 5:9), and bring great strength to the host (Mark 5:4).

But where did these evil spirits come from? In the Old Testament, there is very little explanation of demons. God sends an evil spirit to torment King Saul in 1 Sam. 16:14. Based on Saul's insane behavior it is safe to say he was most likely possessed by that evil spirit (v. 15-23). 1 Kings 22:22-23 reveals that God sends a "lying spirit" into the mouths of false prophets. Demons? Maybe. But certainly subservient to God's interests. Even the satan is depicted as a circumscribed servant of God's will in the Old Testament (Job 1:12). As explained in other Appendices of the Chronicles, pagan idols are sometimes referred to as demonic (Deut. 32:17; Psa. 106:34-37; Lev. 17:7) exposing the spiritual reality behind their earthly façade of graven images and foreign deities.

But other than these few examples, there is a dearth in the Old Testament of the kind of activity we read about in the New Testament, with raging demoniacs being exorcised by Christ and his disciples. It seems like the demons knew that the presence of Messiah was the final countdown of their own demise and they were throwing fits and tantrums. As if the Seed of the Woman was crushing the Seed of the Serpent's head and the body was wriggling in pain.

But they are never described as fallen angels in the Bible.

What then, are demons and from where do they come?

The church father Origen claimed that there was no clearly defined teaching on their genesis in the early church, but that a significant opinion was that "the devil was an angel, and that, having become an apostate, he induced as many of the angels as possible to fall away with himself, and these up to the present time are called his angels."[20]

This common Christian idea of the satan and demons as fallen angels is often proof-texted from Isa. 14:12-15, Ezek. 28:12-16, and Rev. 12:4. But as explained in the Appendix to *Enoch Primordial*, I do not believe these passages apply to a satanic fall from heaven.[21] Isaiah 14 is the likening of the monstrous pride of the king of Babylon to a Canaanite myth of arrogant deities. Nothing about the satan there. And there is no reference to any others joining him either. Ezekiel 28 is a condemnation of the king of Tyre by likening him to Adam's fall in the Garden, *not* the satan. This passage also fails to mention anyone in collusion with the arrogant prince. One has to import an alien notion of the satanic fall into these passages through eisegesis.

Lastly, Revelation 12 is not about a satanic fall or war in heaven *before the Garden of Eden*, or even in some future end of the world scenario. It is an apocalyptic parable that is describing the war of the satan *at the incarnation of Christ*, his ascension to the throne of authority over all principalities and powers, and his suppression of the satan's power as the Gospel goes forth into the world.

So in the Bible there is no evidence of angels falling before the Garden of Eden. There *is* a satanic "fall" or a "casting out" of heaven (John 12:31) and a "throwing down" to the earth of the satan *during the time of Christ* (Luke 10:17-20). But that would be too late in the game to explain the few evil spirits in the Old Testament or their presence before the arrival of Messiah. The only other "fall" of angelic beings in the Bible is the Sons of God, the Watchers, in Genesis 6 coming to earth.[22]

But that presents another problem, namely that the ontological nature or "material being" of the angels as revealed in the Bible would seem to preclude these fallen angels from being the Old Testament or New Testament demons. While angels are multidimensional in their ability to traverse between the heavenlies and the earth, they are described as having flesh that eats food (Gen. 18; 19:1), and can have sexual congress with human beings (Gen. 6:1-4). This is a heavenly flesh that is different from human flesh (1 Cor. 15:39-

---

[20] Origen, "De Principiis," in The Ante-Nicene Fathers: Fathers of the Third Century: Tertullian, Part Fourth; Minucius Felix; Commodian; Origen, Parts First and Second, ed. Alexander Roberts, James Donaldson, and A. Cleveland Coxe, trans. Frederick Crombie, vol. 4 (Buffalo, NY: Christian Literature Company, 1885), 240.

[21] Brian Godawa, *Enoch Primordial* (Los Angeles: Embedded Pictures Publishing, 2013), 367-373.

[22] See the chapter "The Book of Enoch: Scripture, Heresy, or What?" in *When Giants Were Upon the Earth: The Watchers, Nephilim and the Cosmic War of the Seed* (Los Angeles: Embedded Pictures, 2014),.

40), but is flesh nonetheless. This would make angels or divine beings such as the Watchers unlikely candidates for incorporeal spirits seeking flesh to inhabit or possess.

There is no origin of demons detailed in the Bible. There is merely a description of their spiritual nature and evil activities. But there is a tradition of their origin that carries some weight beyond mere speculation. Regarding this origin, the *Dictionary of Deities and Demons in the Bible* says, "The most popular myth, however, is found in the Bible, intertestamental literature, the rabbis and the Church fathers: demons are the souls of the offspring of angels who cohabited with humans."[23] We are right back to that ancient text that keeps rearing its head in the New Testament; the book of 1 Enoch. There we read that the giants had unique ontological status as hybrids of both human and angel. So when they died in the Flood, their spirits became roaming entities seeking bodily possession of humans.

> 1 Enoch 15:8-16:1
> [8] "But now the giants who are born from the (union of) the spirits and the flesh shall be called evil spirits upon the earth, because their dwelling shall be upon the earth and inside the earth. [9] Evil spirits have come out of their bodies. Because from the day that they were created from the holy ones they became the Watchers; their first origin is the spiritual foundation. They will become evil upon the earth and shall be called evil spirits... [12] And these spirits shall rise up against the children of the people and against the women, because they have proceeded forth (from them)... From the days of the slaughter and destruction, and the death of the giants... they will corrupt until the day of the great conclusion, until

[23] G. J. Riley, "Demon," ed. Karel van der Toorn, Bob Becking, and Pieter W. van der Horst, *Dictionary of Deities and Demons in the Bible* (Leiden; Boston; Köln; Grand Rapids, MI; Cambridge: Brill; Eerdmans, 1999), 238. Early church fathers who believed this are Justin Martyr, Athenagoras, Minuciux Felix, Irenaeus, among others: Bo Reicke, *The Disobedient Spirits and Christian Baptism* (New York: AMS Press, 1946), 80-81. Other Intertestamental literature that affirms demons as sons of the Watchers are Test. Of Solomon 5:3; 17:1; Jubilees 10:5; Dead Sea Scrolls 4Q510 v.5; 4Q511 Frag. 35; 4Q204 Col V.2-3 (1Enoch 10:15), that call the demons, sons of the Watchers or "spirits of the bastards." Florentino García Martínez and Eibert J. C. Tigchelaar, "The Dead Sea Scrolls Study Edition (translations)" (Leiden; New York: Brill, 1997–1998), 415, 1029, 1033-35. 11Q11 Col. V.6 calls demons "offspring of man and of the seed of the holy ones." DSS Study Edition, 1203. See Loren T. Stuckenbruck, "The 'Angels' and 'Giants' of Genesis 6:1-4 in Second and Third Century BCE Jewish Interpretation: Reflections on the Posture of Early Apocalyptic Traditions," Dead Sea Discoveries, Vol. 7, No. 3, *Angels and Demons* (2000), pp. 354-37; Ida Fröhlich,"Theology and Demonology in Qumran Texts," *Henoch*; Vol. 32 Issue 1, June 2010, 101-129.

> the great age is consummated, until everything is concluded (upon) the Watchers and the wicked ones."[24]

Chronicles of the Nephilim assumes this Enochic interpretation in its storyline as the last gasp attempt of the Seed of the Serpent to bite the heel of the Seed of Eve. Needless to say, their head is crushed in that attempt.

The God of This World

Chronicles of the Nephilim has largely been based upon the Divine Council worldview that has been explained in several previous Chronicles appendices. This involves the fallen Watchers from God's heavenly host who are called the Sons of God. They led the world astray in the Days of Noah, that led to the Flood as Yahweh's judgment. Deuteronomy 32:8-9, then speaks of how at the Tower of Babel, Yahweh divided the seventy nations according to the number of the fallen Sons of God and placed them under their authority. They became the "princes" (Dan. 10:13, 20-21) or "gods" of those pagan nations (Deut. 32:17; 4:19-21), rulers of those geographical territories.[25]

When earthly rulers battle on earth, the Bible describes the host of heaven battling with them in spiritual unity. In Daniel 10, hostilities between Greece and Persia is accompanied by the battle of heavenly Watchers over those nations (described as "princes").

> Daniel 10:13, 20-21
> The prince of the kingdom of Persia withstood me twenty-one days, but Michael, one of the chief princes, came to help me, for I was left there with the kings of Persia." …Then he said, "Do you know why I have come to you? But now I will return to fight against the prince of Persia; and when I go out, behold, the prince of Greece will come. [21] But I will tell you what is inscribed in the book of truth: there is none who contends by my side against these except Michael, your prince.

When Sisera fought with Israel, the earthly kings and heavenly authorities (host of heaven) are described interchangeably in unity.[26]

---

[24] James H. Charlesworth, *The Old Testament Pseudepigrapha*, vol. 1 (New York; London: Yale University Press, 1983), 22.

[25] See Appendix, "Sons of God," in Brian Godawa, *Noah Primeval* (Los Angeles: Embedded Pictures, 2011, 2012), 280-289.

[26] See also 2 Kings 6:15-17 where Elisha's servant has his spiritual eyes opened to see the myriad of heavenly warriors surrounding Israel preparing to battle Syria.

Judges 5:19–20
"The kings came, they fought; then fought the kings of Canaan…From heaven the stars fought, from their courses they fought against Sisera.

When God punishes earthly rulers, he punishes them along with the heavenly rulers ("host of heaven") above and behind them.

Isaiah 24:21–22
On that day the LORD will punish the host of heaven, in heaven, and the kings of the earth, on the earth. They will be gathered together as prisoners in a pit; they will be shut up in a prison, and after many days they will be punished.[27]

Though this notion of territorial archons or spiritual rulers is Biblical and carries over into intertestamental literature such as the Book of Enoch (1 En. 89:59, 62-63; 67) and others,[28] it seems to lessen at the time of the New Testament.

Walter Wink points out that the picture of Watchers over nations is hinted at in 1 Cor. 4:9 where the apostle explains their persecution has "become a spectacle (theatre) to the world, to angels and to men." He explains that "the image of the Roman theater conjures up hostile and jeering crowds," and the angels are "heavenly representatives of the Gentile nations and people, who watch, not without malicious glee, the tribulations endured by the apostle to their peoples."[29]

The epistles speak of the spiritual principalities and powers that are behind the earthly rulers and powers to be sure (Eph. 6:12-13), but it appears to be more generic in reference. And after the death, resurrection, and ascension of Christ, these spiritual powers have been disarmed and overthrown (Col. 2:15, Luke 10:18), at least legally losing their hegemony (Eph. 1:20-23). The fallen angelic powers are still around, but have been defanged with the inauguration of the Messianic kingdom of God.

---

[27] Interestingly, this passage of Isaiah is not clear about what judgment in history it is referring to. But the language earlier in the text is similar to the Flood when it says, "For the windows of heaven are opened, and the foundations of the earth tremble. 19 The earth is utterly broken, the earth is split apart, the earth is violently shaken. 20 The earth staggers like a drunken man; it sways like a hut; its transgression lies heavy upon it, and it falls, and will not rise again." So this may be another passage that uses a Flood reference tied in with the Watchers and their punishment.

[28] See also Jubilees 15:31-32; Targum Jonathan Deut. 32, Sect. LIII; 3Enoch 48C:9, DSS War Scroll 1Q33 Col. xvii:7, Targum Jonathan, Genesis 11, Section II.

[29] Walter Wink. *Naming the Powers: The Language of Power in the New Testament* (The Powers : Volume One) (Kindle Locations 394-396). Kindle Edition.

But there is one of those fallen angelic powers that seems to rise up and grab extraordinary authority in the New Testament: The satan (which translated, means, "Accuser"). The Accuser's choice of Belial as a proper name in *Jesus Triumphant* is well-attested in Scripture and other ancient Jewish writings, especially the Dead Sea Scrolls from Qumran.[30] He is also called Beliar, Mastema, and Sammael in other Second Temple literature.[31] Throughout the Old Testament, the Hebrew word *belial* is used as a personification of death, wickedness, and treachery, as well as "an emotive term to describe individuals or groups who commit the most heinous crimes against the Israelite religious or social order, as well as their acts."[32] The Apostle Paul uses the proper name of Belial for the satan (using language similar to the Dead Sea Scrolls) in 2 Corinthians 6:14–15: "Do not be unequally yoked with unbelievers. For what partnership has righteousness with lawlessness? Or what fellowship has light with darkness? What accord has Christ with Belial?"

Three times in the Gospel of John, this Accuser named Belial, is called "the ruler of this world" (Jn. 12:31, 14:30-31, 16:11), in 2 Cor. 4:4, "the god of this world." In Eph. 2:2 he is called the "prince of the power of the air, the spirit that is now working in the sons of disobedience." In fact, when Jesus was tempted by the satan in the desert, he offered Christ all the kingdoms of the world for his own "domain and glory; for it has been handed over to me, and I give it to whomever I wish" (Luke 4:6). It seems as if the satan is the only Watcher god in authority over the nations, like he has all the power. What happened to all the other ones?

Walter Wink points out a possible key to the solution. In the intertestamental period "much tradition identified Satan as the angel of Rome, thus adapting the angels-of-the-nations idea to the situation of Roman world-

---

[30] Especially in the War Scroll (1QM) and the Thankgiving Scroll (1QH). Florentino García Martínez and Eibert J. C. Tigchelaar, "The Dead Sea Scrolls Study Edition (translations)" (Leiden; New York: Brill, 1997–1998), 113-178.

[31] C. Breytenbach (I, IV) and (I–III) Day P. L., "Satan," ed. Karel van der Toorn, Bob Becking, and Pieter W. van der Horst, *Dictionary of Deities and Demons in the Bible* (Leiden; Boston; Köln; Grand Rapids, MI; Cambridge: Brill; Eerdmans, 1999), 72; S. D. Sperling, "Belial," *DDD*, 169; J. W. van Henten, "Mastemah," *DDD*, 553. On Sammael: M. A. Knibb, "Martyrdom and Ascension of Isaiah: A New Translation and Introduction," in *The Old Testament Pseudepigrapha and the New Testament: Expansions of the "Old Testament" and Legends, Wisdom, and Philosophical Literature, Prayers, Psalms and Odes, Fragments of Lost Judeo-Hellenistic Works, vol. 2* (New Haven; London: Yale University Press, 1985), 151.

[32] S. D. Sperling, "Belial," ed. Karel van der Toorn, Bob Becking, and Pieter W. van der Horst, *Dictionary of Deities and Demons in the Bible* (Leiden; Boston; Köln; Grand Rapids, MI; Cambridge: Brill; Eerdmans, 1999), 169. "Such crimes include: inciting one's fellows to worship foreign gods (Deut 13:14); perjury (1 Kgs 21:10, 13; Prov 19:28); breach of hospitality (Judg 19:22; 1 Sam 25:17); lese-majesty (1 Sam 10:27); usurpation (2 Sam 16:7–8; 20:1); abuse of Yahweh's sanctuary by female drunkenness (1 Sam 1:13–17); and the cultic misappropriation and sexual harassment of women by priests (1 Sam 2:12–22). Refusal to lend money on the eve of the Sabbatical year (Deut 15:9) falls into the category of heinous deeds because it indicates lack of faith in the divine ability to provide." See also, Deut 13:13; Judg 19:22; 1 Sam 1:16; 2:12; 10:27; 25:17; 2 Sam 16:7; Nah 1:15 (2:1); 1 Kgs 21:13.

hegemony. Since Rome had conquered the entire Mediterranean region and much else besides, its angel-prince had become lord of all other angel-princes of the vanquished nations. This identification was already explicit at Qumran, where Rome and the Romans (the 'Kittim' of the War Scroll) are made the specific allies and agents of Satan and his host."[33]

The Dead Sea Scroll 11QMelch interprets Psalm 82 as describing Satan/Belial as the chief of the gods in the divine council to be punished for his unjust authority over the nations.[34] Another Jewish intertestamental document, the Testament of the Twelve Patriarchs, lists in several places Beliar, synonymous with Satan, as holding captive mankind.[35]

In the post-New Testament religious text The Martyrdom and Ascension of Isaiah (1st century A.D.) the name of Satan is used synonymously with the names Sammael and Beliar.[36] But in the later text of 3 Enoch (5th century A.D.), Satan, Sammael, and Beliar are considered separate entities, with Sammael and Beliar being Satan's underlings (3 Enoch 26:12).

But the real twist is that in this same text, Sammael is called *the Prince of Rome*, just as Dubbiel is called the Prince of Persia (remember the "Prince of Persia" from Daniel 10?).

> 3 Enoch 26:12
> Every day Satan sits with Samma'el, Prince of Rome, and with Dubbi'el, Prince of Persia, and they write down the sins of Israel on tablets and give them to the seraphim to bring them before the Holy One, blessed be he, so that he should destroy Israel from the world.[37]

---

[33] Wink, *Naming the Powers*, Kindle Locations 409-412. Of the Qumran War Scroll, Davies says, "Using the term "Kittim," which in the Hebrew Bible is applied to Greeks and then (in Daniel) to Romans, it transparently identifies the Roman Empire as the ally of Belial, the spirit/angel of darkness, and of the "Children of Darkness," and describes their defeat in a great seven-stage battle… At present, there is little consensus on the literary history, though a date in the last quarter of the first century B.C.E. is widely accepted, as is the identification of the Kittim, allies of the "Children of Darkness," as the Romans." Phillip Davies, "The Biblical and Qumranic Concept of War," James H. Charlesworth, Ed. *The Bible and the Dead Sea Scrolls Volume One - Scripture and the Scrolls* (Waco: Baylor University, 2006), 223, 226.

[34] *11QMelch* (1st century B.C.) Geza Vermes, *The Dead Sea Scrolls in English*, Revised and extended 4th ed. (Sheffield: Sheffield Academic Press, 1995), 361.

[35] TDan 5:10-13; TZeb 9:8; TLevi 18:12; Test. Judah 25:3; Assum. Moses 10:1-3. These texts are from the 2nd century B.C.

[36] M. A. Knibb, "Martyrdom and Ascension of Isaiah: A New Translation and Introduction," in The Old Testament Pseudepigrapha and the New Testament: Expansions of the "Old Testament" and Legends, Wisdom, and Philosophical Literature, Prayers, Psalms and Odes, Fragments of Lost Judeo-Hellenistic Works, vol. 2 (New Haven; London: Yale University Press, 1985), 151.

[37] James H. Charlesworth, *The Old Testament Pseudepigrapha*, vol. 1 (New York; London: Yale University Press, 1983), 281.

Just like the satan in the New Testament, Sammael is called the "prince of the accusers who is greater than all the princes of kingdoms that are in the height [heaven]" (3 Enoch 14:2). And just like the satan in the New Testament, Sammael's name means "god of the blind" (2 Cor. 4:4).[38]

So in these texts Sammael is the Watcher prince over Rome under the authority of the satan, or Sammael is the name of the Watcher prince over Rome who also has the heavenly position of being "the accuser" (the satan).[39]

But what about this notion of the ruler (*archon*), or god of this world? Is the world something bigger than the realm of this satanic Prince of Rome? To answer that, we will have to look at the idea of *the world* as presented in the New Testament.

It is common in the Bible to refer to the Roman Empire as "all the world" (*oikoumene*) which meant the known inhabited world under Rome's power. Luke writes that when Caesar ordered a census of the Roman Empire, he made a decree that "all the world (*oikoumene*) should be registered" (Luke 2:1). Jesus said that the Gospel would be proclaimed "through all the world (*oikoumene*) as a testimony to all the nations" (Matt. 24:14). At that time, all the nations (and their allotted Watchers?) were under Roman rule. When Paul writes that within his own lifetime, the Gospel "has been proclaimed in all creation under heaven" (Col. 1:23), it is an obvious expression of *the inhabited world of the Roman Empire,* not the entire globe as we now know it.

Another Greek word occasionally used for the Roman world was *cosmos*. Cosmos was not the physical universe as we would understand it, but rather more like the zeitgeist or the godless "world system" or "world order" of estranged humanity.[40] And that world order was of course Rome. Paul writes that the very Gospel preached in the Roman Empire "has come to you, as indeed in the whole world (*cosmos*)" (Col. 1:6). The Roman Christian's faith had been "proclaimed in all the world (*cosmos*)" (Rom. 1:8), the Gospel "has been made known to all the nations" (Rom. 16:26) at the time of Paul's writing to those Romans in the first century.[41]

In the New Testament, the "world" (cosmos) and the "inhabited earth" (*oikoumene*) as well as other global language was used interchangeably to refer to the known inhabited world of the Roman Empire. All the known nations were encompassed in its power and worldview, so it seems those

---

[38] P. Alexander, "A New Translation and Introduction," in *The Old Testament Pseudepigrapha*, vol. 1 (New York; London: Yale University Press, 1983), 236.

[39] These pseudepigraphal texts do not have canonical status as Scripture. 3 Enoch is gnostic in its orientation. But they do illustrate an interpretive tradition that is in accord with the Biblical cosmic war we have been examining. Textual food for thought.

[40] κόσμοςd Johannes P. Louw and Eugene Albert Nida, *Greek-English Lexicon of the New Testament: Based on Semantic Domains* (New York: United Bible Societies, 1996), 106.

[41] See Gary DeMar, *Last Days Madness: Obsession of the Modern Church 4th edition* (Powder Springs: American Vision, 1999), 87-89.

angelic entities over those nations would therefore also be under the authority of the Watcher of Rome.

If the satan therefore was "god" or "ruler" of that "world," then most likely he had become the angelic authority over Rome, and it would make sense that the New Testament would focus on the satan over the other Watchers. Rome had become the ultimate enemy of God's people and had authority over *all the nations of the world.* So much so that Daniel's vision was of the Messianic stone (Jesus) that would hit the Roman empire and ultimately crush it as the apex of godless empire (Dan. 2:44-45).

This theory is further evidenced in the book of Revelation where the Dragon of Revelation 12, clearly described as "that ancient serpent, who is the devil and the satan" (20:2), is the angelic principality of power that gives authority to both the Beast of the Sea (13:1-2) and the Beast of the Land (13:11-12).[42] Readers of the *Chronicles of the Nephilim* will be very familiar with the sea beast of Leviathan and the land beast of Behemoth. As explained in previous appendices, these are chaos monsters, symbolic of both foreign nations and rulers against whom Yahweh battles to establish his covenanted order.[43] Leviathan's sea dragon imagery is linked with the satan's serpentine chaos nature.

Revelation is notoriously difficult to interpret, and there are a plethora of interpretations of who or what the Land and Sea Beasts represent. But there is a common thread for the interpretation of the Sea Beast among most all the interpretive schools. Robert Mounce explains it:

> There is little doubt that for John the beast was the Roman Empire as persecutor of the church. It comes onto the land from the sea, just as the Roman troops did when they invaded the eastern Mediterranean. The beast is that spirit of imperial power which claims a religious sanction for its gross injustices."[44]

In his book, *The Beast of Revelation*, eschatology expert Ken Gentry points out that the Beast imagery of Revelation paints a fluid picture of both an individual and a kingdom of spiritual chaos and oppression. That kingdom

---

[42] Wink, *Naming the Powers*, Kindle Locations 407-417.

[43] Brian Godawa, *Noah Primeval*, 323-337. See also David E. Aune, *Revelation 6–16, vol. 52B, Word Biblical Commentary* (Dallas: Word, Incorporated, 1998), 732.

[44] Robert H. Mounce, *The Book of Revelation*, The New International Commentary on the New Testament (Grand Rapids, MI: Wm. B. Eerdmans Publishing Co., 1997), 246. See Steve Gregg, *Revelation, Four Views : a Parallel Commentary* (Nashville, Tenn.: T. Nelson Publishers, 1997), Re 13:1–4.

is the Roman Empire that was also embodied in its emperor.[45] The third of other angels that the Dragon's tail cast with him to earth (Rev. 12:4) then become the Watchers of the other nations under Rome and therefore under the satan's authority.

In this understanding, When Jesus the Messiah arrives and inaugurates the kingdom of God, he does so by "binding the strong man" the "god of this world," the satan. His casting out of demons was a herald of casting down the satan's power (John 12:31; Matt. 12:28-29), and taking authority over his world. It was as if one fell swoop of the highest heavenly power over the nations brought down all the enemies with him. He destroyed the one who has the power of death, that is, the devil (Heb. 2:14). But why is he still prowling around like a roaring lion seeking whom he may devour?(1Pet. 5:8).

Because his overthrow is not absolute. It's a qualified binding. Let's take a closer look at the "binding" of the satan.

Magic and the Binding of Spirits

Through the entire *Chronicles* series, I have used a concept called "binding" of angels, demons, and Watchers. This binding is accomplished through imprisonment in the earth or Tartarus.

This binding notion originates theologically from the binding of Satan in the ministry of Christ as noted above in Matthew 12, as well as the binding of angels in "chains of gloomy darkness" in Tartarus in Jude 6 and 2 Peter 2:4. And these New Testament Scriptures are paraphrases of the Enochian narrative of the antediluvian Watchers who at the Flood were "bound" "for seventy generations underneath the rocks of the ground until the day of their judgment" (1 Enoch 10:12).

The idea of binding spirits is a common one in ancient religion and magic. Michael Fishbane notes that in the ancient Near East, incantations and spells were used by sorcerers and enchanters to bind people and spirits in spiritual "traps, pits, snares, and nets," using venomous curses from their lips like serpents. In response to some of these verbal sorceries, the Psalmist himself calls upon Yahweh in similar utterances to reverse the spells upon his enemies that they would be trapped, ensnared and bound by their own magical devices (Psalm 140; 64; 57:4-6).[46] Exorcists of the first century used incantations to

---

[45] Kenneth Gentry, *The Beast of Revelation* 2nd edition (Fort Worth: Institute for Christian Economics, 1994).

[46] Michael A Fishbane, *Studies In Biblical Magic : Origins, Uses And Transformations Of Terminology And Literary Form* (Dissertation) Brandeis University, 1971. See also Edwin M. Yamauchi, "Magic In The Biblical World," The Institute For Biblical Research Lecture, 1981, *Tyndale Bulletin* 34 (1983).

cast out demons in Jesus' name (Acts 16:18), the same incantation used by Demons *against* Jesus before being cast out (Mk 1:27).[47]

Ezekiel 13:18 refers to a specific form of hunting and binding spirits in a practice of women "who sew magic bands upon all wrists…in the hunt for souls!" I reversed this pagan version of using magical armbands by creating a heavenly version of the archangels with armbands of indestructible Cherubim hair for their hunting and binding of evil spirits. The hair is wrapped as bands around the arms of archangels and used like a rope to bind the Watchers' hands and feet.

Scholars have pointed out that the binding of Satan that occurs in Matthew 12 is evidently not an exhaustive or absolute binding, since he is still active after the ministry of Christ and even into the New Testament era (Acts 5:3; Rom. 16:20; 2Cor. 12:7; 1Thes. 2:18; Rev. 2:13). But then how does this continuing satanic activity fit with the notion that Satan "was thrown down to the earth" (Rev. 12:9), "fell like lightning from heaven" (Luke 10:18), was disarmed and overthrown in triumph (Col. 2:15), destroyed along with his power of death (Heb. 2:14), and all of this accomplished through the death, resurrection and ascension of Christ (Matt. 12:28-29; Heb. 2:14)?

Revelation 22:2-3 provides a theological solution to the dilemma. It says that Satan is bound and thrown into a sealed pit for a thousand years, "so that he might not deceive the nations." Deceiver of the world is a Biblical epithet of Satan (Rev. 12:9; 20:7), ever since the beginning in the Garden (1 Tim. 2:14; John 8:44). So perhaps the binding of Satan is the muzzling of his deception over the world, as Jesus now has all authority, so that the Gospel can go forth into all the nations as it is now doing (Matt. 28:18).

This notion of Satan's binding is a problem for those who interpret that act as occurring in the Millennium, which they interpret as not having occurred as of yet. Revelation 20 is notoriously difficult to conclude any eschatological view. But we don't need Revelation 20 to make the point, because Jesus does in Matthew 12:

> Matt. 12:26–29
> And if the satan casts out the satan, he is divided against himself. How then will his kingdom stand?...But if it is by the Spirit of God that I cast out demons, then the kingdom of God has come upon you. Or how can someone enter a strong man's house and plunder his goods, unless he first binds the strong man? Then indeed he may plunder his house.

---

[47] Graham Twelftree, *Jesus the Exorcist: A Contribution to the Study of the Historical Jesus* (Eugene, OR: Wipf and Stock, 2010), 95, 139, 159-60.

Jesus said that his ministry on earth of casting out demons from the Promised Land was a binding of the satan. The satan could not stop the kingdom of God (ie: the Gospel) from inaugurating on earth.

This binding is like a legal restraining order on the satan. In the Old Testament, the satan is a divinely ordained legal role as a kind of prosecutor within God's heavenly court. He would test God's law and righteousness through accusation against God's people (1Kgs. 22; Job 1, 2; Zech 3). In Rev. 12:10, it describes the satan's fall from heaven as "the Accuser of our brethren being thrown down," also at the inauguration of God's kingdom. With the advent of Christ, the satan/Accuser has effectively been exiled from the divine council of Yahweh and no longer has any legal power of accusation against God's people (Rom. 8:1-4).

Yes, many nations are still in the lap of the evil one, but whereas the Kingdom of God under the Old Covenant was exclusively located in a small patch of land in the Middle East, surrounded by pagan Gentile nations, now under the power of the New Covenant, people from every nation are getting saved from all over the earth. The entire earth is Messiah's inheritance, not merely the land of Israel (Psa 2:8). The Good News of Christ is currently drawing all nations into heavenly Zion (Isa. 2; Heb. 12:22). The kingdoms of man are right now becoming the kingdoms of God through the proclamation and spread of the Gospel (1 Cor. 15:24-28; Heb. 2:8-9).

Now, let's take a look at the anointing of that conquering king over the cosmic kingdoms of the satan and mankind.

The Gates of Hades and the Transfiguration

In Matthew 16:13-20 is the famous story of Peter's confession of Jesus as the Christ, who then responds, "I tell you, you are Peter, and on this rock I will build my church, and the gates of ~~hell~~ [*Hades*] shall not prevail against it" (v. 18). Shortly after, Jesus leads them up to a high mountain where he is transfigured.

In order to understand the spiritual reality of what is going on in this polemical sequence and its relevance to the cosmic War of the Seed, we must first understand *where* it is going on.

Verse 13 says that Peter's confession takes place in the district of Caesarea Philippi. This city was in the heart of Bashan on a rocky terrace in the foothills of Mount Hermon. This was the celebrated location of the grotto of Banias or Panias, where the satyr goat god Pan was worshipped and from where the mouth of the Jordan river flowed. This very location was what was known as the "gates of Hades," the underworld abode of dead souls.

The Jewish historian Josephus wrote of this sacred grotto during his time, "a dark cave opens itself; within which there is a horrible precipice, that descends abruptly to a vast depth; it contains a mighty quantity of water, which is immovable; and when anybody lets down anything to measure the depth of the earth beneath the water, no length of cord is sufficient to reach it."[48]

As scholar Judd Burton points out, this is a kind of ground zero for the gods against whom Jesus was fighting his cosmic spiritual war. Mount Hermon was the location where the Watchers came to earth, led their rebellion and miscegenation, which birthed the Nephilim (1 Enoch 13:7-10). It was their headquarters, in Bashan, the place of the Serpent, where Azazel may have been worshipped before Pan as a desert goat idol.[49]

When Jesus speaks of building his church upon a rock, it is as much a polemical contrast with the pagan city upon the rock, as it may have been a word play off of Peter's name, meaning "stone." In the ancient world, mountains were not only a gateway between heaven, earth, and the underworld, but also the habitations of the gods that represented their heavenly power and authority.[50] The mountain before them, Hermon, was considered the heavenly habitation of Canaanite gods as well as the very Watchers before whose gates of Hades Jesus now stood. The polemics become clearer when one realizes that gates are not offensive weapons, but defensive means. Christ's kingship is storming the very gates of Hades/Sheol in the heart of darkness and he will build his cosmic holy mountain upon its ruins.[51]

But the battle is only beginning. Because the very next incident that occurs is the transfiguration (Matt. 17:1-13). The text says that Jesus led three disciples up a high mountain. But it doesn't say which mountain. Though tradition has often concluded it was Mount Tabor, a more likely candidate is Mount Hermon itself. The reasons are because Tabor is not a high mountain at only 1800 feet compared to Hermon's 9000 feet height, and Tabor was a well traveled location which would not allow Jesus to be alone with his disciples (17:1).[52]

Then the text says, that Jesus "was transfigured before them, and his face shone like the sun, and his clothes became white as light. And behold, there appeared to them Moses and Elijah, talking with him" (Matthew 17:2–3). When Peter offers to put up three tabernacles for each of his heroes, he hears a voice from the cloud say, "This is my beloved Son with whom I am well pleased, listen to him" (vs. 4-5). The theological point of this being that Moses and Elijah

---

[48] *Wars of the Jews* 1:405, Flavius Josephus and William Whiston, The Works of Josephus: Complete and Unabridged (Peabody: Hendrickson, 1987).

[49] Judd H. Burton, *Interview With the Giant: Ethnohistorical Notes on the Nephilim* (Burton Beyond Press, 2009) 15-23.

[50] Richard J. Clifford, *The Cosmic Mountain in Canaan and the Old Testament* (Wipf & Stock Pub, 2010), 1-8.

[51] Michael S. Heiser *The Myth That is True First Draft,* Unpublished book, 266.

[52] Clinton E. Arnold, *Zondervan Illustrated Bible Backgrounds Commentary: Matthew, Mark, Luke, vol. 1* (Grand Rapids, MI: Zondervan, 2002), 106.

are the representatives of the Old Covenant, summed up as the Law (Moses) and the Prophets (Elijah), but Jesus is the anointed King (Messiah) that both Law and Prophets pointed toward.

So God is anointing Jesus and transferring all covenantal authority to him as God's own Son. And for what purpose? To become king upon the new cosmic mountain that God was establishing: Mount Zion in the city of God. In the Mosaic Covenant, Mount Sinai was considered the cosmic mountain of God where God had his assembly of divine holy ones (Deut. 33:2-3). But now, as pronounced by the prophets, that mountain was being transferred out of the wilderness wandering into a new home in the Promised Land as Mount Zion (ultimately in Jerusalem). And that new mountain was the displacement and replacement of the previous divine occupants of Mount Hermon. Of course, just like David the messianic type, Jesus was anointed as king, but there would be a delay of time before he would take that rightful throne because he had some Goliaths yet to conquer (1 Sam. 16:13; 2 Sam. 5:3).

Take a look at this Psalm and see how the language of cosmic war against the anointed Messiah is portrayed as a victory of God establishing his new cosmic mountain. We see a repeat of the language of Jesus' transfiguration at Hermon.

> Psalm 2:1–8 (NASB95)
> 1 Why are the nations in an uproar And the peoples devising a vain thing? 2 The kings of the earth take their stand And the rulers [heavenly as well?] take counsel together Against the LORD and against His Anointed [Messiah], saying, 3 "Let us tear their fetters apart And cast away their cords from us!" 4 He who sits in the heavens laughs, The Lord scoffs at them. 5 Then He will speak to them in His anger And terrify them in His fury, saying, 6 "But as for Me, I have installed My King Upon Zion, My holy mountain." 7 "I will surely tell of the decree of the LORD: He said to Me, 'You are My Son, Today I have begotten You. 8 'Ask of Me, and I will surely give the nations as Your inheritance, And the *very* ends of the earth as Your possession.[53]

Like Moses' transfiguration in Exodus 34:29, Jesus' body was transformed by his anointing to shine with the glory of those who surround God's throne (Dan. 10:6; Ezek 1:14-16, 21ff.; 10:9).[54] But that description is no where near the ending of this spiritual parade of triumph being previewed

---

[53] See also Psa. 48.
[54] Michael S. Heiser *The Myth That is True*, 65.

in God's Word. One last passage illustrates the conquering change of ownership of the cosmic mountain in Bashan. Notice the ironic language used of Bashan as God's mountain, and the spiritual warfare imagery of its replacement.

> Psalm 68:15–22
> 15O mountain of God, mountain of Bashan; O many-peaked mountain, mountain of Bashan! 16 Why do you look with hatred, O many-peaked mountain, at the mount that God desired for his abode, yes, where the LORD will dwell forever? 17 The chariots of God are twice ten thousand, thousands upon thousands; the Lord is among them; Sinai is now in the sanctuary. 18 You ascended on high, leading a host of captives in your train and receiving gifts among men, even among the rebellious, that the LORD God may dwell there... 21 But God will strike the heads of his enemies, the hairy crown of him who walks in his guilty ways. 22 The Lord said, "I will bring them back from Bashan, I will bring them back from the depths of the sea.

In this Psalm, God takes ownership of Bashan with his heavenly host of warriors, but then replaces it and refers to Sinai (soon to be Zion). It is not that God is making Bashan his mountain literally, but conquering its divinities and theologically replacing it with his new cosmic mountain elsewhere. In verse 18 we see a foreshadowing of Christ's own victorious heavenly ascension, where he leads captives in triumphal procession and receives tribute from them as spoils of war (v. 18). He will own and live where once the rebellious ruled (v. 18). He strikes the "hairy crown" (*seir*) of the people of that area (v. 21), the descendants of the cursed hairy Esau/Seir,[55] who worshipped the goat demons (as depicted in *Joshua Valiant* and *Caleb Vigilant*).[56] He will bring them all out from the sea of chaos, that wilderness where Leviathan symbolically reigns.[57]

But first, the Messiah must descend into that sea to claim his victory.

---

[55] "Edom," Geoffrey W. Bromiley, ed., The International Standard Bible Encyclopedia, Revised (Wm. B. Eerdmans, 1979–1988), 18. See the Appendix on Satyrs and Seirim in Brian Godawa *Joshua Valiant*, (Los Angeles: Embedded Pictures, 2013), 310-314.
[56] Marvin E. Tate, *Psalms 51–100, vol. 20, Word Biblical Commentary* (Dallas: Word, Incorporated, 1998), 182.
[57] Heiser *The Myth,* 277-279.

Christ's Descent Into Hades/Sheol

One of the most difficult and strange passages in the New Testament is 1 Peter 3:18-22. It's oddity approaches that of Genesis 6:1-4 that speaks of the Sons of God mating with the daughters of men in the days of Noah and breeding Nephilim giants that lead to the judgment of the Flood. Perhaps its oddity is tied to the fact that it is most likely connected directly to Genesis 6 and therefore of particular importance for the Cosmic War of the Seed.

This 1 Peter 3 passage is notorious for its difficult obscurity and lack of consensus among scholarly interpretation. Views are divided over it with a variety of speculative interpretations to pick from. So, let's take a look at it more closely with an attempt to clarify its meaning.

> 1 Peter 3:18–22
> 18For Christ also suffered once for sins, the righteous for the unrighteous, that he might bring us to God, being put to death in the flesh but made alive in the spirit, 19in which he went and proclaimed to the spirits in prison, 20because they formerly did not obey, when God's patience waited in the days of Noah, while the ark was being prepared, in which a few, that is, eight persons, were brought safely through water. 21Baptism, which corresponds to this, now saves you, not as a removal of dirt from the body but as an appeal to God for a good conscience, through the resurrection of Jesus Christ, 22who has gone into heaven and is at the right hand of God, with angels, authorities, and powers having been subjected to him.

The context of this letter is the suffering of believers for their faith under the persecution of the Roman empire (3:13-17). Peter is encouraging them to persevere in doing good despite the evil done against them because they will be a witness to the watching world just as Christ was in his suffering. He then launches into this section as an analogy of what Christ did for us in his journey of suffering, death, resurrection, and ascension.

The questions begin to pile up:

When did Christ go on this journey? (v. 18)

Where did he go to proclaim to the spirits? (v. 19)

What did he proclaim? (v. 19)

Who are the spirits? (v. 19)

Where is this prison that they are in? (v. 19)

I believe the answers to these questions are very much in line with the storyline of the War of the Seed.

When Did Christ Go on His Journey? When Christ "went" to proclaim to the spirits in prison, it says he was "put to death in the flesh but made alive in the spirit, in which he went…" In the original Greek, "he went" does not contain a notion of direction as in ascent to heaven or descent to hell. It can only be determined by the context.[58] So let's look at that context.

Some scholars interpret this being "made alive in the spirit" as a reference to the physical resurrection of Christ from the dead, repeated later in v. 21. As Bible commentator Ramsey Michaels says, "the distinction here indicated by "flesh" and "spirit" is not between the material and immaterial parts of Christ's person (i.e., his "body" and "soul"), but rather between his earthly existence and his risen state."[59] Scholar William Dalton argues that the idea of being made alive in the spirit was a New Testament reference to the resurrection of Christ's physical body *by the power of* the Holy Spirit, not a reference to Christ's disembodied soul.[60] He writes, "General New Testament anthropology insists on the unity of the human person. Terms such as "flesh" and "spirit" are aspects of human existence, not parts of a human compound. Bodily resurrection is stressed, not the immortality of the soul."[61] This venerable interpretation sees Christ proclaiming to the spirits in Hades, as a resurrected body, sometime before he ascended.

Another scholarly interpretation is that Christ's journey of proclamation occurred in a disembodied state between his death and resurrection. While his body was dead for three days, his spirit was alive and in Sheol. This understands the flesh/spirit distinction as a conjunction of opposites. "Put to death in the flesh but made alive in the spirit" is not talking about the fleshly death and fleshly resurrection, but a fleshly death and a spiritual life. The "spirit" in which he was made alive in this view is not the Holy Spirit, but rather his disembodied soul in the spiritual realm. That "spirit" then corresponds to the "spirits" to whom he proclaimed in the very next verse (v. 19).

This view that Christ's soul or spirit went down into the underworld of Sheol between his death and resurrection is the most ancient and most

---

[58] John H. Elliott, *1 Peter: a New Translation with Introduction and Commentary* (vol. 37B; Anchor Yale Bible; New Haven; London: Yale University Press, 2008), 13.

[59] J. Ramsey Michaels, *1 Peter, vol. 49, Word Biblical Commentary* (Dallas: Word, Incorporated, 1998), 204.

[60] Dalton lists these passages: Rom 8:11; Jn 6:63; 1 Cor 15:45; 2 Cor 3:6; cf. also Rom 1:4, For the resurrection as effected by the power of God, see 2 Cor 13:4; Rom 6:4; Phil 3:10; Col 2:12; Eph 1:19–20; Heb 7:16.Footnote 55, William Joseph Dalton, *Christ's Proclamation to the Spirits: A Study of 1 Peter 3:18–4:6,* vol. 23, Analecta Biblica (Roma: Editrice Pontificio Istituto Biblico, 1989) 137.

[61] Dalton, *Christ's Proclamation to the Spirits*, 64.

traditional view, as attested in the Apostle's Creed.[62] The Greek for "made alive" is never used of Christ's physical resurrection in the New Testament, but it is used of the spiritual reality of the believer "being made alive" in Christ (Eph. 2:5-6).[63] Christ suffered the spiritual death of separation from the Father when he died on the cross (Isa. 53:4-6; 1 Pet. 2:24; Matt. 27:46). How the second person of the Trinity can experience separation from the Father remains a Biblical mystery. But in this interpretation, it is Christ's disembodied spirit that makes the journey to proclaim to the spirits, not his resurrected body.

But whether Christ proclaims in his resurrected body or in his immaterial spirit, the next question arises, who are the spirits to which he proclaims and where are they?

Who are the Spirits in Prison? The identity of the spirits has been debated extensively and falls into four possible categories: Human spirits, demons, Watchers, or a combination of the above.

John Elliott debunks the notion that "spirits" refers to human beings by looking at the Greek word for spirits (*pneuma*) in Biblical and Intertestamental texts. He concludes, "use of 'spirits' for human beings is very rare, and even then it is always qualified. In the Bible and related literature, when reference is made to deceased humans in Hades or the underworld, the term used is not *pneuma* but *psyche*."[64]

But another commentator, Ramsey Michaels, shows that "spirits" (*pneuma*) is used of demons frequently in the New Testament for those supernatural beings that Jesus often confronted in his ministry.[65] He points out

---

[62] The Apostle's Creed is the most universally accepted creed of Christendom. For the full text see http://en.wikipedia.org/wiki/Apostles'_Creed. Some of the earliest Christian apocryphal literature supported the interpretation of Christ's spiritual descent into Hades, such as *the Gospel of Nicodemus, the Ascension of Isaiah, the Testaments of the Twelve Patriarchs, the Shepherd of Hermas, the Gospel of Bartholomew, the Odes of Solomon*, among others. Church fathers from the second and third centuries who taught this view included Polycarp, Ignatius, Tertullian, Hermas, Justin, Melito of Sardis, Irenaeus, Clement of Alexandria and Origen. Alfeyev states that every major writer from the Eastern Church fathers of the fourth century "touched in one way or another, on the theme of Christ's descent into Hades," as well as Western Church fathers like Jerome, Ambrose and Augustine. See Metropolitan Hilarion Alfeyev, *Christ the Conqueror of Hell: The Descent into Hades form an Orthodox Perspective*, (Crestwood: NY; St. Vladimir's Seminary Press, 2009). Also, see Richard Bauckham, "Descent to the Underworld," ed. David Noel Freedman, *The Anchor Yale Bible Dictionary* (New York: Doubleday, 1992), 154-158.

[63] Jason M. Hauffe, *An Interpretation of 1 Peter 3:18-22*, Dissertation (Lynchburg, Liberty University, 2002), 46.

[64] Elliott, *1 Peter*, Page 292.

[65] "Matt 8:16; Luke 10:20; "unclean spirits" in Matt 10:1; Mark 1:27; 3:11; 5:13; 6:7; Luke 4:36; 6:18; Acts 5:16; cf. Rev 16:13; "evil spirits" in Matt 12:45//Luke 11:26; Luke 7:21; 8:2; Acts 19:12–13 (for the singular, cf. Matt 12:43//Luke 11:24; Mark 1:23, 26; 3:30; 5:2, 8; 7:25; 9:17, 20, 25; Luke 8:29; 9:39, 42; 13:11; Acts 16:16, 18; 19:15–16)." J. Ramsey Michaels, *1 Peter, vol. 49, Word Biblical Commentary* (Dallas: Word, Incorporated, 1998), 207.

that in 1 Enoch, *pneuma* is used of demons as the surviving part of the giants killed in the Flood.

> 1 Enoch 15:8-10
> But now the giants who are born from the (union of) the spirits and the flesh shall be called evil spirits [*pneuma*] upon the earth, because their dwelling shall be upon the earth and inside the earth. 9 Evil spirits [*pneuma*] have come out of their bodies…They will become evil upon the earth and shall be called evil spirits [*pneuma*].[66]

In this view, the "spirits in prison" are therefore the demonic souls of the Nephilim that are restricted to the prison "holding cell" under the earth until the coming of Messiah. (See below for the definition of "prison" as a holding cell). As 1 Enoch 15:10 reasons, "The dwelling of the spiritual beings of heaven is heaven; but the dwelling of the spirits of the earth, which are born upon the earth, is in the earth."[67]

But what of the angelic Watchers? Are they ever referred to as "spirits"? As the 1 Enoch 15 passage above shows, the spirits of the Nephilim hybrids comes from their angelic Watcher progenitors who are also called spirits. In verse 4 of that passage, Enoch condemns the Watchers for violating their heavenly being as spirits (*pneuma*) and defiling themselves with "the blood of the flesh begotten children."[68]

The Intertestamental book of Jubilees that drew from 1 Enoch also concurs with the spirits being fallen angels:

> Jubilees 15:31-32
> over all of [the nations God] caused spirits to rule so that they might lead them astray from following him. 32 But over Israel he did not cause any angel or spirit to rule because he alone is their ruler.[69]

---

66 Charlesworth, *The Old Testament Pseudepigrapha vol. 1*, 21–22.
67 Charlesworth, *The Old Testament Pseudepigrapha vol. 1*, 22.
68 Charlesworth, *The Old Testament Pseudepigrapha vol. 1*, 21.
69 James H. Charlesworth, *The Old Testament Pseudepigrapha and the New Testament: Expansions of the "Old Testament" and Legends, Wisdom, and Philosophical Literature, Prayers, Psalms and Odes, Fragments of Lost Judeo-Hellenistic Works, vol. 2* (New Haven; London: Yale University Press, 1985), 87.

The only New Testament Scriptures that speak of imprisonment of spirits are Jude 6 and 2 Peter 2:4, *the very passages that most scholarship has revealed are literarily dependent on the book of 1 Enoch.*[70]

Jude	2 Peter	Enoch
Jude 6 (NASB95) And angels who did not keep their own domain, but abandoned their proper abode, He has kept in eternal bonds under darkness for the judgment of the great day	2 Peter 2:4 God did not spare angels when they sinned, but cast them into hell [*Tartarus*] and committed them to chains of gloomy darkness to be kept until the judgment...	1 Enoch 12:4; 10:12 the Watchers of heaven who have abandoned the high heaven, the holy eternal place … bind [the Watchers] for seventy generations underneath the rocks of the ground until the day of their judgment.

Jude not only quotes Enoch outright in Jude 4, but throughout his entire letter, he follows the progression of ideas in 1 Enoch and references memes and motifs of the angelic Watchers' sin and judgment in that ancient text.[71] 2 Peter 2 is considered a paraphrase of Jude with the addition of the word for *Tartarus* as the description of the location of punishment.

Tartarus was well known by the ancients as the lowest place of the underworld where the Titans were bound in pagan mythology. That underworld was referred to as Hades (Greek) or Sheol (Hebrew), and has obvious conceptual links to Jude and Peter's location of punishment (more on Tartarus and Sheol later).[72] It would make most sense that Peter's second letter about angels bound in the prison of Tartarus would have continuity with the "spirits in prison" he is writing about in this first letter.

Some scholars have argued that the link of this passage to 1 Enoch is so strong that it can only make sense if there was a scribal error that mistook the Greek word for "Enoch" as the very similar Greek word for "in which."[73] So Peter had actually written that Christ was made alive in the spirit in the same way as "Enoch who went and proclaimed to the spirits in prison" in 1 Enoch.[74] Even though there is no manuscript evidence for this scribal error theory,

[70] Nickelsburg, *1 Enoch: a Commentary*, 7. Also, E. Isaac, "A New Translation and Introduction," in *The Old Testament Pseudepigrapha*, vol. 1 (New York; London: Yale University Press, 1983); Robert Henry Charles, ed., *Pseudepigrapha of the Old Testament*, vol. 2 (Bellingham, WA: Logos Bible Software, 2004), 178.

[71] See Brian Godawa, "The Book of Enoch: Scripture, Heresy, or What?" in "*When Giants Walked the Earth: The Watchers, Nephilim and the Biblical Cosmic War of the Seed* (Los Angeles, Embedded Pictures Publishing, 2014), 1-30.

[72] See the Appendix of Brian Godawa, *Enoch Primordial* (Los Angeles, Embedded Pictures Publishing, 2013), 336-338.

[73] J. R. Harris, "The History of a Conjectural Emendation," *Expositor 6* (1902): 387-390; E. 1. Goodspeed, "Some Greek Notes," *Journal of Biblical Literature 73* (1954): 91-92.

[74] 1 Enoch 18:10-19:3; 21.

making it unlikely, the strong analogy to Enoch's descent into Sheol is undeniable. So much so that Bo Reicke argued that Peter is casting Jesus as a typological Enoch.[75] Dalton enumerates, "A survey of 1 Enoch reveals a striking and obvious parallel to 1 Pet 3:19–20. In this latter text we have 1. a journey of Christ, 2. a proclamation, 3. to the spirits, 4. in prison, 5. who rebelled, or disobeyed, 6. in the setting of the flood. Now it is precisely in 1 Enoch that we find all these elements bound together in the closest unity."[76]

The spirits are specifically indicated as being those who were disobedient during "the days of Noah while the ark was being prepared." That "days of Noah" is exactly the time period that 1 Enoch speaks of the fallen Watchers and their giant progeny receiving their comeuppance with a binding in Tartarus/Sheol at the Flood.[77]

Chad Pierce makes a convincing argument that the disobedient spirits are not just the Watcher angels, demons, or human spirits alone, but the sum total of all who defied God at that time because cosmic powers are often united with human powers in the ancient world.[78] In the Bible, the angelic power over Persia animated the human kingdom of Persia (Dan. 10:13), The Roman human kingdom in Revelation is granted its power from the satan (Rev. 12-13), and both are destroyed together in the Lake of Fire (Rev. 19:20; 20:7-10).

Wink explains that the ancient mind of the Biblical writers was steeped in a macrocosm/microcosm of "what is above is also below." "Angelic and demonic activity in heaven was reflected in events on earth…These Powers are both heavenly and earthly, divine and human, spiritual and political, invisible and structural."[79] Reicke adds that the "fallen Angels… the Powers, the demons in general, can in a certain way represent the whole world of fallen angels."[80] And Pierce concludes, "the distinction between cosmic and earthly sinners is so blurred they cannot be distinguished. It appears that the author of 1 Pet 3:18-22 has left the recipients of Christ's message purposefully vague so as to include all forms of evil beings. The spirits in prison are thus all the forces of evil which have now been subjugated and defeated by Christ."[81]

1 Peter 3:22 concludes that the context of the proclamation Christ made was the subjugation of "angels, authorities, and powers." Heavenly

---

[75] Bo Reicke, *The Disobedient Spirits and Christian Baptism* (New York: AMS Press, 1946), 100-101.
[76] Dalton, *Christ's Proclamation*, 167.
[77] This would tend to work against the demon view since the demons were released upon the earth *after* the Flood, not while the ark was being built. But it could be argued that 1 Enoch 15 conflates the demons with the Nephilim and the spiritual side of the Watchers. This would mean that Peter may be referring to the disobedient spirits in the Nephilim *before* the Flood while the ark was being built.
[78] Chad Pierce, *Spirits and the Proclamation of Christ: 1 Peter 3:18-22 in Its Tradition-Historical and Literary Context,* (Durham theses, Durham University, 2009), 215-218. Available at Durham E-Theses Online: http://etheses.dur.ac.uk/13/
[79] Walter Wink. *Naming the Powers,*1552-1553, 182-183. Kindle Edition.
[80] Reicke, *The Disobedient Spirits,* 121.
[81] Pierce, *Spirits and the Proclamation,* 218. See also Reicke, *The Disobedient Spirits,* 121.

"principalities, powers, and authorities" is a recurring concept in the New Testament (Col. 1:16, 2:13-15; Eph. 1:20-23). It is a concept that assumes earthly rulers and powers are animated and empowered by spiritual or cosmic rulers and power behind them.

Thus, Paul could encourage those Christians who were suffering from the earthly rulers and powers who persecuted them; "For we do not wrestle against flesh and blood, but against the rulers, against the authorities, against the cosmic powers over this present darkness, against the spiritual forces of evil in the heavenly places" (Eph. 6:12-13). In other words, the real enemies of the persecuted Christians were the spiritual powers behind their earthly persecuting powers. This is not a denial of the human evil, but rather a drawing back of the curtain to see the ultimate enemy with more clarity.

These spiritual and earthly "powers, rulers, authorities, and thrones," are the Seed of the Serpent that had been involved in the cosmic War of the Seed against Messiah. It is these rulers, *both heavenly and earthly*, who did not understand the mystery of the Gospel of redemption through Messiah's suffering. They thought that killing the Chosen One, the Messiah, would bring them victory.

> 1 Corinthians 2:7–9
> But we impart a secret and hidden wisdom of God, which God decreed before the ages for our glory. None of the rulers of this age understood this, for if they had, they would not have crucified the Lord of glory.

So the focus on "powers and authorities" stresses the nature of Christ's cosmic mission against the heavenly powers. But the humans of Noah's day were certainly united in the rebellion of the Watchers and were also marked out by Enoch for judgment along with the angels.[82]

Where is the "Prison"? One interpretation of the prison is that it is a metaphor for human beings on earth who are "imprisoned" in their sin. But the context of the passage mitigates against this view. When the New Testament refers to preaching the Gospel to people on earth, the Greek term for "soul," is used (*psyche*). But this is not a term about a ghost in a machine, but rather an expression of the life of an individual human, their inner being, their "person," or their "self." Thus, Peter writes in 3:20 that "eight persons (*psyche*) were brought safely through the waters" in the ark during the Flood. When Peter preaches the Gospel in Acts 2, it says that "those who received his word were baptized, and there were added that day about three thousand

[82] 1 Enoch 9:10; 20:3, 6; 22:3, 6-13; 98:3, 10;103:4.

souls [*psyche*]… and awe came upon every soul [*psyche*]" (Acts 2:42-43). "Soul" could be used synonymously with "individuals" or "persons."

But in 1 Peter 3, the distinct Greek term for "spirit" (*pneuma*), not "soul" (*psyche*), is used in contrast to the physical flesh. And these "spirits" are those who were disobedient in the days of Noah (v. 20), so they could not be people on earth at the time of Christ. Christ was proclaiming to spirits. During the time of Christ, those who were around in the days of Noah could only be in one place according to the Old Testament: The underworld of Hades or Sheol.

Hades was well known in the Greco-Roman world as the holding cell of the spirits of the dead until the judgment. Sheol was the Hebrew equivalent for Hades so the two could be used interchangeably.[83] Prisons in that time period were exactly that, holding cells for punishment. So when Peter refers to a prison for spirits, this view concludes that he is referring to Hades, just as he did in 2 Peter 2:4 when he said that the disobedient angels were cast into Tartarus, the lowest point in Hades.

There are orthodox traditions of Christian scholars who have supported this passage as referring to Christ's proclamation as occurring at his physical ascension into heaven and others as referring to Christ's spiritual descent into Hades. I take the position in *Jesus Triumphant* that Christ spiritually descended into Hades. So did early church fathers like Tertullian, Augustine, Jerome, Clement of Alexandria, Irenaeus, Cyril, and Origen, as well as Medieval scholastics like Robert Bellarmine, John Calvin, Thomas Aquinas, and modern scholars like Charles B. Cranfield, and Bo Reicke.[84] But I also incorporate the post-resurrection interpretation when it comes to the angelic Sons of God (Watchers) reigning on earth.

William Dalton agrees with Reicke that Jesus is cast as a typological Enoch, but then argues that in 2 Enoch, Enoch visits the bound angels in the lower regions of heaven, not Hades.[85] This is true of 2 Enoch, but unfortunately, the text is of such late origin (2nd century after Christ) that it cannot have been part of the original Enochian corpus used as a source in the Bible.[86]

In contrast, 1 Enoch, which seems to be the source of the Biblical text, does in fact depict Enoch as visiting the place of the condemned Watchers who were "formerly in heaven" (1 Enoch 16:2), and that place is described as

---

[83] Richard Bauckham, "Hades, Hell," ed. David Noel Freedman, *The Anchor Yale Bible Dictionary* (New York: Doubleday, 1992), 14.
[84] Pierce, *Spirits and the Proclamation,* 2-10.
[85] William J. Dalton, *Christ's Proclamation to the Spirits: A Study of 1 Peter 3:18-4:6*. Second Edition. Analecta biblica 23. (Rome: Pontifical Biblical Institute, 1989), 179-81.
[86] Francis I. Andersen, "Enoch, Second Book Of," ed. David Noel Freedman, *The Anchor Yale Bible Dictionary* (New York: Doubleday, 1992), 516–517. Philip S. Alexander, "Enoch, Third Book Of," *AYBD*, 524.

a "deep pit," in the bottom of a mountain, just like Tartarus of Hades (Sheol), "an empty place with neither heaven above nor an earth below" (1 Enoch 21:1-2).[87]

The descent of Christ in 1 Pet. 3:19 is poetically structured to counterbalance the ascent of Christ into heaven in verse 22. In the same way that Christ went down into Sheol, he later ascended up into heaven. But more importantly, if Christ makes a proclamation to the spirits in prison, those dead and bound prisoners are certainly *not* in heaven. They are most likely in Sheol.

Another passage, Ephesians 4:8 quotes Psalms 68:18 about Christ "ascending on high and leading a host of captives." Paul then adds a parenthetical,

> Ephesians 4:9-10
> "In saying, 'He ascended,' what does it mean but that he had also descended into the lower regions, the earth? He who descended is the one who also ascended far above all the heavens, that he might fill all things."

Christ "descending into the lower regions, the earth" can legitimately be interpreted as referring to Christ's incarnation or even his descent in the Spirit on Pentecost.[88] But other scholarship argues that the phrase is better translated as "descending into the *lowest parts of* the earth," in other words into Sheol.[89]

This underworld (Sheol) interpretation would seem to coincide with the memes presented in 1 Peter 3. The contrast of the heights of heaven with the depths of Sheol, and the tying of Christ's death, descent into Sheol, resurrection, and ascension into the totality of his victory over the angelic principalities and powers.[90]

Psalm 68 says that after leading the host of captives, God "received gifts from men," a reference to the notion of ancient victors receiving tribute from their conquered foes. Paul changes that "receiving of gifts" into "giving of gifts" as an expansion of that victory over foes into a sharing of victory with his army, the people of God. Perhaps this is the meaning of the Old Testament saints resurrected at the time of Christ's resurrection (Matt. 27:52-53). They

---

[87] Enoch has a dream vision and ascends to heaven in 1 Enoch 14 and 15. But then he is brought to the place of punishment in chapter 18:10-19:3, which is not in heaven, but is a mountain that leads him down into the pit of Sheol.

[88] For a good survey of the defense of these views, see: Andrew T. Lincoln, *Ephesians, vol. 42, Word Biblical Commentary* (Dallas: Word, Incorporated, 1990), 244–247.

[89] "κατώτερος," Gerhard Kittel, Geoffrey W. Bromiley, and Gerhard Friedrich, eds., *Theological Dictionary of the New Testament* (Grand Rapids, MI: Eerdmans, 1964–), 640; Clinton E. Arnold, *Zondervan Illustrated Bible Backgrounds Commentary: Romans to Philemon., vol. 3* (Grand Rapids, MI: Zondervan, 2002), 325.

[90] Robert G. Bratcher and Eugene Albert Nida, *A Handbook on Paul's Letter to the Ephesians, UBS Handbook Series* (New York: United Bible Societies, 1993), 99–100.

too were sharing in the long awaited victory train of Messiah to free them from Hades and ascend into heaven.

The context of conquest over the angelic powers is also apparent in Eph. 1:20-21, "when he raised [Jesus] from the dead and seated him at his right hand in the heavenly places, far above all rule and authority and power and dominion, and above every name that is named."

Christ's death on the Cross becomes the apparent defeat by God's enemies, led by angelic principalities and powers. But it turns around and becomes a disarming of those spiritual powers and the beginning of his triumph over them (Col. 2:15). In this view, Christ goes down into Sheol (in his spirit or later, in his resurrected body) to make a proclamation to the original minions of evil, now held captive. After he raises from the dead, he ascends into heaven to be coronated as king over all authority and powers of heaven and earth (Eph. 1:20-21). And that victory over spiritual powers brings us to the next element of 1 Peter 3:18-22.

What was the Proclamation? Some have believed it was Christ preaching the Gospel to the Old Testament dead, as if they may have a second chance to repent because they died before Messiah, or even to Old Testament believers who did not yet have the historical sacrifice of Christ to apply to them yet. This brings us back to the human interpretation of the "spirits in prison."

Since there is no place in the New Testament that supports the notion of a purgatorial type of second chance after death (Heb. 9:27), then the proclamation that Christ makes cannot be the "preaching of the Gospel" unto salvation, but something else. That something else is most likely a triumphant proclamation of his victory over the angelic authorities and powers.

In the ancient world, kingly victors would perform a triumphal procession through the streets of a conquered city. They would parade their captive opponents, alive or dead, on carts to show off their power over their enemies. Thus the triumphal procession in Psalm 68 quoted in Ephesians 4:8 as "ascending on high and leading a host of captives." This would also be an encouragement for obedience from the vanquished inhabitants.[91] Triumphal language like this in 1 Peter as well as other passages, reflect this military type victory of Christ over the ruling authorities achieved at the Cross.

---

[91] Clinton E. Arnold, *Zondervan Illustrated Bible Backgrounds Commentary: Romans to Philemon., vol. 3* (Grand Rapids, MI: Zondervan, 2002), 387.

> 2 Corinthians 2:14
> But thanks be to God, who in Christ always leads us in triumphal procession, and through us spreads the fragrance of the knowledge of him everywhere.

This triumph is referred to in the next verse of 1 Peter 3:22. "Christ, who has gone into heaven and is at the right hand of God, with angels, authorities, and powers having been subjected to him." The subjection of the spiritual powers occurs sometime before or during the ascension in this passage, most likely in the prison of Sheol. In Col. 2:15 we read that God "disarmed the rulers and authorities and put them to open shame, by triumphing over them" in Christ's death and resurrection. His death on the cross forgives us the legal debt of our sin, his resurrection unites us in our new spiritual life, and his ascension wraps it all up with a victory lap, towing the bound and defeated principalities and powers of the nations behind him.

One of the premises of the entire *Chronicles of the Nephilim* series is the Deuteronomy 32 worldview that spoke of the allotment of earthly nations to the fallen Watchers, at the time of the Tower of Babel (Deut. 32:8-9; 29:26). God granted territorial authority to these divine beings (Deut. 4:19-20; Daniel 10). But God kept Jacob for himself and then took the land of Canaan as his inheritance. So the picture is one of a world divided up into parcels of land underneath the authority of the fallen Watchers as false gods, with Yahweh having Israel in Canaan as his own.

And this allotment occurred at the division of tongues during the Tower of Babel episode (Duet. 32:8). But one day, the coming Messiah would ultimately take back that Watcher allotment and inherit the entire earth as his territory, along with the nations to be his people.

> Daniel 4:17
> 17 The sentence is by the decree of the watchers, the decision by the word of the holy ones, to the end that the living may know that the Most High rules the kingdom of men and gives it to whom he will.

> Psalm 2:7–8
> 7 The LORD said to me, "You are my Son; today I have begotten you. 8 Ask of me, and I will make the nations your heritage, and the ends of the earth your possession.

The proclamation that Christ made to the spirits in prison was most likely his proclamation of victory and authority over the angelic powers that once ruled the Gentiles. The first of those powers were imprisoned in the Days of

Noah, but their fellow fallen angels continued to rule in their absence over the nations. This inheritance of the earth and the drawing in of the nations would finally commence on the Day of Pentecost when the Holy Spirit would literally undo Babel and the division of tongues and begin to draw those nations to himself (Acts 2).

But why would Christ have to proclaim authority or victory to those who were already imprisoned? Would that not be anti-climactic? Not if their fellow fallen angelic powers still ruled outside that prison on the earth, much like imprisoned Mafioso leaders are still linked to their fellow criminals on the outside. The angelic powers imprisoned at the Flood were the original rebels, the progenitors of the ongoing Seed of the Serpent that continued on in a lineage of evil on earth. They were in bonds, but the resultant War of the Seed that they spawned originated with their fall.

Christ's exorcism of demons becomes the picture of his cosmic authority casting out the occupying evil powers, described as an army (Luke 11;18). And that cosmic authority would ultimately crush the Serpent's head.

> Luke 11:20–22
> 20 [Jesus:] "But if it is by the finger of God that I cast out demons, then the kingdom of God has come upon you. 21 When a strong man, fully armed, guards his own palace, his goods are safe; 22 but when one stronger than he attacks him and overcomes him, he takes away his armor in which he trusted and divides his spoil."

The incarnation and ministry of Christ inaugurated the Kingdom of Messiah, the Kingdom of God. His death, resurrection, and ascension accomplished the atonement of sins for his people (Col. 2:13-15), the crushing of the head of the Serpent (Luke 10:17-19), and the victorious triumphal procession of binding his enemies, from Sheol up to heaven (1 Pet. 3:18-22), as he rose to the ultimate seat of authority over all kingdoms, rulers, and authorities: The right hand of God the Father (Eph. 1:21). From there Jesus reigns victoriously, in which he undid the Tower of Babel (Acts 2) evicted the spiritual authorities over the nations (Deut. 32:8), and began to draw those nations away from their gods unto the new cosmic mountain, Mount Zion (Isa. 2). This is the cosmic War of the Seed, a war of conquering Christ's enemies through the power of the proclaimed Gospel in history…

> 1 Corinthians 15:24–28
> 24 Then comes the end, when he delivers the kingdom to God the Father after destroying every rule and every authority and

power. [25] For he must reign until he has put all his enemies under his feet. [26] The last enemy to be destroyed is death. [27] For "God has put all things in subjection under his feet." But when it says, "all things are put in subjection," it is plain that he is excepted who put all things in subjection under him. [28] When all things are subjected to him, then the Son himself will also be subjected to him who put all things in subjection under him, that God may be all in all.

Chapter 13
The Geography of Hades

When reading the words *Hades* or *Underworld*, most educated readers immediately conjure images of Greco-Roman myth taught in school: A misty and gloomy abode of the dead below the earth where all souls of mortals, both good and evil, went after death. It is ruled over by the god of the same name, Hades, and contains perilous landscapes and dangerous bizarre creatures. Though there is not perfect consistency of geography among the various Greek and Roman authors, some elements repeat.[1]

There are five rivers in the classical Hades. Styx is the most prominent one that circles the underworld. The second one, Acheron, is the one crossed by souls on a boat ferried by the ghostly boatman Charon to bring them to the gates of Hades. Each of the rivers represent what happens to the departed souls.

1) Styx: River of hatred.
2) Acheron: River of pain.
3) Lethe: River of forgetfulness.
4) Phlegethon: River of fire.
5) Cocytus: River of wailing.

The entrance to the underworld is guarded by the three-headed dog Cerberus and other chimeric creatures like centaurs. The rivers then divide the geography into multiple regions with different purposes.

1) Fields of Punishment: Where souls who committed sins against the gods are punished.
2) Fields of Asphodel: Where souls go who were insignificant, neither great nor wicked.
3) Vale of Mourning: Where souls go who were unloved.
4) Elysium: Where the spirits of heroes and the virtuous ended up.
5) Isles of the Blessed: For the most distinguished of souls for eternity.
6) Tartarus: The deepest pit of Hades where the rebel Titans were bound.

---

[1] For a brief introduction to Hades, http://en.wikipedia.org/wiki/Greek_underworld

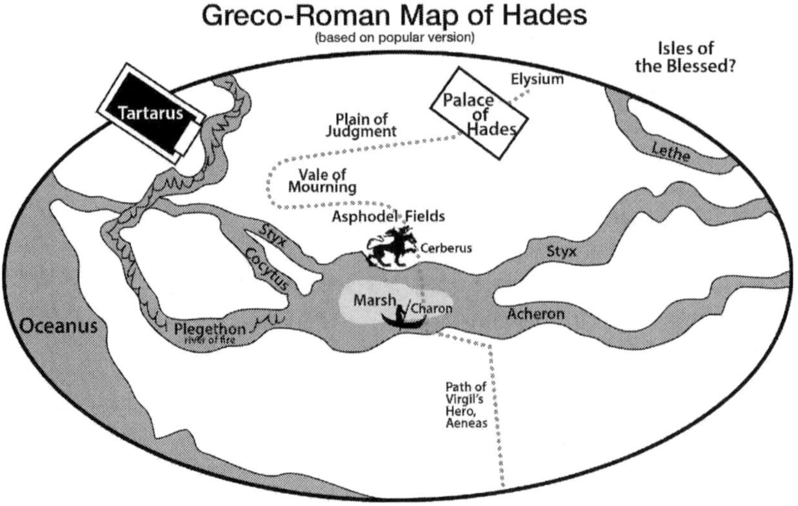

Most modern western pictures of the afterlife, or realm of the dead, come from the medieval punishments of Dante's *Inferno* and Milton's *Paradise Lost*. Levels of torture for sinners meted out by angels or demons, with Lucifer reigning over hell as a more interesting character than God. Sadly, these unbiblical notions have influenced Christian theology in some ways more than the Scriptural text itself. They make for colorful stories, but are not true to Biblical theology.

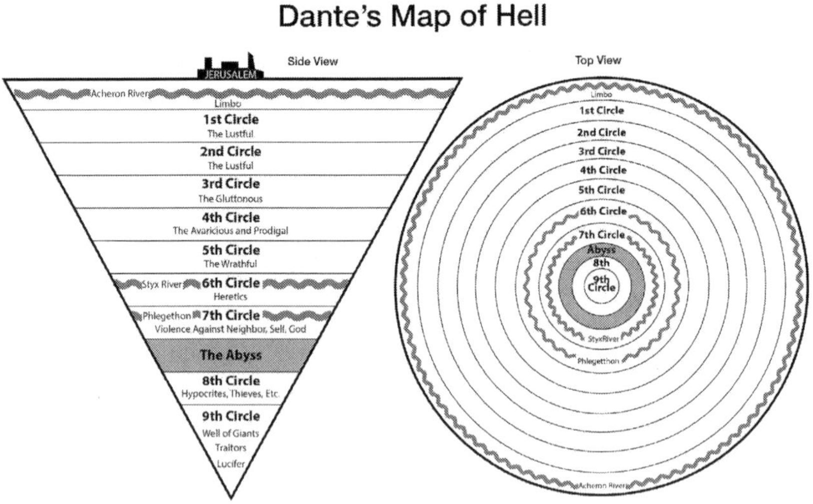

Ancient Hebrew Conception of the Heavens and Earth

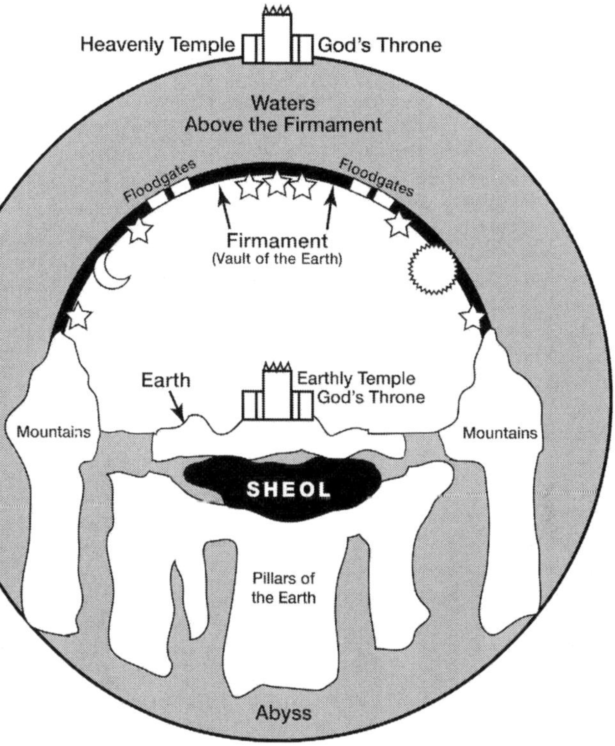

What does the Bible itself say about the underworld? The Old Testament Hebrew equivalent to the Greek *Hades* was *Sheol.*[2] Sheol could be a metaphorical personification of death (Hos 13:14; Isa. 28:15; 38:18, Ps. 49:15) or the grave (Psa. 88:11; Isa. 14:9-11), but it could also refer to a location beneath the earth that was the abode of the dead (Isa 14:9-15). The spirit of Samuel was called up from Sheol (1Sam. 28:13), and the sons of Korah went *down alive* into this underworld (Num. 16:33). People would not "fall alive" into death or the grave *and then* perish if Sheol was not a location. But they would die after they fall down into a location (Sheol) and the earth closes over them in that order.

When the prophet writes about Sheol in Isaiah 14, he combines the notion of the physical location of the dead body in the earth (v.11) with the location beneath the earth of the spirits of the dead (v.9). It's really a both/and synthesis. The term includes several concepts of imagination.

[2] "Sheol," *DDD*, p 768.

Here are some verses that speak of Sheol geographically as a spiritual underworld below the earth in contrast with heaven as a spiritual overworld above the earth:

> Amos 9:2
> "If they dig into Sheol, from there shall my hand take them; if they climb up to heaven, from there I will bring them down.
>
> Job 11:8
> It is higher than heaven—what can you do? Deeper than Sheol—what can you know?
>
> Psa. 139:8
> If I ascend to heaven, you are there! If I make my bed in Sheol, you are there![3]

These are not mere references to the body in the grave, but to locations of the soul as well. Sheol is a multi-layered term that describes both the grave for the body and the underworld location of the departed souls of the dead.[4] In Old Testament times, Sheol did not include any kind of punishment beyond its power to hold souls captive to death (Psa. 18:4-5), separated in some sense from God's presence (Psa. 115:17; 6:5), and one's misery of lost power and glory (Psa. 7:5; Isa. 14:9-16). But fire and bodily torture are absent from this Old Testament worldview.

Shades

One biblical term used for departed souls in Sheol is *rephaim*. It is sometimes translated as "shades," in English. As the *ISBE* puts it, "In Job 26:5 "the shades below" are the dead (cf. Ps. 88:10; Isa. 26:14). They dwell in "the depths of Sheol" (Prov. 9:18), where they live together in "the assembly of the dead" (Prov. 21:16)."[5] That assembly is described in 1Enoch as "four hollows" or pits under the mountain of the dead, where they await their judgment in the last days. One hollow is for the righteous; another hollow is for Abel and those unjustly murdered; a third is for the wicked unpunished in life; and a fourth for the wicked who were punished in life. The souls of the unrighteous dead

---

[3] See also Isa. 7:11; Matt. 11:23; Phil 2:10; Rev. 5:3, 13; 1Pet 2:4-5.

[4] "The ideas of the grave and of Sheol cannot be separated…The dead are at the same time in the grave and in Sheol…Where there is grave, there is Sheol, and where there is Sheol, there is grave." Theodore J. Lewis, "Dead, Abode of the," ed. David Noel Freedman, *The Anchor Yale Bible Dictionary* (New York: Doubleday, 1992), 103.

[5] P. K. McCarter Jr., "Shades," ed. Geoffrey W. Bromiley, *The International Standard Bible Encyclopedia, Revised* (Wm. B. Eerdmans, 1979–1988), 440.

thirst and are frightful of their future judgment (1En. 22:9), but they are not tortured by angels or demons. Righteous souls receive refreshment from a fountain of waters "with light upon them" (1En. 22:9; Luke 16:24).

Another Jewish text of the first century, 4Ezra, describes the departed soul's entrance into Sheol as consisting of seven days to see the future results of their ways before being led to their habitation to wait for judgment. During this time period, the unrighteous…

> 4Ezra 7:80, 87, 101
> …shall immediately wander about in torments, ever grieving and sad…they shall utterly waste away in confusion and be consumed with shame, and shall wither with fear at seeing the glory of the Most High before whom they sinned while they were alive, and before whom they are to be judged in the last times… and afterward they shall be gathered in their habitations.

Another ancient Christian text, The Apocalypse of Zephaniah, describes the angels who draw the shades to their destiny as beings whose "faces were like a leopard, their tusks being outside their mouth like the wild boars. Their eyes were mixed with blood. Their hair was loose like the hair of women, and fiery scourges were in their hands."[6]

This ancient legendary depiction is behind the confused, wandering zombie-like shades in *Jesus Triumphant* who are animated by maggots and worms (Isa. 14:11; 66:24) while wailing and gnashing their teeth (Matt. 25:30), before being brought to the Mountain of the Dead.

In Isaiah 14, a prophetic rant against the arrogant king of Babylon, the "shades" take on an additional meaning…

> Isaiah 14:9-11
> Sheol beneath is stirred up to meet you when you come; it rouses the <u>shades (*rephaim*)</u> to greet you, <u>all who were leaders of the earth</u>; it raises from their thrones <u>all who were kings of the nations</u>. All of them will answer and say to you: 'You too have become as weak as we! You have become like us!' Your pomp is brought down to Sheol.

The Hebrew word for "shades" here is *rephaim*, a word with ties to the Canaanite giants of Joshua's and David's time (Josh. 13:12; 2Sam. 22:15-22),

---

[6] James H. Charlesworth, *The Old Testament Pseudepigrapha*, vol. 1 (New York; London: Yale University Press, 1983), 511.

and mighty warrior kings of Canaanite literature also called *rephaim*.[7] Isaiah's intent is to mock the pomp and vainglory of man, who will end up as humiliated as every other mighty being imprisoned in Sheol.[8] Thus, the appearance of the Rephaim guardians in *Jesus Triumphant*.

Hades in the New Testament

Because the New Testament is in Greek, it does not use the word Sheol, but the Greek word, *Hades*. Jesus himself used the term Hades as the location of condemned spirits in contrast with heaven as the location of redeemed spirits (Matt. 11:23). Jesus referred to the "Gates of Hades" (Matt. 16:18), a well-known underworld concept in ancient Near Eastern and Western Greco-Roman mythology. This was more than a metaphorical reference to the "power of death," because the sacred grotto in Caesarea Philippi, where he spoke those words, was considered a gateway to Hades.[9] The location had a cave with a deep chasm believed to lead to the Abyss and Hades.[10] In the book of Revelation, Jesus claims to capture the "keys of Death and Hades," which is a doublet separating the two words rather than identifying them (Rev. 1:18).

Hades was the location of departed spirits in Christ's parable of Lazarus and the rich man in Hades (Luke 16:19-31). It was from this parable that the term "Abraham's Bosom" came, that indicated the separated location of righteous souls in Hades from the eternally thirsty wicked by a large chasm. This parable has been convincingly proven by some scholars to be a subversive polemic against the common motif of Hellenistic pagan journeys to the underworld and communication from the dead, not a literal geography of Hades.[11] But if it was good enough for Jesus, it's good enough for *Jesus Triumphant* in its imaginative depiction of Hades.

In Greek mythology, Tartarus was another term for a location beneath the "roots of the earth" and beneath the waters where the warring giants called "Titans" were bound in chains because of their rebellion against the gods.

---

[7] Mark S. Smith, "Rephaim," ed. David Noel Freedman, *The Anchor Yale Bible Dictionary* (New York: Doubleday, 1992), 674-75.

[8] Philip S. Johnston, *Shades of Sheol: Death and Afterlife in the Old Testament*, (Downers Grove: IL, InterVarsity, 2002), 128-130.

[9] Michael S. Heiser, *The Unseen Realm* (Bellingham: WA, Lexham, 2005), 267-271; Jimmy R. Watson, *The Religious History of Banias and Its Contribution to an Understanding of the Petrine Confession* (Hardin-Simmons University, Master's Thesis, 1989). 87; George W. E. Nicklesburg, "Enoch, Levi, and Peter: Recipients of Revelation in Upper Galilee," Journal of Biblical Literature 100 (December 1981): 598.

[10] *Wars of the Jews* 1:405, Flavius Josephus and William Whiston, *The Works of Josephus: Complete and Unabridged* (Peabody: Hendrickson, 1987).

[11] Kim Papaioannou, *The Geography of Hell in the Teaching of Jesus: Gehenna, Hades, the Abyss, the Outer Darkness Where There Is Weeping and Gnashing of Teeth* (Eugene, OR: Pickwick Publications, 2013), 112. Richard Bauckham, *The Fate of the Dead: Studies on the Jewish and Christian Apocalypses*, (Leiden, Netherlands: Brill, 1998), 101.

Peter uses a derivative of that very Greek word Tartarus to describe a similar location and scenario of angels being bound during the time of Noah and the warring Titans called "Nephilim."[12]

> 2Pet. 2:4-5
> God did not spare angels when they sinned, but cast them into hell [*Tartarus*] and committed them to chains of gloomy darkness to be kept until the judgment.

From Sheol to Gehenna

Despite this claim of a realm for the dead in both the Old and New Testaments, there is very little specificity of description of its attributes beyond "darkness" (Job 17:13; Lam. 3:6) and "silence" (Psa. 31:17–18; 94:17; 115:17). The one clear certainty about Sheol/Hades is that "he who goes down to Sheol does not come up" (Job 7:9; 10:21; 2Sam. 12:23). As Papaioannou describes:

> First, Sheol/Hades is where everyone goes at death. There is no distinction between the righteous and the wicked... Second, Sheol/Hades is not a place of eschatological punishment, but rather the destiny of all human beings... Third, there is no life or consciousness in Sheol/Hades. In contrast to some cultures that envisioned meaningful existence in the afterlife, the Hebrew Bible portrays Sheol as a place of silence and lifelessness where human existence has come to an end... There is no memory in Hades (Isa 26:14); neither is there any longer a communion with God (Isa 38:18). It is a place of silence, darkness, and oblivion (Job 17:13). Thus, a person who dies in effect ceases to exist (Eccl. 9:6)... With a belief in a bodily resurrection, Sheol/Hades is only a temporary abode—the dead remain there until they are raised.[13]

Richard Bauckham explains the change in understanding that occurred between the Old Testament and New Testament Scriptures regarding the abode of the dead. He points out that the older view did not involve active

---

[12] 1.25 ταρταρόω [*tartaroo*] Louw, Johannes P., and Eugene Albert Nida. *Greek-English Lexicon of the New Testament : Based on Semantic Domains*. electronic ed. of the 2nd edition. New York: United Bible societies, 1996. Bauckham, Richard J. Vol. 50, *Word Biblical Commentary : 2 Peter, Jude*. Word Biblical Commentary. Dallas: Word, Incorporated, 2002, p 248-249.
[13] Papaioannou, *The Geography of Hell*, 87-88.

punishment of souls in Sheol, but merely involved holding the wicked in detention until the last judgment. The newer view, driven by apocalyptic literature included descents to the underworld, where increasingly only the wicked were located:

> The older view allowed for visits to the place of detention in Sheol (1En. 22), visits to the hell which is already prepared for but not yet inhabited by the wicked (lEn. 26:3-27:4; 2En. 10; 40:12; 2Bar. 59:10), and prophetic visions of the casting of the wicked into Gehenna at the last judgment (1En. 41:2; Bar 59: 11). But only the later view enabled a seer to see and to describe in detail the punishments actually being inflicted on the wicked in hell. The later view therefore spawned a long tradition of 'tours of hell,' in which a variety of different punishments appropriate to different categories of sinners is described.[14]

By the time of the New Testament, some Second Temple Jewish literature began to increasingly evidence the notion of punishment for the wicked and reward for the righteous in Hades *before the final judgment.* Bauckham suggests this new notion of immediate recompense upon death in both Jewish and Christian writings may have been the result of Greek influence,"[15] but the fact remains that after the advent of Christ and his spiritual mission, the change took place with the growth of Christianity. In this sense, Christ's descent into Hades, and his victorious triumph over spiritual principalities and the powers of Death and Hades marked the inauguration of God's kingdom that may have included the beginning of rewards and punishment in Sheol/Hades.

The Greek word for "hell" used in New Testament translation is *Gehenna.* Some have believed that this was the name of a garbage dump outside Jerusalem that burned with perpetual flames, and Jesus used it as a metaphor for the fires of judgment. But recent scholarship tends to disregard this thesis as lacking both exegetical weight and hard archeological evidence.[16]

In fact, Gehenna is Greek for "Valley of Hinnom," the valley that bordered the south and western sides of Jerusalem.[17] This valley had a dark history in Israel's past as the location of tophets, or burning places for sacrifice

[14] Bauckham, *The Fate of the Dead*, 34.
[15] Bauckham, *The Fate of the Dead,* 36.
[16] Papaioannou, *The Geography of Hell*, 80.
[17] Duane F. Watson, "Gehenna (Place)," ed. David Noel Freedman, *The Anchor Yale Bible Dictionary* (New York: Doubleday, 1992), 926.

to Molech, the underworld god. Israelites would "pass their children through the fire" as human sacrifice. God became so angry with this abomination that the prophet Jeremiah pronounced a fiery curse on the area destroyed by King Josiah around 632 B.C. (Jer. 7:29–34; 19:1–15). It would become known as the "Valley of Slaughter," and a synonym for future judgment/destruction of people and nations in this life as well as the next. Both Second Temple literature and Jesus' teachings used Gehenna as a reference to the future final judgment (Matt. 13:42, 30; 25:41).[18] So, yes it was a metaphor for fiery punishment, but a far richer meaning than a burning garbage dump. It provided incarnate location for the belief in the eschatological judgment of God upon evil.

Geography of the Underworld in 1Enoch

Apart from Jesus' parable of Abraham's Bosom (Luke 16:19-31), there are no descriptions of the actual geography of the underworld in the New Testament. Rather than drawing from pagan Greek myths to depict Hades in *Jesus Triumphant*, I decided to draw from a respected Jewish source that did provide a "cosmic geography" or conceptual map of the universe that included the underworld. This geography of Hades can be found in the visions of the ancient book of 1Enoch.[19]

Though 1Enoch is not Scripture, I have argued elsewhere for the high regard that the New Testament gives the ancient text as a source for some of its own theological concepts and language.[20] The book consists of several "books," that recount an expanded version of the Genesis 6 story of the Watchers and Nephilim giants, as well as visions that the prophet Enoch allegedly experienced of angels taking him around the earth, up into the heights of heaven, and down into the depths of Hades (which are actually arrived at by going to the "ends of the earth" rather than descending down into the earth). Unfortunately, these visions are obscure, overlapping, and at times contradictory, so scholars have disagreed over their interpretation as well as their actual cosmic geography. I have attempted to use my own reading of the text and integrate it with several of these scholarly viewpoints that can be found analyzed in the book, *A Study of the Geography of 1 Enoch 17-19,* by Kelley Coblentz Bautch.[21] Imagination is required!

---

[18] See 1 En. 10:13; 48:8–10; 100:7–9; 108:4–7; Jdt 16:17; 2 Bar. 85:13.

[19] Though 1Enoch does evidence Hellenistic influence, it retains a unique Jewish perspective throughout its literary style and content.

[20] See the chapter "The Book of Enoch: Scripture, Heresy, or What?" in *When Giants Were Upon the Earth: The Watchers, Nephilim and the Cosmic War of the Seed* (Los Angeles: Embedded Pictures, 2014).

[21] Kelley Coblentz Bautch, *A Study of the Geography of 1 Enoch 17-19: No One Has Seen What I Have Seen*, (Leiden, Netherlands: Brill, 2003).

Since Enoch's "map" is cosmic, it includes Sheol/Hades as well as the heavens and the earth. But some scholars have argued that Enoch's entire journey is to the realm of the dead.[22] So I decided to use the ancient Near Eastern (and Jewish) notion of "on earth as it is in heaven" (Matt. 6:10) or "as above, so below," to apply to the underworld as well. In this way, the geography of Hades that Jesus follows on his underworld journey, is a reflection of the sacred geography of the earth above ("Sacred geography" means that it does not so much follow physical geography as it does theological meaning).

Since the underworld was believed by the Jews to be under the earth,[23] and accessed by the waters of the Abyss,[24] that was the source of the waters above,[25] I have those waters work as a kind of sky in the dome of the underworld (though not in all places). The mountains below rise up from Hades to the earth above. So when Jesus is at Mount Zion in Hades, it rises up and penetrates the ceiling of Hades and becomes Mount Zion on earth above them. This fulfills the ancient Near Eastern notion of the cosmic mountains being an *axis mundi*, a connection between the heavens, the earth, and the underworld.[26]

The circle of Hades matches the circle of the earth above it and likewise has an ocean/river (the Great Sea or Abyss) at its outer reaches that extends beyond the "Four Winds" or "Four Corners" of the earth where the pillars of the earth support the heavens and the earth (1En. 17:5; Prov. 8:27, 29; 1Sam. 2:8; Mark 13:27).[27]

In this conceptual map, Jerusalem, or Mount Zion is at the center of the earth, and has "the accursed valley" (Gehenna) right next to it (Ezek. 5:5, 38:12; 1En. 26:1-2; 27:2).

North from that center resides Mount Hermon, the "rock" (mountain) that Jesus said God would build his new kingdom church upon.[28] This mountain is described as "reaching to the heavens" and as being the celestial storehouse of the luminaries and storms (1En. 17:3). Many rivers flow from it, including a river of fire and a river of "living waters" (17:4-8), and it is guarded by fiery beings who take human shape (17:1). This "source of the waters" is a

---

[22] Glasson, T. Francis. *Greek Influence in Jewish Eschatology*. London: S.P.C.K., 1961, 8-11; Nickelsburg, *Jewish Literature between the Bible and the Mishnah*, (Philadelphia: Fortress Press, 1981) 54–55; 66, n. 26; also *1 Enoch*, 280; James C. VanderKam, *Enoch and the Growth of an Apocalyptic Tradition*. CBQMS 16. Washington, D.C.: Catholic Biblical Association of America, 1984.

[23] Amos 9:2.

[24] Ps. 136:6; Job 41:34 LXX.

[25] Wayne Horowitz, *Mesopotamian Cosmic Geography*, (Winona Lake; IN: Eisenbrauns, 1998), 334-348.

[26] Richard J. Clifford, *The Cosmic Mountain in Canaan and the Old Testament* (Wipf & Stock Pub, 2010). Also, Isa. 14:13-15.

[27] See also Isa. 40:22; Zech. 9:10; Job 38:4.

[28] Matt. 16:18.

reflection of the cosmic Mountain of Eden and it's source of living waters (Ezek. 28:13-14).[29]

In the south are seven mountains of precious stones arranged in a perpendicular layout. The central mountain burns with fire day and night, and is called the "throne of God," where God will come down at the final judgment. These elements suggest it is Mount Sinai (1En. 24-25).

In the west are "wintery winds" and the "great darkness," where another mountain hosts "hollow places" for the souls of all the dead. The righteous are separated from the sinners, much like the chasm separates the righteous in Abraham's Bosom from the sinners in the parable of Lazarus. (Luke 16:19-26; 1En. 17:6; 22:1-14).

In the east are "great beasts and birds" at the ends of the earth (1En. 33:1). Tartarus is further "beyond the edge of the earth," where the earth meets to uphold the vault of heaven (1En. 18:10).[30] This is where the angels who sinned in Genesis 6 are kept imprisoned in gloomy darkness (2Pet. 2:4; 1Pet. 3:18-20). They are in deep pits or chasms that are like fiery pillars. (1En. 18:10-16).

There is much more detail that can be quite confusing to follow, so I have included an illustrated map with some of the major elements adapted from Bautch and my own reading of 1Enoch.

[29] Bautch, *A Study of the Geography of 1 Enoch*, 64-69.
[30] George W. E. Nickelsburg, *1 Enoch: A Commentary on the Book of 1 Enoch, ed. Klaus Baltzer, Hermeneia—a Critical and Historical Commentary on the Bible* (Minneapolis, MN: Fortress, 2001), 286.

Enoch's Cosmic Geography
(adapted from 1Enoch 17-19 & Kelley Coblentz Bautch)

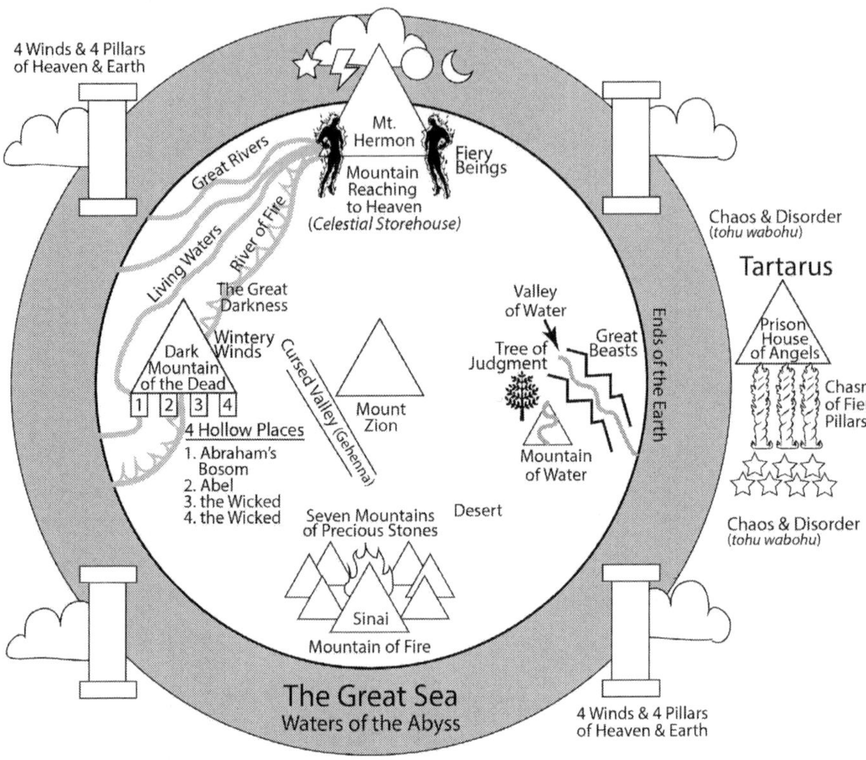

Can We Trust This Ancient Cosmology?

The ancient Biblical cosmic picture is a three-tiered universe with God's throne above the waters of heaven, a solid dome above the flat disc earth, founded on pillars, surrounded by a circular sea, on top of a watery abyss, beneath which is the underworld of Sheol, where souls are trapped in waiting cells for a final judgment.[31]

A natural question arises while examining this ancient cosmology: If the Biblical writers were so "scientifically inaccurate" in their understanding of the universe, then why should we trust what they write about God, the afterlife, and judgment?

Some well-intentioned Evangelicals seek to maintain their particular definition of Biblical inerrancy by denying that the Bible contains this ancient Near Eastern cosmography. They try to explain it away as phenomenal

---

[31] For a detailed examination of this full cosmology see "Appendix D: Mesopotamian Cosmic Geography in the Bible," in the first Chronicle of the Nephilim, *Noah Primeval* by Brian Godawa.

language or poetic license. Phenomenal language is the act of describing what one sees subjectively from one's perspective without further claiming objective reality. So when the writer says the sun stood still, or that the sun rises and sets within the solid dome of heaven, he is only describing his observation, not cosmic reality. The claim of observation from a personal frame of reference is certainly true as far as it goes. Of course the observer describes what they are observing. But the distinction between appearance and reality is an imposition of our alien modern understanding onto theirs. As Seely explains,

> It is precisely because ancient peoples were scientifically naive that they did not distinguish between the appearance of the sky and their scientific concept of the sky. They had no reason to doubt what their eyes told them was true, namely, that the stars above them were fixed in a solid dome and that the sky literally touched the earth at the horizon. So, they equated appearance with reality and concluded that the sky must be a solid physical part of the universe just as much as the earth itself.[32]

If the ancients did not know the earth was a sphere in space, or that there was no underworld beneath their feet, they could not know that their observations of appearances were anything other than reality. It would be easy enough to relegate one or two examples of Scripture to the notion of phenomenal language, but when dozens of those phenomenal descriptions reflect the same complex integrated picture of the universe that Israel's neighbors shared, and when that picture included many elements that were *not* phenomenally observable, such as the Abyss, Sheol, or the pillars of earth and heaven, it strains credulity to suggest these were merely phenomenal descriptions intentionally unrelated to reality. If it walks a like an ancient Near Eastern duck and talks like an ancient Near Eastern duck, then chances are they thought it was an ancient Near Eastern duck, not just the "appearance" of one having no reality.

It would be a mistake to claim that there is a single monolithic ancient Near Eastern cosmography.[33] There are varieties of stories with overlapping imagery, and some contradictory notions. But there are certainly enough commonalities to affirm a generic yet mysterious picture of the universe. And that picture in Scripture undeniably includes poetic language. The Hebrew

---

[32] Seely, "The Firmament," p 228.

[33] Horowitz, *Mesopotamian Cosmic Geography*.

culture was imaginative. They integrated poetry into everything, including their observational descriptions of nature. Thus a hymn of creation such as Psalm 19 tells of the heavens declaring God's glory as if using speech, and then describes the operations of the sun in terms of a bridegroom in his chamber or a man running a race. Creative imagination is inescapable and ubiquitous.

And herein lies a potential solution for the dilemma of the scientific inaccuracy of the ancient cosmic geography in Scripture: *The Israelite culture, being pre-scientific, thought more in terms of function and purpose than material structure*. Even if their picture of the heavens and earth as a three-tiered geocentric cosmology, was scientifically "false" from our modern perspective, it nevertheless still accurately describes the teleological purpose and meaning of creation that they were intending to communicate.

Though there is no literal underworld beneath the earth with rivers of fire and souls trapped in mountains waiting for the judgment, it still communicates the truth, transcendent of that ancient culture yet revealed through it, that those who have died await a future resurrection and judgment before the living God. Jesus' descent into that imagined underworld is a theological narrative explaining the transcendent truth that his death and resurrection paid the price for the sins of his people, and secured his victory over the spiritual powers who rule mankind, and from whom Christ has taken back his inheritance of the earth. Our modern worldview obsessed as it is with empirical science and human reason is so blinded to its own ignorance of transcendent reality and stunted imagination, that it amounts to idolatry, the limited, fallible human mind and senses as god.

Othmar Keel, one of the leading scholars on Ancient Near Eastern art has argued that even though modern depictions of the ancient worldview like the illustration of the three-tiered universe above are helpful, they are fundamentally flawed because they depict a "profane, lifeless, virtually closed mechanical system," which reflects our own modern bias. To the ancient Near East "rather, the world was an entity open at every side. The powers which determine the world are of more interest to the ancient Near East than the structure of the cosmic system. A wide variety of diverse, uncoordinated notions regarding the cosmic structure were advanced from various points of departure."[34]

John Walton has written recently of this ANE concern with powers over structure in direct relation to the creation story of Genesis. He argues that in the ancient world existence was understood more in terms of function within a god-created *purposeful order* than in terms of material status within a natural

[34] Othmar Keel, *The Symbolism of the Biblical World*, Winona Lake; IN: Eisenbrauns, 1972, 1997, 56-57.

physical structure.[35] This is not to say that the physical world was denied or ignored, but rather that the priority and interests were different from our own. We should therefore be careful in judging their purpose-driven cosmography too strictly in light of our own material-driven cosmography. And in this sense, modern material descriptions of reality are more "false" than ancient pictures because they do not include the immaterial aspect of reality: Meaning and purpose.

But even more basic than that, human observation of the universe is always changing, from Newtonian physics to Quantum physics to String Theory. That change is less a change of more precise instrumentation than it is a change of ideas. What we think we see is more affected by our philosophical presuppositions (and theories) than empirical scientists are willing to admit.

Biblical writers did not *teach* their cosmography as scientific doctrine revealed by God about the way the physical universe was materially structured, they *assumed* the popular cosmography to teach their doctrine about God's *purposes and meaning*. To critique the cosmic model carrying the message is to miss the meaning altogether, which is the message. God's throne may not be physically above us in waters held back by a solid firmament, but he truly does rule "over" us and is king and sustainer of creation in whatever model man uses to depict that creation. The phrase "every created thing which is in heaven and on the earth and under the earth" (Rev. 5:13) is equivalent in meaning to the modern concept of every particle and wave in every dimension of the Big Bang space-time continuum, as well as every person dead or alive.

The geocentric picture in Scripture is a depiction through man's ancient perspective of God's purpose and humankind's significance. For a modern heliocentrist to attack that picture as falsifying the theology would be cultural imperialism. Reducing significance to physical location is simply a prejudice of material priority over spiritual purpose.

One of the humorous ironies of this debate is that if the history of science is any judge, a thousand years from now, scientists will no doubt consider our current paradigm with which we judge the ancients to be itself fatally flawed. This is not to reduce reality to relativism, but rather to illustrate that all claims of empirical knowledge contain an inescapable element of human fallibility and finitude. A proper response should be a bit more humility and a bit less hubris regarding the use of our own scientific models as standards in judging theological meaning or purpose.

---

[35] John H. Walton, *The Lost World of Genesis One: Ancient Cosmology and the Origins Debate* (Downers Grove: IL, InterVarsity Press, 2009), 23-36.

ABOUT THE AUTHOR

Brian Godawa is the screenwriter for the award-winning feature film, *To End All Wars,* starring Kiefer Sutherland. It was awarded the Commander in Chief Medal of Service, Honor and Pride by the Veterans of Foreign Wars, won the first Heartland Film Festival by storm, and showcased the Cannes Film Festival Cinema for Peace.

He also co-wrote *Alleged*, starring Brian Dennehy as Clarence Darrow and Fred Thompson as William Jennings Bryan. He previously adapted to film the best-selling supernatural thriller novel *The Visitation* by author Frank Peretti for Ralph Winter (*X-Men, Wolverine*), and wrote and directed *Wall of Separation,* a PBS documentary, and *Lines That Divide*, a documentary on stem cell research.

Mr. Godawa's scripts have won multiple awards in respected screenplay competitions, and his articles on movies and philosophy have been published around the world. He has traveled around the United States teaching on movies, worldviews, and culture to colleges, churches and community groups.

His book, *Hollywood Worldviews: Watching Films with Wisdom and Discernment* has been released in a revised edition from InterVarsity Press. His book *Word Pictures: Knowing God Through Story and Imagination* (IVP) addresses the power of image and story in the pages of the Bible to transform the Christian life.

Find out more about his other books, lecture tapes and dvds for sale at his website www.godawa.com.

Get the First Novel of the Bestselling Biblical Fiction Series Based on This Book!

For a Limited Time Only in eBook

FREE

This is Not Your Sunday School Noah's Ark.

This book you are reading, *When Giants Were Upon the Earth*, is the research for the entire bestselling series, *Chronicles of the Nephilim.*

The first novel in the series is *Noah Primeval*. It tells of the events that lead to the Great Flood, with Noah at the very center of the storyline of God's chosen Seed. See how the Nephilim, the Sons of God and the Watchers fit into the War of the Seed. Faithful to the Scriptures. Open to Biblical imagination. Get it in eBook NOW!

Download Free eBook Here

https://godawa.com/free-noah-book/

Great Offers By Brian Godawa

Get More Biblical Imagination

Sign up Online For The Godawa Chronicles

www.Godawa.com

Updates and Freebies
of the Books of Brian Godawa
Special Discounts,
Weird Bible Facts!

Chronicles of the Watchers

A Series About the Watchers in History.
Action, Romance, Gods, Monsters & Men.

The first novel is *Jezebel: Harlot Queen of Israel*

www.Godawa.com

Video Lectures

The Book of Enoch: Scripture, Heresy or What?

This lecture by Brian Godawa will be an introduction to the ancient book of 1Enoch, its content, its history, its affirmation in the New Testament, and its acceptance and rejection by the Christian Church. What is the Book of Enoch? Where did it come from? Why isn't it in the Bible? How does the Book of Enoch compare with the Bible?

Available on video.

Chronicles of the Nephilim: The Ancient Biblical Story

Watchers, Nephilim, and the Divine Council of the Sons of God. In this dvd video lecture, Brian Godawa explores the Scriptures behind this transformative storyline that inspired his best-selling Biblical novel series Chronicles of the Nephilim.

Available on video.

God Against the gods

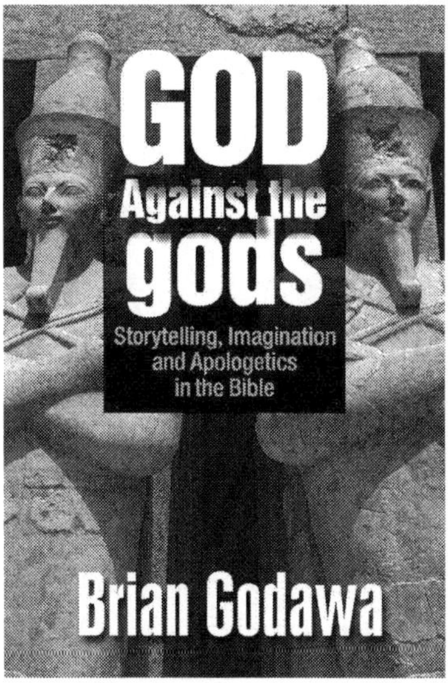

How God Captures the Imagination

This book was previously titled *Myth Became Fact: Storytelling, Imagination & Apologetics in the Bible.*

Brian Godawa, Hollywood screenwriter and best-selling novelist, explores the nature of imagination in the Bible. You will learn how God subverts pagan religions by appropriating their imagery and creativity, and redeeming them within a Biblical worldview. Improve your imagination in your approach to glorifying God and defending the faith.

Demonizing the Pagan Gods
God verbally attacked his opponents, pagans and their gods, using sarcasm, mockery, name-calling.

Old Testament Storytelling Apologetics
Israel shared creative images with their pagan neighbors: The sea dragon of chaos and the storm god. The Bible invests them with new meaning.

Biblical Creation and Storytelling
Creation stories in the ancient Near East and the Bible both express a primeval battle of deity to create order out of chaos. But how do they differ?

The Universe in Ancient Imagination
A detailed comparison and contrast of the Biblical picture of the universe with the ancient pagan one. What's the difference?

New Testament Storytelling Apologetics
Paul's sermon to the pagans on Mars Hill is an example of subversion: Communicating the Gospel in terms of a pagan narrative with a view toward replacing their worldview.

Imagination in Prophecy & Apocalypse
God uses imaginative descriptions of future events to deliberately obscure his message while simultaneously showing the true meaning and purpose behind history.

An Apologetic of Biblical Horror
Learn how God uses horror in the Bible as a tool to communicate spiritual, moral and social truth in the context of repentance from sin and redemptive victory over evil.

For More Info
www.Godawa.com

The Imagination of God

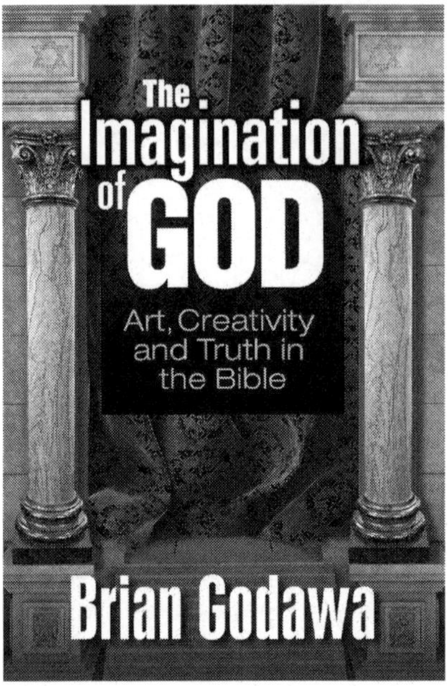

Art, Creativity and Truth in the Bible

In his refreshing and challenging book, Godawa helps you break free from the spiritual suffocation of heady faith. Without negating the importance of reason and doctrine, Godawa challenges you to move from understanding the Bible "literally" to "literarily" by exploring the poetry, parables and metaphors found in God's Word. Weaving historical insight, pop culture and personal narrative throughout, Godawa reveals the importance God places on imagination and creativity in the Scriptures, and provides a Biblical foundation for Christians to pursue imagination, beauty, wonder and mystery in their faith.

This book was previously released with the title, *Word Pictures: Knowing God Through Story and Imagination.*

Endorsements:

"Brian Godawa is that rare breed—a philosopher/artist—who opens our eyes to the aesthetic dimension of spirituality. Cogently argued and fun to read, Godawa shows convincingly that God interacts with us as whole persons, not only through didactic teaching but also through metaphor, symbol, and sacrament."

— Nancy R. Pearcey,
Author, *Total Truth: Liberating Christianity from its Cultural Captivity*

"A spirited and balanced defense of the imagination as a potential conveyer of truth. There is a lot of good literary theory in the book, as well as an autobiographical story line. The thoroughness of research makes the book a triumph of scholarship as well."

— Leland Ryken, Clyde S. Kilby Professor of English, Wheaton College, Illinois
Author, *The Christian Imagination: The Practice of Faith in Literature & Writing.*

For More Info

www.Godawa.com

BLANK PAGE

BLANK PAGE

Made in the USA
San Bernardino, CA
14 April 2020

67923810R00186